A CARNIVAL OF PARTING

A CARNIVAL OF PARTING

*The Tales of King Bharthari and
King Gopi Chand as Sung and Told by
Madhu Natisar Nath of Ghatiyali, Rajasthan*

Translated with an
Introduction and Afterword by
ANN GRODZINS GOLD

UNIVERSITY OF CALIFORNIA PRESS
BERKELEY   LOS ANGELES   OXFORD

University of California Press
Berkeley and Los Angeles, California

University of California Press, Ltd.
Oxford, England

© 1992 by
The Regents of the University of California

Library of Congress Cataloging-in-Publication Data

Gold, Ann Grodzins, 1946–
    A carnival of parting : the tales of King Bharthari and King
Gopi Chand as sung and told by Madhu Natisar Nath of
Ghatiyali, Rajasthan / translated with an introduction and
afterword by Ann Grodzins Gold.
        p.   cm.
    Includes bibliographical references and index.
    ISBN 0-520-07533-1 (alk. paper).—ISBN 0-520-07535-8 (alk.
paper)
    1. Tales—India—Rajasthan. 2. Folk songs, Rajasthani.
3. Nath, Madhu Natisar. 4. Storytellers—India—Rajasthani.
5. Folk singers—India—Rajasthani. I. Nath, Madhu Natisar.
II. Title.

GR305.5.R3G65   1992   91-44882
398.22′0954′4—dc20   CIP

Printed in the United States of America
9 8 7 6 5 4 3 2 1

The paper used in this publication meets the minimum require-
ments of American National Standard for Information Sciences—
Permanence of Paper for Printed Library Materials, ANSI
Z39.48-1984. ⊗

For Adam, Jonah, Eli, and Daniel

Contents

Illustrations

Preface

Madhu Natisar Nath, whose words in translation form the substance of this book, is a Rajasthani farmer, now in his midseventies, with no formal schooling. He is also a singer, a musician, and a storyteller. Madhu wears in his ears the distinctive thick rings associated with the sect of renouncers called, among other things, "split-ear" yogis. A married landowner, Madhu is not a renouncer, nor is he a yogi in the sense of practicing esoteric self-disciplines. Born into the caste of Naths (also called Jogis)—householders whose collective identity is linked to renouncer ancestors—Madhu was persuaded in his early teens to have his ears ritually split by a wealthy landlord who wanted to sponsor the ceremony.

At the center of this book are Madhu Nath's oral performances, which I have rendered into written English, of two linked tales about the legendary kings Gopi Chand and Bharthari. Both these characters, while in their prime, leave thrones and families to be initiated as yogis. Gopi Chand and Bharthari are usually reckoned among the "Nine Naths" whose biographies are major features in popular traditions of North Indian yogis. At some undeterminable point in the development of this lore, the two renouncer-kings became linked as sister's son to mother's brother. The uncle Bharthari's tale precedes the nephew Gopi Chand's in strict chronology. In performance and, I believe, in significance, Gopi Chand's story takes precedence. Madhu acknowledges that it is more popular with his patrons. When the two are spoken of as a pair, which they often are, it is as Gopi Chand–Bharthari, not vice versa. For me, also, Gopi Chand's tale came first in several ways.

Described by Sir Richard Temple as a "wearisome agglomerate of interminable platitudes" (Temple [1884] 1962, 2:1), and by G. A. Grierson as an epic containing "here and there a tiny pearl of interest, hidden amidst the rubbish" (Grierson 1878, 146), the tale of Gopi Chand was immediately engrossing and wholly delightful to me when I first encountered it in Temple's *Legends of the Punjab*. This encounter took place long before I met Madhu Nath or knew of his caste's oral traditions. Temple's version had charmed me in Chicago when I read it for a course; to meet it again as a living performance tradition in a Rajasthan village was for me a momentous but purely serendipitous event.

I have devoted the better parts of several precious fellowship years to crafting the translations, researching the origins, and thinking and writing about the meanings of the Rajasthani versions of Gopi Chand and the companion tale of his uncle Bharthari. Moreover, I have labored thus not for the record, as did Temple, nor for the tiny pearl, as did Grierson, but because I love the whole cycle and am convinced that many other people will also find it gripping, moving, and funny.

What explains the divergence between my aesthetic sensibilities and those of the early British folklorists? Historical circumstances, no doubt, account for much. Temple and Grierson were representatives of a colonial power as certain of its enlightened good taste as it was of its right to tax and rule. I came of age in the United States of the late sixties, part of a generation that routinely embraced and elevated the wisdom of other cultures in its quest for peace of mind, good health, and vital community.

My generation lived in canvas tepees sprayed with chemical waterproofing according to instructions in a how-to-do-it book. We sought wisdom relevant to our own lives in texts as culturally diverse as the *Songs of Milarepa* (poems of a Tibetan Buddhist saint) and G. I. Gurdjieff's *All and Everything* (a twentieth-century Armenian mystic's eccentric history of the cosmos). We massaged our babies according to a photographic manual recommending this time-honored South Asian technique as the key to satisfying parent-child relationships. I have selected these examples from my personal history, but they are fairly representative. While few such ventures were fully successful, cumulatively they broadened our collective horizons. If my friends and I had never heard the expression "anthropology as cultural critique"—indeed I suppose it had not been coined—we were nevertheless immersed during early youth in a direct if unschooled version of such a reflexive enterprise. That it was more or less this same generation who, in the academy, conceived theoretical and practical potentials for such criticism is probably no historical accident but a meaningful conjuncture.

General cultural malaise and hunger for foreign knowledge provide only the loosest frame within which I might offer some explanation for my instant and long-term attraction to the Gopi Chand–Bharthari cycle. I acknowledge, retrospectively, that the particular charms Gopi Chand's tale held for me derive from a confluence of personal and intellectual interests that may be common (but usually go unreported) in the formulation of many academic projects. When I first read Gopi Chand I had but recently returned, after a long spell of nomadic questing, to academia. The tale held for me an instantly appealing message, which in the starkest terms is this: abandoning beloved women for the sake of religion isn't easy.

One of the reasons I liked this message must be because I had—before taking up the academic study of Indian language and culture—parted very painfully from a husband who, as I perceived it, cared more for his spiritual aspirations than he did for me and our child. His aspirations could not have been more different from a yogi's; returning to his childhood roots, he had joined a tradition—the Latter Day Saints—that celebrated eternal family unity. Feeling irrevocably alienated, I fled back to my own roots, which happened to be the University of Chicago. I was certainly drawn to the study of anthropology and of Indian religion in part because both offered luxuriant vistas of fluid cultural and cosmic relativities I had found so gallingly absent from my husband's beliefs.

I suppose I also nursed the suspicion, or hope, that valuing God and salvation more than one's strongest attachments was not a morally certain venture. The Gopi Chand legend confirmed this intuition to my satisfaction. Although Temple's version is significantly less laden with expressions of misery than the one I was later to record, it nonetheless depicts the process of Gopi Chand's renunciation as difficult. These difficulties all derive from the genuine claims on Gopi Chand of wife, daughter, and sister. Although Nath bards—to the extent of my knowledge—have always been males, I sensed hints of a women's perspective in Gopi Chand's story. Many years later I, along with a number of others, began to formulate some ideas about women's perspectives available through folk traditions (Gold 1991, Raheja and Gold, forthcoming; Wadley 1978). In 1978, when I read *Legends of the Punjab*, I had no background in women's studies and no feminist stance.

The fieldwork that took me to India (in 1979–81) and landed me in the village of Ghatiyali where I met Madhu Nath had nothing to do with women's perspectives or with oral traditions, Naths, or Gopi Chand. I had no expectation of finding a living performance tradition of Gopi Chand's tale, and had never even heard of Bharthari as a folk hero—although I had read translations of the elegant poems attributed to Bhartrihari, the Sanskrit poet with whom he is traditionally identified. What interested me was renunciation as a value in householders' lives, and I planned to study this not through translating folklore texts but rather through participant observation in the practice of pilgrimage (Gold 1988).

The introduction to this book provides several sets of backgrounds to Madhu Nath's tales. In chapter 1, I describe how I came to know the bard in the setting of his natal village, Ghatiyali, where I lived for almost two years. I then sketch Madhu's life history, or as much of it as he chose to divulge to me, and describe his usual modes of performance as well as the particular events that I recorded. I go on to recount and reflect on the translation process in its multiple phases and to consider at a more general level the problems of "translating" an oral performance across cultural boundaries. Here I clarify which compromises I have chosen and why.

The two chapters that follow provide a different set of backgrounds, locating the stories of King Gopi Chand and King Bharthari, and their Rajasthani variants, within the moving currents and deep layers of Hindu traditions. In chapter 2, I discuss the Naths or Jogis both as sect and as caste. In chapter 3, I treat the oral traditions they create and inhabit.

There follow my translations of Madhu Nath's performances of Bharthari and Gopi Chand. Madhu himself divides each tale into discrete segments—three for Bharthari and four for Gopi Chand. I give a brief introduction for each of these parts, offering some general orientations and some cross-referencing of themes between the two epics. I annotate the texts themselves on two premises. Primarily, whenever I sense that a non-Rajasthani audience needs additional information to understand a reference (be it mythological, agricultural, geographical, or other) I provide that information. Secondarily, whenever my translator's choices seem more than ordinarily risky or bold, and sometimes when I translate key concepts, I supply an original term or phrase, with or without discussion. I attempt to offer a fluid and unencumbered English performance and therefore retain very few Indian terms. The few that remain are explained on first appearance.

Because I perceived the language and music to be important aspects of Madhu Nath's performances but am myself neither linguist nor musician, I turned to specialists in treating these matters. One of the very few American experts in Rajasthani, David Magier of Columbia University, consented to act as linguistic consultant on my National Endowment for the Humanities translation project. Appendix 1 of this volume contains his concise but comprehensive note on Madhu Nath's language and its relation both to Hindi and to other Rajasthani dialects. David Roche of the California Institute of Integral Studies, an ethnomusicologist who has worked extensively in Rajasthan, helped me to understand Madhu Nath's music in its historical context; his comments inform my brief discussion of the music in chapter 1.

I have found a great wealth of meaning in these stories. Some of my attempts to probe and highlight Gopi Chand alone are published elsewhere (Gold 1989, 1991). Here I offer as an afterword (following with diffidence the precedent set by A. K. Ramanujan in his several volumes of translation) my impressions of the two tales' most poignant themes. These impressions are based not only on taking the texts together as mutually informing but on the years I have lived in and thought about the culture that generated them.

I still have the conviction, a sustaining one throughout the often tedious work involved in this project, that these tales stand on their own as human stories. I encourage readers who do not care for academic trappings to enjoy them as stories, the way Madhu offers them. Although it is not common practice, I reproduce here, with just a few cosmetic changes, a paragraph from the sixty-eight-page proposal I submitted in 1988 to the National Endowment for the Humanities, whose generous support saw me through to the conclusion of this work.

Several times in varied contexts—faculty seminars, undergraduate class-rooms, dinner parties—I have taken advantage of the bard Madhu Nath's gifts to me, and retold the stories of Gopi Chand or Bharthari. As my narrative begins to flow, I lose my dispositional shyness and capture my audience; drawn into the story, they want to know what happens next. During the year that I was typing out a rough translation of Gopi Chand's tale, I retold it every few evenings to my five-year-old son; he would beg to hear the next episode even before it was ready.

When I contemplate these texts and wonder, first why I'm personally so fond of them; and second why anyone whose life work is not rooted in Indological folklore should care about them, the immediate answer that comes to mind is that they are great stories, often funny stories, and above all involving stories. Whatever quality or qualities they possess that endow them with the capacity to move aging professors and little children must be the reason they are important to the humanities.

I am very thankful that the NEH, an independent federal agency, was persuaded by my arguments for a universal interest in these stories—arguments I stand by after another two years' engagement with the texts.

Looking back over these and earlier years, I have a weight of gratitude to express toward institutions, colleagues, friends, and family. A Mellon fellowship from the Society for the Humanities at Cornell University first allowed me to think and write on the Gopi Chand transcripts. A short-term Senior Fellowship from the American Institute of Indian Studies brought me back to Madhu Nath to tape his performance of Bharthari. On that trip Komal Kothari of Rupayan Sansthan, where I was affiliated, was once again a terrific source of advice and knowledge.

As will be clear to anyone who reads this book, it would never have come into existence without the long-term, patient, dedicated, and intelligent assistance of Bhoju Ram Gujar who has made my work his own in a way that I do not know how to acknowledge with sufficient ardor. As scribe for both epics in their entirety, Nathu Nath must once more be thanked and praised. This book is Madhu Nath's before it is mine. His name is on the cover, and his knowledge and art bear their own testimony. Here I thank him only for his cordiality and generous cooperation.

I have been writing and talking about these tales for a number of years, both publicly and privately. Many friends, kin, colleagues, and mentors have read, listened, and contributed their ideas, information, and counsel. Versions of the afterword were presented during the spring semester of 1990 at Cornell University's South Asia Seminar, at the University of Michigan's South and Southeast Asian Center, and as part of a University of Wisconsin lecture series on ethnography and narrative. I thank all who helpfully commented, probed, and applauded in those settings.

Daniel Gold was always the first to read a newly finished piece and has saved me embarrassment more than once by pointing out snags in my syntax, logic, and spelling. All told, he has supported this project, however dubious its merits seemed to him, with great patience and affection. Ruth Grodzins once again put in her share of labor, contributing valuable consistency and lucidity to the language.

Very particular thanks go to Sandra King Mulholland, Frances Pritchett, and David White for close, critical, and kindly readings of the first three chapters in draft. Frannie went on to read the entire manuscript, in installments, and I have acted on the majority of her acutely Hindi-sensitive suggestions, while stubbornly resisting a few of them. At Berkeley, Lynne Withey has encouraged and supported this endeavor since its inception; Pamela MacFarland Holway oversaw the book's production with care, cheer, and energy. Copy editor Edith Gladstone brilliantly tracked, and helped to eliminate, inconsistencies both gross and subtle; I thank her wholeheartedly for her painstaking attentiveness—and especially for telling me she enjoyed the stories.

Others whose comments and criticisms have sustained, inspired, and prodded me at various stages include Roxanne Gupta, Philip Lutgendorf, Kirin Narayan, Gloria Raheja, A. K. Ramanujan, Milton Singer, and especially Margaret Trawick—the one person in Ithaca with whom I can talk about everything that interests me. Susan Wadley has been a generous mentor and gentle critic over the past six years; in countless ways she has helped this project unfold, and its author survive. None of the above-mentioned institutions or persons, but I alone, bear responsibility for remaining errors and infelicities.

The Gopi Chand and Bharthari epics sustain from start to finish a tension between the moral responsibilities and passionate attachments that make family life so valuable to human beings, and the opposing fascination of solitary quests for knowledge, power, and divinity. While I remain inwardly susceptible to those counteral-lurements, my own actions have for many years been ruled largely by a householder's commitments. That is not to say that my family has not often had to suffer my absence and absentmindedness during this book's production. I dedicate it to them whose love, demands, comforts, and charms weave the net of *māyā* around me: Adam Morton Rose, Jonah Malkiel Gold, Eli Kabir Gold, Daniel Gold.

For Madhu Nath, it is always the imperceptible to which all acknowledgment belongs. Madhu often dedicates a segment of his singing to gods and gurus. With him, then, speak: Victory to Bharthari Baba! Victory to King Gopi Chand! Victory to Lord Shankar—Indescribable! Indestructible!

Note on Transcription and Transliteration

Madhu Nath's performance of the tales of Bharthari and Gopi Chand was transcribed by his nephew, Nathu Nath. Nathu had worked for the folklorist Joseph Miller before he worked for me. When not employed by foreign scholars he has made his living through agriculture, clerical jobs, tractor-driving, and temple service. Miller trained Nathu, along with several other young village men, to follow particular guidelines in his transcription work. These included: write every sound each time just as you hear it; don't standardize divergent pronunciations; don't Hindi-ize local dialect. Nathu was meticulous in his adherence to these, by and large excellent, standards. We thus escaped the syndrome, lamented by other folklore-collectors in India—where literate scribes revise as they transcribe, refusing to reproduce irregularities or language they consider unfit to be written down.

However, there are certainly occasional drawbacks to this method. Sometimes the same word, or especially name, is written in several different ways. Bharthari's father is a good example—he appears as *Gandarap Syān*, *Gandaraph Sen*, and *Gandaraph Syāṇ*. I take the obvious decision to standardize this and other instances of phonetic fluidity.

I use a standard system to transliterate from Nathu's Devanagari to English. The question of when to use diacritics is a vexing one, for which there is no accepted standard. The conventions adopted here are as follows: I italicize and give diacritics for all Hindi and Rajasthani words that are not proper nouns whenever I use them, with the exception of those that have come into English—most notably "yogi." Proper nouns appear in plain roman type without diacritics. In appendix 2 I add an alphabetical list, subdivided by category, of important names with diacritics.

Some of the names and terms that appear in these pages belong to a wider Indian tradition and have a number of variant spellings. For the most part, I consistently employ name spellings that are in accord with Madhu Nath's speech, but in chapters 2 and 3 where I treat broader traditions, footnotes offer some of the better-known variants as they arise. I make a few concessions in cases when Madhu's variant is different from everyone else's; for example I use Bharthari where Madhu actually says Bhartari.

In organizing the translated text, I keep the bard Madhu Nath's own divisions and subdivisions. He thinks of, and performs, each epic in major, named parts. In the performance context, each part falls into segments—broken by Madhu's putting down his *sārangī*, evoking the gods and gurus, coughing, and launching his prose explanation. The present text is numbered according to the title of the epic, the number of the part, the number of the segment, and whether it is singing or explanation. Thus GC 1.5.e means the explanation of the fifth segment of the first part of Gopi Chand; Bh 2.1.s means the sung verses of the first segment of the second part of Bharthari.

In the interests of fluidity and space I omit most of the interjections from the designated respondant (*hūṅkār*), or other audience members, that characterize the performance of an explanation. These consist almost always of a monosyllabic "Yes" or "Ah!" or repetitions of a word the bard has just used. If, however, an audience comment does anything other than echo or affirm the content of the performance, it is included, set apart by slashes. A few descriptive notes are provided in brackets—for example: [*Laughter*]. Also bracketed are occasional verbal exchanges that are relevant, but not integral, to the performance.

I will be happy to make tapes or transcribed text available at the cost of duplication to any interested parties. In the case of Bharthari's tale, copies of the tapes are archived at the American Institute of Indian Studies' Centre for Ethnomusicology in New Delhi.

Introduction:
The Tales in Their Contexts

Chapter One

Madhu Nath and His Performance

First Encounters

Try as I might, I cannot remember the first time I met Madhu Nath, the senior author of this volume. That I came to record his performance of Gopi Chand was initiated neither by me nor by him but by his relatives Nathu and Ugma Nathji—some of my closest associates during my residence in the Rajasthani village of Ghatiyali. Madhu, although born in Ghatiyali, settled many years ago in another nearby village, Sadara. Therefore, although he celebrated life cycle rituals among his kinfolk in Ghatiyali, and periodically performed there, he spent most of his time in Sadara. This accounts for my being unaware of him as a special person after over a year's residence in Ghatiyali and a deep involvement with several households of his relatives there.

Because of manifold links between pilgrimage and death, I had been systematically recording "hymns" (*bhajans*) sung on the eve of funeral feasts by the Nath caste and non-Nath participants in the sect which they led. I had grown increasingly interested in the Naths' peculiar approach to death and the liberation of the soul (Gold 1988, 99–123). When Madhu was directly introduced to me as a singer, in January 1981, I was reminded that my *bhajan* recordings of April 1980 were made at hymn sessions, first for his son and then for his wife. I had actually attended both their funeral feasts. This latter significant connection was phrased as, "You ate his son's and his wife's *nuktī*"— *nuktī* being the little sugary fried balls that are one of the most characteristic foods of ceremonial village feasts (called *nuktā*). During these particular feasts I must have seen Madhu, as I have seen so many other hosts at dozens of similar events, harried and anxious to keep all his guests satisfied, with no time for casual conversations. Madhu always wore his pale red-orange turban tied low, almost hiding and also supporting the heavy yogis' earrings that might otherwise have caught my attention.

My memorable and formal introduction to Madhu Nath took place over half a year later when, after six weeks in Delhi and Banaras, where I had been recuperating from hepatitis, I returned to Ghatiyali accompanied by Daniel Gold (then friend and colleague but not yet husband). Daniel, as a historian of religions researching the *sant* tradition in North India, had become interested in Ghatiyali's Naths when I showed him the transcribed texts of their hymns—many of which had the signature (*chhāp*) of the poet-saint Kabir, and some of which employed the coded imagery common to Sant poetry (Gold 1987; Hess and Singh 1983).

Daniel expressed his desire to talk with persons learned in Nath traditions, and my research assistant Nathu Nath introduced to him several members of his family and sect. The last person he brought to us was Madhu, and that evening—Daniel's last in the village— Madhu performed, and I duly recorded, Gopi Chand's *janmpatrī* or birth story. I was immediately intrigued and delighted: here was a living bard singing a story that was obviously about the same character as Temple's Punjabi version, yet evidently startlingly different in certain prominent details. I recalled from Temple nothing about Gopi Chand's being won as a boon by his mother's ascetic prowess or borrowed from the yogi Jalindar. Yet these were the dominant elements that framed the plot of Madhu's "Birth Story."[1]

Until that first evening with Madhu Nath I had largely confined my recordings of folklore to much briefer performances: women's worship tales and songs, and men's hymns. Yet now I felt compelled to obtain the whole story of Gopi Chand, despite its lack of direct relevance to my pilgrimage research, and the perceptible ticking away of my finite time in India. My recording sessions were not continuous; Madhu made a trip to Sadara to look after his fields when he had finished the "Birth Story" (in one night) and the "Journey to Bengal" (in two). Persuaded to return so that I could have the complete tale of Gopi Chand, he next gave me "Gopi Chand Begs from Queen

1. In chapter 3 I discuss how Gopi Chand varies from region to region.

Patam De," which belongs chronologically between the segments on birth and Bengal, and "Instruction from Gorakh Nath"—the conclusion. Seven years later I returned to Rajasthan with the express purpose of recording from Madhu the tale of Gopi Chand's maternal uncle, Bharthari of Ujjain. Despite the gap in time, the circumstances of the recording sessions in 1988 were not very different from those of 1981, except that the loudest crying baby on the second set of tapes belonged not to my host's household or neighbors but to me.

In January 1981 when I came to know Madhu Nath he did not strike me as a man undone by loss and mourning, although in 1980 he had buried first one of his two sons and then his wife. The son had suffered a long and debilitating illness through which he was intensively and devotedly nursed by his mother. She had, I was told, kept herself alive only to serve her child and had not long outlived him. Accompanying this double personal loss, Madhu had incurred the great economic stress of sponsoring two funeral feasts. I saw others driven to or beyond the brink of nervous collapse by just such accumulated pressures.

Yet Madhu Nath was calm, confident of his power with words, always entertaining, and sometimes very humorous. Retrospectively, I wonder if he did not derive some of his solidity, following this very difficult period of his life, from the teachings of the stories that he told so well again and again—stories with the bittersweet message that human life is "a carnival of parting." Another factor in his equilibrium could have been the Nath cult's promise of release from the pain of endless rounds of death and birth, and thus certainty of his wife's and son's liberation.

It is also true, however, that I approached Madhu Nath as a source of art and knowledge rather than as a man who had recently suffered much grief. We never spoke of his family; indeed, we hardly exchanged any personal courtesies of the kind that constitute much of normal village social intercourse. Madhu teased me sometimes—making jokes at my expense during the spoken parts of his performance—but outside the performance itself we did not talk very much in 1981. In short, although he was a wonderfully expansive storyteller, Madhu seemed to me a reserved and veiled person.

I did not attempt to obtain even a sketchy life history from Madhu Nath until my 1988 visit. My experience then confirmed in part the intuition that our lack of personal relationship could be attributed to him as much as to me. My attempt at a life history interview rapidly degenerated, or evolved, into an illuminating session of "knowledge talk," rich in myth but skimpy on biography. What follow here are the bare outlines of Madhu's career as I gleaned them from that leisurely and rambling conversation, supplemented by a few inquiries made by mail through my research assistant Bhoju.

Madhu, a member of the Natisar lineage of Naths, was born in Ghatiyali, but in his childhood he was sent to live with an elder brother already residing in nearby Sadara. His brother was *pujārī* or "worship priest" in Sadara's Shiva temple.[2] The *ṭhākur* or local ruler of Sadara—and this would have been in the thirties when *ṭhākur*s still ruled—came into possession of a pair of yogis' earrings and took a notion to put them on somebody. Madhu, and other Naths who were listening to our conversation, concurred on the consistent if seemingly superficial interpretation that the Sadara *ṭhākur* was endowed with great *śauk* (a term translatable as "passionate interest") in such works. Perhaps more salient, they also suggested that enduring "fruits" (*phal*) accrue to the one who performs such a meritorious act. And they offered as evidence the information that, even today, when independent India's concerted attempts at land reform have greatly reduced the circumstances of Rajasthan's former gentry, there is "nothing lacking" in the Sadara *ṭhākur*'s household.

Whether we see Madhu as beneficiary or victim of the *ṭhākur*'s *śauk*, the rationale for his becoming the recipient of these yogis' earrings appears to have been more economic and social than spiritual. The landlord deeded some fertile farmland to Madhu's family in exchange for cooperation on the family's part. As for Madhu himself, he was young and clearly his head was turned by the attention he received in the ceremony, and the pomp with which it was conducted. Fifty years later he described to me with pleasure the feasts, the processions, and the "English band" that were for him the most impressive and memorable aspects of this function. He stated that, although two "Nath *bābājī*s"[3] were called to be ritual officiants, he had no personal

2. Through much of rural Rajasthan it is Naths, not Brahmans, who serve as priests of Shiva temples. The Nath cult and their lore are strongly, but not universally, identified with Shaivism; see chapter 2.

3. Like *mahārāj* or "great king," *bābājī*, literally "respected father," is a common epithet and term of address for Nath and other renouncers. It has connotations of intimacy that other terms for "father" lack and may also be used affectionately for children.

guru. For Madhu, his own ear-cutting seems to have been completely divorced from the kind of spiritual initiation with which it is consistently associated, not only in the tales he himself delivers but in other published accounts.

Nevertheless, this experience and its visible physical aftermath—the rings themselves—surely set Madhu apart from the other young men of his village world. Although Madhu did not state this in so many words, what he did make clear was that after the ritual he found himself restless and unsatisfied with the life of an ordinary farmer's boy. His brother sent him out to graze the goats, but he felt this was "mindless work" (*binā buddhi kā kām*) and quarreled with him. Evidently the economic fruits of Madhu's ear-splitting were being reaped not by Madhu but by the senior male member of his household. The brother declined to support a non-goatherding Madhu; Madhu declined to herd goats. At this juncture, Madhu decided to set off on his own. As he put it, "There was no one to control me so I had a *sārangī* [the instrument he plays to accompany his performances] made by Ram Chandra Carpenter." Madhu continued, "I rubbed it,"—meaning he did not know how to play properly—"and went to all the big feasts."

Madhu then listed a number of events (weddings, holiday entertainments, and so forth) that he had attended in several villages where Naths performed their tales, both for their own caste society and at the request of other celebrating groups. In the course of these meanderings Madhu hooked up with his mother's brother's son, Sukha Nath, who was already an accomplished performer. Madhu began by informally accompanying and making himself useful to Sukha. Eventually they agreed on an apprenticeship. Madhu said, "I'll go with you," and Sukha said, "Come if you want to learn." Madhu then sought permission from his grandmother in Ghatiyali, telling her—as he recalled it for me—"I'll wash his clothes, I'll serve him, I'll live with him."

Madhu appeared to remember the years of his discipleship fondly, and no doubt selectively. He described eating two meals a day of festive treats for weeks at a stretch when he and his cousin were commissioned to perform for relatively wealthy patrons. It was particularly at such special events—the only occasions when the stories are narrated from beginning to end rather than in fragments as is the usual custom—that he mastered Sukha Nath's repertoire. This comprised the three epics Madhu himself performs: Gopi Chand, Bharthari, and the

marriage of Shiva. Madhu also knows countless hymns and several
shorter tales.[4]

At a time that Madhu estimated to be about five years after he
acquired the yogis' earrings, he was married, eventually becoming
the father of two sons. After his brother's death, the Sadara property
came fully into Madhu's possession, as did the service at the Sadara
Shiva temple. He seems then to have settled into a life divided between
agricultural and priestly tasks in Sadara and exercise of his bardic art
in a group of nine surrounding villages, including Ghatiyali.

Madhu Nath's Performance

Members of the Nath caste in Madhu's area of Rajasthan inherit and
divide the right to "make rounds" (*pherī lagānā*) and to collect grain
donations, just as they do any other ancestral property. When a
father's right must be parceled out among several sons, they receive
it as "turns." The Rajasthani word for these turns is *ausaro*, but
English "number" is also commonly used to refer to them. Of course,
some who inherit the right to perform have no talent to go with it.
For example, Madhu explained to us, when his cousin Gokul Nath's
"number" comes, Gokul seeks Madhu's assistance and they make
singing rounds together, for which Madhu receives a part of Gokul's
donations.

Besides what a performer collects while making rounds, designated
Nath household heads also receive a regular biannual share of the
harvest—called *dharo*—in the villages with which they are affiliated.
In 1990 this share, for Ghatiyali's Natisar Naths, amounted to two
and one-half kilos of grain at both the spring and fall harvests from
every landed household in eight villages. In Ghatiyali itself, where
the Natisar Naths are landed residents, they do not collect *dharo*,
although they receive donations on their performance rounds. Madhu
explained that *dharo* was not allotted to Naths for singing, but rather
for the "work" of removing locusts—a magical power that the caste
claims. Nowadays, he concluded, they sing because there are no

---

4. I recorded Madhu's performance of the "Wedding Song of Lord Shiva" in
1988; the tapes are archived with the American Institute of Indian Studies, Centre
for Ethnomusicology, in New Delhi.

locusts, thanks to a governmental extermination program (clearly a mixed blessing for Naths).

It seems that performing Gopi Chand–Bharthari may have recently been transformed into an inherited right, in order to preserve the patron-client relationship founded on locust removal.[5] By asking the kind of imaginative "what if" question that I always felt was too leading but from which we often learned the most, my assistant Bhoju elicited further support for this interpretation. What, he asked Madhu, would happen were he to practice his art in someone else's territory? Would there be trouble? Madhu responded with a firm denial: "We *jogīs* make rounds; we could go as far as Udaipur. We are *jogīs* so no one could stop us."

Twice a year, when it is his turn, Madhu Nath makes rounds in his nine villages. In any village on any given night, rather than remaining in a single location, he moves from house to house in the better-off neighborhoods, or temple to temple among the lower castes. At each site he sings and tells a short fragment of one of his lengthy tales—choosing what to sing according to the request of his patrons or his own whim.

Madhu is highly respected as a singer and storyteller of rich knowledge and skill who can move an audience to tears. His performance alternates regularly between segments of sung lines, accompanied by music which he plays himself on the *sārangī*—a simple stringed instrument played with a bow—and a prose "explanation" (*arthāv*). In this explanation he retells everything he has just sung, using more colorful, prosaic, and often vulgar language than he does in the singing. The spoken parts are performances or communicative events as clearly marked as the musical portions are. Whereas Madhu's ordinary style of speaking is normally low-key and can seem almost muted, his *arthāv* is always enunciated distinctly and projected vigorously. The *arthāv*, moreover, often incorporates the same stock phrases and poetic conceits that occur in the singing.

During both my 1981 and 1988 recording sessions, Madhu was

5. According to Ghatiyalians, Naths were first invited to settle in the villages round Ajmer because of their magic spells. One of the episodes that definitively localizes Madhu's version of Gopi Chand contains a "charter" for the Nath power over locusts (see chapter 2 and GC 4).

1. Madhu Nath plays the *sārangī* and sings Bharthari's tale.

2. Madhu Nath gives an explanation of Bharthari's tale.

3. Madhu Nath and his son, Shivji, sing Bharthari's tale.

usually accompanied by his surviving son, Shivji, who sang along in
a much fainter voice that was prone to fade away when, presumably,
he did not remember the words. However, there were some occasions—
notably more in 1988—when Shivji carried the words and Madhu
faltered. Shivji played no instrument and did not participate at all
in the *arthāv*.

As I worked on translating Madhu's words, I replayed the tapes
of his original performance. Inspired by Susan Wadley's exemplary
demonstrations and discussions of the ways an epic bard in rural Uttar
Pradesh self-consciously employs various tunes and styles (Wadley
1989, 1991), I began to try, in spite of my musical illiteracy, to pay
attention to Madhu's use of "tune."[6] My initial impression of Madhu's
music had been that it was monotonous; what kept you awake was
the story. This is partially but not wholly true. Compared to the bard
Wadley describes, Madhu Nath's range of musical variations seems
limited; yet he does deliberately modulate emotional highlights of his
story with shifts in melody and rhythm.

6. Other studies that helped me to appreciate the interpenetration of musical
artistry and cultural meanings are Basso 1985; Feld 1982; Seeger 1987.

Madhu uses two patterned tunes, which he calls *rāg*s, in Gopi Chand and two different ones in Bharthari, where he also recycles both Gopi Chand *rāg*s. All four melodic patterns are flexible in that although each engenders verbal verse patterns, the melodic patterns frequently and readily change to accommodate narrative needs. In what I call Gopi Chand *rāg* 1, for example, each verse normally has three similar lines and one longer concluding one. Long narrative sequences, however, may repeat the short lines many more times than three before concluding. And for an emotional or dramatic climax the long concluding line may repeat once or even twice. The main *rāg* identified with Bharthari begins with a prolonged *Rājājīīīī*— "Honored King . . ."—that seems to signal the plaintive voice of the king's abandoned wife. Part 1 of Bharthari is performed in a style different from any of the others, its melody less interesting and less emotional, that seems to me in keeping with its orientation to external action.

Ethnomusicologist David Roche (personal communication 1991) describes Madhu Nath's musical style as one influenced by caste traditions but infused by new influences. He says that the melodic phrases are "pan-North Indian"—not particularly Rajasthani. Madhu Nath's musical style is, according to Roche, a "contemporary *bhajan* style" reflecting the influence of regional religious dramas and mythological films. Roche finds Madhu's music historically influenced by the harmonium—an instrument introduced to India by Christian missionaries from the West in the late nineteenth century and soon passionately adapted to Hindu devotional singing. This influence is apparent to Roche in Madhu's "intonation and diatonicism, with emphasis on major and mixolydian mode tetrachords." Although Madhu uses no harmonium—nor do other Rajasthani Nath epic performers I have met—many of Madhu's relatives and caste-fellows in and around Ghatiyali participate in *bhajan*-singing groups regularly accompanied by harmoniums.

That Madhu employs the term *rāg* to refer to the melodies he plays probably represents a folk usage rather than a significant link to Indian classical traditions. Once Madhu told Bhoju that he "always" sang in *āsāvarī rāg*, a named *rāg* within the classical system. Because I was hearing four distinctive melodies, I hoped that Madhu had a name for each of them. I made clips from the tapes and sent this "sampler" back to the village with Bhoju. Bhoju wrote, "I took that

rāg tape and listened to it with Madhu Nath, Shivji Nath, Ugma
Nath, and Nathu all together, but no one could tell a particular name
of the *rāg*s." Rather, the assembled Naths used labels such as "the
melody of rounds" (*pherī ko rāg*) or "Gopi Chand's melody" (*Gopī Chand
ko rāg*). This seems to confirm Roche's suggestion that Madhu's music
is not to be labeled among any fixed traditional systems but rather
is part of a creative synthesis continually emerging in North Indian
folk music.

It is widely acknowledged that any folk performance situation is
a dynamic, interactive event,[7] and this statement certainly describes
Rajasthani performances in general and Madhu Nath's in particular.
I shall examine the several ways in which Madhu and his audience
sustain this dynamic during individual performances. Before doing
so, however, I wish to suggest some broader contextual factors that
contribute to these occasions but are more diffuse and difficult to
pinpoint.

Rajasthan's regional culture includes a rich and diverse body of
living oral performance traditions. These enliven a daily existence
that may be both monotonous and laborious. On the one hand, an
urban Westerner like myself, landed in a place like Ghatiyali, is
overwhelmed by the abundance of festivals, rituals, all-night singing
sessions, storytelling, and other lesser and greater artistic and communicative events; during my first months in the village I often felt
that I was feasting at a perpetual banquet of live music and theater,
with no tickets required. On the other hand, in 1979–81 the villagers
had no TVs and few radios or tape recorders, while the nearest
cinema was a costly three-hour journey distant. Any performance
event punctuated the humdrum grind of labor-intensive agriculture.

Nath performance traditions must be viewed within this cultural
frame: they exist as one genre in a wealth of related genres; they also
exist as valued entertainment in a society not yet made blasé by
multiple media. Rural Rajasthani society, moreover, venerates religious experts and accords recognition to many from different ranks
and with varying sectarian affiliations. Like most of the region's
popular folk traditions, Madhu Nath's performances meshed with
his audience's twin passions for entertainment and enlightenment.
Although Madhu himself protests that his stories are not *śikṣā*, or

7. Bascom 1977; Bauman 1977, 1986; Seitel 1980; Tedlock 1983.

"instruction," audience members claim that they are. The Nath tales are not unique, nor are they the most highly prized of performances available to Rajasthani villagers. Yet they have a welcome and secure place in the annual round.

Madhu Nath at times refers to the entire tale of Gopi Chand or Bharthari as a *byāvalā,* a term that one dictionary defines as a god's wedding song (Platts 1974). Before returning to Rajasthan in 1987 I speculated that both tales might be so described because they were somehow anti-wedding songs. However, as I was to learn, a third long narrative in Madhu Nath's repertoire is "The Wedding Song of Lord Shiva" (*Śivjī kā byāvalā*); it seems clear that he has named the others accordingly. Most villagers do not use the term *byāvalā* to refer to Madhu Nath's performances and often simply call them *vārtā.* This label reveals their kinship with other epic tales of Rajasthani hero-gods whose singing and recitation may be called *vārtā,* too.[3]

According to the sensible, informed, and flexible definitions proffered in the recent important volume *Oral Epics in India,* the Bharthari–Gopi Chand tales fall beyond doubt in the epic genre. Epics in general are characterized as narrative, long, heroic, and sung (Blackburn and Flueckiger 1989, 2–4; Wadley 1989, 76). In the South Asian context, Blackburn and Flueckiger suggest, the quality "heroic" may be understood in three distinct ways. An epic may exhibit martial, sacrificial, or romantic heroism. Both the martial and sacrificial types "turn on themes of revenge, regaining lost land, or restoring lost rights," and stress "group solidarity"—all of which would apply to other Rajasthani epic-length tales. Romantic epics, by contrast, "celebrate individual actions that threaten that solidarity" (1989, 4–5). Clearly the tales of Bharthari and Gopi Chand belong in the "romantic" category if they belong anywhere. Yet our heroes are hardly traditional, undaunted lovers.

It might seem that the tales celebrate individual action that threatens group solidarity, but as I will discuss in more detail in the afterword, yogis gain nothing from a damaged social order. Rather, they maneuver for an intact social order that supports yogis. What then makes these tales romantic? Unless we consider them as stories of the union between guru and disciple, Bharthari and Gopi Chand are romances of parting. The theme of love in separation is a pervasive

8. See Pande 1963 for the scope of *vārtā.*

one in Indian literature. Longing for an absent lover—whether soldier, ascetic, or clerk in the city—has inspired much poetry on mortal love (Kolff 1990; Vaudeville 1986; Wadley 1983), as well as an entire genre of devotional expression. But most literature inspired by love in separation suggests at least a movement toward, or the possibility of, future reunion. Bharthari and Gopi Chand, by contrast, continuously and irrevocably move farther and farther from their loved ones. Madhu Nath's performances of Bharthari and Gopi Chand can be styled romantic epics celebrating separation rather than union, if we keep clearly in mind that the separation they establish is eternal.[9]

One factor distinguishing these stories from many others heard by villagers is that, although sung and told in the local dialect, they are not indigenous to Rajasthan—a matter I will deal with more extensively in chapter 3, where I attempt to trace their origins. Gopi Chand and Bharthari have been incorporated into Rajasthani traditions, and Rajasthani traditions have been incorporated into them. But these Nath tales are not self-defining epics that contribute to the identity of a regional culture—the kind of tales that people call "ours" (Blackburn et al., eds. 1989; Flueckiger 1989). Indeed, for Rajasthani farmers, Gopi Chand and Bharthari are stories of the exotic, in two senses. First, they are about other lands; second, they are about world-renouncers.

That Gopi Chand and Bharthari were understood in some ways as alien was brought home to me very strongly in 1988 when I asked some village men if they would want to be like Bharthari or Gopi Chand, and some village women if they would like their husbands or sons to emulate those figures. An almost universal answer from both sexes was "No, I wouldn't have the courage." Although some renouncers encountered and interviewed in temples spontaneously referred to Gopi Chand or Bharthari as exemplary in their capacity for *tyāg*, or "relinquishment," no ordinary persons held them up as role models.[10]

There is a real difference between my "induced"[11] performances

9. The only tale considered by the editors and authors of *Oral Epics in India* that belongs to Nath lore is that of Guga. Blackburn categorizes it as a romantic epic with a supraregional spread and places it about midway on the ritual-to-entertainment continuum (1989, 17–20). The same description applies more or less to Bharthari and Gopi Chand.

10. See, however, Kothari 1989 on the unsuitability of many folk epic heroes and heroines as role models.

11. See Goldstein 1967 for the "induced natural context" in folklore fieldwork.

of both tales and the performances that most villagers hear twice a year when Madhu makes his rounds. They hear fragments, and often their favorite fragments are repeated from year to year. People's understanding may be limited by lack of familiarity with the whole story. Most of those whom Bhoju or I questioned were easily able to retell the most popular episodes from both tales.[12] Few villagers, however, had heard either tale from beginning to end from Madhu, although a number had seen theatrical performances at religious fairs. Several members of leatherworker castes (*regar* and *chamār*) claimed to know very little about the stories; one complained that when Madhu came to his neighborhood he only spoke "a few lines" and left again.

My own experience of immediate audience reactions to the performances of Gopi Chand and Bharthari is limited to the context of the event which I sponsored, for I never observed Madhu "making rounds" (although he was recorded doing so by my colleague Joseph Miller). In the setting of my performance the responses were quite limited. After three or four hours of listening, until well past midnight, we would usually hurry home when Madhu ended his singing. Indeed, he often closed a night's session by saying to me, "Now go to bed."

Madhu Nath's Stories in Synopsis

It has been said of at least one Indian epic—and may be true of most—that no one ever hears it for the first time. Western readers, who have not participated from childhood in the culture that produces these stories, may need a "pony." Throughout these introductory chapters I often talk about events and characters in Madhu Nath's versions of Bharthari and Gopi Chand. Therefore, as points of reference for those citations, I offer skeletal plot summaries in advance, segmented and ordered according to Madhu Nath's performance as it is translated in this book (see also figs. 4 and 5).

Bharthari's "Birth Story" (part 1) describes how his father was cursed by his own father to enter a donkey's womb. The donkey suc-

---

12. Episodes for Bharthari included Pingala's *satī* and Bharthari's encounter with Gorakh Nath at the funeral pyre (both in part 2), as well as Bharthari's begging and Pingala's lament (part 3). For Gopi Chand most commonly cited were his mother's instructions (part 1), his begging from Patam De Rani (part 2), his troubles with the lady magicians (part 3), and his farewell to his sister (part 3).

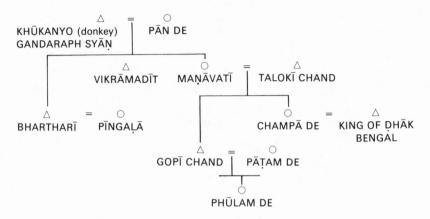

4. Family relationships in the tales of King Gopi Chand and King Bharthari.

ceeds after lengthy efforts in marrying a princess and founding a city, Dhara Nagar, where his three offspring—Bharthari, Vikramaditya, and Manavati—are born.

In part 2, Bharthari is king of Dhara Nagar and married to Queen Pingala. He rides out hunting and kills a stag, whose seven hundred fifty does, widowed, curse King Bharthari that his women will weep in the Color Palace as they do in the jungle. They then hurl themselves on the dead buck's antlers and thus commit *satī*.[13] Bharthari wonders if his own wife is equally devoted. He sends her a handkerchief soaked in deer's blood with the message that he is dead. Pingala knows this is a test but decides to die anyway. Bharthari has other adventures in the forest but eventually returns home to find Pingala a heap of ashes. He goes mad with remorse, until the yogi guru Gorakh Nath arrives, demonstrates the illusory nature of life and death, and finally restores Pingala to the king.

Part 3 finds Bharthari sleepless and unsatisfied. Convinced that nothing in the fluctuating world matters, he abandons his wife and renounces his throne to seek initiation from Gorakh, who sends him back to the palace to beg alms from Pingala and call her "Mother."

---

13. Although the common image of a *satī* is of a woman who chooses to be cremated alive on her husband's funeral pyre, any style of death may be called *satī* if through it a female follows a beloved male.

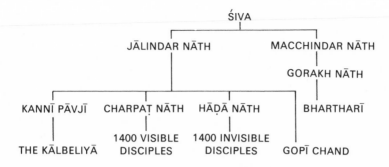

5. Nath guru-disciple lineages in the tales of King Gopi Chand and King Bharthari.

She reproaches him but gives the alms. This difficult task accomplished, Bharthari returns to Gorakh Nath's campfire.

Gopi Chand's "Birth Story" (part 1) opens with Manavati (Bharthari's sister, married into "Gaur Bengal") instructing her only son, Gopi Chand: "Be a yogi." She then reveals in a long flashback how she obtained the boon of a son from Lord Shiva although no son was written in her fate. In order not to break his promise, Shiva allows her to borrow one of the yogi Jalindar Nath's disciples, and she chooses Gopi Chand. The loan has a limit: after twelve years of ruling the kingdom, Gopi Chand must become a yogi or die. As a wandering ascetic, however, he will gain immortality. Gopi Chand, possessing eleven hundred wives and sixteen hundred slave girls, is not pleased with his mother's bargain.

In part 2 Gopi Chand tries to get rid of the guru by putting him down a well. But it is Gopi Chand who dies, and only the power of yogis saves him. Restored to his palace, he follows his mother's instructions and has his ears cut by Jalindar. The guru then sends him to beg alms from Queen Patam De, his chief wife, and to call her "Mother." Although Patam De finally fills his alms bowl, when her mother-in-law literally twists her arm, Jalindar has to rescue Gopi Chand from the palace, where he is surrounded by weeping women.

Against his mother's and guru's advice, Gopi Chand heads for Dhaka in Bengal to say goodbye to his sister, Champa De Rani (part 3). On the way he is harassed by seven lady magicians who transform him into various animals and abuse him. Jalindar sends a party of yogis to rescue him but it fails. The guru himself then accompanies a second group, which succeeds. Gopi Chand proceeds to his sister's; she dies of grief in his arms but is brought back to life by Jalindar. Gopi Chand spends some happy time with her and then leaves alone.

In part 4 a dispute arises between Jalindar's disciple Kanni Pavji and Gorakh Nath. Kanni Pavji tells Gorakh that his guru, Machhindar Nath, is enjoying women and fathering sons in Bengal; Gorakh tells Kanni Pavji that his guru, Jalindar, is at the bottom of a well. Gorakh goes to Bengal and rescues Machhindar, destroying his wives and sons along the way. Gorakh then brings seven species of locusts out of the well, tricks Jalindar into giving immortality to Gopi Chand and Bharthari, and convinces him to emerge. All the great yogis then feast one another. At Gorakh Nath's "wish-feast" Kanni Pavji's disciples wish for improper foods and are degraded.

Madhu Nath's Performances for Me

It is winter. We assemble in that part of the Rajasthani village house called a *pol*—a covered entranceway wide enough to form a room that lies between street and courtyard, often with raised platforms on either side for storage or sitting. This area is a shady breezeway in the summer and a shelter in the winter. By the time we gather there after the evening meal it is already dark and slightly chilly. Everyone, male and female, has wrapped a shawl or blanket over his or her usual daily attire. In the center of the *pol* is a small fire of dry sticks that burns low, even its frugal warmth a luxury in this wood-impoverished region.

In January 1981 I had already lived fifteen months in the village, but recording Madhu Nath was my first experience as performance patron. I received a quick education in how to fulfill this role with appropriate liberality. I must supply the singer and his son with a "bundle of *bīṛīs*"—*bīṛīs* being harsh, leaf-wrapped cigarettes smoked by almost all males who have not taken a vow of abstinence. I must treat performers and audience to tea each night, which involved purchasing tea leaves, sugar, and milk in advance—the last item not always easy to buy in the evening. In addition, a quarter- or half-kilo of *guṛ*, unrefined brown sugar, was indispensable. The singers required *guṛ* to soothe their throats (Madhu had an awful cough, which did not deter him from relishing the *bīṛīs*). A generous patron should pass small lumps of *guṛ* round to all the listeners once or twice in the course of an evening.

At the beginning of our recording sessions my comprehension of the sung segments of Madhu's performance was very limited. How pleased I was to benefit from the custom of *arthāv* or explanation, in which Madhu repeated everything he had sung and elaborated on much of it. During the *arthāv*, members of the audience who have passively listened to the sung portions are more actively engaged by a vital performer. A formalized element of performer-audience inter- action in Rajasthan is the part played by the *hūṅkār*. A *hūṅkār*, which can only be awkwardly glossed as someone who makes the sound *hūṅ*—a kind of affirmative grunt—is a standard feature of any story- telling event, from women's worship stories to men's informal anecdotes.

At first I thought the *hūṅkār*'s function was to offer a perfunctory reassurance to the performer that at least one person was really listen- ing. Given the distracting surroundings of many village performances— often including clamorous childern and simultaneous competing activities—such assurance may indeed be needed. However, after being pressed more than once into fulfilling this role myself (which my frequent misunderstandings at times made me bumble or fake quite awkwardly), I began to perceive that a good *hūṅkār* can elicit a tale-teller's enthusiasm whereas a poor one can discourage a full telling.

A *hūṅkār*'s responses can shape the performance content as well as its quality. This too I learned from personal experience. On relistening to my tapes it was evident to me that when I played *hūṅkār* to Madhu, if he was in a generous mood, his *arthāv* was noticeably changed: he used more standard Hindi (versus Rajasthani) vocabulary; he ex- plained cultural phenomena he thought I might not understand; he glossed terms he suspected I was failing to grasp. For example, to my uncertain grunt following the line "Gopi Chand ruled the kingdom," he added, "Gopi Chand ruled, like Indira Gandhi rules."

The opposite case, a situation far more comfortable if sometimes less educational for me, would be when someone who knew the story well acted as *hūṅkār*. That person might even supply key lines if Madhu seemed to be dallying before giving them. During climaxes other audience members chimed in, adding their bit to the *hūṅkār*'s own responses, which also became less perfunctory. Thus when King Bharthari surveys the seven hundred fifty magically created look- alike Queen Pingalas—a vision both awesome and slightly comical—a number of spontaneous commentators (audible on the tape but only selectively included by the scribe) added their exclamations to the *hūṅkār*'s: "They looked just alike, all seven hundred and fifty!" "Their faces were exactly the same!"

Madhu deliberately evoked audience participation by identifying persons in the story with persons in the audience.[14] One way he did this was by caste. For example, when Jalindar Nath's disciples arrive in Bengal they encounter a gardener. Since there was a man of the gardener caste in the audience, Madhu named the gardener in the story with his name. Besides naming story characters after audience members, Madhu sometimes named audience members after story characters. Thus throughout the Gopi Chand performances he gently teased a younger relative by calling him "Charpat Nath" after one of the powerful yogi figures. This stuck, so that when Bhoju or I met that young man outside the storytelling context, we would call him Charpat.

The entire performance of Gopi Chand took five recording sessions, each from three and one-quarter to four and one-half hours long; it filled the better part of eleven 90-minute cassettes—or over sixteen hours of tape. Each night's session was broken up by short intervals of *bātchīt* (conversation), during which the recorder was shut down, usually following the *arthāv* and preceding a new sung section, but sometimes coming between singing and *arthāv*. During one of the breaks strong sweet tea would be passed round and eagerly swallowed, its caffeine and warmth both welcome.

The first part, the "Birth Story," was recorded in its entirety on 24 January 1981. It took two sessions, on the nights of 26 and 27 January, to record the whole "Journey to Bengal" episode. This was followed by a twelve-day hiatus in our recording (during which much transcription and translation work went forward). Madhu then performed "Gopi Chand Begs from Queen Patam De" on the night of 9 February and "Instruction from Gorakh Nath" on 10 February.

When I returned to Ghatiyali at the end of 1987, after an interlude of almost eight years, it was in order to record Madhu Nath's version of the tale of Bharthari, and my arrival was no surprise. I had written well in advance to Nathu and Bhoju. There were several surprises in store for me, however—one so serendipitous that, looking back, it seems like a most improbable stroke of fate. The very aged mother of

---

14. K. Narayan very delightfully describes the expert practice of this technique by a North Indian guru (Narayan 1989).

Nathu Nath, my former research assistant, had died. His caste had decided to hold a major funeral feast to which Naths from villages all over the area were invited. Because this feast coincided almost exactly with the time I had to spend in Ghatiyali, it was certain that Madhu would be there, and not in Sadara as I had feared. It also presented a remarkable opportunity for Daniel Gold and me to meet many knowledgeable Naths. Much of my understanding of that caste's identity, presented in chapter 2, is the result of our conversations with Nathu's guests.

Word circulated among those attending the funeral feast that a foreigner was interested in their verbal art, and their caste lore in general. Several groups of strangers knocked at my door, a number of whom announced their capability and willingness to perform Gopi Chand–Bharthari. Even Nathu, who seemed to be annoyed with Madhu for reasons that never became clear to me, strongly suggested that I should record someone else's version. But I held out for Madhu, feeling that the continuity of my translation project required the same bard and that all these other potential singers presented an almost frightening distraction.

It was out of the question to record in Nathu's house, as we had in 1981, because the rooms were virtually overflowing with guests and all seating and tea-making resources were seriously overtaxed. Instead, we spread a carpet on the newly plastered courtyard of the Rajput house that had been my home in 1979–81 and was my camp this trip. We thus had cloistered Rajput women in the audience, and I was able to compensate for an old injury done to my former landlady. She had been angry with me eight years ago for not inviting and escorting her to the Gopi Chand sessions. Now she was able to savor Bharthari in the comfort of her own home.

Again, it was winter and we wrapped ourselves in shawls, savored our tea breaks, and sucked on *gur*. Madhu's performance got off to a somewhat slow start; Bharthari's birth story has more repetition in it than any other segment of either text. But soon Madhu warmed to his themes. His rendition of the central part of Bharthari—containing the best-loved climax when the king madly circles Pingala's pyre—was perfectly delightful and aroused much audience appreciation. Besides myself, Daniel, and our two inattentive sons, our gathering always included my research assistant Bhoju; my landlady; her daughter-in-law, grandchildren, and nieces; and a variable number of neighbors and friends, who wandered in by plan or chance. Nathu, immersed in the work of the funeral feast, was unable to attend.

Madhu completed Bharthari's tale in three recording sessions held on the nights of 28, 29, and 30 December 1987. This represents approximately eight hours of recording, filling five and one-half 90-minute tapes. On the whole, the performance atmosphere for Bharthari was very similar to that for Gopi Chand eight years before, with only a few perceptible differences. Madhu's cough seemed a little worse; Shivji's singing seemed a little better; Bhoju was the *hūṅkār* most of the time and played his part vigorously.

Translation in Practice and Theory

Toward the conclusion of part 1 of Madhu Nath's Gopi Chand, Manavati Mother has at last won the boon of a son. She goes to select from among the yogi Jalindar Nath's fourteen hundred visible disciples the one that pleases her the most; then Jalindar will loan him to her by having him reborn as her child. But until she spots beautiful Gopi Chand, the queen is far from delighted with her prospects as she scans the meditating yogis. Her words—as Madhu Nath narrated them and I recorded them in 1981—were as follows: "What will I do with such bearded fellows? What will I do with such twisted limbs, or ones like this who don't even understand speech (*bolī hī na hamjai*)? What will I do with them?"

When Madhu Nath thus elaborated the queen mother's expressions of distaste there was laughter among our small company—laughter that was dutifully noted in parentheses by Nathu Nath when he transcribed the recording. Why was there laughter? Because, as Madhu enunciated "those who don't even understand speech," he gestured toward me. True to his characterization of me as uncomprehending, although I laughed along with the rest, I did not catch this quick jest at my expense. I thought we were laughing at the images of yogis as unattractive, defective persons not likely to make it in the world. But Bhoju, my research assistant, explained Madhu's jibe to me, as kindly as possible, when we read the transcribed text together a week or so later and the scene was still fresh in his memory. Over the words "those who don't even understand speech" I penciled "like Ain-Bai," my village name (this third-person notation symptomatic I suppose of self-alienation common in fieldwork experience), and soon forgot about it.

Six years later, as I embarked on a Mellon postdoctoral fellowship that centered on the Gopi Chand tale, I rediscovered Madhu's little "joke" and paused to ponder this characterization of me—a confident, well-funded translator and published ethnographer—as someone who didn't even "understand speech." It brought to my mind a moment described in the preface to my book on pilgrimage: my first evening in the company of Bhoju Ram Gujar, the young village man who was later to become my closest assistant, pilgrimage brother, and eventually coauthor. During this night he had excited and tired us both by steadily imparting to me in lucid grammatical Hindi the mystical and multiple meanings of esoteric Rajasthani hymns as they were being performed during an intense all-night singing party celebrating the new benign identity of a restless ghost.

When it became apparent to this young man, around two or three in the morning, that I was exhausted and had ceased to absorb his explanations, he chided me by quoting a Rajasthani saying. "For you," he said, "all this is 'brown sugar for a deaf-mute' (*gūṅge kā guṛ*)." Steeped as I was in the rich village world, consuming its sweets but unable to hear its language clearly, where would I find the tongue to tell of it? In my published preface I exclaim, "What a perfect metaphor for the anthropological enterprise!" (Gold 1988, xiv). This metaphor, simultaneously evoking inexpressible delight and human disability, seems equally applicable to the efforts of translation—especially the translation of a multidimensional, interactive communicative event into a linear, soundless, printed story. In the remaining pages of this chapter I examine the phases of my translation efforts, returning in the end to some other metaphors—of hopelessness and possibility.

The first round of translation for Gopi Chand was certainly the most enjoyable. During February and March 1981 except for two short trips, each of a few days' duration, to wrap up loose ends in my pilgrimage research, and the usual distractions of festivals, rituals, and the interpersonal psychodramas that I had finally come to accept as part of village life, my time and attention were remarkably centered on the recordings and rapidly emerging written text of Gopi Chand.

I employed both Nathu Nath and Bhoju Gujar full time during this period. Ugma Nathji, nonliterate but more knowledgeable than Nathu in his caste's teachings, was also often on the scene. We worked in two neighboring rooms, each opening on the same courtyard but not adjoining the other, as was the architectural custom in the village. Nathu (with or without Ugma Nath) would sit in one room, listening to tapes and transcribing Madhu's words with painstaking accuracy. In the other room Bhoju and I sat side by side at a small desk doing our "translation work" (*anuvād kā kām*)—as we explained it in most unsatisfactory fashion to the many skeptical questioners who wondered how we passed our days. This work involved reading through the pages Nathu had transcribed and stopping everywhere I had a problem with the Rajasthani. Bhoju would then endeavor to clarify my confusions with explanations and glosses in Hindi. I made notes in pencil directly on the transcription, in an *ad hoc* mixture of English and Hindi.

Occasionally, when confronted by something extremely puzzling, we would resort to the nine-volume *Rājasthānī Sabad Kos* (Lalas 1962–78; hereafter *RSK*) with its ponderous definitions in Sanskritized Hindi. Far more often I just wrote the meanings of words as Bhoju dictated them to me. Sometimes he embellished his verbal descriptions with sketches, demonstrating, for example, the design of a kind of earring or the shape of a particular clay pot.

In midafternoon scribe and translators all took a long tea break together and often talked and joked in terms of the stories and the bard's language. If Nathu, whose caste identity was Nath or Yogi, had to go somewhere, Bhoju would recite the bard's favorite couplet: "A seated yogi's a stake in the ground but a yogi once up is a fistful of wind." Gossiping about the passion of an illicit lover when aroused by his woman, Nathu might say, "It was just as if a wick were lit to one hundred maunds of gunpowder"—parroting the bard's stock metaphor for Gopi Chand's emotional crises. Thus the text's special language merged as I learned it with everyday life.

I had not the slightest sense of what I would do with the results of all this effort. But I found the protracted routinized translation work to be very soothing. It filled my days and kept my mind from dwelling on all the things I would never be able to finish, or even begin, as time ran out. Inevitably but nonetheless abruptly, when we were but a few pages into part 4, I at last had to leave Ghatiyali. I did not spend any time with the text again until 1987—six years later. The summary of Gopi Chand's story, which I included in my dissertation (Gold 1984) and ensuing book (Gold 1988) as well as in the article that I coauthored with my husband (Gold and Gold 1984), was done from memory. As I discovered to my chagrin when I did return to the text, it contains a few errors, the result of my imperfect comprehension and memory lapses, combined with Madhu's occasional vagueness. For example, I stated in that summary that Jalindar Nath rescues Gopi Chand from Death's Messengers; actually it is Gorakh Nath who, after taunting Jalindar with the news that his given disciple is dead, frees Gopi Chand so dramatically.

The second round of translation work, still only for Gopi Chand, began in 1987 when, supported by a Mellon Foundation Fellowship at Cornell University, I sat daily at a computer with Nathu's transcription in my lap and typed directly onto the screen a rough and literal English version. I never lifted a dictionary during this stage but worked entirely from my own knowledge of the language and Bhoju's glosses that I had jotted down six years earlier. By late summer 1987 I had a 250-page double-spaced English typescript. The last 80 pages were by far the roughest since they covered the final segment that I had never read through with Bhoju. I think of this as the "reading-for-meaning" phase of my translation. At this point I felt I had a full understanding of the story and wrote several interpretive essays (Gold 1989, 1991).

Convinced, however, that nothing I said about Gopi Chand's story would be fully valid unless I knew Bharthari's as well, I made plans to return to Rajasthan over winter break 1987–88. During that hectic six-week trip I had nothing comparable to the earlier daily routine of eight or nine hours in which I used to sit peacefully reading with Bhoju. I did manage to go over and solve most of the problems encountered in part 4 of Gopi Chand. Although I set the transcription process in motion for Bharthari, I left the village with only twelve pages on paper. Nathu completed the rest after my departure; Bhoju made interlinear notes in red ink and forwarded it to me.

Later still (from June through September 1989) supported by an NEH translation grant, I entered yet another phase, during which I relistened to all the tapes. The tapes made me aware of nuances of meaning totally lost in transcription and helped me to relive interactive dimensions of the performance in which I had participated but which I had forgotten during my subsequent fixation on the story. As Madhu's wonderfully gruff and expressive voice, or his minor-key melodic *sārangī* riffs filled my ears, and I stared at flat words on the grey shrunken screen, I despaired over the inadequacy of all translation.

While my ethnographic self retreated, stymied, I became obsessed with definitions. During these months I compulsively read dictionaries, searching for every word I did not "know"—a category arbitrarily comprising every word for which I was relying solely on Bhoju's glosses—in a series of dictionaries (Rajasthani-Hindi, Hindi-Hindi, Hindi-English as required). I made alphabetical lists with cross-references. Words that I found in none of these references, or whose dictionary definitions did not coincide with Bhoju's, I listed, and every month letters filled with these queries flew back to India. Bhoju often consulted Madhu himself or Madhu's son, Shivji, before responding.

Toward the end of this unpleasant and laborious period, another translator and I were able to bring Bhoju to America. I had the uncanny experience of sitting in my Ithaca office, subzero temperatures outside, with a village voice in my ears. By then my involvement in these stories and the tradition that generated them extended beyond firsthand ethnographic experience; I had read numerous variants from other regions and times and was working out my interpretations. No longer did I passively take dictation from Bhoju; occasionally I found myself arguing with him.

When Gopi Chand's wife reproaches him for becoming a yogi, she says: "Grain-giver, I taste bitter to you, but you think that yogi's just swell. He shoved a loincloth up your ass and put these earrings on you. He pierced your ears and put these great big earrings in them." In the village in 1981 Bhoju told me that the word the queen used for "earring" meant "yogis' earring" because of course that's what she was referring to—the yogis' earrings her husband wore. But the word itself, *murakā*, refers to a small earring worn by ordinary men. It is not one of the several special words for yogis' earrings, most often called *darśanī* or "divine visions." I thought the queen was being deliberately disrespectful by using this word, as she surely was about the loincloth up the ass—employing a crude term for anus. Bhoju, however, said she was just an ignorant woman who didn't know the right word for yogis' earring.

Later in the scene Gopi Chand calls on his guru for help and threatens that if the guru doesn't come he'll go back to taking care of his kingdom and get rid of his "earrings-and-stuff"—calling them *murakyāṅ vurakāṅ*—thus further exaggerating the queen's disparaging terminology. The echo-word formation readily implies "earrings and all the rest of this yogic paraphernalia." To me it seems to confirm

Gopi Chand's interpretation of the queen's language, adopted when he is momentarily swept over to her perspective (and I see him as constantly backsliding thus from a yogic to a householder's viewpoint). The bard is quite unlikely to have used the wrong word by accident as he himself wears these "divine visions" and is extremely conscious of their special power. Bhoju was still not convinced.

I relate this dispute because it reveals nicely how much of a translator's problem lodges not so much in words but in contexts. To translate *murakā* as yogis' earring—even though that is what it refers to—would be simply wrong. But to translate it as "earring" also leaves something out: the fact that it is the wrong word for the type of earring referred to. Any solution to such moments must transact a compromise between fluidity and semantics. As is no doubt too often the case, I resorted here to a footnote where I gave both sides of the argument.

Eventually I arrived at the most challenging and vexing task: to take the repetitive, awkwardly phrased, but reasonably accurate product of all this labor and transform it into something palatable, pleasurable, charming. After all, Madhu's performance was all those things. I no longer feel quite deaf and dumb, but what I have to offer is not exactly brown sugar. My first decision was to use the written word and the printed page traditionally. I respect and admire the groundbreaking efforts of Dennis Tedlock (1983) and Elizabeth Fine (1984) among others, who have tried to develop innovative ways of putting oral performances on paper. Yet I myself find it difficult to enjoy their productions aesthetically. Such devices as uneven type sizes, slanting lines, and coded symbols do provide a far better record of oral performance than plain linear print. But as access to an aesthetic experience, for me at least, they fail. My immediate reaction to uneven type and arcane symbols is an almost automatic blurring or skimming impulse rather than transformed awareness. Whether this is common or idiosyncratic I do not know. In any case, I have taken a different route.

Surrendering music and largely surrendering audience interaction, in a sense I gave up on sustaining an oral mode; readers will have to supply that from my descriptions and their own imaginations. What I tried to reproduce is the rough charm and spontaneous flow of Madhu's speech, without falsely embellishing it. The fourth round was literally countless rounds, for I could not say how many times I went over the English version, rearranging, rewording, and cutting.

Eventually I had to make substantial cuts, by which something is certainly lost, but much is gained for all but the most patient English readers.

I cut in three ways, or at three levels. On the grossest of these, I made the decision—after translating the entire performance—to omit the sung portions except for those that open and close each of the seven parts of the two epics. A few other maverick segments of sung text slipped in because they advance the plot significantly with no spoken explanation covering the same ground. Normally, however, the explanation gives all that was sung and more. The singing does not present beautiful poetry; it lacks rhyme and its meter is strongly subordinated to the *sārangī rāg*s. The pleasure in it, I have come to believe, both from discussions with Madhu's audience and from my own experience, is largely musical. But the pleasure of the *arthāv* is intentionally verbal—and is therefore a pleasure much more easily translatable to the printed page.

The second level of cutting involved condensing most of a particular scene when it replicated almost exactly another that was fully translated. Such scenes are limited. The biggest reduction from the original involved the encounter between a begging yogi and a group of slave girls that occurs once in Bharthari and three times in Gopi Chand. Of these four instances, two were substantially condensed as noted within the text. Another highly repetitive moment is the contest between yogis and lady magicians; I gave Gopi Chand's initial encounter fully but condensed whenever possible, and so noted, the subsequent encounters between Charpat Nath, followed by Hada Nath, and their Bengali enemies.

The third level of cutting is the one that makes me as a folklorist most uneasy, but its execution may contribute most to making this text generally accessible. This is the excision of innumerable internal repetitions—repetitions that give the oral performer time to think, that give his audience time to take it all in, but that on the printed page become rapidly tedious. My aim was to retain enough of these to leave the English with a colloquial, oral "flavor," but to remove enough to keep the story moving at an acceptable pace.

Let me give an example, from the opening scene of Gopi Chand. The queen has just told her son to be a yogi, and he is questioning her knowledge of yoga. My translation in this book is as follows:

Then Gopi Chand said, "But mother, you live in purdah inside the palace, and yogis live in the jungle. They do *tapas* by their campfires in the jungle. But you live in the palace. So, how did you come to know any yogis?"

Madhu Nath's original speech translated word for word goes like this:

Then Gopi Chand said, "Oh, Manavati Mata, you live in purdah inside the palace and a yogi, yogis, they live in the jungle. They live in the jungle performing *tapas* by their campfires, and you stay in the palace, so how did you come to know yogis? How do you know them? Yogis live in the jungle, in the woods. And you live inside the palace, so how did you get to know them, you?"

I think this example speaks for itself, and it is perfectly typical.

Pottery Lessons

The act of translation is often enough metaphorically maligned, in images that include the translator as executioner, bigamist, and traitor.[15] Fortunately, more benign images also exist. Perhaps the most pleasing of these, especially to an anthropologist steeped in notions of empathy, is that of the translator as friend, sharer, intimate— evoked by Kelly, who cites Rosecommon's seventeenth-century essay. Kelly writes of a "sharing between friends" that is "not merely informational: friends add to the information they share, a joy in the act of recounting it and a vicarious sharing of each other's experience on terms special to the friendship" (Kelly 1979, 63).

If part of a positive vision of translation is intimacy, another part is craftsmanship. Yet it is just such praiseworthy traits as skill, technique, and knowledge that contribute to the translator's self-image problem. If translation is skill then it is something less than art, a secondary act. Among all the metaphors proposed for translation, one of the most elegant and subtle is that of Walter Benjamin, whose essay "The Task of the Translator" begins with the skilled but artless act of gluing together pot shards but moves rapidly beyond this mundane figure into luminous visions.

15. For translator as killer see Nabokov cited in Zvelebil 1987, vi; the bigamy image is one among several in Johnson 1985, 143, whose subtle exegesis I do not touch here; traitor is of course from the Latin pun-proverb.

Fragments of a vessel which are to be glued together must match one another in the smallest details, although they need not be like one another. In the same way, a translation, instead of resembling the meaning of the original, must lovingly and in detail incorporate the original's mode of signification, thus making both the original and the translation recognizable as fragments of a greater language, just as fragments are part of a vessel.

Later in the same paragraph Benjamin continues: "A real translation is transparent; it does not cover the original, does not block its light, but allows the pure language, as though reinforced by its own medium, to shine upon the original all the more fully" (1969, 78–79).

Several metaphors are working on several levels here. On the one hand matching the pieces of a broken pot is like the reproduction of meaning in translation; and on the other the original and the translation are themselves both fragments, not wholes. Abandoning the pots with their shapes, Benjamin goes on to speak of covering and translucency. The translation does not cover the original but allows light to shine through—not from it, however, but upon it. There appears to be, in that light, a premise of a reality bigger than both translation and original. When I read Benjamin it reminded me of a broken pot in the Rajasthani bard Madhu Nath's own stories—a pot that can be neither glued together nor replicated.

This pot appears in King Bharthari's tale in the central episode of part 2. Here the yogi Gorakh Nath mourns for his broken clay jug, deliberately mocking King Bharthari's mourning for his cremated queen. The king says the jug is easily replaced, and the yogi retorts that the queen is too. They agree that the yogi will restore Queen Pingala to life if the king replaces the jug. The king commandeers the labor of scores of potters, but the yogi uses his "divine play" (*līlā*) to spoil the potters' work so they fail to get the original jug's color just right. When cartloads of jugs are delivered by exhausted potters, Gorakh Nath scorns them, holding up his shards of a slightly different color, and demanding once more a jug just like the one that broke:

So King Bharthari grasped his feet and prostrated himself. "Grain-giver, I've done the best I could, good or bad, I've ordered what I could. Now, Grain-giver, that's enough. Good or bad, black or fair, make me a Pingala. Just as I've brought these jugs, black or yellow, so bring her, black or yellow."

Of course, the yogi is able to summon up not one but seven hundred fifty identical queens and the sameness of their faces, clothes, and jewelry are elaborated upon to the audience's considerable wonder. On the surface the point seems to be that yogis are more powerful than kings or potters: without divine power, a king can't even replicate the form and color of a common clay jug; with it a yogi can infinitely multiply the form and color of a human being who has burned to ash.

Gorakh Nath's pottery lesson, however, goes beyond such trumpeting of yogis' magic power. For even perfect reproductions are illusions, if there is no graspable reality in the original. This lack of reality operates on several levels. We do not even know whether any of the seven hundred fifty Pingalas is the real Pingala—since she burned up and all these may just be Gorakh Nath's *śaktis*, enslaved female spirits in Pingala's form. But, even if one of the restored queens is the real one, she is still no better than a whore (as Gorakh Nath makes clear) because no human love endures forever. All of them, perfect copies though they are, are just as false as the cartloads of jugs that do not match the original jug. They represent distractions from higher or calmer realities for which the yogi's unblemished and irreplaceable jug of pure cool water may itself be a sign.

Walter Benjamin's pottery lesson indicates that translating from one language to another might be like the act of matching fragments to rebuild a shattered whole, but that this work is neither perfect reproduction nor an illusory effort doomed to failure. Ultimately, Benjamin's images push our thoughts beyond the translator and his work, to consider the relation between languages, suggesting that a shared human capacity for communication exists beyond particular tongues.

Why do I thus laboriously juxtapose these very different uses of broken-pot images emerging from different cultural discourses and created for different didactic aims? One solid if small reason is that it seems to me auspicious that for both Nath yogis and European literary criticism a broken pot and its reconstruction or replication may become metaphors for the possible and the impossible, indicators of communication between two worlds (whether of French and German poetry, or of yogis and kings, or of Rajasthani peasants and Western readers). One ephemeral but larger reason for this pottery lesson is that *both* Benjamin's and Gorakh Nath's metaphors point beyond cycles of disintegration and reconstruction to some more stable area of light or truth. For those of us who spend our days translating texts and cultures, this is encouraging.

Yellow or black, I have tried to make these tales stand up. Lacking yogis' magic along with much other knowledge and skill, I have labored even longer and harder than Bharthari's potters. I can only hope that the imperfect results presented here are, as Benjamin advises, limpid to the light of the original.

Chapter Two

Naths or Jogis in North India

The preceding chapter introduced Madhu Nath, the storyteller, as an individual and located him in the rural society of Rajasthan where he lives, sings, and explains his tales. Here I shall selectively explore some broader contexts of Madhu's knowledge, while continuing to touch base within the corpus of his performed texts. The tales of Gopi Chand and Bharthari as sung and told by Madhu Nath belong to a loosely bounded but nameable tradition whose roots reach back at least to the tenth or twelfth century. I shall speak of this as the Nath tradition, but its adherents or practitioners are often popularly designated *Jogī,* or in some areas *Jugī*—vernacular derivatives of *yogi.*

Throughout this book I use English "yogi" rather than *jogī,* unless referring to a specific caste in a specific region by its name of record. And I use the terms Nath and yogi interchangeably, except when focusing on the significance of their respective etymologies. Nath teachings and stories flow as one stream within popular Hinduism, contributing to and drawing from several others. The purpose of this chapter is to give readers of Gopi Chand's and Bharthari's tales a sense of these stories' roots, and of the bard's roots, within such broader cultural, historical, and religiohistorical patterns.[1]

One way of understanding the popular stories of the Naths, including Madhu's tales, is to consider them as didactically motivated representations of renunciation. In these representations both a high

---

1. The progression of this chapter very deliberately leads to the tales that are our central focus. Others have written about Naths themselves as a focal topic; those seeking a fuller and more "disinterested" treatment are referred to them: Briggs 1973; Dvivedi 1981, n.d.; Mahapatra 1972, 75–96; Pandey 1980.

evaluation of world-renunciation and an appreciation of the sacrifices entailed by acting on that evaluation are transmitted for the edification and entertainment of householders.[2] The stories provide an interface between two distinguishable although intricately linked social and religious universes.

In thus formulating as separable but interwoven the lifestyles and worldviews of householders and yogi ascetics, I do not intend to address directly the big issues of "man-in-the-world" versus "world-renouncer" in pan-Indian thought. These issues have been elegantly if misleadingly formulated by Louis Dumont and worried over by many others including myself.[3] Although the following discussion may shed some light on those vexed matters, my focus is on a smaller-scale but still complex contrast. This is the contrast between householder or *grihasthī* Naths who form hereditary castes (*jāti*s), and renunciatory or *nāgā* Naths—using *nāgā* here in its unmarked sense of celibate member of a Nath sect.[4] It seems no accident that it is frequently *grihasthī* Naths who purvey—not only to their own communities but to society at large—the stories of Gopi Chand and Bharthari, in which the central figures are, or become, *nāgā* Naths.

I begin by considering the term Nath as it is applied to renouncer members of a *sampradāy* or religious sect.[5] In this context the category

2. For an interpretive approach to these issues, see the afterword. See also Gold and Gold 1984.

3. For Dumont's formulation see Dumont 1970; for some reflections on, reactions to, and conflicts with Dumont see, for example, Bradford 1985; Burghart 1983a, 1983b; Das 1977; Gold 1988, 3–4; Madan ed. 1981.

4. Meaning four under the masculine noun *nāgau* in the *RSK* is *nāth sampradāy kā vah vyakti jo vivāh nahīṅ kartā hai*—"a member of the Nath sect who does not marry." During interviews in the winter of 1987–88 I heard both Rajasthani renouncer and householder interviewees regularly employ *nāgā* in opposition to *grihasthī*. Used thus, *nāgā* does not refer to the particular sect of Shaivite renouncers who go naked (the primary adjectival meaning of *nāgā*) or to the "fighting *nāgā*s"—famous battalions of these unclothed ascetics, whose participation in local military struggles is recorded in Rajasthan and elsewhere.

5. Some scholars argue that "sect" may not appropriately translate Hindi/ Sanskrit *sampradāy*. Barz, following Wach, shows etymologically that *sampradāy* refers positively to a "vehicle for transmission of doctrine" whereas "sect" has negative implications of a splinter group. However, *sampradāy* also suggests a "refuge" from the ordinary world, as sect may; Barz continues to use it (Barz 1976, 39–40). More recently, van der Veer prefers "order" or "monastic order" to sect because the "church–sect dichotomy" is so alien to Hinduism (van der Veer 1988, 66–71). Like Barz, I find it convenient to use "sect" here; like van der Veer, I warn against a false jump to Christian parallels.

"Nath" is a rubric that may cover any number of loosely organized associations of Shaivite renouncers, sharing certain orientations and practices.[6] Besides referring to a sectarian identity, the term Nath evokes a particular set of ideas concerning the merged physical and spiritual perfection possible for humans, and how to achieve it. And, not the least important in relation to our tales, Naths are strongly associated in popular thought with certain visible emblems, appurtenances, and behaviors.

I turn then to the phenomenon of householder Naths: castes whose group identity is rooted in renunciation. Such is Madhu Nath's birth group (*jāti*), and it is not unique. Similar castes are present throughout India and Nepal.[7] The distinction between Nath as sect or path and Nath as caste is pronounced and critical in indigenous accounts. However, as will soon become apparent, it is also imprecise, plastic, and subject to collapse at several levels.

Nath Renunciatory Traditions in Story and History

Nāth may be simply defined as "master" and the Naths as " 'Masters' (of yogic powers)" (Vaudeville 1974, 85). Other sources report various complex etymologies deriving from possible syllabic deconstructions of the word *nāth*, producing meanings such as "form of bliss established in three worlds" or "he who removes ignorance of Brahm and is absorbed in truth-consciousness-bliss" (Lalas 1962–78).[8] A yogi is an adept, a practitioner of yoga—deriving from a Sanskrit root meaning "yoke," carrying implications of self-discipline as well as union. Yoga

6. Classifications and descriptions of various and variously organized groups of Nath renouncers are available elsewhere (Briggs 1973; Dvivedi 1981; Oman 1905, 168–86; Sinha and Saraswati 1978, 113–14; Tripathi 1978, 71–74); Nath traditions, rather than monastic organization, are my focus here.

7. For two interesting examples see Bradford 1985, a discussion of how the South Indian Lingayat caste maintains its renouncer identity through historical and social changes; and Bouillier 1979, an ethnographic study of a renouncer caste in Nepal. On relatively recent fieldwork with other North Indian Jogi performers see Champion 1989; Henry 1988; Lapoint 1978. That a number of Jogi groups are nominally Muslim is a phenomenon well worth investigating, but I lack data and space to do it justice here.

8. For other definitions and etymologies of Nath see also Dvivedi 1981, 3; Singh 1937, 1; Upadhyay 1976, 1–6.

is one of the six *darśana*s or major classical philosophical systems known in Indian thought.[9] But in relation to Nath traditions it refers particularly to various physical and meditative techniques for self-realization.[10]

Most scholars treat the terms Nath and yogi as interchangeable when dealing with the sect and its teachings (for example Vaudeville 1974, 85–86).[11] Many, for the sake of clarity, settle upon one or the other to use when speaking of that tradition.[12] The terms Nath and yogi are far from exhausting the descriptive designations applied to Naths. Briggs discusses "Gorakhnāthī," "Darśanī," "Kānphaṭa," and "Nātha"—all categorizations with identical or overlapping references that at times designate members of the sect(s) with which he is concerned (Briggs 1973, 1–2). Whereas the first in the series refers to the founding guru, the second two highlight the most visible and distinctive emblem of the group—their large earrings (*darśanī*) worn in split ears—the descriptive meaning of *kanphaṭā*.[13]

The origins of Nathism dissolve in the mists of a presumed selective merging of Buddhist and Hindu tantra, Shaivite asceticism, and yoga philosophy and practice that took place somewhere in the tenth or eleventh century (Briggs 1973; Ghurye 1964; Schomer 1987). A shadowy but imposing figure looming in those mists is Gorakh Nath—who probably lived but whose biography is totally overlaid with myth and magic.[14] Although some locate Gorakh's birthplace in northwestern India (Sen 1954, 74; Singh 1937, 22) and his lore certainly flourished in Punjab, merging with indigenous tales much as it has done in Rajasthan, most cultural historians agree that the real Gorakh came from the east. Briggs, who mustered most of the sources available in his time in admirably systematic fashion, concludes that "Gorakhnāth lived not later than A.D. 1200, probably early in the 11th

9. Sources for yoga as philosophy include Dasgupta 1924, 1974; Woods 1972; Raju 1985, 336–76.

10. See Eliade 1973; Varenne 1976; Sinh 1975.

11. Yogi, of course, may and often does have myriad associations unconnected with Naths.

12. Ghurye uses "jogi" (Ghurye 1964, 114–40) and Oman "yogi" (Oman 1905, 168); Dasgupta prefers Nāth (Dasgupta 1969, 191–210).

13. I follow Dvivedi 1981 and Sundardas 1965 in spelling the sect name; others use *kānphaṭa* (Briggs 1973) or *kānphāṭā* (Ghurye 1964).

14. For a full hagiography of Gorakh Nath (also Gorakhnāth; Gorakṣanāth) in simple Hindi see Gautam 1986; see also Briggs 1973, 179–207; Dikshit n.d.; Pandey 1980; Sen 1960, 42–54.

century, and that he came originally from Eastern Bengal" (Briggs 1973, 250; see also Dvivedi 1981, 96–97).

Sukumar Sen characterizes the Nath cult as "an esoteric yoga cult based on austere self-negation and complete control over the vital, mental and emotional functions" (Sen 1960, 42). But as Nath teachings spread within popular Hinduism, both their content and mode of transmission changed. From secret instructions imparted by guru adept to select disciple, Nath ideas passed into folklore. There, these teachings are strongly associated with the "perfection of the body" (*kāyā siddhi*) and the quest for immortality (Eliade 1973; Maheshwari 1980, 101).[15]

There exist numerous and conflicting stories of the origins and guru-disciple lineages of the early Nath gurus. One popular version with which Madhu Nath's tales coincide is that Gorakh was a disciple of Machhindar Nath who obtained his knowledge directly from Shiva (known as the *Adi-Nāth* or original Nath), although he did it by trickery.[16] This association of the founding Nath guru with a wily coopting of divine power fits well with the general character of most Nath gurus in popular lore. In part 4 of Madhu Nath's Gopi Chand we see Gorakh playing all kinds of tricks on his own guru, Machhindar himself. Although he acts thus for the guru's good, such behavior none-theless runs counter to ordinary Hindu piety that prescribes nothing but diligent obedience in the disciple role. Most striking of all in the Gopi Chand tale, Gopi Chand and Bharthari obtain immortality only through Gorakh's devious tricking of Gopi Chand's angry guru Jalindar.[17]

There exist texts, including technical manuals of esoteric yogic practice in Sanskrit and the vernaculars, whose authorship is attri-buted to Gorakh Nath himself, and to others closely associated with his teachings.[18] The connection between Gorakh the folk trickster

15. Some expounders of Nathism as philosophy explicitly bar such vulgar physical aspirations (Singh 1937, 28).

16. For summary versions of the story of Machhindar Nath (also Macchendranāth, Mīnanāth; Matsyendranāth) see Bhattacharyya 1982, 285; Mahapatra 1972, 82–83; Sen 1960, 43–44.

17. Jālandhar.

18. For extensive catalogs and discussions of literary works attributed to Gorakh Nath and his disciples see Briggs 1973, 251–57; Singh 1937, 35–39; Upadhyay 1976, 134–79. An English translation of one important text is Sinh 1975. For the *Gorakṣa Samhitā* in Sanskrit verse with a simple Hindi explanation see Gautam 1974.

hero and Gorakh the author of esoteric yoga manuals may seem slim
but has relevance for an understanding of the folk traditions. The
popular reputation of Nath yogis is of persons who have benefited,
mysteriously but enormously, from their secret knowledge of just such
techniques. If the epic texts presented in this volume make little or
no reference to specific techniques, they nevertheless assume their
results: magical powers and physical immortality.

Madhu's texts posit some crude but handy stereotypes for what a
yogi is and does. These tales reveal two kinds of yogis: the powerful,
well-known few and the powerless, nameless many. Thus, the yogis'
world can seem as hierarchical as that of householders, with rank based
not on birth or wealth but on ascetic prowess. Ordinary yogis, if they
are described at all, are often portrayed in most unflattering ways
(Gopi Chand parts 1 and 3). A polite way for a householder to greet
a yogi is to tell him he doesn't look like just any old yogi.

What all yogis have in common is a lifestyle outside the domestic
and social realms of marriage, work, and caste and a dedication to
meditation or divine recitation. Thus all yogis sit by a campfire
(*dhūnī*)—understood as an ascetic act in a tropical climate—with
lowered eyelids (*palak lagāyā*) and repeat divine names (*samaraṇ*).
When ordered by the guru to do so, they go into villages, towns, or
castles and beg for alms (*bhikṣā māṅgnā*). The powerful among them—
Jalindar, Machhindar, Gorakh, Kanni Pavji,[19] Charpat, and Hada,
whose names and characters (except for Hada) are part of wider Nath
traditions—possess the capacity to perform miracles. They can bring
the dead to life and turn rocks to precious metals. Madhu's audience
loves it when Charpat Nath whacks a stone with his tongs and it glit-
ters as pure gold, or when Jalindar casually restores flesh and breath
to a crumbling heap of bones.

An obvious cause-and-effect relation exists between the lifestyle
and miraculous capacities of yogis. The primary conditions for, if not
the sole sources of, yogis' miraculous powers are their ascetic practices
or ardor (*tapas*), often simply construed as unbroken meditation by
the campfire. The ability to pursue such activity singlemindedly is in
turn grounded in detachment from the worldly snares of women and
wealth. If the hundreds of nameless, faceless, sheeplike disciples have
not attained such powers, the tale suggests—if only obliquely—that

19. Kānhūpā, Kriṣṇapād, or Kānphā.

it is because they have not fully overcome the physical and mental snares that bind mortals to an illusory world.

In physical appearance the yogis of Madhu Nath's tales look very much like members of the Nath sect described in earlier ethnological accounts (Ghurye 1964, 134; Risley 1891; Rose 1914). Their emblems of identity include a begging bowl (*khappar*), a deer-horn instrument (*singī nād*), a "sacred thread" made of black wool (*selī*), iron tongs (*chīmṭā*), wooden sandals (*pāvarī*), a body smeared with sacred ash (*bhabhūt*), and thick crystal earrings (*darśanī; mudra*). The earrings are especially important. For Naths, full initiation is marked by cutting the disciple's ears, and this cut is said to allow a yogi to bring his senses under control.[20]

Less frequently referred to in the tales is the one emblem that the present-day Nath caste in Rajasthan retains, although only in the token form of their turbans: the wearing of ochre-colored cloth, called *bhagvā*. Reference to yogis as wearers of *bhagvā* occurs only in part 4 of Gopi Chand, when Gorakh Nath is prohibited from entering Machhindar Nath's kingdom because the roads are closed to all those clothed in ochre. Unlike the deer-horn instrument, which figures in almost every mention of a yogi's appearance, ochre robes are of course worn by many non-Nath renouncers, which might account for their relative neglect in the texts.

None of the yogis in Madhu's tales, including the gurus, are particularly well spoken; indeed they curse more freely than any other characters in the epic. They never attempt to impart wisdom or enlightenment through reasoned or impassioned words; rather their language is blunt, direct, and action-oriented. They give abrupt commands, and recalcitrance is met with shocking demonstrations of miraculous power. Beyond miraculous power, yogis also assert and exercise brute physical strength. When Jalindar's superiority in hurling spells is challenged by the lady magicians of Bengal, he rouses his cowardly disciples by proclaiming, "Well, sister-fuckers, if you can't win with magic and spells, then use your tongs, give those sluts your tongs, beat them." And indeed, more than once in the tales an angry

---

20. Not all Nath renouncers wear *darśanī*. The term *aughaṛ*—although it has a number of general meanings evoking such qualities as "lazy," and "carefree"— refers to a Nath yogi whose ears are not split. Briggs understands this as a "first stage" (1973, 27), but it can also refer to particular sects whose practices are less "restrained" and closer to Tantric.

yogi wields his tongs—worshiped symbol of ascetic practice by the campfire—as a club. Beyond that, all the yogis like to smoke hashish and eat sweets. And even the greatest of the gurus are not above quarrelling with, competing with, and deceiving one another.

Clearly, Madhu Nath's tales of Nath yogis do not teach their audiences any practical or spiritual disciplines. Nor do they focus on relationships between human beings and God. Although Madhu Nath invariably utters a fervent "Shiv! Gorakh!" or "Victory to Mahadev!" at the close of each sung portion of his performance, thus framing it in devotion, references to divine grace and religious emotions are scant within the stories. Yet like the framing prayers, presuppositions of spiritual discipline, human-divine relationships, devotional feelings, and grace form the backdrop before which audience members see and evaluate the yogis' actions. This evaluation is clearly based on moral standards different from those appropriate to householders— or perhaps more accurately, on a clearly defined but unresolved tension between householders' dharma and renouncers' paths.[21]

Teachings of yoga philosophy and techniques, attributed to Gorakh Nath and his followers, are not of immediate relevance in understanding Nath folk epics. On the level of allegory, popular Nath stories may indeed contain some mystic messages. For example, the unusual name of Bharthari's queen, Pingala, suggests an association with yogic physiology where the subtle channel called Pingala represents the right side, the sun, and violent action.[22] Such an association, however, never surfaces in Madhu's explanations or in any villagers' reception of the tales, to the extent that I have investigated these.[23]

The stream of Hindu thought most strongly and consciously associated with Nath teachings in rural Rajasthan is not esoteric yoga but *nirguṇ bhakti* or devotion to a God perceived as "without qualities." *Nirguṇ bhakti* is important to village religion, and one of the sects that promotes it is led by Naths (Gold 1988). The diffusion of Nath yogis and their lore antedates by several centuries the emergence of *nirguṇ bhakti* as preached and sung by medieval poet-saints called *sants*.

---

21. I discuss this irresolution more fully in the afterword.

22. David White (personal communication 1990) suggests that Gopi Chand's many women and his struggles to come to terms with them may have to do with the "awakening, taming and sublimation of the female energy within the yogic body."

23. Members of Nath *bhajan* parties and their listeners will, by contrast, readily discuss esoteric, mystical, or subtle interpretations of the language of hymns.

Because of this chronology, the relation between Nath and Sant traditions is usually seen in terms of Nathism's influence on the icono- clastic teachings of the fourteenth- and fifteenth-century Sants.

The external trappings and postures of Naths were denigrated by Sant poets, who found them as false as any other exterior forms of religion.[24] Most scholars of medieval Hindi literature acknowledge, however, that early Sant poets such as Kabir were conversant with Nath teachings, and that Nath esoteric imagery is important in Sant poetry (Barthwal 1978; Gold 1987; Schomer 1987; Vaudeville 1974, 88–89). Barthwal cites a respectful reference to Gopi Chand and Bharthari in Kabir's verses (Barthwal 1978, 141).

In the village where I recorded Madhu's tale, the situation is curiously reversed. Rather than an active Sant tradition retaining traces of Nath influence, in Ghatiyali the Naths as caste, as leaders of a local sect, and as members of loosely organized hymn-singing groups, seem to have appropriated and become the purveyors of a somewhat altered Sant tradition. Their "*bhajan* parties" have an extensive repertoire of hymns including many with the signature of Kabir; others are stamped by Gorakh and Machhindar. Sometimes, the same *bhajan* will bear on different occasions either a Sant or a Nath signature, probably depending on the orientation of the lead singer. Madhu, living as he did in another village, was not often a participant in the *nirgun bhajan* sessions in Ghatiyali. However, several times during his Gopi Chand performance he presented interludes of *nirgun bhajans*. Clearly he felt his repertoire of Nath tales and Sant compositions to be unitary.

But Nath and Sant traditions can seem profoundly different. Sants teach surrender to divine grace; Naths, although they invoke Shiva as the original Nath and first guru, stress not devotional feeling but austere practice and a transformation of the physical being. The quest for bodily immortality with which popular Nathism is strongly asso- ciated would appear to be a very different enterprise from the spiritual development fostered by the Sants. Yet in village traditions Nath and

24. See for example Kabir's poem translated by Hess and Singh, that begins "How will you cross, Nath, how will you cross, so full of crookedness?" (Hess and Singh 1983, 76). Centuries earlier than Kabir, the South Indian poet-saint Allama is said to have demonstrated to Gorakh Nath the superiority of his inner devotion to the yogi's "solid diamond-body" (Ramanujan 1973, 146–47; thanks to David White for reminding me of this example).

Sant teachings blend together, are referred to loosely as *nirguṇ bhakti*, and are taught by Nath gurus.

Several significant cosmological and practical elements common to the two traditions help explain their close merging in popular thought. Foremost among these would be the concept of divinity as formless and indescribable (*niranjan; nirākār; alakh*), and the idea that only a guru can help human beings to realize their identity with that unknowable divinity. The reliance on a guru is greatly stressed in Nath *nirguṇ* hymns, where the "true guru within" may be invoked as in Sant poetry. Reliance on and submission to an external guru inform the plot structure of both of Madhu Nath's tales. The single element of practice stressed in the epic tales, that of *samaraṇ* or divine recitation, is also an important part of the meditative practice that Sant poets taught and followed.

Madhu Nath and participants in his sect identify themselves simultaneously as worshipers of Shiva and followers of *nirguṇ bhakti*. They do not see these two persuasions as incompatible. And indeed, Naths' worship is iconographically and mythologically unelaborated, in keeping with *nirguṇ* ideas. Shiva does appear as a minor character in both Bharthari's and Gopi Chand's epics, but he appears as a yogi, or just another guru, a step higher up in the power hierarchy and chain of command from Gorakh or Jalindar Nath, and lower than an unnamed *bhagvān*—the Lord.[25]

Both Nath and Sant traditions disdain social norms and caste ranking, at least in relation to God.[26] Gorakh, like most of the early Sant poets, is said to have come from a low level of society.[27] However, teachings of human equality are notably absent from village Nath lore. Village society in the 1980s was still caste-ruled in many respects, and radical messages, publicly proclaimed, would probably not have been welcomed. Although Bengali traditions explicitly identify Gopi Chand's guru as a sweeper, Rajasthani versions give no indication

---

25. The third long tale in Madhu's repertoire, "The Wedding Song of Lord Shiva," is almost solely concerned with deities in mythic time. This tale is not usually included in general Nath traditions, but many versions figure in Shaivite mythology (O'Flaherty 1973). When speaking of or invoking Shiva, Madhu Nath often calls him Lord Shankar; less frequently he says Mahadev or Bhola Nath.

26. For examples see Gokhale-Turner 1981; Zelliot 1981.

27. See Singh 1937, 23–24. The pervasive legend that Gorakh was born from a pile of cow dung testifies, some suggest, to humble origins.

that Jalindar is an untouchable. Yet a secret cult (of which I have no evidence beyond much gossip from many sources) with which Naths were often associated was said to feature as its central rite intercaste eating from a single pot. That this significant defiance of hierarchical codes should be elevated to powerful but hidden ritual speaks both for its importance to Nath belief and its untenability in the public domain of ordinary village life.

The influence of Nath sects on community life in Rajasthan has varied greatly over time and space. But it does not seem ever to have been a radical one, in the sense of undermining the socioeconomic status quo. However, the history of the Nath sect in Rajasthan is not divorced from political events. Indeed, in Rajasthan as elsewhere in India, historical research uncovers more and more political and economic roles played by supposedly otherworldly monks and yogis.[28] Madhu Nath's texts propose that kings may be influenced by yogis, and such has certainly been the case at times.

Stemming from their reputed powers as religious adepts, miracle workers, and gurus but obviously supported also by a skillful command of statecraft and diplomacy, some members of the Nath sect have acquired considerable influence over ruling families and have been directly involved in affairs of state. The most notorious instance of Naths' political activities in Rajasthan unfolded during the rule of Raja Man Singh of Jodhpur.

Man Singh, the Maharaja of Marwar in western Rajasthan from 1803 to 1842, initially obtained the Jodhpur throne with the powerful aid of the yogi Ayas Dev Nath. Whether this aid was effected by prayer or by poison is unclear. Whatever the case may be, Man Singh's grateful resolve was to "rule Marwar strictly in accordance with the advice of the Naths" (Sharma 1972, 155). During Man Singh's reign, members of the Nath sect acquired unprecedented wealth and power in his kingdom, and their numbers swelled (1972, 177). That some at times abused their privileged position, indulging in luxury and sensuality, is history. The story of how the British attempted to diminish Nath influence in Jodhpur, even as the Maharaja's own behavior

28. Historical studies discuss worldly parts played by many renouncer sects, including Naths; these include active participations in trade, politics, and diplomacy as well as military ventures (Bayly 1983, 183–85; Ghosh 1930; Sarkar n.d.; Singh 1937, 23–24).

became more yogi-like, is not the tale I have to tell here.[29] Yet Man Singh's case demonstrates that the gap between story and history is not so great as it may appear to Western readers of Madhu Nath's tales.

The last few lines of Madhu's performance of Gopi Chand include some auspicious predictions for the followers of Jalindar Nath (as opposed to those of Kanni Pavji who have been degraded to nomadic snake-charmers). One of these predictions is: "When armies die then we make the king a disciple and bring his army back to life. We bring it back to life, and make the king a disciple." The history of Man Singh's Jodhpur demonstrates that yogis have indeed at times swayed the beliefs and actions of kings, and when the tale-teller boasts of his sect's potential temporal influence he is not just spinning fantasies.

But let us beware of reading either story or history one-sidedly. Another lesson from Man Singh's reign is that yogis are susceptible to corruption, and this could serve as a cautionary tale about the alluring world of illusion to which yogis are not immune (the theme occurs too in Gopi Chand part 4). With the accumulation of wealth and property come worries over inheritance—increasing the temptation to abandon celibacy, beget a lineage, and return, even if only partially, to a householder's existence.[30]

Horace Rose complains in his discussion of Jogi divisions and subdivisions (in an ethnographic survey of Punjab and the north-western provinces compiled at the end of the nineteenth century) that "Though professing Jogis are forbidden to marry, many of them do so, and it is impossible to disentangle the jogis who abandon celibacy from those who do not profess it at all and form a caste" (Rose 1914, 410). Rose, as a surveyor who must produce a neat alphabetically organized glossary of castes within his appointed region, is evidently peevish over these blurred categories. But his failure to "disentangle" yogis who form a caste from renouncers who have abandoned celibacy highlights one of the perpetually shifting boundaries between house-holding and renunciation.

29. At one point a British officer, Ludlow, observed that "the Maharaja would have passed anywhere for a 'religious mendicant'" (Singh 1973, 82–83). See D. Gold 1992 for a full discussion of this revealing drama of cultural confrontations.

30. For processes of "sedentarization" among *Ramanandi* monks of Ayodhya see van der Veer 1988, 126–30.

Nath Jātis

Nāgā Naths as renouncers are celibate ascetics whose traditions must be passed on through recruitment and guru-disciple transmission. Theoretically, such associations have nothing to do with *jāti*, or birth-given caste status, but only with separate human beings' decisions to follow a particular path to divinity. In considering the distinction between householder and renouncer, however, it should also be kept in mind, as recent studies by Burghart and van der Veer have amply demonstrated, that there are many kinds of renouncers, many degrees of asceticism, and many transitions, both gross and subtle, between those degrees (Burghart 1983a, 1983b; van der Veer 1988). For example, it is not unusual for a renouncer to keep a mistress and subsequently appoint his natural child by her to be his chief disciple and successor.[31] How did castes of married yogis come to exist? "Abandonment of celibacy" is certainly one common explanation.[32]

Renouncer Naths, who may regard householder groups with a certain amount of disdain, tend to formulate the transformation explicitly as a process of degradation. Householder Naths are fallen ascetics whose ancestors could not resist the blandishments of women and domestic life. As one renouncer with whom we spoke expressed it, "Householder life is like honey, it attracts flies."

Risley provides several origin stories of Jugi castes in Bengal, all of which reinforce the proposition that these groups were engendered by a fall from ascetic perfection. In these stories the fall is attributed to seduction of the yogis by irresistible females. In one instance the caste is the product of the union of former ascetics with widows of the merchant caste; in another *yoginīs* (female yogis) tempt *siddhas* (perfected male yogis) and their intercourse results in the ancestors of the caste (Risley 1891, 355–58).

Gorakh Nath is, according to Bengali legend, the only one of five original Naths to resist the attractiveness of women and all that they

31. Komal Kothari reports groups of householder Naths in western Rajasthan who call their children *chelās* or "disciples"—a nice twist on the kinship metaphor that dominates the nongenetic guru-disciple relationship (personal communication 1988).

32. See, however, Vaudeville who argues that "married" Jogis are not necessarily fallen ascetics because Nathism itself is "a kind of anti-Brāhmaṇical, half-Buddhistic creed" (Vaudeville 1974, 87), by which she implies, as did many householder Naths, that asceticism is no prerequisite for the spiritual achievements to which Naths aspire.

represent and offer (Sen 1960, 45). As we have already noted, in Madhu's tales, Gorakh's own guru, Machhindar Nath, becomes a not-so-unwilling "victim" of Bengali queens—an episode appearing in most Nath traditions and popularized in theater and romantic literature. It is only with great difficulty that Gorakh is able to pry Machhindar away from his householder's life. Of course, mythological explanations that shift the blame from male weakness to female allure offer a rationalization that may appeal to the male bards who usually perform and transmit caste origin stories.

The ancient Hindu pilgrimage center of Pushkar, located in Ajmer district, Rajasthan, has thousands of temples, many of which are associated with a particular caste and provide guestrooms and priestly services for pilgrims of that caste. Here, the Nath *sampradāy* and the Nath *jāti* have separate accommodations. Renouncers do not patronize the householders' temple, nor do householders normally visit the renouncers' location. In January 1988, just following our extensive conversations with Naths from many villages who had assembled in Ghatiyali for the three-day funeral feast in December, Daniel Gold and I interviewed householders and renouncers, resident priests and wayfarers at both these Pushkar temples. We also visited a retreat of *nāgā* Naths on the outskirts of Pushkar.[33]

Despite the preliminary nature of this round of fieldwork, we were able to note certain consistent patterns in responses to our inquiries about the differences between *gṛhasthī* and *nāgā* Naths. *Nāgā* Naths often vehemently expressed a conviction that there existed a world of difference between them and *gṛhasthī* Naths. One of them formulated this distinction in a terse but illuminating fashion. He said that for him and his fellow renouncers everything is interior and "hidden" or "secret" (*gupt*) whereas householders need external props. "Renouncers don't have to sing hymns or hold knowledge talks," he asserted. "They can just be *mast* (carefree, intoxicated): eat, drink, sleep." This is consistent with the impression given in Madhu Nath's tales that being an ordinary (non-miracle-working) yogi doesn't call for any particular aptitude.

Folklore and classical satire on renouncers often judge their exter-

---

33. On this trip our time was limited. We considered these interviews preliminaries to a future depth study of Rajasthani Naths but learned a lot from the many persons who kindly agreed to talk with us.

nal trappings (ashes, beads, muttered prayers, and so forth) to be the hollow insignia of professional hypocrites. According to ascetics, however, householders are the ones whose religious postures belie their worldly concerns. Ascetics insisted that householders must perpetually, and by and large futilely, struggle to control their bodies and minds in order to draw their attention away from the ever-pressing and seductive concerns of the world of flux. Renouncers have none of these concerns and thus relax.

Householder Naths expressed their own strong convictions that living in the world offers no impediment to spiritual achievement. One of them, for example, told me that there is absolutely no difference between death rites for married members of the Nath caste and *nāgā* Naths.[34] He claimed that the use of "*Gāyatrī* mantras" at these rites— powerful spells known to sect gurus—ensures the highest Hindu aim of liberation (*mokṣa*) and that one's worldly condition, whether householder or renouncer, is of no account.[35]

That this speaker took death rites as the critical conjunction of renouncers and householders is no accident. Their death rites are the most distinctive feature of the Nath caste, setting them apart from other Hindu villagers.[36] Naths bury their dead near their homes, rather than cremating them outside the village as is the custom for other Hindu castes. Moreover, the place of burial, although unmarked by more than a pile of stones, is referred to as a *samādhi*—a term usually reserved for monuments memorializing the final resting place of powerful world-renouncers.

Madhu's caste calls itself Nath, and all its members take the surname Nath, while other villagers use Nath as a term of reference for them. In the tales of Gopi Chand and Bharthari, however, although Nath occurs as a surname for renouncers, it is used less often as a general term of address or reference for people. Rather *jogī* and the inter-

34. Sandra King Mulholland who has done extensive fieldwork among Nath ascetics in Uttar Pradesh comments that "not all ascetic Naths indulge" in spells and rituals (personal communication 1990).

35. The *Gāyatrī* mantras spoken of by members of the Nath caste and sect are a set of powerful secret spells used particularly in death rituals. They should not be confused with the Sanskrit prayer recited each day by orthodox Brahmans. According to the householder Naths we interviewed in Ghatiyali, there are twenty-four *Gāyatrī* mantras and someone who knew them all could bring the dead to life; but no one today possesses that knowledge.

36. See Gold 1988, 99–105, for more about Nath death ceremonies.

6. Ogar Nathji, a *nāgā* Nath and Madhu Nath's paternal cousin, at the grave site (*samādhi*) of Nathu's mother during her funeral rites.

changeable *jogīṛā* are constantly employed. When "Nath" is used to address an ordinary yogi it occurs significantly in situations of exaggerated politeness—those in which the addresser compliments the yogi as appearing "princely" and "established." Besides being used as a surname, Nath sometimes occurs in the texts in reference to Lord Shiva, the "true Nath."

Pre-independence census data and various ethnographic surveys usually do not present Nath as a caste name. Nineteenth-century British sources report castes called Jogi (or Jugi) in Bengal (Risley 1891), Rajputana (Census of India 1921), and the Punjab and North-West Frontier Province (Rose 1914). A Hindi census from Rajasthan, however, lists Naths as one of six subgroups under the broader heading of Jogis (Marwar Census n.d.). Commonplace throughout Indian history is the manipulation of status by castes through name changes, among other strategies. Several of the nineteenth-century sources attribute low rank and bad reputation to Jogis (Risley 1891; Rose 1914). In general, their image appears to be strongly associated with wandering minstrel-beggars, fallen ascetics, or low-status weavers. The term Nath clearly carries fewer of these pejorative associations. It is understandably preferred by the present-day Naths of Rajasthan, many of whom are prosperous farmers and serve as Brahman-like priests in temples patronized by clean castes. The current preference for Nath as a caste name in Rajasthan, then, represents a move toward greater respectability consonant with an improved economic condition.

If today's Rajasthani Naths are dissociating themselves from the negative images of begging *jogīs*, they are in no way interested in unlinking their identity from the powerful yogi gurus whom they accept as founding ancestors. Madhu and all of his caste fellows with whom I spoke have a clear pride in this special identity, one explicitly emerging from the same roots as the Nath sect, although now distinct from it. Moreover, the traditional part Naths play in village society is based on their credentials as spell-wielding magicians—credentials rooted in their descent from yogis.

According to people with whom we talked (I cannot document this), several hundred years ago local *ṭhākurs* or landlord-rulers invited families of Naths to live in their villages and gave them land grants in exchange for their magical services. Naths possess verbal spells to avert plagues of locusts and hailstones whenever they might threaten the village crops. As this power was explained to me, it consisted not in

making these plagues disappear but in sending them down the road
a way. Therefore, it is not surprising that any village ruler who
could afford the land grant might be interested in having a family or
two of Naths settle within his dominion.

The text of Gopi Chand contains, as we shall see, the "mythic
charter" for Naths' power over locusts and their right to eat well as
a result of this power. Gorakh Nath commands seven species of locusts
to obey yogis of both sexes: "Brothers, when yogis tell you go, then
go. And maintain the honor of robe-wearers. Help them to earn their
livings.... And keep their stomachs full of bread." By the 1980s when
I first met them, Ghatiyali's Naths were lamenting the loss of their
status as locust-removers owing to the government's successful use of
pesticides to eradicate this perpetual agricultural hazard, Yet, some
Naths still claim a power over hailstones and drought, and several
Nath women whom I knew possessed effective spells to remove the
pain and ill effects of scorpion stings.[37] Moreover, in Ghatiyali Naths
are hereditary priests at two of the three shrines most closely associated
with the physical well-being of the village and its livestock (Gold
1988, 44–58). It is still in their interests to maintain their special
identity even though they now derive most of their income from agriculture. Many are educating at least one of their sons for white-collar
professions, and whether the part of resident magicians will continue
to appeal to them remains to be seen.

It should by now be evident that, although the Nath *jāti* and the
Nath sect have separate temples and their members may express
strong opinions concerning their nonidentification with one another,
in other ways they are closely associated, and at times they merge.
Members of the Nath caste often become householder initiates into
sects led by Nath renouncers, and participate in sect rituals, although
these may be performed under the direction of a renouncer-guru.
Such participation can be a powerful force in the lives of householders.
One way the Nath sect recruits members is through the offering of
children by devotees who have received favor, and householder Naths
are perhaps more disposed than other castes to offer their children up
in this fashion to become Nath renouncers. In Madhu's case (chapter 1)

---

37. The efficacy of these spells is not simply in their words but must be cultivated
by the person who wields them through an initial period of constant repetition
accompanied by ascetic self-discipline.

we see another intersection: a young member of the Nath caste is given an initiation appropriate to a renouncer yet continues on a householder's life course.

Although caste origin myths and the comments of many living renouncers explicitly posit human frailty and moral debasement at the root of householder Naths' existence, the Nath *jāti*'s lore that comprises this book sympathizes intensely with those attracted to worldly life.[38] Moreover, it perpetually vacillates in its evaluation of that attractiveness, which derives from much more than simple animal sexuality. Domestic love, and the ever powerful Hindu ideal of continuity in the male line, are values that the Nath caste's lore treats with respect. Pingala's lament, acknowledged as one of the most powerful scenes in King Bharthari's tale, has a moral force not easily refuted.

The teachings of the Nath sect are best known not through religious texts but through their stories. And purveyors of those stories, all over India, are often members of Nath or yogi castes. What makes this lore distinctive is that it is about renouncers but plays largely to householders. Thus the continuities established in the preceding discussion of sect and caste will continue to inform our investigation of Nath oral traditions.

---

38. Who first told the stories of Nath yogis to whom is a tantalizing but unanswerable question. A cross-referencing of householders' and renouncers' values is, I believe, at the core of these traditions.

Chapter Three

Naths in Folklore and the Folklore of the Naths

The figure of the ascetic or world-renouncer is a remarkably pervasive and persistent one in Indian literature, spanning regions, languages, centuries, and genres. Wandering holy men—whether genuine selfless saints, pompous and self-important platitude-spouting preachers, or fraudulent self-serving rascals—are stock figures in classical Sanskrit theater, simple vernacular tales, and oral epics. Moreover, modern Indian fiction shows a remarkable fascination with such characters and often skillfully probes the psychological ambiguities and individual quirks that may underlie unkempt hair and ochre robes.[1]

Among the large numbers of ascetics in narrative literature, Nath yogis comprise a minor subcategory. At first glance, Naths are exemplary of a certain fairly homogeneous type: the master of showy "supernatural" powers. If these powers are accepted as genuine, then the yogi is an awesome and godlike being with control over the phenomenal world. If they are shown as pretense, then the yogi is pure sham and his otherworldly scorn for convention is readily construed as a perfect orgy of self-indulgence.[2]

---

1. The many fictions involving renouncers include Ganguli 1967; Markandaya 1960, 1963; Narayan 1980. For an illuminating discussion of other fictional accounts see Madan 1987, 72–100.

2. Siegel 1987, 191–96, discusses and translates fragments of hilarious Sanskrit satires on ascetics and their practices; Narayan 1989 provides performance context and audience exegesis for stories of true and false gurus. See also Bloomfield 1924.

Assessments of the parts played by yogis in Indian folklore have become more sophisticated over time. Writing in 1914, Rose cites a Mr. Benton who declares: "The Jogi is a favourite character in Hindusthani fiction. He there appears as a jolly playful character of a simple disposition, who enjoys the fullest liberty and conducts himself in the most eccentric fashion under the cloak of religion without being called in question" (Rose 1914, 389).

About ninety years later, Zbavitel in his history of Bengali literature sees Nath stories as representing "the extreme of non-realistic trends in Bengali literature." He continues:

They are fruits of an almost unbounded imagination, withdrawing from the hard facts of life. No wonder that in the atmosphere of the 17th and 18th centuries which for most inhabitants of the country were a period of the utmost poverty, insecurity and misery, their attraction grew, because it offered an escape from the facts of everyday life which were not at all bright and pleasant. (Zbavitel 1976, 191)

Still more recently, Gill, whose endeavor is interpretive and psychological, discusses the Punjabi legend of Puran Bhagat, in which Gorakh Nath plays a major part. He finds there that "the touch of the yogi doesn't heal but inflicts sharper cuts to open wounds" (Gill 1986, 137). That is, Gill sees the yogi figure in this well-known Punjabi legend as neither jolly nor escapist but rather as embodying painful conflicts inherent in the human condition as construed within a Punjabi worldview.

Each of these differently couched, differently oriented, and differently motivated appraisals of yogis in stories speaks to Madhu Nath's Rajasthani versions of Gopi Chand and Bharthari. If we look for "liberty" and "eccentricity," we do indeed find a cavalier imperiousness about the yogi gurus. They throw their weight around with impunity (remember that *guru* means heavy), and they are heedless of common "morality," whether it be honesty, compassion, or familial loyalty. As for Nath tales being products of, or outlets for, an efflorescent and even escapist imagination, certainly a measure of delight for Madhu Nath's audience derives from pure fantasy. An imperious donkey stamps its foot and an entire city is surrounded with double walls of copper and brass. Given the job of grazing oxen, a yogi in disguise waits until his employers leave, then urinates. Where the stream falls lush green grasses spring up; he then lounges about while the animals in his charge grow sleek and fat. The audience revels in these moments, and they do indeed contrast with ordinary life.

But it is Gill's insight into the yogi's figure as a painful one that seems still more germane to the Rajasthani tales of Gopi Chand and Bharthari. Gopi Chand's sufferings dominate his story; Queen Pingala's heartbreak is acknowledged by all to be the climax of Bharthari's tale. These stories fully acknowledge that yogis not only experience pain but inflict it. Indeed there is far greater stress on the sufferings of Pingala than of Bharthari; and Gopi Chand's personal trials are enormously magnified by his empathy with those who mourn his departure.[3]

The powerful Nath does not play exactly the same part in every story in which he appears. Different yogis have distinct personalities and histories and exhibit among themselves varying relationships of alliance and animosity. Moreover, those who follow them do so for different reasons in different stories. Even within Madhu Nath's own repertoire, repetitive as it is in some ways, the personalities, motivations, and sensibilities of various yogi figures emerge as extremely variegated.

Gopi Chand is pushed into renunciation by his mother and his fate; a vainglorious and uncontemplative king, he becomes a despondent and powerless yogi, buffeted about by the designs of friends and enemies. Bharthari, by contrast, is decisive both as king and yogi; he stands firm and is even stubborn whereas Gopi Chand repeatedly, helplessly yields. Gopi Chand is readily moved by the persuasions of all his loved ones; Bharthari acts on principle and reveals no empathic responses. Neither renouncer-king displays the kinds of authoritative yogic competence and commanding guru nature that give characters such as Gorakh and Jalindar Nath their particular auras. Gorakh and Jalindar are often worshiped as gods in temples, Gopi Chand and Bharthari only rarely. And even the perfected yogis do not present a homogeneous category or type: their personalities and predilections are evident. Gorakh, for example, is a sometimes devious trickster but Jalindar is forthright and forceful.

Stories that are part of the Naths' own performance repertoires,

---

3. Frances Pritchett points out that the sorrows of an abandoned or neglected suffering woman are pervasive in Indian literature (personal communication 1990). The Nath tales' special twist is that neither war's glories nor a courtesan's favors but rather a guru's teachings and an ascetic life are the cause of males' defections.

like those of Gopi Chand and Bharthari (as well as Gorakh Nath himself and Guru Guga),[4] focus squarely on Nath heroes. There are many other tales in many regional traditions where Naths have peripheral but critical roles as advisors or aides to heroes who are not themselves renouncers, or who become renouncers only temporarily and for instrumental reasons.[5]

When yogis appear in folklore, worldly aims and renunciative modes of being combine and recombine in diverse motivational configurations. Mortal love and worldly ambition, genuine self-sacrifice and spiritual questing are not opposed but juxtaposed.[6] Folklore often capitalizes on a yogi's potential to be sexually desirable and martially victorious. Such elements are muted, but not imperceptible, in Madhu's Gopi Chand–Bharthari cycle. Madhu's tales give precedence to emotions rather than sexuality, to familial responsibilities rather than royal or military duties. In common with most popular traditions, these tales too reveal the ambiguities that surround any attempt by human characters to free themselves from worldly entanglements.

Bharthari and Gopi Chand

I turn now to a closer examination of the particular origins of Bharthari and Gopi Chand. For Madhu Nath, both tales are part of a unified, integrated repertoire. The two are linked not only in the similar patterns of their stories—both are kings who turn yogi—but genealogically, as sister's son to mother's brother (see figure 1). Indeed the *janmpatrī* of Bharthari reports the birth not only of Bharthari but also

---

4. Guru Guga's life story is little known in Madhu Nath's area of Rajasthan but is found elsewhere in that state as well as in Uttar Pradesh and Punjab (Kothari 1989; Lapoint 1978; Temple 1884, 1:121–209, 3:261–300).

5. For example, in the Rajasthani Pabuji epic one character, Harmal, turns yogi in order to complete a dangerous journey and another, Rupnath, is raised as a renouncer but uses his power to support a battle for family vengeance (Smith 1986, 1991; Blackburn et al., eds. 1989, 240–43). In the Punjabi Hir-Ranjha tale (Shah 1976; Swynnerton 1903, 3–67; Temple 1884, 2:507–80) and in the ballad of Malushahi and Rajula from Himalayan Kumaun (Meissner 1985), frustrated lovers become yogis in reaction to the hopelessness of their romantic quests but also in order to further these quests.

6. Van Buitenen's classic essay on the Vidyādhara hero in Sanskrit stories (1959) made this point; see Lynch 1990 for some reformulations. See also Kolff 1987 for a very interesting and comprehensive discussion of temporary renunciation as an important aspect of the Rajput warrior's identity.

of Manavati, Gopi Chand's mother; and the end of Gopi Chand's
tale finds him splitting the fruit of immortality with his uncle. This
link between the two renouncer-kings is posited not only in Madhu
Nath's stories but throughout most of popular Nath lore. The two are
familiarly referred to as a unit: *māmā-bhāññej* or "mother's brother–
sister's son."

For Madhu and his audience, the stories of Bharthari and Gopi
Chand, performed in a familiar dialect, belong to local lore. My original approach to interpreting these tales was a parochial one: I wanted
to understand their meanings for Ghatiyalians. But even that limited
endeavor necessitated broadening my horizons. For example, Gopi
Chand's tale is largely concerned with one or more lands called Bengal.
True, the women of Madhu Nath's Bengal dress in the red and yellow
wraps characteristic of Rajasthani women (rather than less garish
Bengali saris) and knead and roll out wheat bread (rather than boiling
rice). Nonetheless, Gopi Chand's journey to Bengal is very much a
journey into fabled and remote territory. Bharthari's entire story is
also located elsewhere—in Malva, a fairy-tale kingdom to Rajasthanis.

In this respect the stories of Bharthari and Gopi Chand differ
strikingly from epic tales of regional hero-gods that take place in a
familiar landscape. It was possible for me in 1980 to spend several
weeks journeying through a storied countryside where the god Dev
Narayan's life history was geophysically embodied. A slightly indented
rock was reverently identified as the hoofprint of Dev Narayan's
magic mare, Lila; a simple stone well was known as the divine warrior's
bathing place and thus a source of healing mud and water; a row of
slanted stones bowed as Devji passed by; a modest hilltop pool
marked his miraculous birthsite.[7] Such imminence is not available
for Bharthari and Gopi Chand. Events preceding their renunciation
are not indigenous and thus not enshrined. I have, however, visited
a number of sylvan shrines dedicated to Shiva in Ajmer and Bhilwara
districts, near Madhu Nath's home, featuring caves where Bharthari
and Gopi Chand are said to have meditated together, or spots where
their *tapas* is memorialized by divine footprints or by a *dhūnī* or
campfire shrine with yogis' tongs.[8]

7. For Dev Narayan as worshiped in Ghatiyali and environs see Gold 1988,
154–86; for a summary of his epic tale see Blackburn et al., eds. 1989.
8. Such shrines to yogi gurus are of course found in many other parts of India
as well.

7. Bharthari Baba's divine footprints (*pagalyā*) at a shrine near a well (its engine-driven pump is visible) in a field belonging to a *nāgā* Nath community in Thanvala, Nagaur district, Rajasthan.

Nath stories and the characters who inhabit them have lives of their own that reach beyond what is available in a single telling or a single bard's knowledge. Madhu Nath's performances for me are moments in a long history. The ongoing process of transmission and diffusion through time and space brings about countless permutations. Here, I shall very briefly consider some of these permutations in order to illuminate the unique performances that are my subject. My intention is by no means to present an exhaustive inventory of extant versions but rather to highlight interesting trends in the complex history of an oral tradition.[9] I hope thereby to convey the ways that

9. The research for this chapter led me across more than one regional and linguistic boundary. In the case of Bharthari, it also led from vernacular oral tales back to Sanskrit texts. For Sanskrit, Punjabi, and Bengali I depended on translations, or English summaries; the comparisons I offer here are necessarily circumscribed by these linguistic constraints. I found references to versions of Gopi Chand's tale in Oriya, in Marathi, and in South Indian languages (Chowdhury 1967, 186–87; Sen 1954, 73–74; Sen 1974, 68)—none of which I discuss here.

one performer's version of an oral tale emerges from multiple streams of tradition and yet has a coherence and weight of its own.

Because of their evident origins in different places, probably on different sides of North India, I shall treat the two tales of Bharthari and Gopi Chand discretely. The issue of when, where, and how they came to intersect and partially fuse—somewhere in the middle of North India—is a mystery upon which little light can be shed; that union appears to date back at least several centuries. Although in terms of the bard's repertoire, Gopi Chand is the favored performance, chronologically and conceptually Bharthari precedes it. For when Gopi Chand, advised by his mother to renounce the world, demands to know what king had ever been fool enough to become a yogi, his mother is able to cite her brother, Bharthari, as a role model. There-fore, although until now I have given precedence to Gopi Chand for several reasons (it was first in my heart and my studies, and first in the favor of Madhu Nath's audience), here I shall begin with Bharthari.

Bharthari

Tradition identifies King Bharthari as the former ruler of the real city of Ujjain, located in what is today Madhya Pradesh. Ujjain and its surroundings—an area that Rajasthani villagers even today call by its traditional name of Malva—is a frequent point of reference in local lore. Dhara Nagar, another name for Ujjain, is often the kingdom inhabited by any king who appears in Rajasthani women's worship stories. Bharthari's birth story, as told by Madhu, includes the founding of Dhara Nagar, by the grace of Nath gurus and the acts of a haughty donkey who is Bharthari's progenitor, Gandaraph Syan,[10] cursed by his father to enter a donkey womb.

Bharthari, the legendary king of Ujjain who turns Nath yogi, is generally considered to be identical with the Sanskrit poet Bhartrihari, renowned for three sets of eloquent verse on worldly life, erotic passion, and renunciation.[11] The legends surrounding the poet Bhartrihari

---

10. As Nathu transcribed Madhu's pronunciation, this prince's name is some-times *Gandarap* and sometimes *Gandaraph*, sometimes *Syāṇ* and sometimes *Sen*. I regu-larize this.

11. Whereas books about the Sanskrit poet often refer to the legendary king, the legends of Bharthari rarely refer to the Sanskrit poet—an exception being Duggal's retelling (Duggal 1979). Miller, who gives us some beautiful translations of Bhar-

identify him, as Madhu identifies his Bharthari, as the elder brother of the Hindu monarch, Vikramaditya; Bharthari's decision to renounce the world brings Vikramaditya to the throne. The name of Vikram is associated with a fixed point, 58–57 B.C., from which one major system of Hindu dating, the Vikrama era, begins. However, King Vikramaditya's status as a historical personage is also open to doubt.[12]

The tale of Bhartrihari's renunciation takes up but a few pages in the cycle of Sanskrit stories surrounding Vikramaditya. These have been translated and retold in English and are often summarized in introductions to collections of the Sanskrit poet's work.[13] The plot involves a circular chain of deception that will inevitably recall to Western readers the French farce and opera plot evoked by the title *La Ronde*.

A Brahman, as a reward for his intense austerities, receives the fruit of immortality from God; he presents this prize to King Bhartrihari, who gives it to his adored wife, Pingala.[14] She, however, passes it on to her paramour, and he to a prostitute who offers it once more to the king. Having extracted the truth from each link in this chain, and stunned not only by his queen's perfidy but by the generally fickle ways of the world, Bhartrihari decides then and there to pursue a more stable reality, turning the rule of his kingdom over to Vikramaditya.[15]

Madhu Nath's version of Bharthari's story does not include any

---

trihari's poems, notes, "In spite of the legend, the content of the verses suggests that the author... was not a king, but a courtier-poet in the service of a king" (Miller 1967, xvii). Bhartrihari the poet may be the same as Bhartrihari the Sanskrit grammarian, author of a famous treatise, the *Vākyapadīya*. Coward 1976 and Iyer 1969, 10–15, both favor this identification; Miller 1967 is more skeptical.

12. For the historicity of King Vikramaditya see Edgerton 1926; Sircar 1969.

13. See Edgerton 1926 for translations from the Sanskrit; see also Bhoothalingam 1982 who adapted a Tamil version of the Sanskrit for young readers in English. For an elaborate, embellished retelling in Hindi see Vaidya 1984, 7–24. Versions of the story are also referred to in Miller 1967; Kale 1971; Wortham 1886.

14. As a woman's name, *Pīngaḷā* is rare. The *RSK* lists a variant, *Pingaḷā* as a name of the goddess Lakshmi as well as the name of Bhartrihari's wife. Its primary meaning, however, is one of three main, subtle channels in the human body described by yogic physiology.

15. Some elaborations on the story have Bhartrihari first exiling Vikramaditya after the debauched queen accuses him of assaulting her honor in order to cover up her real indiscretion. Then Bhartrihari must recall Vikramaditya and exonerate him before following the guru Gorakh Nath to a renouncer's life (Duggal 1979).

reference to this circle of illicit connections. Pingala here is an impec-
cably true wife. Rather than woman's infidelity, the premise of Madhu
Nath's tale is that even the most faithful woman is part of the illusory
nature of the universe and thus not worth loving. Jackson in a note on
the lore surrounding Bharthari's Cave—a famous shrine in Ujjain—
and Rose in his ethnographic survey of the Northeast both relate
stories similar to Madhu Nath's in which Pingala is true (Jackson
1902; Rose 1914). Gray translates a fifteenth-century Sanskrit play,
the *Bhartṛharinirveda* of Harihara, that also has a plot very similar to
the Rajasthani folk telling (Gray 1904). However, to my knowledge
all the popular published dramas and folk romances (*kissas*)[16] about
King Bharthari and Queen Pingala center on the fruit of immortality
and Pingala's deceit (but she usually reforms in the end).

Although I have called attention to a dramatic dichotomy between
types of Pingalas in Nath traditions, let me note that these striking
differences mask an underlying symmetry. In the end, it is women—
true or false, beloved or despised—whom yogis abandon. Madhu
Nath's version actually seems at one moment in the *arthāv* to consider
Pingala's fanatic fidelity as yet another dangerous feminine wile.
Gorakh Nath implies that by becoming *satī* Pingala was trying to kill
her husband. And yet if we shift perspectives once again, we may view
both types of Pingalas as the impetus for Bharthari's enlightenment,
and thus as valued positive forces in these tales of renunciation.[17]

Bharthari and Gopi Chand's relationship—both as maternal uncle

16. For popular folk romances based on the Vikram cycle, including brief references to Bharthari and the fruit of immortality, and an insightful discussion of
"women's wiles" in this genre, see Pritchett 1985, 56–78.

17. With a script that explains Bharthari's infatuation and Pingala's perfidy
through predestination, one version of the tale actually makes such a collapse nicely
logical. Dehlavi's Hindi play *Bharthari Pingalā* frames the fruit-of-immortality circle
with a glimpse into Bharthari's previous birth as one of Gorakh Nath's disciples,
Bharat Nath. While on an errand for his guru, Bharat Nath is distracted by a beautiful
fairy and sports with her in the woods. The fairy is punished for misbehaving with
a yogi by Indra, the king of the gods, who forces her to take a human birth. Bharat
Nath is given the same sentence by his guru. Indra tells the fairy that she will deceive
her husband and cause him to renounce the world, consequently suffering the heavy
sorrow of widowhood in her youth (Dehlavi n.d., 32). To mitigate Bharat Nath's
misery, Gorakh promises his errant disciple that the same beautiful female who
caused his downfall will bring about his reunion with the guru (26). In this frame
Pingala's infidelity represents not lack of character but a cosmic plan. Bhoju reports
hearing a very similar version from a Brahman schoolteacher who saw it performed
in Alwar; that tale tidily made Pingala's lover an incarnation of Guru Gorakh Nath.

and nephew, and as two Naths with immortal bodies—is mentioned in several versions other than Madhu Nath's (Dehlavi n.d.; Dikshit n.d., 264). In Rajasthani folklore not contained within the epic tales themselves, Bharthari and Gopi Chand are paired as immortal companions still wandering the earth. Thus they appear as the authors of hymns (*bhajans*) to the formless lord (Gold 1988, 109) and are recalled in proverbs: "As long as sky and earth shall be / Live Gopi Chand and Bharthari" (*Jab tak ākāsh dharatī, tab tak Gopī Chand Bhartharī*). Most of the longer versions of Bharthari's tale make some reference to his gaining an "immortal body" (*amar kāyā*), but none is particularly illuminating about the nature of this immortality. Madhu Nath never refers to immortality in telling the tale of Bharthari, but when Gopi Chand receives the blessing (or curse) of immortality from Jalindar Nath, in part 4 of his separate tale, Bharthari is with him and shares in the fruit.

Distinctive to Madhu's telling is a general concern for mundane detail: many descriptions of actions and relationships, well understood or easily imagined in village thought, that do not advance the story line but rather situate it in familiar experience. These include a gathering of village elders in time of crisis; the technology of potters; the negotiations of patrons and clients; the mutuality and interdependence of subjects and rulers. Such familiar scenes or situations may, moreover, be suddenly spiced with magical occurrences or divine intervention: donkeys talk to village elders, a guru's play spoils the carefully crafted pots; messengers come from heaven to straighten out the king and save his subjects. It would seem that Madhu and his teachers, in adapting a traditional tale for village patrons, elaborate both the familiar and the magical to strike a captivating blend. And yet, as we will see, although Gopi Chand's story certainly shares some stylistic and thematic qualities with Bharthari's, it follows a different recipe.

Gopi Chand

In Madhu's version as well as all others except those originating in Bengal, Gopi Chand is described as the king of "Gaur" Bengal. Gaur was an ancient Bengali kingdom that fell to Muslim invaders in the thirteenth century (Sarkar 1948, 8). Although there is no evidence pointing to an association of a historical Gopi Chand with the kingdom of Gaur, attempts have been made to link Gopi Chand with various

Bengali monarchs of the Pala or Chandra dynasties (Grierson 1878; Majumdar 1940); however, too many conflicting details preclude any certain confirmation of these indentifications (Chowdhury 1967, 186–87; Sen 1954).

Versions of Gopi Chand do not divide neatly into two types, as versions of Bharthari do according to Pingala's good or bad character. However, a number of motifs in Bengali versions consistently contrast with those recorded or written down in western India.[18] For example, Gopi Chand's sister is a significant figure in Madhu Nath's tale as well as in other tales from western India but is never mentioned in Bengali versions. As the stories are told in Punjab, Rajasthan, and Uttar Pradesh, Gopi Chand must go east to Bengal to meet his sister. She is thus married into a Bengal that is alien to the Bengal that Gopi Chand rules, a doubling of distance and foreignness.

I might speculate that the journey to a sister who inevitably dies of grief, to be revived by Jalindar's magic, accrues to the non-Bengali versions in order to lend a sense of completion or closure to the king's renunciation. In two Bengali versions, Gopi Chand parts with difficulty from his wives but eventually goes back to them; in the western Indian traditions he leaves the world and women for good, after parting from his sister. Attachment to the sister is, as Madhu's Manavati Mata firmly instructs her son at one point, a far more serious matter than any bond to wives.

Like the visit to the sister, the motif of Gopi Chand burying his guru in a deep well and covering him up with horse manure occurs in all but the Bengali versions. Moreover, this episode is almost always linked, as it is in Madhu's tale, with the subplot of Gorakh Nath's journey to Bengal to rescue his guru Machhindar from magician-queens. That is, the two gurus are ignominiously trapped in two different ways, and their respective disciples compete as to who will rescue his first.[19]

18. I draw on Grierson 1878 and Sircar n.d. for translations from Bengali; Temple 1884 translates a Punjabi oral drama; Dikshit n.d. and Yogishvar n.d. respectively provide Hindi prose and drama versions.

19. In all versions but Madhu Nath's that include the guru-in-the-well motif, the deliverance of both gurus (Machhindar from Bengal and Jalindar from the well) occurs *before*, not after, Gopi Chand's initiation. Thus, Jalindar's magical power to be up and about and active in Gopi Chand's tale, despite being down a well and buried under horse dung (which we must accept in order to follow Madhu's plot line), is unnecessary in these more "logically" structured versions. Perhaps somewhere en route to Rajasthan the plot sequence was rearranged.

I initially thought that the lengthy episode concerning those trouble-some females, the seven low-caste lady magicians of Bengal, was unique to the Rajasthani Gopi Chand. As some of these characters appear in other Rajasthani folk traditions, this surmise seemed plausible.[20] However, although no other versions give anything near the weight and the detail that the Rajasthani does to Gopi Chand's female adver-saries or place them as obstacles between the king and his sister, Bengali and Hindi texts do have Gopi Chand's progress obstructed by one or more lowborn, low-living, magic-wielding females. I have argued elsewhere that the Rajasthani version, which allows both king and audience to develop so much sympathy for Gopi Chand's kins-women, especially needs the lady magicians to make parting from virtuous females less cruel. The Bengali magicians are women the Rajasthani village audience loves to hate (Gold 1991).

One element that all six versions notably have in common is the dynamic instigating role played by Gopi Chand's mother. In all versions Gopi Chand's mother is a religious adept—although her role may range from immortal, wonder-working magician to dedicated devotee. In all versions it is she who makes the fateful decision that her son should become a yogi—an idea that would obviously never have occurred to Gopi Chand of his own accord.[21] Thus, Gopi Chand is propelled toward renunciation, just as is Bharthari, by a woman.

In the Bengali versions of the tale—which we may accept as prob-ably closer to an "original" version insofar as they are produced in the hero's native region—Manavati is a powerful *yoginī* who has learned the secret of immortality. This is in accord with Bengal's reputation in the rest of India as a place of powerful females.[22] Never-

---

20. See Bhanavat 1968 for an episode concerning Gangali Telin, one of the lady magicians who torments Gopi Chand, in Rajasthani lore on Kala–Gora Bhairu or "Black Bhairu and Fair Bhairu."

21. An exception I encountered as this volume goes to press is a new report on fieldwork among Naths in Bhojpur (eastern Uttar Pradesh); C. Champion describes a version of Gopi Chand, "completely different from the Bengali" in which his mother, "confronting her son's decision to become a renouncer tries only to interfere by invoking all the arguments in her possession" (Champion 1989, 66; my translation).

22. For a discussion of legends about an Eastern kingdom of women see McLeod 1968, 110–12. Even travel literature of this century may capitalize on such legends and their possible anthropological realization. In one such account Bertrand refers to Bengalis' fear of "sorceresses having the power to change men into animals" (Bertrand 1958, 173); see also Dvivedi n.d., 53–54. In a comprehensive survey of women in Bengali literature, Rowlands 1930 discusses Gopi Chand's mother and wives.

theless, even in Bengal it is not so easy for a woman to be a guru. Sircar's unpublished translation from the Bengali contains a vivid rendition of this plight of the divinely powerful yet domestically power-less woman. She describes to her son how her husband, Gopi Chand's father, preferred death to having his wife as a guru: "You are but the wife of my house, / but I am the master of that house. / If I accept wisdom from a housewife / How can I call her guru and take the dust off her feet?" (Sircar n.d., 13).[23]

Chief among the distinctive aspects of Madhu Nath's account are a critical plot feature and an attendant emotional timbre. Madhu's is the only text that explains Gopi Chand's birth as a loan to his mother (although others do ascribe it to his mother's devotions or asceticisms).[24] Although all the versions have Gopi Chand initially resist the idea of renouncing the world, Madhu's is the only one in which Gopi Chand perpetually laments and sorrows, calling on his guru like a child at every difficult moment. These two factors are in constant interplay in Madhu's text. By portraying Gopi Chand as doomed to yogahood but attached to the world, by having his feelings oppose his destiny, Madhu's tale creates a space for resistance and generates the human drama (or melodrama) that made me wish to translate this tale as a counterpoint to prevailing images of resolute renouncers.

In other versions it is women who display most of the emotion; Gopi Chand passes through their pleas and reproaches with a certain dignified detachment (much as Madhu's Bharthari hears out and denies Pingala). But Madhu Nath elaborates on the king's inner turmoil, not only by returning again and again to the rainstorm of tears in his eyes, but also by providing trains of consciousness (*veg*) or reveries when Gopi Chand expresses his regret, despair, and simple shame.

Like his telling of Bharthari's story, Madhu's Gopi Chand tale incorporates some familiar details of daily rural life: the ways that barren women seek divine remedies; the washerwoman's rounds to

23. See O'Flaherty 1984, 160, 280–81, for a case from Sanskrit mythology rather than Nath folklore in which a wise wife must resort to extreme subterfuge in order to act as her husband's guru.

24. David White (personal communication 1990) pointed out to me that the idea of a human life as a loan is a very ancient one in Hindu thought. See Malamoud for a comprehensive discussion of "a theory of debt as constitutive of human nature" in Sanskrit texts (Malamoud 1989, 115–36).

8. Gopi Chand's queen faints as her husband in yogi's garb begs for alms; faded cover illustration for Balakram Yogishvar's published Hindi play of *Gopi Chand*.

collect laundry; the companionable filling of water pots by groups of women. But, while these mundane details can seem to dominate his Bharthari performance, generating more interest than do the chief characters and their problems, in Gopi Chand's story the setting is always subordinated to character and interpersonal dynamics.[25]

In Madhu's version of Bharthari, magical moments are embedded in a realistic tapestry of rural life—a life inhabited by largely two-dimensional characters. In his Gopi Chand, events in the world float on the surface of deeply reverberating internal spaces and highly charged interpersonal channels. These inner worlds, moreover, are not bounded. That the same bard can present two tales of renouncer-kings so differently suggests that the tales themselves, despite being part of the common lore of the Nine Naths, have retained distinctive features of their disparate origins.

Uncoupling

Taken together Madhu Nath's tales of Bharthari and Gopi Chand offer a surprising variety of impressions of and information about yogis, even as they use stock images and repeat certain events. A striking example comes from the almost identically framed scenes in the two tales when the king arrives as a yogi outside his wife's palace. Both Gopi Chand and Bharthari have trouble communicating with their former slave girls before crossing enough portals to meet their former queens. Indeed, this is so obviously the same episode that Madhu sings it for Bharthari in the Gopi Chand tune. But the actual encounter between husband and wife is a different story. Gopi Chand's resolution dissolves; he is tormented, wavering, tearful, and plaintive. Bharthari stands firm. Nor are the queens to be merged. Pingala is a more formidable lady than is Patam De Rani, and her lament has its own quality. When she launches it, as if to accentuate this difference, Madhu Nath switches from a Gopi Chand tune to the characteristic *Rājājī* melody of Bharthari.

25. In a recent insightful and provocative paper Brenda Beck observes in Indian folk epics a general stress on "the world of emotion and inner mental states," and suggests that the audience appreciates these emotions not through direct expression but through "understanding the structure of situations in which characters find themselves" (Beck 1989, 155). Such would be true of Bharthari; Gopi Chand presents emotions in unusually forthright fashion.

The identities and histories of Bharthari and Gopi Chand appear to resemble each other more when contrasted with the renouncer-king of a related popular tradition. In the preceding chapter I discussed some mutual influences of Nath and Sant traditions in popular Hinduism. Among the "garlands" of devotees whose life histories form an important part of Sant devotional literature is Raja Pipa (McGregor 1984, 42; Sharma 1983, 184–85). As counterbalance to all the variations we have just observed in the tales of Bharthari and Gopi Chand, it is instructive to consider Pipa's career.

Like Gopi Chand, Pipa has several wives. When he decides to become a renouncer they first try to stop him and then beg to accompany him. Where Pipa's story fully diverges both from Bharthari's and Gopi Chand's is that one of his wives, Sita, is so devoted and virtuous that she submits to the double requirement to come without belongings and naked, and does go with him. Together, Jack Hawley suggests, in a thought-provoking analysis, they point to a possible change in the social order deriving from *bhakti* or devotion. As Hawley puts it: "What is wanted instead is a new understanding of what one already is, and a genuinely new society in which the roles of house-holder and renunciation are not polarized.... Pīpā and Sītā form the nucleus of that society." They remain married but devote their lives to others—a kind of "mutual self-renunciation" (Hawley 1987, 64).

Whatever the variety and religious dedication of their female characters, Nath tales do not allow women to accompany men in renunciation. Indeed, the men must be rid of them at all costs. Whenever a woman does beg to go along (as do Bharthari's wife, Pingala, and Gopi Chand's sister, Champa De), she is admonished in many ways that women have no place in the wandering life of a yogi. Yet women in these tales often can and do go separately, gaining power as independent beings rather than as companions to males.

It is not, therefore, that Madhu's tales deny spiritual progress to women; quite the opposite. But they do indeed deny spiritual progress to couples. Following Hawley's point, it would seem that to accept a couple's capacity for spiritual selflessness might be to break through to a redefined social order such as *bhakti* proposes. This would be a world where human relationships other than the privileged guru-disciple bond were not so thoroughly devalued as they are in Nath teachings. Nath stories do not make that leap. In them, proper yogis are consistently without interest in society beyond their enjoyment of its cooking. And yet—as we shall at last find out, for the story is about to begin—Madhu Nath's tales tell us far more about the problems and pleasures of that social universe than they do about the world of detached perfected immortals.

The Tale of King Bharthari

Part 1

Bharthari's Birth Story

Introduction

Bharthari's birth story[1] is a beauty-and-the-beast fairy tale of how a rude and bold donkey wins a princess-bride. It is also a saga with political and social insight, depicting the play and consequences of various power strategies in families and kingdoms. This chronologically first segment of the Bharthari and Gopi Chand epics has a different flavor from the other parts of both tales. As if to mark its distinctiveness, Madhu performs the entire birth story except its single opening stanza in a tune that never reappears elsewhere. Each of the other three major melodies he employs in at least two, and often several, parts of his performance.

Bharthari's birth story is largely concerned with external actions. It lacks the high emotional pitch and deep psychological reflections that prevail through most of Gopi Chand's tale and emerge sporadically in the other two parts of Bharthari's. No yogi characters appear here, whereas all other parts of both epic texts either feature or star ascetic gurus. Nonetheless, Bharthari's birth story orients its audience to a cosmology where yogis hold the keys of power: the donkey Khukanyo's[2] magic, upon which the action hinges, derives from the all-powerful name of Guru Gorakh Nath.

The opening scene of Bharthari 1 is mysterious. Why does

---

1. *janmpatrī;* usually a horoscope, here *janmpatrī* clearly has a broader sense: how someone got born, the circumstances or story of a birth. See Blackburn 1988, 1989 for discussions of birth stories in and beyond South Indian oral epic tradition.

2. This is Gandaraph Syan's name in his donkey birth, also pronounced *Khūkanyā* and, when used affectionately or intimately, *Khūkanyū.*

Gandaraph Syan's father object to the prince watching his plays being performed? This violent encounter between a defiant rebellious son and a strict repressive father pushes even a nonbeliever in Freudian readings toward psychoanalytic explanations. Surely, such intense wrath on the father's part would not be evoked merely by his son's witnessing a public theatrical performance. Surely, he must have witnessed and, as he forthrightly avows, found "wondrous," what Freud calls a "primal scene." One variant of the tale (see chapter 3) supports an interpretation of Gandaraph Syan's offense as intruding on his parents' sexual domain. It presents the Gandaraph figure as a Gandharva in heaven who embraces one of King Indra's dancing girls and is punished with a donkey birth for giving way so shamefully to uncontrolled sexual urges.[3]

When I asked my research assistant, and through him the bard and his son, whether the "play" could in fact be an allusion to sexual activity on the part of Gandaraph's father, I found them dedicated to a face-value interpretation. Bhoju explained to me that filial disobedience is the central issue here. It doesn't matter what was forbidden; the point is that a son must obey his parent.

Whether Gandaraph Syan's crime was disobedience or voyeurism, his punishment is to go into a "donkey's vagina"—that is, to be born from a donkey. Why a donkey, we may as well ask now, for that humble beast of burden appears with surprising frequency in Madhu Nath's tales—often as the transformation of a human being, either male or female. Bharthari's father is a donkey; Gopi Chand is turned into a donkey (GC 3); Charpat Nath's fourteen hundred disciples are turned into donkeys (GC 3); Hada Nath turns all the women (and later, men) of Bengal into donkeys (GC 3); Gorakh Nath grazes a potter's donkey and later forces one of Machhindar Nath's queens to remain a donkey forever (GC 4).

The donkey is, on the one hand, a pathetic, overburdened, mistreated creature. This is succinctly summed up by Gorakh Nath's instructions when he hands over his guru's former captor and wife, in the form of a donkey, to the potters who will keep her: "Load her heavily and feed her little." Such is the donkey's destiny. Its plaintive

---

3. Both that variant and the present text portray a murderous energy directed from an elder to a younger male. See A. K. Ramanujan's suggestions on the cultural contours of an "Indian Oedipus" complex (Ramanujan 1983).

bray—rendered many times by Madhu Nath as *ṭibhū ṭibhū* (Rajasthani for "hee-haw")—is ever comical. Just as in Western animal stereotypes, a donkey in India is stubborn and stupid and ugly. Its sexuality, if not so blatant as a goat's, is nonetheless powerful. To call someone "donkey" or "donkey's progeny" is a common minor insult in the village, much like our "stupid ass."

But Gandaraph Syan, embodied in the donkey Khukanyo, is not wholly a figure of fun. He wants a wife, and eventually he gets one. People are frightened when he threatens to turn the city upside down with his hoofs and spare no living creature. The ambivalence with which villagers approach yogis' power may be part of what motivates the donkey-transformation motif in general, and Gandaraph Syan/Khukanyo's character in particular. There is a way in which it is appropriate as well as ridiculous to see yogis (and lady magicians) as asses. The donkey's unintelligible braying—in Gandaraph Syan's case a prelude to his demands, threats, and manifestations of power—may resonate with popular double opinions about yogis' magic spells. These are reflected in the term *mantra-tantra*, which may mean, according to context, either "mumbo jumbo" or "powerful verbal spells." The handsome, desirable, and fertile prince emerging from the skin of a donkey could also relate to the extraordinary sexuality that yogic adepts may hide beneath their ochre robes.

That the donkey's ally should be a potter is predictable in the cultural context of rural Rajasthan. Donkeys as beasts of burden are traditionally associated with potters, who figure almost as frequently as donkeys in Madhu Nath's tales (Bh 1, Bh 2, and GC 4). Potters, like donkeys, are lowborn. Yet they possess and manifest creative power in ways that demand respect, and they play important parts in community and domestic ritual life. How highly the villagers value their potter's services is impressively dramatized in Bharthari's birth story.

Bharthari 1 may not carry us to the heart of the human dilemmas concerning love and renunciation about which the corpus of Madhu Nath's tales revolves. Yet, despite all the extraordinary and magical occurrences in the narrative, the birth story takes us some way into the heart of traditional village society. A good example would be the frightened potter's attempt to leave the city and his neighbors' mobilization to prevent his untoward departure. Here we see vividly the integration and interdependence of members of a community, the power of individual resistance, and eventually the king's own dependence on his people. Princess Pan De's father is no absolute monarch but rather a man who takes advice from his servants and negotiates with his subjects. Indeed, the ultimate authority in these tales often appears to lie with royal servants (*darogās*) rather than with the monarch. Presented not only as doing the king's work but as having his ear, the royal servant caste exercises significant influence upon affairs of state.

Another configuration of interdependency in this opening segment, which will be echoed throughout both tales, is that of king and countryside. When the donkey builds a wall with no opening, the bard's portrayal of angry villagers who need to relieve themselves but can't get out to the fields to do so in sanitary privacy, is hilarious. For all its slapstick quality, however, it states a simple truth that villagers live day in and day out: without the countryside life is impossible. Both to deposit wastes and to obtain nourishment for their livestock—and of course, through farming, for themselves—villagers maintain constant intercourse with the lands surrounding them.

Bharthari's birth story contains, as another touch of realism, a synopsis of some key moments in the prolonged Rajasthani marriage ritual. Such capsule weddings appear frequently in local lore, including women's stories and some of the other regional epics. The events of the wedding sequence—the feasts, the preparation of the bride's and groom's bodies with turmeric anointment and henna designs, the striking of the marriage emblem by the groom, the role played by Brahmans, and the importance of the gifts and "send-off" from the bride's father—are strange to Western readers and require an overload of ethnographic footnotes. But it is well to remember that for Madhu's regular audience these are cherished details of the utterly familiar, laden with positive and pleasant associations.[4]

The personality of Princess Pan De is not highly developed, compared with that of other significant women in Madhu's two tales. Nevertheless, Pan De's part, especially the ambivalent quality of her

---

4. I recall touring the Jaipur Museum in 1980 with a group of villagers, many of whom had never been in such a place. Goggling at the exotic was satisfying in its way, but their favorite display was of a Rajasthani wedding. They clustered before the glass case with its lifesize panorama, pointing to important ritual paraphernalia and familiar items of clothing and jewelry. Just as those recognizable elements had value in a very strange environment, so in Madhu Nath's tales such wholly familiar moments may bring a story of yogis' magic close to home.

relationship with her husband, prefigures in some ways other female roles in these traditions. At first Pan De appears to be a perfect wife, accepting her parents' decision about her marriage, protecting her *pati dev* or husband-god from abuse, displaying appropriate modesty toward her potter father-in-law. The neglect of Pan De by her parents, following her marriage, would be considered a very grievous breech of village society's ideology that care and gifts are owed to daughters.

In the new city of Dhara Nagar, however, as her children are born, slurs are levied against Pan De's character. And even though these slurs are unjust, for she is no adulteress, the snickering by Madhu and his audience here (its theme, How can a donkey sire a prince?) shows more relish of the gossip's nasty implications than appreciation of the maligned woman's virtue. The public backbiting is attributed to women, but it is Pan De's mother who remains loyal to her daughter ("Though sinner she be / She belongs to me!") when the father turns his back on her.

Almost immediately, however, with yet another quick and subtle switch in a female character's moral nature, the devoted mother becomes the agent of her donkey son-in-law's untimely demise. This event recalls innumerable fairy tales the world over—including many with beauty-and-the-beast motifs—where bad advice from one's natal female kin spoils, or almost spoils, a happy if strange marital union. In the particular context of the approach to domesticity in Nath tales, this cross-cultural pitting of natal versus marital loyalties is reconfigured as an explicit demonstration of how love-in-the-world backfires. Pan De's mother wants only to secure her daughter's happiness; Pan De desires only to possess completely the human form of the husband she loves. Yet these valid desires conjoin to widow Bharthari's mother.

That Pan De's devotion to her donkey-husband turns out so badly for both of them is the first moment of many to come in Madhu Nath's tales where the plot is skewed by a devaluation of familial love. Relationships in the world are unstable and untrustworthy; even good women's actions are potentially destructive. Yet beneath, or above, such manifestations of human instability is the sense of a cosmic program. All of this was preordained.

After Pan De crumbles the donkey's charred skin to dust between her palms, she finds that her hands are "printed with the sun and the moon"—perhaps foreshadowing the birth of her grandson Gopi

Chand with his attributes of celestial radiance. Gopi Chand too is destined to die, more than once, in the midst of adoring women. But he will reach immortality, along with his uncle Bharthari, by the grace of a yogi guru as cantankerous, dangerous, and well endowed with magical power as the vanished donkey-prince.

Text

Honored King[5]...
Wealth and youth are guests, heroic husband,
In no time at all they're gone,[6]
    you must realize, Bharthari.
You must realize, Bharthari Panvar of Dhara Nagar,[7]
You're my wedded lord, but
You've gone and left me destitute.[8]

In Dip Nagar lived King Ranjit[9]
Oh yes[10]...
Who had a son, a prince.

<hr/>

5. *Rājājī...;* this address, always sung prolonged as *Rājājīīīīī...* marks the beginning of each verse sung in the *Rājājī rāg.* For part 1 it is the single opening verse; in part 2 it continues throughout several sung segments; in part 3 it is a frame, coming at the beginning and end. It is thus the sole *rāg* to appear in all three parts of Bharthari.

6. The meaning of these lines, as of the words they contain, is open to more than one interpretation. Bhoju consulted Madhu and Shivji Nath, who concur that Queen Pingala is "explaining" to Bharthari that he ought to enjoy the good things of life during their brief duration. This exegesis interprets *māyā* as "wealth" rather than "illusion" and gives it a positive valuation. The opposite, yogic, thrust to these words would be: don't put your faith in transient, illusory pleasures.

7. *Panvār* (which Madhu Nath pronounces sometimes *Puñvār,* or *Puṅvār,* and the *RSK* lists as a variant of *Paramār*) is a lineage (*kul*) of the Sun branch of Rajputs. Here and throughout the text it is used as Bharthari's surname. Along with Avanti or Avantipuri, Dhara Nagar is identified with the modern city of Ujjain that will be founded by Bharthari's father the donkey in this birth story.

8. These two lines are part of Pingala's lament, foreshadowing the action in part 3. A wife without her husband is totally destitute.

9. Ranjit is Bharthari's father's father, according to Madhu; Dip Nagar, literally "Lamp City," is his place. I found no references to him or his city by these names in other versions.

10. Characterizing the *rāg* of Bharthari part 1 only is the refrain *haṅ jīīī,* literally "yes sir...," in a prolonged drone that recurs after every several lines of narrative song. To avoid the military ring of "yes sir" but retain whatever positive meaning accrues to this repeated affirmative, I simply use "Oh yes...."

The king had plays performed
In the Chapala Garden[11]
But the father wouldn't let his son watch.
Oh yes...
The son, too, had plays performed,
and the king didn't watch.
Oh yes...
Now one time it chanced
that the young prince hid
in the Chapala Garden
in a bamboo clump.
Oh yes...
He sat and watched the play, and
the king his father said,
"Today the play is spoiled!"
Oh yes...
"Run and look, servant lads!"
But they couldn't find
the young prince anywhere.
Oh yes...
Then one servant ran
to the bamboo clump
where the young prince sat.
Oh yes...
He seized the prince
and took him to the king.
Oh yes...
Then the king said, "Gandaraph Syan,
Why were you watching my play?"
Oh yes...
"Father, I liked your play,
I thought it was wondrous,
That's why I watched it!"
Oh yes...

11. Chapala can mean a *pīpal* tree and is also a name of the goddess. It seems to be a generic name for a garden near a city. The "Chapala Garden" is where Pingala burns in Bharthari 2 and appears in Gopi Chand's Gaur Bengal as the place where Jalindar and other yogis camp, not far from the palace.

The king cursed him:
"Gandaraph Syan,
you spoiled my play.
Oh yes...
"You must go right now
in a donkey's vagina."[12]
Oh yes...
The father cursed the son.
Oh yes...
As soon as he cursed him, Gandaraph Syan
fell over and died.
Oh yes...
Ahead is Ganga City.
In that city lived a Potter[13]
and that Potter had a she-ass.
In that she-ass's belly
the young prince fell.
Oh yes...
One month passed for the she-ass,
Oh yes...
Then the second and third months passed,
The fifth month passed for the she-ass.
Oh yes...
Now nine months passed for the she-ass[14]
and her Prince Khukanyo was born.
Oh yes...
"Tibhu tibhu,"[15]
the prince brayed.
Oh yes...
Shiv! Gorakh![16]

(Bh 1.1.s)

12. That is, take birth as a donkey.
13. Within Madhu Nath's tales I capitalize caste names such as Potter; they occur both as social types and as surnames.
14. Such recounting of the passage of months during human gestation is common in tales and songs. It repeats below for all three pregnancies of Bharthari's mother.
15. This sound is always a bit comical—particularly linked with "prince" as it is here, or "yogi" or "king" as it will be in Gopi Chand.
16. Madhu often closes a sung portion with a chanted invocation to deities or gurus.

In Dip Nagar lived King Ranjit, and he had a son, Gandaraph Syan. The young prince was a boy of ten or twelve years. That king's habit was to have plays performed in the garden. The father didn't let his son watch his plays. And the young prince had plays performed that he didn't let the king see.

So matters went along in this way. But once the ruler was having a play performed in the Chapala Garden—a play that he wouldn't let his son see.

And it chanced that the young prince thought to himself, "What kind of plays does my father have performed? Let me just sneak in and see today."

In the garden, a little distance away from where the play was proceeding, the young prince found a bamboo clump, and he slipped into it and sat down.

So over there the king was seated on his chair, and over here the young prince was watching, and the play was going on. But the king got suspicious. "Uh oh! What obstacle is interfering with my play? The play is no good today. The play is spoiled."

"Grain-giver,[17] the play is just fine," the players said. "It's fine, it's great."

"No, today the play is spoiled!"

The king said to his Royal Servants,[18] "O Royal Servants, run into the garden and see if the young prince is watching the play."

The Royal Servants ran off. Five or ten of them went looking. He had slipped into a clump of bamboo and was watching. Who? The young prince. As soon as they found him, they grabbed him by the arm and took him to His Majesty.

His Majesty said, "Why were you watching my play?"

"Father, I liked it, I liked it. I said to myself, 'What are my father's plays like? How does he have them performed?' I found it very beautiful. So that's why I sneaked in and watched."

"All right, sister-fucker![19] You go into a donkey's vagina!"

So the father cursed his son—his son, whose name was Prince

17. *annātā;* a term of address used for any master, king, god, superior person, or power.

18. *darogā;* I translate this caste name always as "Royal Servant." In the sung section above, the king used a term for servant (*chākar*) that is not caste-linked.

19. *bahin-chod;* this is Madhu Nath's favorite insult. It does not have quite the shock power in Hindi or Rajasthani, where it is common, that it does in English.

Gandaraph Syan. He cursed that boy, and as soon as he uttered the curse, his son dropped dead on the spot. As soon as the father cursed, "Go to a donkey's vagina, go!" the son breathed his last.

In another city there was a Potter named Pachyo Potter. He had a she-ass, and Prince Gandaraph Syan fell into that donkey's belly.

He fell into her belly, and one month passed, two months passed, three months passed—the fifth, sixth, seventh, eighth—and in the ninth month the she-ass had a child. The she-ass had a child and he cried, "Tibhu tibhu!" and suckled the breast.

Now one month passed and two months passed and three months passed and six months passed, and he grew into a fine healthy colt. He was a healthy colt, and then he began to speak with Pachyo Potter. The donkey's son began to bray at midnight.

(Bh 1.1.e)

At midnight he brayed, "Tibhu, tibhu! Listen Pachyo Potter, go . . . you have a king: marry me to his daughter. She has grown into a blooming maid, and her braids are turning white.[20] So go and tell your king to marry me to his daughter. And if he marries her to a donkey, then I will surround his city with double ramparts of copper and brass. And I will build him a gold and silver palace, and I will excavate mines of seven metals.

"But, if he won't marry Pan De[21] to me, I'll knock his country and his city upside down with my hoofs."

This is the vow the donkey made to Pachyo.

When he heard this, Pachyo said, "Sure! I will marry this girl to a donkey!"

He took his wheel-turning stick and began to raise welts on him. On whom? The donkey.

He said to the donkey, "Some neighbors might be listening, and if they go to the king and tell him that the Potter's donkey is saying, 'Marry me to the Princess Pan De,' then he will send me flying from a cannon's mouth, or else he will bury me and have me trampled by horses. My son![22] You are saying very improper things! What if the king finds out?"

---

20. In other words, it is high time she gets married.

21. This is the princess, Bharthari's mother; her name does not occur in other tales of Bharthari's parentage. In Rajasthani folklore, but not in ordinary life, the suffix "De" is very common after women's names.

22. *māro beṭo;* a "small insult."

So he took his stick and beat him, and the donkey was quiet. But the next day came, and the next midnight. And the donkey did the same thing. He kept doing this for six months, calling "Tibhu tibhu" every midnight. Who? Khukanyo, the Potter's donkey.[23]

So the Potter regularly raised his stick, "Take that, your mother's...,[24] you Khukanyo, sure I will get you married!" And he beat him badly every day.

Matters continued this way, and the Potter grew distraught because the donkey called him every night. So he decided to leave the village.[25]

"What to do? Let's leave this city. Let's go somewhere else and settle there, ten or twenty miles[26] away, and let's take the donkey with us. There won't be any king in that village, so the donkey won't call out."

The next day the Potter and the Potteress loaded up the donkey and the buffalo and filled a cart with all their bedding and junk. Then they left the village. "Let's go, or else the donkey will be the death of us."

(Bh 1.2.e)[27]

Pachyo Potter reached the outskirts of the city.[28] But when he got to the border, ten or twenty persons had gathered there.

"Oh no, we have only one Potter and he is leaving the village. And he doesn't say what the trouble is. Why has he left?[29] Suppose someone dies tomorrow...where will we get our new clay utensils? We will need water pots and other vessels.[30]

---

23. Here I delete a repetition of the entire midnight scene.

24. A serious insult if completed: "your mother's vagina."

25. Here and throughout both tales Madhu Nath interchanges the terms "village" (*gaṅv*) and "city" (H. *śahar*, which he pronounces *sair*); his stories take place in cities but his orientations, like those of his listeners, are to villages.

26. A measurement of distance used throughout both tales, *koś* (H. *kos*) equals two miles. I double the numbers Madhu uses to translate in miles.

27. Although omitting each part's sung segments between the first and final one—except those that significantly advance the narrative—I number every new segment of explanation so the reader remains aware of where Madhu Nath makes his breaks.

28. *phalsā;* the agricultural land belonging to a particular populated area, but without dwellings; it lies between the actual city or village and the border of its residents' landholdings.

29. The neighbors believe that Pachyo leaves to protest mistreatment or underpayment, a familiar yet extreme recourse for members of artisan or servant castes who are unhappy with working conditions.

30. After a death in a household, all clay utensils are broken and replaced because they are polluted.

"Now we have a Potter, but if he goes there won't be one. Let's bring him back. He won't tell us what the trouble is, and this is a very fine city of ours. Is it because of grain? But everyone gives him grain, every month.[31] And the king is very good, the king doesn't cause any trouble, so then why has he quit the village and gone?"

So ten, twenty, forty, fifty villagers gathered at the boundary and they blocked the Potter's path.

"Brother Potter, we won't let you go! Tell us your trouble, whether it's from the city or from the king. What's the matter? If someone hasn't given grain, then we will give it. And if it's trouble with the king, then he has a court and we will go and have that trouble removed. But, Potter, we won't let you go, brother."

"Grain-givers, I have no trouble with the city. I have only one answer."

"Oh my son! Whatever answer you give us, we'll accept it."

"Yes, Grain-givers, I'll give it to you."

"So what's the matter? Let's go back."

"I'll give you a really powerful answer."

The Potter saw that he had an opportunity to reveal his trouble. So he joined his hands[32] to all the village elders[33] and all the people of the village, and said, "Grain-givers, I am joining my hands to you. Take me back if you like. But I can't speak about my trouble. Just sleep outside my place tonight. All of you, elders and villagers, sleep outside my place, and you yourselves pronounce judgment. You yourselves listen, and you will learn about my trouble—it is so bad that I can't speak of it."

How could the Potter tell that—about marrying the king's daughter?

"Fine, we'll sleep outside your place, one day or five days."

They took him back. The villagers didn't let him go. They brought his carts and bedding, and the donkey, and they unpacked everything and put away all his junk. Evening came and everyone brought their bedrolls over there. "Brother let's go to the Potter's house—we'll sleep

31. The social context for the dismay over Pachyo Potter's departure is the traditional patron-client or *jajmanī* system where artisans such as Potters serve the agricultural castes in exchange for fixed shares in the grain harvest.

32. To press one's palms together is a gesture of respect and entreaty (as well as ordinary greeting).

33. *panch;* according to context this may be translated as village council or as the elders who constitute such a body.

in that Potter's courtyard." There they sat. And they said, "OK, brother Prajapat,[34] tell us your trouble."

"Grain-givers, wait until midnight, and then listen!"

Now midnight came and all the people of the city were there, and now the donkey speaks.

(Bh 1.3.e)

At midnight that donkey, Khukanyo, began to bray. "Tibhu tibhu, tibhu, tibhu," he brayed. "Listen Pachyo Potter."

"Brother Khukanyo, I'm awake. Tell me your news."

Pachyo Potter turned to all who were sitting there, "Listen, this is the very trouble that made me go... but I couldn't speak of it myself, so now listen, people of the village!"

"Listen, Pachyo Potter, go and tell your king that his daughter Pan De's braids will be white, and he should marry her to me, the donkey. Brother, if he marries his Pan De to me, then I will build a palace of silver and gold for that king, and I will excavate mines of seven metals and I will surround the city with double ramparts of copper and brass, nine yards[35] tall.

"But, if he doesn't marry the Princess Pan De to me, listen Pachyo Potter, three days from today I will use my hoofs on this city and knock it upside down. I won't spare a single animal, nor will I spare a single human being. I'll really knock this city upside down."

After making this vow, that was it; the donkey was silent.

Then the Potter said, "O Village Elders, this is my trouble, this is why I am leaving. Grain-givers, this is why I shall go, this is why this city is impossible for me. So, Village Elders, think about this."

"But what's there to think about? Three days from now he will knock the city down, and he won't spare a single man or woman, not a single animal, nothing. So why die over here? Let's leave with Pachyo, let's leave, tomorrow even. We'll go together and leave the whole village deserted."

Some filled carts with their grains and bedding, and some loaded up buffalo.

"Let's follow that Potter. No one will be left here but the King, all alone."

---

34. Prajapati is the name of a Vedic creator-god. As Potters, too, shape things out of formless substance, they may be politely addressed as "creator."

35. *gaj;* a unit of measure equal to three feet.

Because who is going to tell the king: Marry your daughter to the Potter's donkey?

"If we tell him that, he'll send us flying from a cannon's mouth."

So, the next morning at the break of day, the whole village set forth with their donkeys and buffalo and carts loaded up with grains and bundles. The whole village was emptied.

And now they went and complained to the king. Who? The Royal Servants who stayed behind.

                                                              (Bh 1.4.e)

The only people left were in the fort, where the king and a few Royal Servants remained. Where would they go?

The others had filled carts with their bedrolls and grains and all. They took their livestock—their oxen and all—and they went forward until they reached the border.

Meanwhile, a couple of Royal Servants addressed the king: "A complaint, a complaint! Great King."

"O Royal Servants, what complaint have you brought?"

"Grain-giver, over whom are you ruling here? Only owls are left here in the village, only owls hooting.[36] The whole city is empty. Not even a child remains."

"Why?"

"Who knows why they left. But, I'm telling you, sir, there are no human beings left here."

"So they left. Well what was troubling them?"

"Who knows? They told of no trouble. They left and went to the border. So you'd better send your agents, brother, and if they can't go, then you yourself go. Find out what the trouble is. Take every care."

So the king asked for his horse and mounted it and galloped ahead until he reached the border. There the king turned around and blocked their path. He blocked their path and said, "Why brothers, who gave you trouble? Where are you going?"

"Grain-giver, we have quit this city, and we ask your forgiveness."

"Why are you asking forgiveness? What is your trouble? Are my land taxes too big? Am I taking too much royal food? Are my guards or my messenger[37] afflicting you?"

---

36. A hooting owl is an inauspicious omen.
37. *Syāṇā bāmī;* this pair of terms recurs throughout Bh 1. It refers to two positions

"Grain-giver, you're a very good king. We're troubled neither by taxes nor by your guards and messenger."

"So why are you going then? Why are you quitting this city?"

The king got off his horse and stood in the way of their buffalo and carts.

"I won't let you go, you can't quit the city, what is the meaning of this? Tell me the meaning of this meaningless act."

Then all the villagers, five elders,[38] gathered.

Here is our chance, they thought. They said to the Potter, "Here is a chance for you to tell him, like you told us."

The elders of the city sat in council, and then they said, "Grain-giver, are you taking us back?"

"Yes, I shall take you back, I won't let you go. You may go only if you tell your trouble."

"Grain-giver, our trouble is unspeakable, and that's why the city is impossible for us. But if you want to take us back, then pitch your tent at Pachyo Potter's house today. There sit and listen to our trouble. Otherwise, you're wasting your efforts in trying to bring us back."

"Hey you sister-shamed[39] people of the city, you want me to stay one night at Pachyo Potter's?"

"Yes, please stay for one night, and then you will hear our trouble."

"Why only one night? I'd stay for five. Is Pachyo Potter's house such a bad place? Let's go, O city people!"

So they turned around. "I will listen at Pachyo Potter's house. We will pitch twelve tents there. You people of the city, come there too."

"All right, we will each go to our own houses first, and then we'll sit with you over there. Let's go."

So the ruler brought them back.

He was the king, and so he made them turn around and bring back

---

held by servants of the king: guard (variously *syāṇā; sahanā; sāṇā; hāṇā*) and crier or messenger (*bāmī; bhambī*). The latter is a caste name for a group of weavers, who have traditionally held the role of town crier or king's messenger. The implication of the king's question is: Are my men abusing their privileged place by giving the populace a hard time, extracting bribes and so forth?

38. It takes five elders (although many more may come) to constitute a council meeting.

39. *bāṇkā margāvo;* an insult Bhoju translates as Hindi *bahan ke dvārā māre hue* or "beaten on account of one's sister"; someone whose bad reputation is attributable to his sister's bad character.

their livestock—women and husbands and boys and girls, all returned, and he left them at their own houses, at their doors.

The people said, "Let's not bother to unpack because tomorrow we'll have to leave again. Will the king marry his princess to a donkey? Why should we waste our efforts unpacking?"

Now the king, with his courtiers, came to Pachyo Potter's place and set out his mattress and pillow. "Now let me hear your trouble! What is the people's trouble?"

All the villagers came to Pachyo Potter's house. They wanted to listen and see what the king would say. All the villagers came, from every house. The courtyard filled up, and the king too was there, sitting and talking, and midnight came. The donkey began to bray. And the people said, "Hey Grain-giver, Your Majesty, listen! Everyone be quiet!"

(Bh 1.5.e)

And the donkey brayed at midnight: "Tibhu tibhu tibhu. Listen Pachyo Potter, are you asleep or awake?"

"Brother, I'm awake! Donkey, tell your news!"

"Go to your king and tell him that his daughter is full grown, and he should marry her to me, to the donkey. The Princess Pan De should marry me, and I will make the king a gold and silver palace. And I will excavate mines of gold and silver inside the palace. And I will surround the city with double ramparts of copper and brass, nine yards tall. He should marry the Princess Pan De to me.

"If he doesn't, then three days from today I will use my hoofs to knock the city upside down. And I won't spare a single human being. Not a man will I spare—no livestock, no animals, none at all. Your castles and your court and your houses, I will scatter like little pebbles. I won't leave a trace of a human being."

He said this and was silent. Who? The donkey. Now the whole population said to the king, "Grain-giver, this is the problem. This is our trouble, King-Father, this is why we were leaving. Keep your princess and we will leave. You may stay by yourself, Grain-giver."

Now the king was silent, thinking: My son! Is this some kind of a ghost or is it a donkey? It seems to me to be a ghost. My son! "I will turn the city upside down, the whole place, and I will marry the princess, and I will build a gold and silver palace. And I will excavate mines. And I will surround the city with double ramparts, nine yards tall, of copper and of brass." Now how will he make them?

"People of the city, say something."

"Hey, Grain-giver, if you have any hope then tell us. If not, we won't unload our carts. Tomorrow, along with Pachyo Potter, we go, and you stay and die. You stay alone, with your princess and your queens. Keep your Royal Servants with you, and die. Let him turn you upside down, day after tomorrow. Who wants to stay here and die?"

Now the king thought, Son of a . . .[40] If I marry the princess to this donkey, the world will say it's bad. They will say that the king married his daughter Pan De to a donkey. But if I don't marry her, then he will kill us. Now what to do?

Then the king said, "O people of the city, what do you want?"

"Grain-giver, you tell us—our only hope is to fill our carts and leave tomorrow along with Pachyo Potter. If you marry her, then we'll stay—if you marry your daughter to the donkey. Otherwise, tomorrow morning we'll go."

The king saw how it was. "Son of a . . . All the people will go. Then there will be a couple of Royal Servants and my queen and princess, and we alone will remain. Day after tomorrow is the third day, and he will turn us upside down with his hoofs. Then there will be nothing left for us but to die. I should save the city."

"Grain-giver, we won't stay here and die. Why should we? We will go to another country, there are many—why do we need your fields and wells and land and charity? It's not worth dying for."

The king thought, If I marry the princess to him, he will build gold and silver palaces and excavate mines of gold and silver. Then what else do I need? I'll have wealth and riches in abundance. And I'll have double walls for the city. What else do I need? I'll marry the princess to him.

Then the king said, "People of the city, this is my decision."

"Yes, Grain-giver."

"If, within three nights from today, he builds me a gold and silver palace, and if he excavates mines of seven metals, and if he makes double walls of copper and brass, then on the fourth day I will marry him to the princess. But first he must do all this.

40. *mārā beṭā kī*, literally "my son's . . . ." The feminine possessive *kī* implies "my son's daughter," making this a variant on "father of a daughter." Although the unfinished English expletive "Son of a . . ." is not a perfectly literal rendering, I believe it achieves a similar level of irritated or surprised but not enraged speech.

"And if he doesn't, then I will bury this Potter and his wife and children and let horses trample them, or else I will send them flying from a cannon's mouth."

Now all the people of the city agreed: "Grain-giver, marry her if in three days and three nights there's a gold and silver castle and mines of seven metals and double walls."

"And if not, I will bury this Potter and Potteress and their boys and girls in the ground and have horses trample them, or I will send them flying from a cannon's mouth."

So now a judgment was reached.

Then the king and his Royal Servants picked up the cots and quilts they had spread, and the villagers, too, went to their houses.
The women asked their husbands, "What happened?"

"The Potter and Potteress are dead."

"Why?"

"Because on the third day he will bury them and have horses trample them. It has turned out strangely. The poor Potter and Potteress! He will kill them for sure."

Now Pachyo Potter took his little stick in his hand, the one he used to turn his wheel, and he began to beat the donkey: "For many days you've been calling me, Khukanyo: 'Marry me to the princess or else I will turn the city upside down.' You will be the death of me. What can be done in three days? You had better build a gold and silver palace, and excavate gold and silver mines and build double ramparts today! Then I'll have faith; if not, then you will have been the death of me."

(Bh 1.6.e)

Pachyo Potter took his wheel-turning stick and whap whap whap, he beat him.

"Your mother's...! Khukanyo, six months have gone by while you've been calling me, but now we have reached the conclusion. Sure, you'll get married... the king says 'Build it in three days,' and on the fourth day I'll die. Who has that kind of patience? If you don't build it, then I'm dead. The king is gone and the people are gone and what can happen in three days? So, I shall beat you till your flesh flies, or else you make good today."

Then the donkey spoke, "Listen Potter, it won't get built by beating."

"Yeah, so will it be built in three days? Who can do it?"

"Don't beat me, but do what I tell you to do: load me with one saddlebag of yellow dirt[41] and one saddlebag of ashes. And take me outside the village and poke a little hole, this big, in each bag, and make me run all around the city. Then I shall make the double ramparts."

At once, Pachyo Potter filled up one saddlebag with yellow dirt and he filled up the other one with ashes, and he took the donkey outside the village. He took him outside the village, and . . . as if he were starting from that tamarind tree[42] . . . he made two lines, and circled all around the settlement until the lines met. The Potter remained inside the lines.

The donkey brayed, "Tibhu tibhu," and recited the name of the Sovereign Guru Gorakh Nathji.[43] And with a "Tibhu tibhu," he stamped his hoof.

Then double ramparts of copper and brass sprang up, nine yards tall—even a bug couldn't get out of walls like those, with no windows. He left no opening.

Then Pachyo Potter said, "Father of a daughter![44] Donkey, we need a window or a door."

The donkey said, "I won't make those before the marriage. First I'll marry the Princess Pan De, then I will make a door. Don't agree to do it."

Then the Potter had some faith. "Son of a . . . ! Really he is some kind of deity." So he took him to the fort.

He took him to the fort, and "Tibhu tibhu tibhu," the donkey brayed three times, and stamped his hoof and took the name of the Sovereign Guru.

Then up rose a sparkling gold and silver palace, and mines of seven metals were excavated. The palace was so big and so tall, and there was a lot of gold and silver in the mines, enough wealth to really throw around!

41. *pīlī;* a particular kind of dirt often used, mixed with cow dung paste, to plaster courtyards for cleanliness, auspiciousness, and beauty.

42. Madhu Nath points to a large tree that grows behind the compound where we are seated, helping his audience to envision an encompassment of our village.

43. To avoid confusion, I translate *rājā* as "king" and *mahārāj*—used to describe and address Gorakh Nath and other yogi gurus throughout—as "sovereign." All the donkey's magic is accomplished in the name of Gorakh Nath but Madhu Nath never explained the connection between this guru and Gandaraph Syan.

44. A mild curse with obvious sexist implications.

Finally the Potter had some faith. "Wow! The donkey, my son! He's a miracle worker! He called me and said, 'Marry me to Pan De!' And now I see that he's a miracle worker."

"Now, Potter, go and wrap yourself in a twelve-foot blanket and sleep without care; don't wake up! When someone has to go to the latrine they will beat their head on the wall. As for the livestock, how will they take them to graze? Where will the people go to shit? When it's dark they can squat near the wall, but where will they go once it's light?"

So Pachyo Potter gave the donkey some fodder and wrapped himself in a twelve-foot blanket and lay down. That was it, he slept, snoring peacefully.

Then the people started to go out to wash their hands and faces.[45] Those that went in the dark squatted, but now it was daylight and where could the others go? "Oh no! What has happened?"

There was no window anywhere, no window and no door. So how could they go out? And they needed to take the livestock to graze, but where could they take them? Sheep, goats, cows, buffalo, oxen, all stayed inside. How could people get to their fields when there were ramparts, nine yards high?

Now the whole village gathered. "Oh, what has happened?"

They saw no window, no door. "So let's go." The whole city gathered and went inside the fort. They said, "Grain-giver, where is the window or door? There isn't one anywhere, tell us if there is. We have to shit, to wash our hands and faces, but there is no place to do it. And our sheep and goats are bleating, and our cattle are mooing, and our oxen are right here; how can we take them to the fields and forests?"

"Say brothers, what has happened?"

"We'll tell you what happened: double walls nine yards high! And a sparkling palace, of gold and silver! So, Grain-giver, you're the king, you've got a gold and silver palace and you're feeling happy. But as for us, we're in trouble. How can we get out, how can we go to the fields and jungle?"

"So go and call Pachyo Potter, brother. He's my in-law[46] now. Go wake him up and bring him."

---

45. The most common euphemism in the village for going to defecate.
46. *biyāī;* any person with whom one is connected through marriage.

So the messenger and the Royal Servants went to Pachyo Potter's. "Let's go, the king is calling."

"Brothers, I'm still sleeping. I'm sleeping right now because all night I was awake. Right now I won't go."

"Come on, get up, elder brother, our animals are bleating, and you're sleeping!"

"Brothers, I can't come now, go back."

So they went back and the king asked, "What did he say?"

"He said, 'Right now I'm sleeping.'"

"Bring him, brothers, bring him!" So they went back again.

Then he said to Khukanyo, the donkey: "They keep calling me, one after another they keep coming, so what should I say?"

"Refuse: Wedding rounds[47] before I pierce a single door!"

"But what if they say, 'First the window and the door, and then we'll get you married'?"

"Let the girl be mine, then a window's fine! Tell them this: 'I won't open any door anywhere, until you agree to the marriage.' If you like, say that the donkey refuses and says he must be married first."

So Pachyo Potter hurried to the fort, and the king said to him: "Hey Pachuji[48] Potter. Father of a daughter! why didn't you leave a window? Why didn't you leave a door?"

"Grain-giver, what could I do? That donkey didn't leave one. That was it! He made ramparts nine yards tall that neither man nor animal can climb, and there is no hole big enough for an ant to get out. But why should you be unsatisfied? You have a sparkling palace of gold and silver. And you have mines of seven metals."

"Yes, that's true, but you must make a hole."

"First the marriage, sir. He refuses and says:

Wedding rounds before,
I pierce a single door!

That's all there is to it, sir! Without the marriage, he refuses to open it, King. He says, 'First I must take my marriage rounds; otherwise I won't open it.'"

---

47. *pherā;* the culminating and binding moment of the marriage ritual: the turns round the sacred fire taken by bride and groom, knotted together and led by the priest.

48. The king now uses this form of address, echoed later by the princess and her servants; it combines intimacy and perhaps a patronizing or ingratiating respect.

"But what about the villagers? Father of a daughter! They have to stay in here for the whole day?"

"Yes, let them stay here. And let all the prenuptial rites and feasts[49] take place today. Half the village can sit on the bride's side, and half the village can go with the groom's party, the donkey's party. Just cut wet bamboo[50] and don't bother about it. Prepare the lady with turmeric and henna."[51]

(Bh 1.7.e)

Now over here the princess was adorned with henna and rubbed with turmeric. And over there they held henna and turmeric ceremonies for the donkey.

So usually the rounds are held on a different day from the feasts, but he got married all in one day.

Half the village came to the Potter's place and prepared to join the donkey's wedding party. And half the village stayed over there, on the bride's side.[52]

Then they ornamented the donkey and made him a groom and brought him up to the fort and he really did a nice job of striking the marriage emblem.[53] And they had the Vedas and Shastras[54] recited. They set up a fire altar and called Brahmans and—the king got the donkey married with great celebration. After all, he was a king. So he gave a lot of gifts[55] to Pan De, in fine fashion: he gave land gifts,

---

49. Two kinds of feasts are referred to here, the *māṇḍā* and the *mel*. The former is given by the groom's father to non-castefellows two days before the departure of the groom's party for the bride's village, and to castefellows one day before departure. The latter is a feast given by the bride's father to his own castefellows.

50. *ālā tīlā bāṅs kaṭār;* a local expression used for doing something in a hurry, without elaborate preparations, and by implication not in proper fashion.

51. *pīṭhī māndī; pīṭhī* refers to any anointment that softens and beautifies the body, but in the context of wedding festivities it means rubbing the bride's body with turmeric paste to make her "fair"—usually done several days before the wedding. The application of henna (*māndī*) to her hands and feet, often in elaborate designs, is a separate event that usually takes a whole evening. Both have counterparts in the groom's village. Wedding arrangements in rural Rajasthan are affairs of many days and many stages. This paragraph's purport is that the wedding of Pan De and Khukanyo will be done in a most improper hurry.

52. *māṇḍā taḷā,* literally, "beneath the *māṇḍā*," here refers to part of a temporary structure erected for the wedding ceremony.

53. *toraṇ;* a wooden emblem placed above the door to the bride's house that the groom strikes with his sword before entering to participate in the rituals.

54. Sanskrit texts of prayers and laws.

55. *dān;* a term specifically applied to gifts made for religious reasons, sometimes connoting the transfer of inauspiciousness from donor to receiver.

he gave gifts of wealth, he gave cow gifts. He was attentive to dharma, so he gave her slave girls too. He gave a chariot and oxen and Royal Servants.

And now, the wedding rounds were over, and he was ready to give them a send-off. Then the king said to Pachyo Potter, "Brother, Pachuji Potter, now you have become my in-law. And now you have to leave this village. Go tomorrow, brother, I'm giving you a send-off: leave the village and settle in whatever village pleases you."

Right after the marriage Pachyo Potter took the donkey, who brayed "Tibhu tibhu" in all four directions and four doorways opened. And he said to the people, "Stay well. That's it, my donkey is married."

And so, driving the chariot with the donkey tied behind, Pachyo Potter left that village. Now he is going toward the jungle, and all the people said, "O brother Pachyo Potter, keep well brother! Now we can't stop you. Now that the king married his princess to you, no one can stop you."

They went twenty-four plus twenty-four, forty-eight miles into the desolate wilderness. But then the donkey balked. What's going on? The Royal Servant is driving the chariot, and Princess Pan De is seated inside behind a curtain, and the donkey is tied to the back of the chariot, and they are going twenty-four plus twenty-four, forty-eight miles into the wilderness.

(Bh. 1.8.e)

They had come to a desolate place, and little remained of the day. The donkey was tied to the princess's chariot. And the driver was driving, but the donkey stood stock still; he stopped short and wouldn't move.

The oxen didn't stop, they kept pulling, and so the donkey slid along. The princess saw this, and said, "Tell Pachuji Potter[56] the donkey isn't going."

Then the Royal Servant said, "Pachuji Potter, that donkey isn't going, and he's begun to slide."

So the Potter got his wheel-turning stick and gave him a few blows. But even so he just sat down. He sat down and then they began to drag him, and then the princess, Queen Pan De, said, "Tell my father-in-law Pachyo Potter: Let's stay right here. Let's pitch our tents right

---

56. She addresses the Potter indirectly, via the Royal Servant; village etiquette prescribes that a new bride shall never speak to her father-in-law.

here and do our cooking, and our Royal Servants will keep watch. Let's spend the night here. Don't beat my husband-god.[57] He doesn't want to go on, so let's stay right here."

So they pitched their tents right there and did the cooking and fetched water. For forty-eight miles in each direction wilderness was all around them. But they cooked and washed and ate and drank and went to sleep.

At midnight the donkey brayed, "Listen Pachyo Potter, are you asleep or awake?"

"I'm awake."

"Why, Pachyo Potter, where are you taking me? Where are you taking me by beating me?"

"There are some villages ahead, so we can get out of the jungle."

"But here in the jungle we can have houses. Who will give you housing in the villages? Listen to what I say, load my saddlebags on me and fill one with black clay and fill one with yellow clay and we'll build our own city right here in the jungle. We'll rule right here. So make me run around four, eight, or ten miles—we'll make the ramparts."

So he loaded the donkey and filled one saddlebag with yellow mud and one with black mud and poked small holes in them. Then he went over here . . . here is Khejari and Napa Khera and over here, Mori and then as far as Sawar,[58] and so right there he settled the city of Dhara Nagar.

And when the two lines met, the donkey took the guru's name and stamped his hoof and double ramparts of copper and brass rose up, nine yards high.

Then he said to the Potter, "Now draw the market square." So Pachyo Potter made the donkey run around, and he drew a magic circle,[59] and he made the streets. In the middle he put a mark for palaces. Then the donkey took the Guru Sovereign's name and brayed "Tibhu tibhu" and stamped his hoof. Up rose a golden and silver palace, along with several bungalows and gold and silver mines. In the middle of the city he stamped his hoof and took the

---

57. *pati dev;* the conventional respectful term for husband.

58. Madhu Nath is mapping out a circular area by naming local villages.

59. *kār ghalāno; kār* often refers to a circle inscribed on the ground by exorcists to contain spirits or protect those within from spirits outside.

Guru Sovereign's name and copper mansions rose up. There were streets going this way and that way, with copper mansions all of a kind.

The donkey said to the Potter, "O Pachyo Potter, let's go into the jungle." And he opened up a big doorway in the wall, and he took the Guru Sovereign's name and stamped his hoof. Throughout the jungle, wells and step-wells[60] with stairways emerged from the ground.

Then the donkey said to Pachyo Potter, "You be my chief minister," and he sent the queen into the palace.

"I am Gandaraph Syan, that's my name. King Gandaraph Syan is ruling."[61] As soon as the day broke, he sent his Royal Servants to all the villages in different directions: "Bring tenant farmers. Tell them there are ready-made mansions, mansions of copper and brass, for them to live in, and there are wells and step-wells for their care. Let them clear the land. For five years I will forgive the taxes, and I'll support this land and take care of these mansions."

So a copper city was built: Dhara Nagar. In Dhara Nagar there are mansions of copper and brass. So all the people's minds were spoiled[62] and they abandoned their grass huts.

"Let's live here! There are fine, beautiful copper and brass mansions and we can keep them, and there are fine wells and step-wells and no taxes for five years, no taxes at all! In this kingdom you can earn and eat and enjoy life."

Well sir, within twelve months that city filled up, people crowded together like a folding gate. The whole city was populated, and there were numerous markets, and tenant farmers came and began to farm. Its name was Dhara Nagar.

And Princess Pan De lived in the Color Palace, and the donkey was tied up nearby and fed on betel leaves. King Gandaraph Syan's orders were law, and Pachyo Potter was the chief minister.

---

60. *kūā* are the round deep wells most Westerners can picture; *bāvaṛī*, which I translate as "step-wells," are wells with stairs going down into them. These pleasant places for washing and drinking are vital to the system of irrigation by bullock and bucket still used in much of Rajasthan.

61. This first reference to the original name of Bharthari's father since his soul was transported into the donkey comes, significantly, after he has established his kingdom.

62. By greed.

Now let's see, midnight came and let's see what things come to pass.

(Bh 1.9.e)

The donkey was tied up on the terrace[63] with betel leaves for fodder, and the queen was inside the gold and silver castle, sleeping on a cot.

Midnight came and the donkey brayed, "Tibhu tibhu tibhu," and he said to the queen, "Come, Queen Pan De."

"Brother, is the donkey calling?"

"It's the donkey, who else could it be?"

So the queen came and asked, "Grain-giver?"

"Grab the tips of my ears and pull."

So the queen grabbed the tips of his ears and pulled.

As soon as she pulled . . . a man came out, as splendid as the full moon. Oh my! the queen thought, he is like one of the sun's rays, and the queen shut her eyes tight. Oh my! Now I'll have some good fortune.[64] I am a human being and my father married me to a donkey, but now I'll have a better fate.[65] The queen shut her eyes tight.

Then they went inside, and she fixed him a meal, and they talked.

"Grain-giver, how did you come to be in a donkey's skin? Are you a deity of some kind or other? How did you get into a she-ass's vagina?"

"Queen, I was cursed by my father, he gave me a curse. My father said, 'Gandaraph Syan, sister-fucker, go into a donkey! You saw my play and so you will go into a she-ass's vagina.' It's because of my father's curse that I am in a donkey's skin. Don't tell anybody that I can become human. I won't see the sun's rays. I must go back into the skin when the morning star rises and the rooster crows. I must be in the donkey's skin before I see the sun's rays or I'll breathe my last.

"Don't be ashamed, no matter what the world says of you. You have enough, I am a king, there is no trouble. You have wealth and goods and no losses. You have a gold and silver castle, and gold and

---

63. *cobārā;* an open-air "room" on the roof that the *RSK* notes is used by newlyweds for sleeping quarters.

64. *bhāg khulgyo āpno;* literally, "my future destiny has opened up."

65. *tagdīr;* another word for fate, of Urdu origin, yet common in Hindu speech. Here it seems interchangeable with *bhāg,* from Sanskrit.

silver mines, and many tenant farmers have settled here. So what's your loss? There is none."

"Grain-giver, I was married so you are my husband-god." So that's how they lived and kept on living.

(Bh 1.10.e)

So she pulled the tips of his ears, and Prince Syan came out, bright as a full moon, and they played a lot of parcheesi[66] and feasted in the night.

Then the queen got pregnant. One month passed, the second month passed, the third and fourth and fifth and sixth, the seventh and eighth, and in the ninth month King Bharthari was born, a young prince! The Brahmans came and carefully found a name,[67] and they read the Vedas, and many meritorious gifts[68] were made: horse gifts and grain gifts and diamond and ruby gifts. And in all the houses of the kingdom there was joy and celebration.

"Oh my! A prince was born in the castle! A prince was born!" But the women, they said [*Here Madhu is chuckling and the audience is chuckling and making remarks*]: "But how can a donkey sire a prince? What has happened? What impropriety has happened, that a donkey fathers a prince. It's weird! We have a donkey's prince." The women said these things: "A donkey's prince! Oh my! What has become of our queen's good character?"

(Bh 1.11.e)

One and a quarter years later the queen was pregnant again. One month passed, two months passed, three, four, five, six, seven, eight months passed, and in the ninth month the hero Vikramaditya[69] was born. He was born and they gave lavishly: horse gifts, elephant gifts, gold and silver gifts. Then they called the Brahmans to find a name. They found the name Vikramaditya and said, "Queen, now you'll have a good future destiny. A very fine prince is born, under

66. "Playing parcheesi" appears in many Rajasthani stories and songs as a euphemism for sexual intercourse.

67. By custom all villagers, not just royal families, consult a Brahman astrologer to determine if not what name, then with what letter the name of a new child should begin, according to his or her horoscope.

68. *dān-puṇ.*

69. *bīr Vakaramādīt;* for this legendary king and his part in Bharthari's legend see chapter 3.

a very good sign,[70] and his name will be known in the world: Hero Vikramaditya. It is a future of riches. Your future destiny is good."

But people put their mouths close together: "So, a donkey fathered a prince!" [*Snickers from the audience*] Who can stop people from talking? Well, sir, one and one-quarter years later a princess was born.

(Bh 1.12.e)

A princess was born, a maiden, and they named her Manavati.[71] After a few months, Queen Pan De wrote a letter and sent a man. She thought, Now my own mother and father ought to feel joyful. I've had three children, boys and a girl, but others take care of me. They married me to a donkey and sent me away. And since then no mother comes, no father comes, no one comes to take care.

So she thought, I will send a man. She wrote a letter and sent it. The letter reached the king, and the king read it. "I had three children, boys and a girl, and I'd like to see you and the queen. Please come! Even though you haven't taken care of me, you are still my mother and father. You married me to a donkey and didn't take care of me."

Then the king was very angry. "Who needs a daughter like that? Yes, I married her to a donkey, so where did these princes come from? [*Madhu snickers*] Three children! Two princes and one princess . . . I won't travel in that slut's direction."

But her mother said:

> Though sinner she be
> She belongs to me!

The flames of love are greater in a mother. "Fine, Grain-giver, you don't have to go, but I will go. Harness the chariot and I'll go and take care of the princess. I'll get there and see what it's like and come back."

So the queen harnessed the chariot, and Pan De's mother went to visit her.

(Bh 1.13.e)

> Now the queen
> harnessed her chariot.[72]

---

70. *nakhatarāṅ;* Hindi *nakṣatra.*
71. Thus Manavati Mata, Gopi Chand's mother and Bharthari's sister, is born. She plays no further part in Bharthari's tale.
72. This begins the final sung segment of Bh 1.

Oh yes...
They hung up a curtain
And the queen sat behind.
Oh yes...
When she reached Copper City[73]
She ascended to the palace.
Oh yes...
Mother met daughter,
Mother met daughter.
Oh yes...
Now the daughter Pan De spoke:
"You didn't come see me for so many years!"
Oh yes...
"Daughter, your father
is angry at you!
Oh yes...
"A donkey fathered a prince?
Where did you get this prince?"
"Mother, listen to my news
Just wait till the day's end.
Oh yes...
"Then I will show you the king
At the day's end."
Oh yes...
The queen went in the night,
pulled the tips of his ears.
Oh yes...
and the king came out
Like a full moon.
Oh yes...
The king entered the castle
And prostrated to his wife's mother.
Oh yes...
Now this queen saw and wondered
"How did he come from a donkey's skin?"
Oh yes...

(Bh 1.14.s)

73. *Tāmbavatī;* yet another name for Ujjain, used only here, deriving no doubt
from the copper mansions already described.

She drove in her chariot to Copper City. She drove into Copper City and got down from her chariot and ascended into the palace, and mother and daughter met each other.

And they conversed. "Mother, I've had three children but you never came to visit me. You married me to a donkey and didn't take care of me."

"Daughter, what could we do? It was your written destiny.[74] We had to marry you to a donkey. But you wrote a letter and sent a man and your father got angry: 'A donkey's son? How does it happen?' From whom did you get this boy?"

"Mother, you won't believe the truth. But just spend a few days here, and then you'll see! Let the end of the day come, and in the night I will show you your son-in-law."

So in the night the queen pulled on the tips of the donkey's ears, and he came out, shining like the full moon, a bright light shone in the castle. And then he went and prostrated himself, respectfully greeting his mother-in-law: "Mother-in-law, you have come to visit us after so many days?"

The queen squeezed her eyes shut: "Oh my! What kind of event has taken place?"

Then she asked him, "Bridegroom-prince, what are you doing in a donkey's skin?"[75]

"Mother, my father cursed me. Because of this curse I am in a donkey's skin, I had to take a donkey birth. Otherwise I am King Gandaraph Syan, Gandaraph Syan is my name. My father cursed me."

Thus the queen-mother-in-law spent five or ten days, and she saw how her daughter pulled the ears nightly. And they spent the nights very pleasantly, eating and playing a lot, and having fun. But that was it! When the morning star rose and the rooster crowed, then he returned to his donkey skin.

Now she saw how they lived. Who? The mother-in-law. And she said to Pan De, "Son,[76] this is what you should do: divert his mind

---

74. *lekh.*

75. From this point the explanation goes beyond the final sung segment, as often happens at the end of a major part. I am unsure whether this happens because Madhu is in a hurry to finish and skips the singing, or because no sung portion matches the events narrated.

76. Mothers often call their daughters "son" when they want to express closeness and care.

and take the donkey skin and burn it up. Throw it on kindling and burn up the donkey skin. Light a wick to it. Then rub that skin into powder between your hands and scatter it to the wind from the castle roof. Do that, and then he will stay a man, he won't go back in the donkey skin. He will stay a man."

This was the trick she taught her. She will make her a widow.

The mother spent five or ten days with her daughter, and then she went back to her own place. They gave her a send-off. But meanwhile she had told this cleverness to her daughter, to Pan De. So when her mother had gone, Pan De did this: she obtained a bundle of firewood. Then she pulled on his ears and when he was a king they played a lot of parcheesi and feasted and lay down. Afterwards the king went to sleep.

She said [to her servants], "Bring a bundle of kindling."

"Why, Princess, what are you going to do?"

"Oh don't call out. Don't tell."

/Yes, bring it quietly./

"Bring it quietly." While the king was sleeping she asked for a bundle of kindling, and she put it on top. What? The donkey skin. And then she lit it and burned it up, sir. So the donkey skin burned up and turned to ash.

When it had turned to ash, the queen rubbed the ashes between the palms of her hands and put them on a platter and went to the roof of the palace and scattered them, and her hands were printed with the sun and the moon.

She scattered them. Then the king awoke and the rooster crowed, and he said, "Queen, Queen, oh bring my skin!"

"O girls, where did you put it? O girls, slave girls where did you put it?"[77]

But she was calling "Bring the skin" meaninglessly. If there were a skin they could bring it; but where will they bring it from?

"Oh, the girls put it somewhere, Grain-giver, who knows where they put it? Where did you put it, girls?"

"We know nothing about it."

Then day began to break.

"Oh, you slut, what's going on? Tell me what really happened."

"Well, Grain-giver, my mother came, and she told me this trick:

77. Pan De pretends she knows nothing.

'Light a wick to it, and burn it on kindling.' So I burned it and rubbed it and this moon and sun were printed on me and I scattered it from the roof."

"Oh you slut, what have you done? You made yourself a widow. You destroyed the skin with your own hands, and now I have no hope of living. When I see the light of day my life is over."

"It is?"

"Yes. You made yourself a widow with your own hands. It seems you called your mother-widow[78] here just to kill me."

There was no cure. As soon as he saw the sun's rays, Gandaraph Syan's life was over.

"Oh, the king died, the king died, our king died, King Gandaraph Syan died!"

They sat King Bharthari on the throne, and he performed the cremation rites.

(Bh 1.14.e)

78. *māṅrāṇḍ;* an insult

Bharthari's Detachment

Introduction

Madhu Nath labels this central part of the epic "Bharthari's *vairāgya*," which I translate "detachment." The king does not actually leave the world until part 3. Part 2 is in essence an account of the events that propel him toward that destiny and create in him a renouncer's orientation toward worldly life. The word *vairāgya* can refer to such an orientation, as well as to actual steps toward renunciation.[1]

Part 2 makes no reference back to the birth story and does not attempt to fill in the blanks between Bharthari's infancy and his condition here as Ujjain City's ruler, married to Pingala. However, several strands of image and meaning link the events of the birth story with this central part of the epic. Bharthari 2 opens with Queen Pingala's taunting her husband because he never goes hunting. To this sung reproach the *arthāv* adds that he never plays parcheesi with her in the palace—parcheesi being, as we already know, a regular euphemism for sexual intercourse. In sending her husband out to the forest where kings should sport at hunting, Pingala also sends him into the domain of yogis and precipitates a series of events that will be wholly disastrous to her wedded happiness. Thus, as was the case with Pan De, her desire that her husband be more of a king and a lover has the opposite effect.

Much of Bharthari 2 is concerned with the ambiguities of marital

---

1. The term *vairāgya* is not part of Madhu Nath's usual vocabulary. Its use here may recall the title of one of the Sanskrit poet Bhartrihari's famous sets of verses, *Vairāgya*.

love and the possibilities for mutual violence that lurk within it. In that sense the tale takes off directly from the end of the birth story. Pan De unwittingly destroyed her husband's life by means of fire when she incinerated the donkey skin and scattered its ashes to the winds. After Pingala dies, herself destroyed by Bharthari's thoughtlessness and by her own fanatic dedication to pushing husband-devotion to its limits, Gorakh Nath scatters her ashes to the wind. Ashes are the other side of mortal passion, and they appear in many contexts in these tales.

Ashes represent death but also the potential for a new and different life. Pan De the husband-killer finds that the donkey skin's ashes have left the auspicious marks of the sun and the moon on her palms. Out of Bharthari's madness upon finding Pingala nothing but a pinch of ash comes a new consciousness that will bring him immortality. Later, in Gopi Chand 4, the guru's death curse—"Ashes!"—when it fails twice, is followed by the pronouncement "Immortal!" "Third time proves all," announces the gamester Gorakh Nath, and thus do Bharthari and Gopi Chand gain immortal bodies. Every yogi rubs his skin with ashes, hiding the beauty that arouses mortal passion while showing his affiliation with, and indifference to, fire and death.

Much of Bharthari 2 is a narrative meditation on the act of *satī*—another reduction of flesh to ash that results in divinity. In general, members of the rural audience for this tale respect the tradition of *satī* as a manifestation of the goddess. This does not mean that they do not share Westerners' horror at the thought of a familiar female undertaking such a step. Nevertheless, I urge that readers temporarily suspend judgment of *satī* as oppression of women, in order to appreciate the reasons that yogis devalue *satī* even while they recognize it as an extreme, and dangerous, manifestation of divine female power.

Whereas other Hindu texts may perceive *satī* as the ultimate expression of wifely perfection and woman's dharma (Leslie 1988), this yogic tradition throws it into question in several ways. *Satī* is above all enjoined upon noblewomen (Harlan 1992). But in Bharthari part 2, forest animals and a low-caste or tribal meat-eating huntress precede Queen Pingala in becoming *satī*. None of these *satī*s, not even Pingala's, is quite right. The narrative not only questions whether any males are worth dying for but more obliquely hints that the motivations of the women who choose such deaths may have more to do with power than love. In the afterword these issues are more fully and speculatively explored.

Bharthari 2 contains the epic's best loved and most frequently performed scene: when Gorakh Nath "takes away the king's stubborn-ness" by mocking his mourning and then demonstrating the superior power of yogis and the illusory nature of life and love. This is the origin of Bharthari's detached attitude. Gorakh Nath creates—literally "makes stand up"—seven hundred fifty Queen Pingalas. He then demands that Bharthari put his hand on his own. Madhu's rendering of this scene puzzled me, especially the end, when the last remaining Pingala attempts to jerk King Bharthari up to the sky and Gorakh Nath curses her. My confusion came from the assumption that one of these Pingalas actually was the "real" one.

However, long consultations with Bhoju and Bhoju's further questioning of Madhu Nath made it clear that in creating the seven hundred fifty look-alike Pingalas, Gorakh Nath had not restored a dead queen to life. Rather, he had commanded his female powers or *śaktis*, to appear in Pingala's form.[2] When he tells the king to put his hand on the real one, then, he is setting him an impossible task; none is real. But the yogic message goes beyond this, for the "real" Pingala was no more real than the magic replications of her form. Bodies are not real. Name and form are not real. In part 3, Pingala plays the role of abandoned wife to the hilt and arouses sympathy; we forget that she is not the original devoted wife. Here, however, as one of the fairy-Pingalas she is just another slut.

Bharthari's character, as it is built up in this part of the epic, is stubborn and insensitive—perhaps providing one more direct link to his birth tale. He is, after all, the son of a donkey. He also appears in certain ways as incompetent. When he does go hunting, it is not with great success. The only kill he makes walks right in front of him and advises him on how to shoot. The constant refrain of the sung verses, "You must realize, Bharthari" (*Samajho Bhartharī*), may be a comment on the king's hard-headedness and need for repeated instruction. In this he is quite different from Gopi Chand, who wavers perpetually

2. According to Bhoju, yogis really can bring the dead to life but not after their cremation. For example, Jalindar restores Manavati from a pile of bones, and Champa De from a new corpse. Gorakh Nath revives Machhindar's sons from piles of bone and skin. Jalindar Nath is able to reverse the effects of his own "turn-to-ash" tin with his elixir-of-life tin, but that may be a special case.

and changes course at the slightest push from another person. Where Gopi Chand's weeping arouses great empathy, Bharthari's is made out to be laughable.

Here as in part 1, Madhu Nath's elaboration of workaday details is deliberate and effective. One good example is the description of the potters who, on Bharthari's order, try to replicate Gorakh Nath's broken jug. Like the wedding in Bharthari 1, the work of the potters— digging clay, kneading it, turning it on the wheel, baking it in the kiln—offers listeners down-to-earth and well-known activities. Coming as it does shortly after a rather long detour through the courts of heaven, the potting interlude puts things in perspective. Yogis have their detached attitudes and their miracles; the householder's world has domestic networks and the mundane but fondly recalled details of everyday life. Madhu Nath's performance deftly interweaves and contrasts these alternatives.

Text

Honored King[3] . . .
My husband, you never go hunting lions,
and you never ride pregnant mares, King Bharthari,[4]
You must realize, Bharthari Panvar of Dhara Nagar,
You're my wedded lord, but
you've gone and left me destitute.[5]

Honored King . . .
With seventy-eight hundred servants and
      seventy-two courtiers, the king

---

3. Most of part 2 is sung in the *Rājājī rāg* particularly associated with the tale of Bharthari; in segment 7 Madhu Nath switches to GC *rāg* 1 and then to GC *rāg* 2 for the concluding segment.

4. Although this verse was never explained during the recorded performance, Madhu Nath later told us that a Brahman read in Bharthari's horoscope that he would be a renouncer. The Brahman advised Bharthari's mother that in order to avoid this fate her son must never go hunting; but if he hunts he must never go north; and if he goes north he must never ride a pregnant mare. Later we will find the pregnant mare taboo enumerated by Bharthari himself as one of his personal rules.

5. This entire verse is addressed by Pingala to Bharthari. The first two lines initiate the immediate action, and the last three are the much-repeated refrain of Pingala's lament, here evoking the disastrous consequences of Bharthari's hunt.

Went hunting lions for sport, King Bharthari
went hunting lions, King Bharthari,
You must realize, Bharthari Panvar of Dhara Nagar,
Ujjain City's ruler killed nothing.

Honored King...
He didn't find a lion, King Bharthari, my King Bharthari,
He raised a boar upon the hill, King Bharthari.
He raised a boar upon the hill, King Bharthari,
You must realize, Bharthari Panvar of Dhara Nagar,
Dhara Nagar's ruler: Don't kill me.[6]

Honored King...
Chasing the boar, he whipped his horse, the king went
    after the boar.
King Bharthari whipped his horse and chased the boar.
You must realize, Bharthari Panvar of Dhara Nagar,
Ujjain City's ruler, you've gone and left me destitute.

Honored King...
His seventy-eight hundred servants
    and seventy-two courtiers,
his army was left behind, you must realize, Bharthari,
his army was left behind, you must realize, Bharthari,
Only one servant stayed with him, King Bharthari,
You must realize, Bharthari Panvar of Dhara Nagar,
You're my wedded lord, now don't kill me.[7]

Speak Victory to Bharthari Baba!

(Bh 2.1.s)

So this is what happened. The queen, Pingala...Queen Pingala
nagged him. "Hey, King Bharthari. You are the king, but you never
come into the palaces to play parcheesi. And you never enjoy hunting
lions. Your kingship and your life are worthless."

---

6. The boar speaks to the king, giving the first indication that Bharthari will
have a difficult time hunting, because all the animals have a human consciousness.
7. Here Madhu merges the speeches of Pingala and the boar, whether out of
forgetfulness or because both suffer at the king's hands, I cannot say.

The queen's barb pierced him. So on the very next day he said, "OK, Queen, I'll go this morning."

In order to sport at hunting King Bharthari took seventy-eight hundred servants and seventy-two courtiers along with him.

He took the army and such, and he went to sport at hunting. The ruler went hunting. He went lion hunting, but he met no lion.

He met no lion. Only a boar was raised. One boar was raised, so the king beat his horse, and King Bharthari chased after the boar. He chased after the boar, "I've got you, I've got you, I've got you!" The boar was going along like that and he came to a terrain of streams and ditches.[8] There, among the streams and ditches, my son! he lost him! That boar never came within range of the king's spear.

So he had lost the boar, and just one servant boy remained with him. They were on horseback. That servant was his special favorite. The army got left behind. And there was only that boy with King Bharthari, and now they had lost their prey. Now how could they enjoy hunting?

Then he said, "Servant."

"What, Grain-giver?"

"Where's the army?"

"The army got left behind."

"Where?"

"Near Kekari; they've come to Ghatiyali.[9] And, Grain-giver, now we're out of business with hunting. There was a boar, but it got lost. And we haven't found a lion to hunt."

"Well the army's been left behind. But how can I go back empty-handed? The queen will speak harshly to me."

"Certainly let's go on, let's keep hunting."

"We will hunt."

"OK, Grain-giver. We're still in the jungle. So let's wander around the jungle."

So he whipped his horse until he came upon seventy hundred female deer. In their midst was a single stag. Among seventy hundred there was just one, Moti Stag.

---

8. *khaḷḷā khochorā;* a particular land formation with many little rivulets or gullies where water flows in the rainy season and plants grow during the rest of the year. Animals may graze and also hide in these ditches.

9. This joke also localizes the tale. Kekari is a nearby town where Ghatiyalians often take their business.

The servant's gaze fell on him.

"Grain-giver, there is a male. Let's kill the male."

(Bh 2.1.e)

There were seventy hundred does, but only one stag. Now the does said to that stag, "O Husband-god, run away! You can leap seven hedges in one jump! Run away, because King Bharthari has come. And he is hunting and he will kill you, but he won't kill even one of us does. Run away from the king, Moti Stag, hide yourself! Leap over seven hedges, calamity-bringer! Run! What are you doing here? What will happen to us, to you, today? He will kill you and he won't kill us. It is King Bharthari and he doesn't kill females, he kills only males. He won't kill us, so run away!"

/Yes, you run away or we will all be widowed./

Then Moti Stag spoke: "O Does, why are you afraid of dying? The one who knowingly goes to face death is called a man, he is called a man. And whatever the Guru Sovereign does, that's what happens."

Then the does ran and surrounded the king's horse... "Yes, Bharthari, kill us—kill ten, twenty, forty, fifty, King Bharthari, but don't kill our one Moti Stag. Kill us, as many as you want. But if you kill Moti Stag then all seventy hundred of us will be widows. So kill us."

"Look, Does, I have vowed three things. These are my rules. One is that I don't drink the water of running rivers. And, I don't ride on pregnant mares. And the third is that I never shoot and injure females. If there's a male, then I shall kill only the male. You females, maybe you will come right under my horse's feet, but still I won't kill you. I was born a man and I only kill men, I don't injure women."

Then the does said to Moti Stag, "Burn up! What are you doing here? Run away, leap over seven hedges!"

"O sluts,[10] you belong to the female species, but I shall go and face death. What is there to fear from death? Whatever the Guru Sovereign does, let it come to pass." So he approached Bharthari, coming two *dorī*[11] closer.

King Bharthari wanted to kill him, so this made the king happy.

"Oh ho! It's very fine that the hunt has come in front of the king! Wonderful!"

---

10. *rāṇḍ;* an abusive term whose meanings range from "widow" to "prostitute."

11. A *dorī* is a unit of measure; 16 *dorī* equal one mile.

Moti Stag came before King Bharthari and said, "Hey King
Bharthari, hear my words. My death is in the third arrow. Now I
shall make my promises[12] and you must grasp them."
/Pay attention!/
"Pay attention."

(Bh 2.2.e)

Then Moti Stag spoke, "Look, King Bharthari, you will kill me,
yes, I have come in order to die. So, King Bharthari, listen to what
I have to say. My death is in the third shot. And give these feet of
mine to cowards and thieves. Let them boil and eat them, and then
they'll be able to run away and save their lives. No one will catch
them.

"And as for my skin—in the jungle where some yogi is performing
tapas, some *sādhu*, then he can wrap half around himself, and he
can spread half to sit upon while repeating prayers. That will be my
passage to liberation.

"And look, King Bharthari, my horns, which are so big, give my
horns to Gorakh Nathji, and he can cut off the tip and make a horn
instrument.[13] So he may go from house to house calling '*Alakh!*'[14] Let
Gorakh Nathji Sovereign make the horn and sound it and call
'*Alakh!*' and then I'll get release, passage, I will go to enjoy myself in
Heaven.

"And this flesh, distribute it among the Rajput families.

"And my eyes, my piercing eyes, go and give them to your queen,
and she can eat them and then people will call her deer-queen."
/Deer-eyed./
Yes, deer-eyed.

"Sure, brother." So then he fixed his arrow. Who? King Bharthari.
But Bhairu Nath[15] made the first one of his arrows miss its mark.
Bhairu was his favored deity. Whose? The stag's. He fixed the second

12. *vachan;* although it may be translated as "promise," *vachan* can also mean any
"strong words" or "true words."

13. Here is the origin of the famous deer-horn instrument that we encounter
throughout both tales and that is one of the chief emblems of Nath yogis.

14. "*Alakh!*" which yogis cry when on their begging rounds, means "the imperceptible." The verb used with it, *jagarno*, means to wake up; the implication is
this cry rouses people to an awareness of invisible realities, known to yogis, as well
as the visible reality of a beggar who must be fed.

15. Bhairuji is an important deity in rural Rajasthan, associated with both Shiva
and the goddess, and often does their work in the world for them (Gold 1988,
257–58).

arrow and the Guru Sovereign Gorakh Nathji made it miss its mark. But the third arrow struck him in the middle of his forehead,[16] it struck the middle of Moti Stag's forehead, and he breathed his last.

He breathed his last, and while he was dying, those does said, "O Husband-god, father of a daughter! Turn your neck up and keep it that way! We told you to run away, but you refused to run. Now keep your neck up for a little while, as long as you are conscious." So the stag turned his neck up and his horns were sharp as sharp can be, and the does came jumping and threw themselves on his horns. Jumping and leaping, they became *satī*.

/They gave up their lives./

Yes, they gave up their lives, and their souls were released.[17]

The king thought, Oh ho, what a weird thing has happened! Seventy hundred does are wailing in the jungle.

They said, "King Bharthari, just as we are wailing, we does of the woods, so will they wail in your Color Palace. We will curse you: Be a yogi, in your early youth, and call '*Alakh!*' from house to house. And just as we does of the forest are wailing, so in your dwelling will they wail. We will curse you, King Bharthari." They cursed him.

So the hunter hardly knew, the hunter thought, These sluts are just barking, they are animals, what kind of spirit do they have? So King Bharthari didn't pay attention to what they said, and leaping and jumping the does died.

King Bharthari had a handkerchief.

Those does were stuck, caught, on the horns, and he pulled them off and tossed them aside, and he took his cloth, his handkerchief, and put it in the blood. He soaked it in deer's blood.

"Son of a . . . ! Even these does of the forest become *satī*, but I wonder about my own queen . . . will she? Let's find out. Let's give Queen Pingala a test[18] and see if she will become *satī* too. If these

---

16. *talak lalāṛ* (H. *tilak*), there is more significance than "shot in the head" in these words. A *tilak* is an auspicious religious mark made on the center of the forehead at the close of a ritual; and the word *lalāṛ* is also used for fate, which is written on the forehead. The implication is not only that Moti Stag's death was fated but that it was an auspicious and ritualized death.

17. *muk hogī;* that is, they became *mutki* or free from eternal cycles of redeath and rebirth.

18. *parikṣā;* the theme of a test, very often by a more powerful being demanding supreme sacrifice from a worshiper, is common in Hindu myth and legend. A synonymous term, *ajamāīs*, is also used below.

does of the forest do it, my queen ought to become *sati* too."[19]

So the king soaked his handkerchief in blood and gave it to the Royal Servant who was with him: "Go to my city of Ujjain, and give it to Queen Pingala, and tell her the king was killed in battle. And if she is a *sati*, then this is the moment."

"Hey, Grain-giver, you're standing before me and you haven't even got a splinter stuck in you anywhere, so how can I go and tell the queen that the king died?"

"Go! It's none of your business! You just go and give it to her and see if she becomes *sati* or doesn't."

Well . . . when the king gives a summons old women come running . . . [20]

That Royal Servant went. "The king gave an order and sent me." That Royal Servant took the handkerchief with deer's blood in it.

And this is what King Bharthari did. The does of the woods were wailing. He lifted the stag onto his horse, and then he too sat on his horse. "Let that Royal Servant run away. We will keep on going slowly."

He had chased the servant away, and that servant went and gave the handkerchief to the queen.

(Bh 2.3.e)

> Honored King . . .
> He set the stag before him on his horse,
> My king, before him,
> and the king rode through the jungle.
> He is coming slowly through the jungle,
> O King Bharthari,
> You must realize, Bharthari Panvar,
>   you must realize, Bharthari.

> Honored King . . .
> Baba Gorakh is coming through the jungle:
>   "Listen to this matter, King."
> On his feet he's wearing sandals, in his hand are tongs,

19. Bharthari's perception of what has happened changes somewhat, between not taking the does seriously and deciding to test Pingala.

20. This proverb appears in a completely different context in Gopi Chand 1. Its purport is that, even if a king's work appears meaningless or amoral, it must be done.

On Gorakh's shoulder is a sack,
   you must realize, Bharthari,
You must realize, Bharthari Panvar of Dhara Nagar,
Dhara Nagar's ruler: "Listen to my words!"
Now Gorakh Baba approached him.

Honored King . . .
"Why did you kill a harmless animal?
Why did you kill him, King?
One stag and seventy hundred widows,
You made seventy hundred widows today, King Bharthari."

Honored King . . .
"Did they destroy your fields?[21]
King, listen to my news:
Why did you kill the animal? You'd better listen, Bharthari,
Listen, Bharthari Panvar of Dhara Nagar."

Honored King . . .
The king said to Gorakh Nath, "Listen Gorakh Nath
I killed him, but now listen,
I killed him, but listen, Gorakh Baba."

Honored King . . .
Gorakh Nath came. "Listen Baba Nath,
You can make him live again, listen Gorakh Baba,
Make him live again, listen Gorakh Baba."
Now Gorakh Baba told Bharthari, "Put down the deer, King,
Why did you kill that harmless life?"
You must realize, Bharthari,
Gorakh Baba made Bharthari put down Moti Stag.

Honored King . . .
Gorakh Nath wrapped it with a sheet,
now Gorakh Nath sprinkled it with elixir of life,
   you must realize, Bharthari,
He sprinkled it with drops of the elixir of life,
   you must realize, Bharthari,
He took off the sheet and Gorakh Baba . . .

21. That is, what harm did they ever do you?

Honored King...
He made him live, the stag got up, listen to me, King,
He leapt over seven hedges,
   you must realize, Bharthari,
You must realize, Bharthari Panvar of Dhara Nagar,
He lost his prey, you must realize, Bharthari [*Laughs*],
You must realize, Bharthari Panvar of Dhara Nagar,
Listen, Dhara Nagar's king, you must realize, Bharthari.

(Bh 2.4.s)

So he sent that Royal Servant, to the queen. He went to Queen
Pingala, "Queen, Queen, take this handkerchief, take it, and become
a *satī*—this is the moment. King Bharthari was killed. He was hunting
deer for sport, but he got sliced into pieces. A lion killed King
Bharthari. So this is the moment to be a *satī*."

Queen Pingala had a magic tree. She had planted a magic tree,
and if King Bharthari had a mere splinter, one of its branches would
wither.

/The magic tree's./

The magic tree's. Now the queen looked at the magic tree, and it
was blossoming and blooming as usual.

"O Royal Servant, King Bharthari, my husband-god, hasn't even
a splinter. You are lying."

"You are always watering that tree, so how could it wither? If you
pour water on a tree, if you give it liquid, then the tree will never
wither. If you are a *satī*, then this is the time. This is the king's blood.
He filled the handkerchief and sent it to you, so if you want to be a
satī, then be one; if not, then, that's your wish. It could be you are a
hypocrite... You said, 'I won't eat bread without you, without seeing
your face, but you told lies. You women are a heartless race.[22] If
you're a *satī*, then burn, burn, because King Bharthari died."

Then Queen Pingala realized what was going on, "Oh my, it's
strange, he is testing my *satī*-power.[23] Who? King Bharthari is testing

---

22. *begam jāt; begam* could also mean "empty-headed."

23. Pingala uses the word *sat* here. Although it can mean "truth," "divinity,"
"essence," several definitions of *sat* in the *RSK* relate it directly to the power of a *satī*.
Thus, meaning 4: *satī hone ke kāraṇ āne vālā joś, umang va bal* "the intoxication,
excitement and strength caused by being *satī*"; meaning 5: *strī dvārā pati yā putra kī
lāś lekar citārūḍh hone kī kriyā yā bhāv* "the act or intention of a woman to take her
husband or son's corpse and be cremated." See Flueckiger 1989, 44–45, for a
discussion of *sat* as "female truth power" in the Lorik-Candā epic.

my *satī*-power. 'Let's see if my queen will be a *satī*.' So it's a test!"

Now Queen Pingala served Lord Shankar. She was a devotee. Of whom? Of Shankar and of Parvati. She served them regularly and recited their names. Queen Pingala recited their names only. So she went and threw herself into Lord Shankar's shelter. "Hey Grain-giver, Shankar, Lord, now give me *satī*-power."

Lord Shankar was in her heart, so she was able to speak to him, face to face.

Lord Shankar said, "Queen Pingala, on whose account are you asking for *satī*-power?"

"Grain-giver, give me this power, I will be a *satī*."

"Queen Pingala, your husband is alive so how can I give you *satī*-power? You will die, and then your King Bharthari will come, and ask for Pingala, and who will give her? Where will we get a Pingala to give him?"

"No, Grain-giver," she said, "he sent a towel, a handkerchief with blood in it. The king is dead, and he sent the Royal Servant. So Grain-giver, give me *satī*-power. This is it! Yes, certainly, I will burn, for my husband-god is testing my *satī*-power."

"Go then into the Chapala Garden,[24] and set up a funeral pyre and be a *satī*."

Lord Shankar gave her *satī*-power. "Go and burn up, sister-fucker!" So Queen Pingala became *satī* over there. And King Bharthari, King Bharthari, over here, even his game was snatched away.

[*The bard is laughing here; an audience member comments:* His game came back to life and ran away.]

It came to life and ran away, and King Bharthari tramped along with a glum face. He had lost his game. He had met no lion in his hunt, nothing; he didn't kill the boar, and even the deer that he had killed—Gorakh Nath had brought it to life and it ran away.

Now what to do? He was afflicted by great thirst in the jungle. And it was a hot day, and where was water? Nowhere in the jungle. There were twenty-four plus twenty-four, forty-eight miles of desolation!

Then King Bharthari saw a heron circling. "Over there surely there's some water." So King Bharthari whipped his horse and went

24. Why the funeral pyre should be in the garden instead of the cremation ground is not explained but may bear on the association of the Chapala Garden with yogis throughout both tales.

to where the heron was circling, and there was a banyan tree and a step-well.[25]

"Thank God, here is some water. I've found some water." So King Bharthari tied up his horse, and went down into the step-well and had a drink. He had a drink, and he thought he'd rest a little in the shade of the banyan tree.

(Bh 2.4.e)

So, he lay down in the shade, but the king couldn't sleep. He was just lying down, thinking, Let's have a little rest.

Now a Hunter[26] came along. Who was the Hunter? A *bāgaryo*.[27] And he had ten or twenty rabbits and ten or twenty deer, oh my, oh my, dangling from both his shoulders. He threw them down under the tree.

King Bharthari saw this, and thought, But I had only one...

/And that one ran away./

...which Gorakh Nath brought to life and chased away. But this fellow, my son! How and where did he collect so many? He has piled up as many as ten or twenty deer and ten or twenty rabbits under the banyan tree.

The Hunter lay down, he stretched himself out. He had told his wife, the Huntress, "I'll come to such and such a banyan tree and step-well, so bring my food there. I'll come there after I've killed animals." So the Huntress is coming with his food. And that Hunter looked up into the banyan tree and upon it, upon the banyan tree, sat a cuckoo.[28]

Now the cuckoo sat in the tree and above a bird of prey was circling. What was it? A hawk. A hawk was circling, thinking, Brother, I'll kill that cuckoo. Brother, if he flies up then I'll kill him.

---

25. These two accommodations appear very frequently in Rajasthani folklore; in GC 4, Gorakh Nath and Machhindar Nath rest in such a setting.

26. *phārdī*.

27. This is a caste (*bāgarī, RSK*) of hunters or hunters' helpers. According to Bhoju a number of them live near Sawar and buy and sell male buffalo for meat. Thus Madhu Nath identifies the tale's Hunter with an unsavory but familiar local *jāti*.

28. *paphiyo;* Hindi *cātak*, defined as *Cuculus melanoleucus*. This small black bird occurs frequently in Rajasthani folk songs, associated with romance and moonlight, as it sings sweetly in the night. Hearing its voice, women yearn for their absent husbands and therefore sometimes address the bird as "enemy."

Now down below the Hunter too took aim. The hawk was circling, and it too might come into his line of fire. He wanted to kill both the cuckoo and the hawk with one arrow. He thought, The hawk is circling and when he comes into line with the cuckoo, then, that's it! I want to kill them both with one arrow. So he fixed his arrow.

Then the cuckoo prayed to God: "*Pīv pīv pīv pīv*,"[29] the cuckoo said:

> The Hunter's fixed his arrow,
> above flies a bird of prey,
> Hey Lord, where and how can I save my life today?

The cuckoo prayed once, twice, four times, he prayed. To whom? To God.

"Hey God, how, how can I save my life? If I fly upwards then the hawk kills me, and if I don't fly then that Hunter is fixing his arrow, and he will shoot me down."

So the cuckoo remembered the Guru Sovereign and Lord Shankar with his voice. God heard that cuckoo's voice. His God heard his voice. Whose voice? The voice of the cuckoo praying. So, from the roots of the banyan tree a poisonous snake emerged. And it struck him right on the back of the head,[30] even as he was taking aim.

/The Hunter./

Yes, the Hunter.

It struck him on the back of the head when his attention was on his aim, and pulled out the Hunter's breath.[31]

/Oh my!/

So even as he aimed, he gasped for breath and tumbled down and died. The Hunter died. The snake pulled out his breath and drank it, and the Hunter died.

That Hunter wrapped himself up. As soon as he was struck, he covered his face, he covered his face and breathed his last and he died.

Meanwhile, the Huntress came bringing food. She came and cried,

---

29. The call conventionally attributed to this bird is thought to sound like "beloved" (*pīu pīu*)

30. *coṭī nakhai;* literally, upon the braid. The spot high on the back of the head, where high-caste or twice-born Hindus keep a long lock of hair, is a very unlikely place for a snake to bite, according to Bhoju; and a hunter would be unlikely to have such a braid.

31. *sās khānchtāī;* if a snake is very poisonous people believe that the victim of its bite cannot take another breath.

"Alas alack! What kind of heap did you take today? Ten or twenty deer and ten or twenty rabbits—you have so much, who can eat it? We are only two persons, two eaters, and how will we use so much? You have sinned, you have. killed the whole earth and gone to sleep. Get up, have some food."

But he didn't speak. Then the Huntress grabbed his foot and pulled it, "Get up!" But he still didn't get up.

Now she uncovered his face, and ants were going in and out of his mouth.

"Oh, you killed these deer, sinner, you killed all these deer and rabbits, and you haven't even eaten them. You died and these ants are going in and out . . . Now, Lord, what will I do? What kind of arrangement can I make?"[32]

That Huntress didn't even cry. Immediately, she will be a *satī*.

/Right over there./

Right over there, beneath the banyan tree.

/Oh my!/

Even beneath the banyan tree. It was uninhabited land, jungle, so there were lots of cow pies lying around. Cow pies were lying around, cow dung, manure, and she kicked them, and they turned into coconuts and went rolling.[33] And many branches fell from that banyan tree, and she used them to build a pyre. She brought the coconuts, and she collected cow pies by the basketful, and she made a pyre, and ignited it. How? She struck fire with flint.

She lit the pyre, she lit it, sir, she lit it! And now this is what that Huntress did: she took a dagger, son of a . . . ! She took a dagger and she began to recite "Shiv! Gorakh! Shiv! Shankar, Shankar!" and she circumambulated it.

/The pyre./

The pyre. King Bharthari was watching. "Son of a . . . ! Why is she circumambulating it? Let's see, she is becoming *satī*, maybe she will become *satī?*"

Now King Bharthari was watching. And she took the dagger, and the pyre was burning, her husband's, and she lifted him and placed him in the middle of it, and she took the dagger, and she cut off her breast and threw it, brother.

---

32. That is, how will I cremate him?

33. Because of her decision to become *satī* she is already like a goddess; hence the miracle of cow dung turning to coconuts.

/Into the pyre./

She threw it into the pyre. King Bharthari saw this: "Oh, son of a . . . ! She cut off her breast and threw it. What is going on?"

Meanwhile she cut her second breast also and threw it also in the pyre.

"Oh, son of a . . . ! Will she not become *satī?*" Meanwhile, she cut off one hand. With the dagger, she sliced it and cut it off, and that hand went rolling. She cut it off and threw it in the pyre. Who? This Huntress.

"O son of a . . . ! She is cutting off her hands and feet and throwing them down."

And now, she cut one leg from the knee. She cut and separated that knee with the dagger, son of a . . . ! and threw that foot, too. [34]

/Into the pyre./

Into the pyre.

Now she is hopping on one foot, while King Bharthari is looking: "Oh, son of a . . . ! She has become a *satī!* She is cutting off her hands and feet and throwing them. Now let me ask her for predictions for the coming year,[35] let me find out the news.

She was hopping along and swaying, and she went and fell into the middle of the pyre.

"Har! Har! Har! Shiv! Shiv! Shiv! Shiv!" she kept saying. Then King Bharthari asked that Huntress:

"Come, Lakshmi,[36] are you going to be a *satī?*"

"Yes, if King Bharthari says it."

He said, "What are the predictions for the coming year? Tell me. You have become a *satī,* so tell me your predictions for the coming year."

"King Bharthari, the coming year will pass in great bliss, a very fine year lies ahead . . . and say, King Bharthari, do you think I'm giving a show?"

---

34. Bhoju points out that Madhu should have her cut her feet before her hands; how can she hold the dagger after the hands are cut? The audience, clearly involved in this scene, did not question the sequence, however.

35. *sammatsāl;* during the fall worship of the goddess in Ghatiyali and other Rajasthani villages, persons possessed by the goddess give predictions about crop yields and grain prices and so forth for the coming year. Bharthari behaves rather crassly here, wishing to profit from this tragic and violent moment.

36. To address the Huntress as Lakshmi—consort of immortal Vishnu and goddess of prosperity—carries a certain irony, but Bharthari has prosperity on his mind.

"Yes I am sitting here, so I am seeing this show."

"O King Bharthari, you may be watching this show, but your Queen Pingala burned up over there in the Chapala Garden. She has become a pinch of ash. And the people . . . there are five hundred, maybe seven hundred villages in your domain, and all the people including women and young men are filling the Chapala Garden. Your Queen Pingala burned up, and the world is watching, and sister-fucker you are watching my show!"

He said, "Is it true?"

"It is; your Pingala burned up."

/Oh my!/

King Bharthari ran from there. He saddled and bridled his horse, he untied his horse and sat on it, and King Bharthari gave it a kick, he gave it a kick, and brother, he came to Ujjain.

He came to Ujjain, and went into the garden, oh my! It was filled up with people! men, boys, little boys, and they were saying "*Rām Rām Rām* our Queen Pingala burned up."

She became *satī* . . . and now the king's horse appeared and everyone said, "Look, there's our king, he is coming."

/He's alive!/

"But our queen burned up."

Something improper had happened. King Bharthari came and got off his horse, and the grooms took it, somebody tied it up. Then he began to circle the funeral pyre.[37]

(Bh 2.5.e)

So the pyre is burning, the pyre is burning and as soon as Bharthari came there he began to circle round it.

"Alas Pingala, alas Pingala!"[38] He was circling all around the pyre. He was being stubborn, King Bharthari was being stubborn.

Big lords and officials came—kings came too, very big ones.

---

37. *rati;* although the pyre the Huntress built is called by the common term, *chitā,* Pingala's pyre in the following episode is always designated *rati.* Bhoju glosses *rati* as "a pile of ashes from a burning corpse," but this meaning does not appear in the *RSK.* Rati is the name of the love god Kama's wife and often refers to sexual pleasure. This idiosyncratic usage may unite Bharthari's passion for his deceased wife with the yogic message that passion's objects inevitably become ash.

38. *Hāy Pīngalā;* the king's mad cry is one of mourning; thus I translate *hāy,* an exclamation, as "alas."

Even kings who were his equals came: "Hey Grain-giver, hey King Bharthari, where is Queen Pingala now? Where is Queen Pingala? You did it with your own hands, so whom will you blame?[39] You sent the handkerchief with your own hands, and she burned up at her own hands and where is Queen Pingala now? You sent the handkerchief and nobody burned up Pingala by force.

"You knew what you were doing when you sent the handkerchief, so she burned up and now . . . did you mean to kill her so you could be a *sato*?[40] Yes, you 'killed her on purpose to be a *sato*.'[41] You meant to kill her, you sent the handkerchief, and Queen Pingala burned up. She burned up, and now you keep going on: 'Alas, alas Pingala! Alas Pingala, Pingala!' Where will she come from now? She has become a pinch of ash."

So the king circled the funeral pyre for three days and three nights, crying "Alas Pingala, alas Pingala!" Then God's throne began to tremble.

Why? Because they are dying of hunger, while the king is circling over here.

/How to light the cooking fire? [*obviously, this audience member is prompting Madhu*]/

How to light the cooking fire?[42] Women and men and boys and girls were swooning and dying, "Oh misery, we're hungry for bread!" Three nights and three days had gone by, and how to light the cooking fire when the king is over here crying, "Alas Pingala!"?

---

39. Literally, to whom will you give the "sin"—as *doṣ* is often translated. But *doṣ* usually implies a mistake, and the point here is that Bharthari can attribute the mistake resulting in Pingala's death only to himself.

40. *Sato* would be the masculine equivalent of *satī*—that is, a husband who burns himself on his wife's funeral pyre. According to Bhoju the act is not unheard of, and at least one Rajasthan village has shrines to *sato*s. See Vaudeville for a moment in the *Ḍhola-Mārū* epic where Ḍhola is about to choose cremation along with his beloved Māruṇī when a passing yogi restores her life, chiding him: "Est-ce à l'homme à se brûler avec sa femme? C'est la femme qui se brûle avec l'homme!" (1962, 96).

41. The proverb *maṇas mārar satī honā* implies that a bad woman will cause her husband's death in order to become *satī*. Gender-reversed here, it suggests that Bharthari deliberately killed his wife in order to follow her as a *sato*.

42. During this inauspicious period while the king mourns, no one can cook or eat; a state of death pollution prevails for the whole kingdom. Or, as Bhoju puts it, "When the king goes hungry lamenting, how can the subjects go home and cook?"

God's throne trembled. When his throne trembled, God said to Naradji,[43] "O Narad?"

"Yes Grain-giver."

"Go and see what's happening in the three worlds.[44] What's going on, what great ascetic was born, causing my throne to tremble?"

So Narad Sovereign ran off, and as he went running and wandering he came to the city of Ujjain. In the city of Ujjain—its rule was over five hundred, one thousand persons, and there were five hundred, thousands of villages that belonged to it—people from the whole district had gathered—women and young men. And there was the king crying, "Alas Pingala, alas Pingala!"

And they were dying of hunger, their eyes watering. The boys and girls were wailing, dying of hunger, rolling around here and there.

But how to light the cooking fire?

Oh my, Lord Narad thought; something weird has happened! Things are stirred up and people are dying.

Having seen this, Narad hurried back to God's city of Vaikunth.[45] Going in there he said, "Grain-giver, hey Lord, something extremely shocking has happened."

"What happened?"

"What happened? Well, Queen Pingala burned up, she became a *satī*, and King Bharthari came and found that the queen had burned up into a pinch of ashes, and he let his horse go, and he has been circling the funeral pyre crying, 'Alas Pingala! Alas Pingala! Alas Pingala!' for three nights and three days. That's all King Bharthari wishes to do, and he won't accept any counsel, and the people are dying of hunger. The king is acting this way, so how can they light the cooking fires? The boys and girls and women and men are rolling around from starvation, and their eyes are watering—they're dying of hunger, but how can they abandon the king? This is the state of affairs."

Then God said, "Call the thirty-three *karor* of deities."[46]

So they called the thirty-three *karor* of goddesses and gods.

43. Narad is a familiar mythological figure, often a go-between for heaven and earth.

44. Conventionally: heaven, the world of mortals, and the underworld.

45. *vaikunth;* one of several commonly used names for heaven or paradise.

46. A *karor* is ten million; this conventional figure describes the multitude of Hindu gods.

When they came, God asked, "Now which one of you gave *satī* to Queen Pingala? Who gave her *satī?* which one of you thirty-three *karor* of goddesses and gods?"

"Grain-giver, no one, none of us gave *satī* to Queen Pingala."

Well, who gave her *satī? Satī* is given on death. Who gave her *satī* when her lord of the house[47] was living?"

"Hey Grain-giver, who has this information? We know nothing at all about it. So let's see, . . . God, call Lord Shankar."

God called Lord Shankar and asked him, "Hey Shankar, Innocent Storehousekeeper,[48] didn't you give it to her? Who gave *satī* to Queen Pingala? And her husband was living, so he's crying 'Alas Pingala! Alas Pingala!' and people are dying. Shankar Baba, you gave her *satī*, didn't you?"

"Yes I gave Queen Pingala *satī*-power."

"So Baba, how could you give her *satī*-power when her husband is living? Now King Bharthari is asking for Pingala—how could you give it to her with a living husband?"

"Well, she was my devotee. Who? Queen Pingala. She served me, she was my devotee, so she fell at my feet and said 'Give me *satī*-power!' and 'He tested me, he tested me, King Bharthari wants to find out if I will be a *satī*.' So, the sister-fucker, she wanted to burn so she burned!"

Then God said to Lord Shankar, "Well Baba, you gave her *satī*-power?"

"Yes, I'm the one who gave her *satī*-power."

"So give back Pingala, give back Pingala, and take away that *satī*-power you gave her. Take it away from her. Have them light the cooking fires and then come back. If they don't light the cooking fires then they will all die."

Now Mahadevji said, "Oh, sister-fucker! What kind of a mess have I gotten myself into?"

"Into just this kind of a mess—why did you give *satī*-power? You should have thought, 'Well, brother, her husband is alive, we will hardly give her *satī*-power.' So Baba, this sin will stick to you."

Then Lord Shankar called Gorakh Nathji and said to him, "O brother Gorakh Nath!"

47. *ghar ko dhaṇī;* the most frequent term for husband in village speech.
48. *bholā bhaṇḍārī;* another epithet for Shiva.

"Yes, Baba."

"Go over there to Ujjain where Queen Pingala burned up, and put an end to King Bharthari's stubbornness. And light the cooking fires."

"But Baba, that King Bharthari, he won't quit being stubborn."

"So give that sister-fucker a couple of blows on his ass with your tongs, and tell that sister-fucker, 'This is how I'll take away your stubbornness!'"

"So the king is stubborn, but I can be just as stubborn—I won't allow him to do what he's doing. I'll beat him with my tongs and I'll make him quit being stubborn, I'll make him forget Queen Pingala."

"Go, Gorakh Nath, and light the cooking fires and stuff, because I'm at fault."

"Baba, you're sending me, so send me—but whatever I say, it should happen[49]—then you can send me. Or else I won't go."

"Go, son, and whatever you say will happen."

"If it's like that, then I'll go."

(Bh 2.6.e)

As soon as Shankar Baba gave the order, Gorakh Baba went right away.

He took his sack-and-stuff, the Guru Sovereign took his tongs-and-stuff, he put on his sandals-and-stuff[50] and blew his horn. The Guru Sovereign prostrated himself respectfully to Lord Shankar. A seated yogi's a stake in the ground, but a yogi once up is a fistful of wind.[51] The Nath took the wind's own form and turned his face toward[52] Ujjain.

He crossed one forest, he crossed a second forest. In the third forest he came to Ujjain City and he entered the Chapala Garden.

As soon as he entered the Chapala Garden, he saw it was filled with people, women and men.

---

49. The actual phrase, "should stand up," would sound peculiar in English but foreshadows Gorakh Nath's miraculous restoration to life of the dead queen.

50. Madhu uses Hindi echo-words here; a literal replication would be "sack-wack, tongs-wongs, sandals-wandals." One implication of the echo-word formation is "et cetera."

51. This phrase, a rhymed couplet, occurs every time a yogi travels: *baiṭhyā jogī to khair kī khūṭi; uthyā jogī paṅvan kī mūṭhī.*

52. *sūratī lagālī; sūrat* may simply refer to a face but in esoteric yogic terminology is a particular kind of "consciousness." While this stock phrase certainly implies a magical directing of the yogis' consciousness, the more literal translation is smoother; the consequences of immediate transportation are contextually clear.

Bharthari Baba was crying, "Pingala Pingala!" and Gorakh Nathji came and as soon as he came, Gorakh Nathji said, "King Bharthari, why are these people dying? You sister-fucker, you killed Pingala. You killed Pingala, but why are you killing all these people? What will you rule then?

"Three days and three nights have passed, and they are dying of hunger, and these boys and girls and women are trembling and dying. Aren't you sorry for them? You're crying, 'Alas Pingala!' but this Pingala has become a pile of ash."

Then he filled both his hands with ash and scattered it to the wind, and the ashes of the funeral pyre flew away.

"King Bharthari, where is your Pingala? You sister-fucker, you burned her up with your own hands, and now you are crying 'Pingala Pingala,' sister-fucker, and it looks as if the people are dying."

But Bharthari Baba[53] didn't listen, still Bharthari Baba didn't listen. He kept on with "Alas Pingala! Alas Pingala!" and he didn't listen—he didn't even know that Gorakh Nathji had come, and he wouldn't shut up.

Gorakh Nathji got mad. "So be stubborn and what will be will be," he said. He had a clay drinking-water jug, like this, just this big, and that jug fell on a big rock and broke; he broke it. He dropped it on a rock. King Bharthari, a little distance away, had been going around the funeral pyre with his "Alas Pingala!" for a long time. He was tired, three days and three nights had passed. Gorakh Nathji, a little ways away, dropped his jug, its little fragments fell, and he circled round them crying "Alas my jug! Alas my jug!"—chanting.[54]

He was chanting, and to King Bharthari's one round he made twenty rounds, he circled the jug chanting, "Alas my jug! Alas my jug!" He was chanting so loud that nobody could even hear Bharthari Baba. Gorakh Nathji's chanting went right up into the sky. He kept chanting "Alas my jug! Alas my jug!" and it was heard all over the world.

So now people began to laugh, "Hey, that sound is coming from the sky! The sky is speaking: 'Alas my jug!' and that chanting reaches down here, too. Now what's going on here?"

53. This epithet presages King Bharthari's transformation to a *sādhu* or *bābājī*.
54. Bhoju glosses the term used here, *raṇoṭī*, as "continuous and loud vocalization" and suggests its relation to *rūṅkhaṛ*, meaning the repeated recitation of the name of God, or any religious recitation.

Bharthari Baba got mad, and he stopped in his tracks, and as soon as he stopped he said to Gorakh Nathji: "Yogi, you're making fun of me! Very important people are gathered here. Very big kings are gathered, and this yogi is making fun of me."

To the assembled people Bharthari said, "Why aren't you able to stop him? These policemen have authority and all these important men are seated here and this yogi is making fun of me, but you aren't able to stop him."

They answered, "Who will fight with a Baba? This is a Baba and who will do it? He is a yogi, so how can we do anything to him? And Grain-giver, you should be patient with him. You did it yourself and caused us all misery and now you're saying 'Alas Pingala!' and demanding her, but where will she come from?"

Then King Bharthari got mad, and he called to Gorakh Nathji, "Hey, you're a yogi and I am King Bharthari and you are making fun of me."

But Gorakh Nathji didn't hear him. He just kept crying, "Alas my jug! Alas my jug!"

Now he burst out in anger at Gorakh Nath. Who?

/Bharthari./

King Bharthari, "Hey yogi, you are making fun of me."

Even so, Gorakh Nathji didn't listen, he didn't leave off his chant: "Alas my jug! Alas my jug!"

The third time King Bharthari said to Gorakh Nathji, "You are totally ruining my reputation. You are crying about your jug of mere clay, but my Queen Pingala burned up, and that's what I am crying about. You are crying over your clay jug and not letting me be heard, yogi."

When he said this three or four times, then Gorakh Nathji stopped.

"What's the matter, King Bharthari?"

"Well, my Queen Pingala burned up, and I'm crying about that but you are crying about a clay jug."

"OK, King Bharthari, what work did your Queen Pingala do?"

He spoke then to King Bharthari.

"King Bharthari, you sister-fucker, you killed her with your own hands. You sent the cloth soaked with deer's blood and killed her, sister-fucker. You killed the deer Moti Stag, sister-fucker, and you sent Moti Stag's blood in a handkerchief to see if your queen would burn or not burn, and she burned.

"Why are you crying? Compared to your queen my jug is a very great and useful thing. What was your Queen Pingala like? What work did she do? She made your food and gave it you, and she slept with you in your women's quarters; that's the work she did.

"But my little jug, when my soul feels thirsty, then if I say so she puts her neck in a noose. This little jug puts her neck in a noose and then she goes fifty hands deep and she strains the water and brings it—good, pure water.[55] Afterwards, as soon as she comes out, I drink up the water, glub glub glub glub. She alone is my body's caretaker, and now she has died, so shouldn't I cry for her? She took care of my body. Far better than your queen is my little jug."

Then King Bharthari said, "Gorakh Nathji, I can get seven hundred and fifty clay jugs just like yours."

Gorakh Nathji said, "King Bharthari, you won't get one."

"No, Gorakh Nathji, I will order seven hundred and fifty jugs just like yours."

Gorakh Nathji picked up the broken pieces of his jug and said, "If you order a jug just like this, then I will make seven hundred and fifty Pingalas just like yours stand up."

"How can I believe that?"

He said, "King Bharthari, seven hundred and fifty . . . "

"Gorakh Nathji Sovereign, I shall order seven hundred and fifty jugs exactly like your jug."

"King Bharthari, you'll order a jug just like this one?"

"Yes, exactly like it."

"Then I will give you seven hundred and fifty Pingalas, every one of them just like yours. Do you think I'm just any yogi? If you ask for seven hundred and fifty Pingalas, I'll get you just as many as you ask for."

Meanwhile, King Bharthari called, "O all you village Potters!" He ordered the village Potters: "Go and bring clay jugs just exactly like this one."

But Gorakh Nathji was saying, "King Bharthari, where are the jugs? Right now the Potters are dying of hunger. It has been four days now, and women and men are dying of hunger. These Potters should go and roll out bread and eat it. They have been hungry for

55. That is, he uses the jug, tied to a rope, to bring up water from a deep well; its narrow neck admits no debris.

four days, they're upset, so they should sleep for a little while. Later the Potters will take their donkeys and go to the mines. They'll go to the mines and dig out clay, and load it on their donkeys and bring it, and later they will come to their homes and break up the lumps of clay, and later they will add water.

"They'll add water, and later they'll knead it. The clay from the mines. And after kneading it, they'll make balls and then turn them on the wheel and it won't be dry for four days... What? Those jugs that they make. After drying, then they will decorate them, and put them in the sun, and later they will bake them, so meanwhile ten days will pass.

"So, will you keep them sitting here for ten days? Who? All these people, they'll die."

Gorakh Nathji said, "Go, everybody go and light the cooking fires. When I make Queen Pingala stand up, on that day come back and see the show, but meanwhile go light the cooking fires and feed the children. Who knows when the jugs will be ready? Go, brothers. All the sin of this district will be removed, as 'When the evil sinner Shivo Khuvas died...' "[56]

When you suffer hunger, your spirit leaves. So Gorakh Nathji told them, "Go and light the cooking fires. Who knows how many days it's been since the queen died and he's been killing everyone with his 'Alas Pingala!'"

(Bh 2.7.e)

So they lit the cooking fires in the village, and the Potters all ate their bread and drank and had a little rest. Then the Potters took their pickaxes, and their buffalo and donkeys and went to the mines to dig. They dug clay and brought it back and threw it in a trench. Breaking the lumps apart, they added water to the clay. They put in water and dissolved it, and finally they began to knead it.

Gradually they prepared it, and when it was ready they shaped it into balls,[57] and then the Potters put these on the wheel and began

---

56. *papaḷāno kor maryo Shivo Khūvās;* an uncommon saying, according to Bhoju, referring to a wicked barber named Shiva whose death released his whole community from sin. I do not know his story; the point is simply that one sinner can ruin a whole kingdom, as Bharthari's crazed mourning has caused so much trouble in his domain.

57. *piṇḍā,* H. *piṇḍā;* any round object. The term is laden with creative meanings: an embryo is a *piṇḍā,* as are special food offerings to the spirits of recently deceased persons that create bodies for them. *Piṇḍā* is also a Shiva lingam, and the ball of clay on the potter's wheel is said to resemble a Shiva lingam.

to turn them. But, that was it! Gorakh didn't allow them to make them nice and straight. He messed them up and made them all crooked.

/He has many kinds of divine games, how would he let them come out right?/

The Potters made the jugs very nicely, but as soon as they cut one and lifted it from the wheel and set it down—of its own accord it became crooked.

Later they dried them in the sun. They dried them in the sun, and the Potters made designs on them and applied color. They applied color and designs to the jugs. They decorated the jugs but he would not allow that particular color to come. Then they baked them in the kiln, to make them firm. They covered them, and they used cow-dung cakes to bake them.

Then they loaded their donkeys, piled them up—the Potters of every village, every district of the kingdom of Ujjain—all the Potters loaded their buffalo and donkeys and brought jugs and more jugs.

/All brought them./

Yes, they brought jugs and more jugs and put them in the Chapala Garden.

It was a huge heap, like you see at a Potter's kiln. Then the king said, "Grain-giver, look! Gorakh Nathji, look! The jugs have come."

But Gorakh Nathji lifted up the shards of his jug and said, "King Bharthari, demand a jug of this color. These Potters haven't brought any of this color, the color of these shards. If you want to have a Pingala just like your Pingala, order me a jug of just this color, and then you'll get your Pingala."

The King said, "O Potters, take these shards and bring me just such a color."

They said, "We have plenty of shards but this color won't come. We've already gone to a lot of trouble, making these jugs. Brother, five or seven days have gone by—by the time we dried them and loaded them on the buffalo, fifteen days have gone by."

Fifteen days had gone by, and what could King Bharthari do? Now the jugs had come, the buffalo came loaded and the donkeys came loaded and Grain-giver Gorakh Nathji Sovereign looked and said, "O King Bharthari, order a jug just like this jug."

So King Bharthari grasped his feet and prostrated himself. "Grain-giver, I've done the best I could, good or bad, I've ordered what I could. Now, Grain-giver, that's enough. Good or bad, black or fair,

make me a Pingala. Just as I've brought these jugs, black or yellow,
so bring her, black or yellow."

So King Bharthari fell at his feet, at Gorakh Nathji's feet, and said,
"Grain-giver, just like this, black or fair, make her stand up. I offered
you what I could make. So Grain-giver, you give me Pingala, black
or fair."

(Bh 2.8.e)

> Gorakh Baba
> worshiped Shankar.[58]
> Gorakh Baba worshiped Shankar,
> "Yes, Shankar as I worship, come, Baba Nath,
> And make Pingala stand."

> Gorakh Baba had worshiped Shankar,
> then he stood up, Gorakh Baba stood up.
> Yes, Gorakh Baba lifted his tongs from the campfire
> and struck seven times.

> He struck his tongs seven times
> upon the funeral pyre.
> Yes, he hit the ashes.

> Baba hit the funeral pyre
> seven times with his tongs,
> Gorakh Nath hit the funeral pyre,
> Yes, and seven hundred and fifty
>   sluts with fairies[59] inside
> Stood up over here.

> Now they descended from
> their palanquins,[60] and
> seven hundred and fifty Pingalas were standing.
> All the Pingalas, all of them

---

58. This begins the final sung segment of Bh 2.

59. The term Madhu uses here is *puriyāṅ* or *pariyāṅ* (f.pl.), a cognate of English
"fairy," I believe. Hindu mythology associates these female spirits with Indra.
However, Bhoju's investigations determined that the "fairies" mentioned here are
actually *śaktis*—"powers" subject to control by the perfected yogi Gorakh Nath.
They are denigrated as "sluts," for they are no better than his slaves.

60. *pālkyā* or "sedan chair," which bearers usually carry on their shoulders.
Here, however, the image is of fairies flying through the sky in automotive chairs.

looked like one another.
All looked like all, and all looked like Pingala,
with just one face.
All of them had just one face,
they all had Queen Pingala's face.

Gorakh Baba said to King Bharthari,
"Now listen, Bharthari,
Seven hundred and fifty Pingalas are standing here,
Grab the one that's yours by the hand.
Grab that one only, for if you grab another
by the hand, King,
I'll make your skin fly with my tongs."

(Bh 2.9.s)

So, King Bharthari fell at his feet: "Hey Guru Sovereign, hey Gorakh Nathji, Sovereign, I had the black and white jugs made, as best I could, I brought them."

"So like that, black or fair, shall I make seven hundred and fifty Pingalas stand up—gorgeous or black?"

"Yes, Baba, that's what I'm asking you to do."

"Good, King Bharthari."

So Gorakh Nath stood up. He stood up and took the name of Lord Shankar and struck the funeral pyre seven times with his tongs and called, "*Hāy laṇḍī*"[61] and seven hundred and fifty Pingalas stood up.

The Pingalas got down from their palanquins, and all seven hundred and fifty Pingalas stood up. They formed two rows, one in front and one in back. All seven hundred and fifty Pingalas stood, and all of them were dressed the same, the ladies were dressed in long skirts just like this lady's.[62]

And they all had blouses just like this, and bangles, and were wearing wraps like this. And their eyes all looked the same. All seven hundred and fifty had Queen Pingala's face, Queen Pingala, who burned up, her exact face—not one of them was missing something. /Or else the king might not have recognized her./

---

61. *Laṇḍī* is a variant of *raṇḍī* or "prostitute," an insulting yet more accurate epithet for these female spirits than "fairy."

62. Madhu gestures to Suraj Kumar, the daughter of our hostess; she wears a *lāṅgo*—the traditional ankle-length skirt of women from the Rajput caste.

All seven hundred and fifty Pingalas stood there with the same face. Good. Then Gorakh Nathji Sovereign gave an order: "King Bharthari, here are seven hundred and fifty Pingalas. Put your hand on the one that is yours. Don't touch any of the others. Your Pingala is here, so grab her hand, and watch out! Because if you put your hand on another, sister-fucker, I will beat you with my tongs and make your skin fly. Don't touch any other Pingala, but only yours. Grab the one who is your Pingala."

"Hey Grain-giver, they all look the same. They all have the same face."

"What, you don't recognize the Pingala you were crying for?"

"Yes I recognize her."

"Then grab her."

King Bharthari thought, Now Gorakh Nathji said that if I touch the wrong one "I will beat you sister-fucker." But they all have exactly the same face.

He looked at their faces, but they all looked the same.

/One like the next one./

This one looked like the next one who looked like the next one. It was her face.

"Their faces are just like hers—all seven hundred and fifty Pingalas that I see. Her color, her form, son of a . . . ! Which one should I grab? Should I grab this one or this one?"

So King Bharthari went between the two rows of all seven hundred and fifty Pingalas, and he looked and looked, and then he came back. He came back to the Guru Sovereign.

"Well, King Bharthari, grab her, sister-fucker."

"Baba, they are all mine. All the Pingalas are mine."

"Hey sister-fucker, what do you mean, all seven hundred and fifty Pingalas are yours? You were crying for one, you weren't crying for seven hundred and fifty."

"Grain-giver, Guru Sovereign, I can't recognize her, and if I put my hand on another one, if I grab another one, then you will beat me with your tongs, so what should I do? Grain-giver, I can't recognize her, they all look the same. Therefore they are all mine, because she had a face just like that."

"Go, sister-fucker King Bharthari. You were crying and crying for just one Pingala and now you say 'All seven hundred and fifty are mine.' You sister-fucking greedy king."

"So Grain-giver, I won't grab them all, I will only the grab the one you say I should."

"Good, brother."

He blindfolded him tightly. "Now, go, go, and your Pingala will come into your hand. The one that comes into your hand, hold on to her tightly or else she'll take you flying. Grab her forcefully."

So, blindfolded, he went back and grabbed Pingala, brother, he grabbed one, only one. He grabbed her tightly by the wrist.

And Gorakh Nathji struck his tongs again and chased them away. "Go back where you came from, *laṇḍī*. Run away all you Pingalas, fly away."

But the one that King Bharthari had grabbed started to take him up with her, she went flying with him. Then Gorakh Nathji said, "Yeah, you sister-fucking whore, did you kill your husband on purpose to become *satī*,[63] Pingala, sister-fucker? He was asking for Pingala. Did you want to make your husband fly with you to Vaikunth? Will you take the king?"

Gorakh Nathji said, "Sister-fucker, husband-killer, you became *satī* and went over there to Vaikunth. But stop, here comes your husband!"[64]

He gave Pingala back to Bharthari, "Here is your Pingala, King Bharthari, take her and don't say, 'Alas Pingala! Alas Pingala!' Now go into the castle and take care of the kingdom."

Who made this pronouncement? Gorakh Nathji said it. "Take care of your kingdom. And take this Queen Pingala."

This is Ghatiyali Village, and Madhu Nathji has finished this Bharthari right here.

Gorakh Nathji Sovereign made a dead Pingala stand after fifteen days, after fifteen days he gave her into King Bharthari's care, after she had burned. That's the kind of king Gorakh Nathji Sovereign was.

(Bh 2.9.e)

---

63. *maṇasa mārar satī hor;* here the saying previously applied to Bharthari is turned on Pingala.

64. If none of the Pingalas are real, and the one Bharthari has grabbed is only a slave-spirit, then Gorakh is just being rude, as usual, to his enslaved female spirits. If it is the real Pingala then he is imputing dark motives to the faithful queen.

Part 3

The Guru's Lesson

Introduction

This part opens with Bharthari tossing and turning in his royal bed—perhaps the single moment of the tale in which the audience sympathizes with his character. Comparing Gorakh Nath's power over life and death to his own kingly potency, Bharthari concludes, as have a number of other legendary and mythological Indian kings, that royal dominion is nothing but dust.[1] The lesson begun by Gorakh Nath at Pingala's pyre reaches fruition here in Bharthari's resolve to leave the palace.

Titled by Madhu Nath "The Guru's Lesson" or "sermon" (*upadeś*), part 3 does show Bharthari falling at Gorakh Nath's feet to receive initiation and a little good advice. But most of the action actually concerns the ex-king's confrontation with his former slave girls and wife. Of course, these experiences too are part of the guru's lesson: it is Gorakh Nath's order that the king should bring alms from the hands of Queen Pingala after calling her "Mother." This would seem to be a powerful lesson, indeed. Yet in the event, not Gorakh Nath's but Pingala's words are the most eloquent and memorable, although ultimately futile.

Both Madhu and his audience usually cite "Pingala's lament," which is not a soliloquy but a dialogue between eternally severed husband and wife, as a favorite scene in the epic. It is judged second in appeal only to the initial encounter between Gorakh Nath and

---

1. See Gold 1989 for a discussion of and references to renouncer-kings in Hindu myth.

Bharthari at Pingala's funeral pyre. Whereas the latter is a scene of comic and magical drama, Pingala's lament is high melodrama—certainly the most emotionally touching episode in Bharthari's epic.

In between Bharthari's initiation and his final encounter with Pingala is the episode in which the king, as yogi-beggar, confronts his former slave girls. This entire scene very closely replicates three encounters between begging yogis and slave girls appearing in Gopi Chand's tale. I decided to condense the yogi–slave girl dialogue here, because I am convinced that it is more intrinsic to the Gopi Chand story, where I fully translate two of its three occurrences (in parts 1 and 2). When Madhu Nath performed this encounter in Bharthari 3, he not only used the Gopi Chand *rāg* but several times said Gopi Chand's name by mistake, as well as calling Pingala "Patam De." The end of Bharthari's encounter with the slave girls, where I return to a full text, does depart from Gopi Chand's two encounters. Far from breaking down and wailing for his guru, Bharthari unlike Gopi Chand is able to take care of himself even in such taxing circumstances.

When Bharthari finally meets Pingala, we are more clearly back in his proper story; at this very moment Madhu shifts the *rāg* back to the *Rājājī* melody characteristic of his Bharthari performance. Pingala's challenge to Bharthari is couched in a persuasive rhetoric different from Patam De's to Gopi Chand. Just as Bharthari did not cry when the slave girls attacked him, he does not waver before Pingala's powerful onslaught. Rather, he matches her complaints and demands with appropriate rejoinders.

Nonetheless, audience sympathies are with Pingala. In Gopi Chand the encounter between husband turned yogi and devastated symbolically widowed wife is mediated by the interference of Manavati Mother, who is trying to manipulate them both into following the guru's commands. There, too, the acute passion of Gopi Chand and Patam De as husband and wife is diffused from personal to collective sorrow, if intensified in volume, by the loud chorus of concubines and slave girls. Here, in contrast, Bharthari and Pingala have a one-to-one encounter.

The task of calling one's wife "Mother" and bringing alms from her hands is a standard trial for new yogis in popular traditions. Why this should be, when initiation as a renouncer involves a shedding of past identities and kinship connections, is again a question I take up (though hardly answer) in the afterword. Let me, however, call the reader's attention to the final lines of Madhu Nath's text: "Baba, now feast on your food, from the queen today, from my Queen Pingala." Just at the moment when the guru has promised that his yoga will be fulfilled, Bharthari uses the language of his ruling times: "my Queen." Thus, although Bharthari seems to have internalized the guru's lesson far more readily and thoroughly than did his nephew Gopi Chand, this speech suggests a lingering irresolution. It could be a verbal accident, or it could be yet another expression of how difficult it is to let go of past possessions and relationships, even for a fated and strong-willed renouncer-king.

Text

Honored King...
Your throne and bed are pleasant, King,
Your storehouse filled with pearls, King Bharthari,
Your storehouse filled with pearls, King Bharthari.
You must realize, Bharthari Panvar
King of Dhara Nagar,
Nobody is immortal!

Honored King...
At midnight the king had a dream,
He dreamed he saw Gorakh Nath,
    you must realize, Bharthari,
He dreamed he saw Gorakh Nath,
    you must realize, Bharthari.
You must realize, Bharthari Panvar,
King of Dhara Nagar,
Nobody is immortal!

Honored King...
At night he dreamed he saw Shankar,
Lord Shankar appeared to the king in the night,
    to King Bharthari,
And Baba Gorakh Nath appeared,
    you must realize, Bharthari.
You must realize, Bharthari Panvar,
King of Dhara Nagar,
You're my wedded lord, but
you've gone and left me destitute.

Honored King...
The king had dreams at midnight: Listen King Bharthari!
Honored King...
You'll go to hell[2] if you rule the kingdom,
my king, straight to hell.
Now you be a yogi, you must realize, Bharthari.
You must realize, Bharthari Panvar,
King of Dhara Nagar,
Ujjain City's ruler, you must realize, Bharthari.

(Bh 3.1.s)

Meanwhile, the kingdom and Queen Pingala were given back into Bharthari's care. He is king, and he does not lack diamonds or rubies, his warehouse is filled with pearls. But now the king can't sleep. King Bharthari can't sleep. In his dreams he sees Lord Shankar and he sees Gorakh Nathji Sovereign.

Gorakh Nathji Sovereign appears to him: "Oh King, why are you holding on to these things when you should hold on to yoga?"

The king agreed. "There's something in the condition of yoga but nothing at all in rule."

"King, nothing comes of ruling! You just accumulate sin. You eat dharma.[3] You put cows in the lockup and then collect a fine. Whoever commits any crime or sin, you fine them fifty or one hundred rupees. So you eat dharma and then you fall into hell. King, ruling is the same as hell, but yoga is the same as ruling. Previously you earned yoga, you earned yoga and so you became king.[4] But by ruling you fall into hell."

The king agreed, but for five, ten, fifteen, twenty days, for an entire month it went on like this. He stayed, but King Bharthari couldn't sleep. "Oh, this is all a bundle of sin! And sister-fuck! What to do inside of it? Look, take Gorakh Nathji, he is wise, and he lives as a yogi, so why should I live as a king? In the forest he brought Moti Stag to life and sent him running. Gorakh Nathji Sovereign brought a dead deer to life. Oh my, what a yogi! When my own Queen Pingala burned up, she was really a pinch of ash, and he scattered it, but

2. *narak;* in Gopi Chand the alternative to yoga is not hell but death.

3. *dharma khānā;* a phrase often used to mean "to commit injustice." Here the implication seems to be that the ruler (like any petty village official) lives off of unfair penalties imposed on others.

4. This may be a reference to Bharthari's previous birth as a yogi, not ever mentioned explicitly in Madhu's performance but part of a framing tale in several other versions (see chapter 3).

fifteen days later he made seven hundred and fifty Pingalas stand up!
Oh my, this yoga is great. To hold on to yoga is great, but to live as
a king is nothing at all. It is just a fall to hell."

Now King Bharthari agreed. "All right, I'll be a yogi, I'll do it,
because this life of rule is nothing but dust. I shall go behind the
queen's back. Otherwise, if I try to leave in front of the queen and
all the others, there isn't a chance that they'll let me go."

[*An older woman in the audience, not the* hūṅkār, *comments,* Yes, they
won't let the king go! Who would let him go?]

"Now I won't rule. I won't rule and I will put the auspicious mark
of rule[5] on my brother, Hero Vikramaditya."

"Hey Grain-giver, where did you get such an impossible notion?"
/He had a younger brother./

Yes, his younger brother was Hero Vikramaditya.

"We ought to crown Vikramaditya. I won't rule anymore, so I'll
call my brother Hero Vikramaditya and crown him. He will be the
master of the kingdom."

King Bharthari couldn't sleep, or he slept restlessly, and he saw
Gorakh Nathji and agreed with him. His desire fixed on yoga. "Compared to yoga the ruling life is nothing at all. In the ruling life you
fall into hell." King Bharthari agreed with this. So let's see now, at
midnight, he got up and is going into the jungle...

                                                        (Bh 3.1.e)

Honored King...
At midnight Bharthari got up, my King Bharthari
He went out of the palace, the king went out,
    you must realize, Bharthari,
The King is leaving the city,
    you must realize, Bharthari,
The King is leaving the city,
    you must realize, Bharthari,
You must realize, Bharthari Panvar of Dhara Nagar,
Ujjain City's ruler wandered in the jungle.
He went wandering in the jungle,
    you must realize, Bharthari.

Honored King...
He crossed one woods, the king crossed another,

5. *rāj talak;* that is, ritually install Vikramaditya as king.

He crossed the third woods and then,
   you must realize, Bharthari,
The king crossed the third woods,
   you must realize, Bharthari,
The king went wandering in the jungle,
   you must realize, Bharthari,
Over here a lion roars, you must realize, Bharthari.
Now he fixed his mind on Gorakh Baba,
Now he fixed his mind on Gorakh Baba,
He is crying in the jungle now, O King Bharthari.

Honored King...
On the mountain his campfire[6] is burning, O King Bharthari,
He went straight to that campfire, King Bharthari
He went straight to that campfire, O King Bharthari.

Honored King...
He went to the campfire, King Bharthari, my King Bharthari,
He fell at the campfire and called, O King Bharthari,
He fell at the campfire and called, O King Bharthari,
You must realize, Bharthari Panvar met Gorakh Baba,
He met Baba Gorakh Nath, you must realize, Bharthari,
You must realize, Bharthari Panvar of Dhara Nagar,
Dhara Nagar's king bowed flat to Gorakh Nath,
he bowed flat, you must realize, Bharthari.[7]

The king bowed flat to Gorakh,
   he fell at his feet.
"Yes Baba raise your eyelids, Dina Nath,
   and make me your disciple.

"My guru raise your eyelids,
Baba Gorakh Nath
Make me your disciple."

When Bharthari said this,
Gorakh Baba raised his eyelids,

6. The term I translate "campfire" is *dhūnī* and refers specifically to the fires by which yogis sit, as a form of ascetic practice. Shrines to renouncers often center on their former campfires.

7. At this point Madhu gave a longer than usual musical interlude and switched to GC *rāg* 2.

Now he raised his eyelids,
Yes, Baba raised his eyelids, Gorakh Nath,
and saw King Bharthari at his feet.

"King, I already took care
of your queen
so why have you come again?"
"My guru make me a disciple
Gorakh Baba Nath
Please make me a yogi."

"King, your queen
will wail in the Color Palace.
Yes King, she will be *satī*, so why then
are you standing here again?
Your queen will wail
in the Color Palace.
Go back and rule!"

"My guru in a life of rule
I fall into hell,
my honored guru Gorakh,
But Baba, in a life of yoga, Baba Nath,
I'll get immortality.

"Now make me your disciple,
Baba Gorakh Nath,
for I can't ever sleep."

(Bh 3.2.s)

So whenever King Bharthari tries to sleep then, always, Lord
Shankar appears to him, and always Gorakh Nathji appears.

The king really found out that if there is anything at all, it is in
the yogi's life. But in the life of a ruler there is nothing at all—all it
amounts to a pile of hell.

"So Guru Sovereign, initiate me as your disciple.[8] I get to sleep only
with great difficulty, and if I do get to sleep, then Gorakh Sovereign,
you appear. I was wandering lost in the wild woods, wandering lost

8. Note how the transition from Bharthari's wakeful thoughts to his falling at
Gorakh Nath's feet is completely blurred here. In the sung portion he leaves the
city and crosses three forests. But in the explanation his passage is a mental one.

and with difficulty when your bright campfire appeared. Your bright campfire appeared, so Guru Sovereign, I have come.

"I called, 'Hey Baba Gorakh, Baba Gorakh Nath,' while I was in the jungle, and lions and tigers were roaring and I had no weapons with me, nothing at all. But Baba, I thought only of you, and you kept the lions and tigers from eating me. Baba, I was lost in the jungle when this hill with your campfire on top appeared, and so Guru Sovereign, I have tied myself to your holy feet and fallen there. Guru Sovereign, initiate me as your disciple."

"Hey King Bharthari, sister-fucker, always you are wailing like a queen. First you cried, 'Alas Pingala, alas Pingala,' and now you are following me? Queen Pingala will weep."

"Let her weep if she weeps. Make me a yogi."

"Oh yoga is very difficult work, King Bharthari. I will thrust a dagger through your ears, and then I will thrust these wooden plugs[9] in the holes. Following a yogi's rules is very difficult; it is the blade of a sword."

"No Baba, no matter what, I will take hold of yoga."

"OK, I will make you a yogi."

"Yes Baba I will certainly be a yogi."

"Now I will thrust the dagger in your ears ... but are you sure this heat won't burn you?"[10]

"No Baba."

"Good, son, but your soul doesn't go to your queens?"

"No, it doesn't."

"Your soul doesn't go to your brothers, your family?"

"No, it doesn't."

"So sit down King Bharthari, now I will make you a yogi."

(Bh 3.2.e)

So to make him a yogi he seated him in the *ūkaṛū* position,[11] like this [*Madhu demonstrates*]. Gorakh Nathji Sovereign took his dagger and thrust it through Bharthari's ear. He pierced his ear and pushed

---

9. *guṭṭā;* wooden plugs put into a new initiate's ears until the wounds heal.

10. *tap nahiṅ bhalegā;* Bhoju suggests that *tap* here covers all the difficulties included in initiation: the pain of cutting, the heat of the campfire, the sorrow of leaving his family.

11. Sundardas's dictionary (1965) describes this position taken with knees bent, soles of feet touching the ground, and buttocks resting on heels.

in plugs made of *nīm* wood, as big as a big toe. Plugs of *nīm* are pushed in first.

So, he put in the plugs. "Yes, sister-fucker! Now look, you will remember your life of rule."[12] And he ignited flames in a half-pot[13] and put it on his head. First he took a head pad and put it on his head, and then he ignited flames in a half-pot and placed it on top, and the flames reached his ears. It didn't burn his head, but it kept his ears very warm. Keeping his ears warm, he took him to Badari Narayan.[14] Who? Gorakh Nathji Sovereign.

He took him to Badari Narayan. They went very slowly, by foot, and they were barefoot too. Bharthari had many blisters on his feet, and the pot was burning on top of him, and he was sweating too, with the heat coming onto his ears.

The king thought, Sister-fucker! Ruling was really great.

[*Much laughter from the audience*]

"Oh my, yoga is very big and difficult work. Yoga is very big and bad work. Oh, flames are heating my ears."

The guru was going in front. He took him to Badari Narayan. It took them ten, fifteen days to reach there, maybe a month. So he took him to Badari Narayan, and there he took *darśan* of Badari Narayan. They prostrated themselves and gave respect to Badari Narayan. Then Gorakh Nathji Sovereign took permission from Lord Shankar... and he put an iron platter[15] on his head and they went to make offerings to Hing Laj Mother.[16]

To worship Hing Laj Mother they had to go by foot. Previously there were no motor cars, no airplanes [*Laughter*], no motors or cycles,

---

12. There is no mention here, as there is in Gopi Chand, of one ear "bleeding" milk and the other blood—the blood indicating that Gopi Chand's mind had wandered to his ruling time. However, the guru uses the future tense "will remember" (*yād āyegī*). Perhaps the pot of flames is intended to prevent such memories in Bharthari's case, whereas in Gopi Chand's it is supposed to cook them out of him.

13. *dhībaro;* Bhoju says this is the bottom half of a clay water pot that sometimes holds small fires in winter.

14. An important pilgrimage shrine in the Himalayas that is especially famed for its difficult access, Badari is a site dedicated to Vishnu, but these Shaivite yogis visit it first.

15. *tagar;* this term, used for the container of flames placed on Gopi Chand's head by Jalindar Nath, now seems to replace the original clay half-pot.

16. A goddess whose worship is central to the Nath sect in the village; her shrine is in Pakistan and no Rajasthani pilgrims visit it today. See Gold 1988, 102–4.

no way to go but by foot, and the platter was burning on his head, and the flames were striking his ears. It took about a month for them to get there. Where? To worship Hing Laj Mother.

They went by foot, and he had blisters on his feet. Some places they found water but some places there was no grain, no water, nothing at all. It was very difficult for King Bharthari. "Oh me, oh my! A very weird thing has happened. In truth, the life of yoga is very hard work."

Afterwards they came back to the campfire in the Kajali Woods.[17] And then Gorakh Nathji took the platter down from King Bharthari's head.

"Enough! Sit down, King Bharthari. Now you don't have a platter on your head and your ears are healed. The heat burned away the blood, and they're healed. Now let's put *darśaṇī* in your ears."

Enough! He took out such *darśaṇī!* Who? Gorakh Nathji Sovereign. There were diamonds sparkling in them, and he put them in his ears for him to wear.

"Good son, I will give you *darśaṇī* like these to wear, King Bharthari." So he gave him *darśaṇī* to wear, and he was a yogi. "Recite prayers and sit." He taught him to turn his prayer beads and gave him ashes to rub on himself and gave him a loincloth to wear. He gave Bharthari Baba prayer beads to turn, made of *rudrākṣa*,[18] and he gave him a deer-horn instrument on a rope[19] and yogis' earrings to wear.

"OK, son, Bharthari."

"Yes Guru Sovereign?"

"Son, your yoga is still not fulfilled."

"So Guru Sovereign, how will it be?"

"Go to your Queen Pingala's palace and bring alms from your queen's hand. And say 'Mother,' 'Honored Mother,' call your queen 'Mother.' [*This is spoken with high drama.*] 'Drop in alms, Pingala Mother!' Then your yoga will be complete."

"Hey Guru Sovereign, my Queen Pingala is my wife, she is my wife, she is my wife, so how will I call her 'Mother'?"

<hr />

17. *kajaḷī van;* this location appears frequently in Nath lore as a gurus' retreat. In the *RSK* it is a forest of banana trees; the name may also evoke darkness and mystery, as *kajaḷiyo* means dark or black.

18. A special dried seed used by Shaivite renouncers only for their prayer beads.

19. *selī singī nād;* see chapter 2 for characteristic paraphernalia of yogis.

"Yes, sister-fucker! The queen was your wife, when you lived as a ruler, she was your Queen Pingala, but now you have become a yogi. Now you have become a yogi, and she has become your mother. So call her 'Mother' out loud, and bring alms. Then your yoga will be complete."

"Fine, Guru Sovereign, I shall go."

"Look son, come on the roads and go on the roads and call all women 'Mother' and 'Sister.'[20] And don't bring shame to your yogi's robes. Get alms from your Queen Pingala. Call her 'Mother,' and take alms and hurry back."

"Fine, Grain-giver."

So, let's see what happens with Pingala.

(Bh 3.3.e)

Honored King[21]...
The king...a seated yogi's a stake in the ground,
but a yogi once up is a fistful of wind.
He took his sack, the yogi
picked up his tongs,
he put on his sandals,
and sounded his deer-horn instrument.
Baba sounded his horn,
and bowed his head to the guru.
Yes Baba wandered into the jungle, Bharthari Nath,[22]
and turned his face toward Ujjain.

Bharthari Baba crossed one woods,
the yogi crossed a second woods,
then he crossed the third woods.
Yes, in the third woods, Lord,
Baba came to the boundaries of Ujjain.

(Bh 3.4.s)

20. That is, don't stray from the path and don't look upon any females as sexual beings. These lines are the normal parting words from guru to disciple setting forth. See Narayan 1989 for tales of disciples who set out on a guru's errands only to be distracted by women.

21. Madhu began with one off-key "Honored King..." and then settled into GC *rāg* 2. I give only three verses of the singing that are not covered in the *arthāv*.

22. This is sung very dramatically, stressing the king's new identity, no longer as *Rājājī* but as Bharthari Nath. The last syllable is drawn out: "Naaaath."

King Bharthari had become a yogi, but in the jungle Bharthari Nath remembered the things of his ruling times. The white, white castles appeared, and he remembered the things of his ruling times. "Oh my, I used to sport at hunting lions in this very jungle, with how many soldiers and armies, and workers and servants! I sat in a throne on an elephant's back with whisks waving over me and many Royal Bards[23] praising me. And today in what poverty I have come!

"On my fair[24] body a loincloth[25] is tied, and on my fair neck tangled locks spread, and my whole body is smeared with ash. Just look at the poverty Fate has given me: in my hand tongs and on my feet sandals and on my shoulders a sack. I'm wandering in the jungle and there is no herald for me, there are no humans at all."

So King Bharthari was remembering the things of his ruling times and crying hard, his eyes filled with Indra's misty rain. Water poured from his eyes.[26] Who was there to talk with in the jungle?

"Oh my guru, Fortune has inscribed this destiny in my karma with thick writing: immortal fakirhood.[27] There is no one to remove it."

But he kept up his faith, telling himself, "Quit remembering the things of your ruling times, and keep your mind on prayer. Let's go brother, with a strong chest!" And King Bharthari went on his way.[28]

A seated yogi's a stake in the ground, but a yogi once up is a fistful

---

23. *chāraṇ bhāṭ;* an important caste of poet-historians in Rajasthan.

24. *bhūryā sā;* literally brownish but implying a favorable contrast with dark and unattractive skin—thus fair.

25. *langoṭi;* for an extensive discussion of folklore surrounding and meanings carried by ascetics' loincloths see Narayan 1989.

26. Indra is the Vedic deity associated with rain. This description of bitter weeping, in three stock phrases, recurs dozens of times in Gopi Chand.

27. *vidhātā āpaṇ likh diyā moṭā lekh ar karma me likh diyā amar fakīrī.* English-speaking Rajasthanis often identify *Vidhātā* as "Goddess Fortune" and equate it with *Bemātā*—the female divinity who inscribes all infants' foreheads with their destinies. However, as usually understood in Sanskrit and standard Hindi, *Vidhātā* is male and impersonal. "Thick writing" (*moṭā lekh*) may mean the "main" thing written or, more literally, something written in letters that cannot be erased, as the following sentence implies. Popular thought often merges the concepts of *fakīrī* and *jogā*, although *fakīr* is an Islamic term for a practitioner of asceticism. There exist census reports of castes desiring to switch their name of record from *jogī* to *fakīr* (see chapter 2). Here as in Gopi Chand's tale, *fakīrī* appears associated with immutable fate.

28. In GC 2 and GC 3 we will see Gopi Chand in an identical situation, but absolutely unable to proceed without the guru's comfort. Bharthari pulls himself together independently.

of wind. The Nath took the wind's own form. He crossed one woods, and a second woods, and in the third woods he entered the city of Ujjain.

King Bharthari entered with tongs in his hand and locks this long hanging down, and he went along smeared with ashes, but keeping up his courage. Over there nobody even said "Victory to Shiva!"[29] Who would? "Brother, it's just some poor *sādhu.*"

"There is no one to announce my own name, they don't even remember Bharthari Baba over here. That is what the world of flux is like. There was a day when I used to go out riding, and then they called before me, 'Mercy, Grain-giver, mercy, Grain-giver!' But now look! My own people see me in this poor clothing, in yogi's robes, and nobody even says 'Victory to Mahadev!' This is the ocean of cosmic flux."

Thinking in this way, he went into the Jewel Square.[30] He passed through one portal, he passed through a second portal, he went to the top of the third portal and set up his meditation seat and lit his campfire.

Having lit his campfire in the third portal, Bharthari Baba stood up and cried *"Alakh!"* He cried *"Alakh!"* and blew his deer-horn instrument. As soon as he blew his deer-horn instrument, and cried *"Alakh!"* it resounded in Queen Pingala's ears.

And as soon as it resounded in Queen Pingala's ears, she called her eleven slave girls.[31] Queen Pingala had eleven slave girls among whom her favorite's name was Motiji.

"Motiji."

"Yes, Lady?"

"Go, son, today some great soul has come to our door, a yogi has come. And he is calling '*Alakh!*' He has sounded his deer-horn instru-

---

29. This would be a polite greeting for a Nath renouncer, because Naths are known as a Shaivite sect.

30. *māṇak cauk;* an image of splendor that occurs often in folksongs and stories in reference to the main square of a city.

31. Madhu Nath uses two terms for slave girl, *dāsī* and *golī.* According to Bhoju, *dāsī* refers to virgin girls included in a dowry given to a great king, and *golī* refers to the female offspring of Royal Servants or *darogās.* Although Madhu's usage appears to be random, in order to replicate the word variation I translate *dāsī* as slave girl and *golī* as bondwoman. At points in both tales, *golī* appears to have more derogatory implications.

ment. Go, son, fill a platter with diamonds and rubies and take it. Put on fine clothing and then go, don't go like this. You put on nice clothes and go. Take a platter of diamonds and rubies, and go, give the yogi alms. Go quickly because if you don't then the yogi will leave our door empty-handed and give a curse.

"Now we don't know, for he didn't tell us, where our own king is. He became a yogi . . . who knows how we failed to serve him[32] . . . our own king became a yogi, or so they say, though we didn't see it with our own eyes. He went out in the night, and who knows where he went. Two months, two and a half months have passed and he hasn't come back."

(Bh 3.4.e)

So the queen sent Moti Dasi to give alms, and she started a fight. [Moti Dasi dresses in her finest and offers Bharthari a platter of diamonds and rubies. When he refuses them she insults him, and eventually he loses his temper and strikes her. She goes weeping to the queen, who arms all her slave girls with bamboo sticks and sends them to drive away the violent yogi. They surround him and threaten him with their sticks. For an identical encounter featuring Gopi Chand and his queen's slave girls see GC 2. I return now to Madhu's words.]

(Bh 3.5–6.e)

So they surrounded him and prodded him. Then Bharthari Baba thought, Before these sluts thoroughly spoil my honor, I will show them the face of my ruling times. So he wet a square of cloth from his gourd[33] and wiped the offering-ash off his whole body. He wiped the offering-ash from his face too. He said, "Sluts, you saw my garments of poverty. That's why you came with bamboo sticks. Who would recognize me? Sluts, raised on my scraps, you are holding bamboo sticks over me!"

Oh my! As soon as they saw King Bharthari's face, all the sluts fell at his feet. And they threw down their bamboo sticks. "Hey Grain-giver, we have become your ungrateful wretches."[34]

---

32. *kāṇā khaī saivā me cūk paṛgī;* it might also be construed as "who knows what lack of service he is suffering?"

33. Wandering renouncers carry dried, hollow vegetable gourds as water containers.

34. *lūn harāmanyā;* those who have eaten one's salt and then treated one badly.

/*vā sā vā!* [*exclamation of satisfaction and approval*]/

"We threatened you with bamboo sticks, and we have become ungrateful wretches."

So then as soon as they said this, the bondwomen went running, the slave girls. They ran wailing, and the queen said, "Girls, I sent you laughing so why have you come crying? What kind of a yogi is it, a magician, a death-spell wielder? Did he feed you some kind of roasted hashish that you have come stoned and wailing?"

"Lady, no, the yogi is no magician, no death-spell wielder, and he did not feed us roasted hashish. But your fate has split and the king, King Bharthari, has come as a yogi. He has long matted locks spreading, and in his ears he is wearing yogis' earrings. And there are ashes smeared on him and—take your ivory armbands and throw them away, and put on a long blouse![35] The king has become a yogi!"

"O sluts, many yogis come, and they all look the same! Yogis keep coming, crying '*Alakh!*' Sluts, now I will beat you with the whip, and I will make your skin fly off. The king will never be a yogi. He will never come."

What he became now we'll see.

(Bh 3.7.e)

Now Pingala came too.[36]
She passed through all the portals,
and all the slave girls
went with her.
Yes, Lady, go and take your husband's *darśan:*
Your husband-god[37] has come as a yogi.

She crossed one portal, the queen
crossed the second portal,
then she came to the third portal.
Yes, in the third portal, Lord,
King Bharthari was standing.

---

35. Because a renouncer "dies" to his past life, his wife becomes a widow. Broken bangles especially, and the removal of all ornaments, are signs of widowhood. A "long blouse" (*lāmbī kāṅchaḷyā*) summarizes what we might call "widow's weeds."

36. Madhu begins in GC *rāg* 2, then switches to *Rājājī*. I include this and all remaining sung portions because they comprise Pingala's lament—considered to be the emotional peak of Madhu Nath's Bharthari performance.

37. *pati dev* takes on pain and irony; he has become a *darśan*-worthy renouncer but is no longer her husband.

He picked up his sack, Baba,
and lifted his tongs,
and picked up his cup.
"Yes, Mother Pingala, give me alms today,
it is the guru's powerful command!
My mother, give me alms,
Pingala Mother,
it is the guru's powerful command."

Honored King[38] ...
Misled by a yogi
he is standing, he has come,
my husband has come.

Honored King ...
Had I but known you were
born to be a yogi,
my king, had I but known,
I would have stayed with my father,
and thus spent my life,
   you must realize, Bharthari.
You must realize, Bharthari Panvar of Dhara Nagar,
you're the master of my union but
you've gone and left me destitute.

Honored King ...
Eat and drink and accept wealth,[39]
   my husband, accept it,
Treat your soul with love, you must realize, Bharthari,
treat your soul with love, you must realize, Bharthari.
You must realize, Bharthari Panvar of Dhara Nagar,
you're the master of my union but
you've gone and left me destitute.

---

38. Here Madhu switches to the *rāg* that is characteristic of Bharthari, just at the moment when his story diverges significantly from similar scenes in Gopi Chand.

39. As in the very first stanza of Bh 1, the interpretation of these lines plays on the double meaning of *māyā* as wealth and illusion. Presumably Pingala tells him to "enjoy life" (as Bhoju puts it) but the words *māyā māṇlyo* could hint at the illusory qualities of the very things she urges him to accept.

Honored Queen ...
Don't stand there and quarrel, my beautiful queen,
My company's leaving for Badari Nath.[40]
Quit being stubborn, O Queen, for
my company's leaving for Badari Nath.
Quit being stubborn, just like a woman,[41]
and accept what I say.

Honored King ...
When I was a virgin, many grooms sought me, my king,
    many grooms sought me.
But nobody marries a married woman,
    you must realize, Bharthari,
Nobody marries a married woman,
    you must realize, Bharthari.
You must realize, Bharthari Panvar of Dhara Nagar,
you're the master of my union but
you've gone and left me destitute.

Honored King ...
For whom shall I wear these dangling earrings,
    my husband, dangling earrings?
And for whom this tasseled armband?
    you must realize, Bharthari,
For whom this tasseled armband?
    you must realize, Bharthari.
You must realize, Bharthari Panvar of Dhara Nagar,
you're the master of my union but
you've gone and left me destitute.

Honored King ...
If you must be a yogi then
I am your yogini, my husband, your yogini.
We'll cooperate in yogic practice,
    you must realize, Bharthari,
We'll cooperate in yogic practice,
    you must realize, Bharthari,

---

40. That is, "I'm about to leave on a pilgrimage" and am therefore in a hurry.
41. *tariyā kī jāt;* literally "female species."

You must realize, Bharthari Panvar of Dhara Nagar,
take me with you, master, you must realize, Bharthari.
You must realize, Bharthari Panvar of Dhara Nagar,
you're the master of my union but
you've gone and left me destitute.

Honored Queen . . .
If I take you with me, the world will speak badly,
    my queen, they'll speak badly.
The world will think me a householder,
    you must realize, female.
You must realize, female species,
    you must realize, Bharthari.
You must realize, female species,
    and accept what I say.

(Bh 3.8.s)

Baba lifted his sack and lifted his cup, "Ho, Pingala Mother,
don't quarrel with me, give me alms, Pingala Mother. It is my Guru
Sovereign's powerful command. Give me alms my mother!"

As soon as he said this she fell into lamentation, "Oh my, this is
really an outrage! Now you said 'Mother.' Hey, husband-god, am I
your mother or am I your woman? Could this have come to pass in
just a few days?"

He said, "Now you're not my queen or anything, now you are my
mother."

Then she lamented, "Hey Honored King, eat and drink and
accept wealth, and treat your soul with love. The pleasures of a
human birth will not come again.

"Honored King, for whom do I wear these dangling earrings, and
for whom this tasseled armband? And Grain-giver, what is this
outrage you've committed? I burned up in the garden, and you had
me brought back to life. It seems you had me brought back to life in
order to make me weep, in order to leave me here lamenting."

[*Several members of the audience, of both sexes, make sympathetic comments.*]

Then he said, "You have your young brother-in-law,[42] who? Hero

---

42. *devar;* husband's younger brother, with whom sexual joking is permitted
and a marriage after widowhood might be approved.

Vikramaditya. The auspicious mark of rule was given to him and you can live with him in bliss."

"King, a craving for mangoes isn't satisfied by tamarinds. King Bharthari, if you must be a yogi, then take me with you. I'll be your yogini, and we'll cooperate in yogic practices, we'll both live in the condition of yoga."

"Hey Queen, if I took you with me the world would understand us as householders and the world would speak badly."

"I will be a yogini."

"If you become a yogini it won't look good. We can't live together. I have taken on fakirhood, immortal fakirhood, and you are my mother, so how could I take you with me?"

Now the queen said, "Hey King, if I had known you were born to be a yogi I would have stayed with my father, and I would never have got married. How was I to know that you were born to be a yogi?

"I would never have got married, I would have stayed a virgin, and worshiped the *pīpal* tree[43] at my father's house. But you are leaving me in the middle."

"Queen, don't stand there quarreling, because my company is about to leave for Badari Nath. Why are you standing there and quarreling? Fortune wrote in my karma, and she wrote 'immortal fakirhood' and there is no remover."

So that's the way the queen lamented. Then the king said, "Queen, don't lament, and give me alms, I must have alms, it is my guru's powerful command, so don't delay."

Hey, Guru Sovereign! Indescribable! Indestructible!

(Bh 3.8.e)

Honored Queen . . .
Feast me a meal from your hand, my queen,
    from your hand,
And make the guru's portion too, Queen Pingala.
You must realize, female species, and accept what I say!
Accept what I say, female species.
Quit being stubborn, female species, and
    accept what I say!

43. Worship of the *pīpal* tree is associated with virgin daughters.

Honored King . . .
Place your campfire in the Cloud Castle,[44]
   my husband in the castle.
Place your meditation seat in the portal, and
   do *tapas*[45] at my door.
Oh yes, do *tapas* only here, ruler,
   You must realize, Bharthari,
you must realize, Bharthari Panvar of Dhara Nagar,
Ujjain City's ruler, you've gone and left me destitute.

Honored King . . .
What is moonlight without the moon,
   my husband?
What is night without the stars?
   you must realize, Bharthari.
What is night without the stars?
   you must realize, Bharthari.
You must realize, Bharthari Panvar of Dhara Nagar,
you're the master of my union but
you've gone and left me destitute.

Honored Queen . . .
If I place my campfire here, the smoke will fly up,
   my lovely queen, it will fly up.
The Color Palace will be blackened, Queen Pingala,
the Color Palace will be blackened, my Queen Pingala.
You must realize, female species, and
accept what I say.

Honored King . . .
If the kingdom be blackened,
or the palace, my husband,
I will double their color,
   you must realize, Bharthari,
I will double their color!

---

44. *bādaḷmahal;* described in the *RSK* as the "best and most beautiful castle,"
and a "place of merriment and pleasure."

45. *Tapas* is often translated as "ascetic feats"; literally it is heat or ardor. I retain
it in the original throughout this translation where it usually vaguely indicates appropriate yogic practices.

You must realize, Bharthari Panvar,
do *tapas* at my door.
Yes, do *tapas* at my door, ruler,
You must realize, Bharthari.

Honored King . . .
Who tied the yellow wedding bracelets,
    my husband, the wedding bracelets?
Who tied the wedding crest on your head?
    you must realize, Bharthari,
Who tied the wedding crest on your head?
    you must realize. Bharthari.
You must realize, Bharthari Panvar of Dhara Nagar,
you're the master of my union but
you've gone and left me destitute.

Honored Queen . . .
The Brahman tied the yellow wedding bracelets,
    my queen, the bracelets.
The Barber tied the wedding crest on my head,
    you must realize, female.
You must realize, female species, and
accept what I say.

Honored King . . .
Let lightning strike the Brahman,
    my husband, lightning,
Let a black snake bite the Barber,
    you must realize, Bharthari,
Let a black snake bite the Barber,
    you must realize, Bharthari.
You must realize, Bharthari Panvar of Dhara Nagar,
you're the master of my union but
you've gone and left me destitute.

(Bh 3.9.s)

So she had lamented all this much, but even so what happened?
He said, "Queen, now you have lamented about everything, and you
want lightning to strike down the Barber, you want a black snake to
bite whomever, whatever you want, but if you are going to prepare a
meal and feast me at this campfire, do it, or else I will pack up and

go right now. Today you see my face, but afterwards you will not
see it."

So, weeping, the queen went back and prepared food. She prepared
food and came back and fed it to Bharthari Baba. She fed him and
she put down a special portion for the Guru Sovereign.

"Hey, King Bharthari, I didn't know you were born to be a yogi,
and I burned up, so why did you make me stand up again?"

[*The audience laughs at this bitter irony*]

She fed him and kept up her lamentation. After the food was
prepared, she took him inside the castle and feasted him a good meal.

"Take the special portion for the Guru Sovereign and go, sir, go."

She gave him a send-off and he went back to the campfire.

/To Gorakh Nath's campfire./

To Gorakh Nath's.

(Bh 3.9.e)

Honored King[46] . . .
My blouse was never wet with milk, husband,
   my blouse,
And a boy child never played in my lap,
   you must realize, Bharthari,
A boy child never played in my lap.
You must realize, Bharthari,
You must realize, Bharthari Panvar of Dhara Nagar,
Dhara Nagar's ruler left me destitute.

Honored King . . .
Feast on food from my hand,
my husband, from my hand.
Take the guru's portion, O King Bharthari,
Then give me *darśan* once again, Innocent Nath,
   you must realize, Bharthari.
You must realize, Bharthari Panvar of Dhara Nagar,
You're the master of my union but
you've gone and left me destitute.

Honored King . . .
He picked up his campfire

46. This is the final segment of Bh 3.

from the portal now, King Bharthari,
he shouldered his sack,
King Bharthari.
Now the yogi got up, you must realize, Bharthari.
[*A brief musical interlude in GC* rāg *2, and a return to it*]

A seated yogi's a stake in the ground,
but a yogi once up is a fistful of wind.
Yes Baba became the wind's own form
and turned his face toward the Kajali Woods.

He crossed one woods,
Bharthari crossed a second woods, then
he crossed the third woods.
Yes in the third woods, Lord,
Baba reached the guru's campfire.

He reached the campfire
and bowed his head to the guru,
he bowed his head.
"Baba take this special portion of Pingala's,
My guru, feast on my food.

"My guru I stayed on the road, Baba,
I stayed on the road.
I called everyone
'Mother' and 'Sister.'
Yes Baba take this food, Gorakh Baba,
I called the queen 'Mother' and brought it.

"Baba, now feast on your food,
from the queen today,
from my Queen Pingala."

Speak: Victory to Bharthari Baba! Speak: Victory to Guru Gorakh
Sovereign! O Lord Shankar, now Bharthari Baba is complete.

(Bh 3.10.s)

The Tale of King Gopi Chand

Gopi Chand's Birth Story

Introduction

Just as we learn nothing of Bharthari himself in his birth story, we learn very little of Gopi Chand in the first part of his tale. However, Gopi Chand's destiny is shaped more explicitly than is Bharthari's by the circumstances of his birth. A number of critical motifs are introduced in this briefest of the tale's four parts: Gopi Chand's personal beauty, the guru's love for him, and most of all the fact that he is "borrowed" by his mother. Gopi Chand literally "owes" his life to the guru Jalindar. He was a yogi before his birth and is destined to return to that state. Gorakh Nath plays a backstage part in Bharthari's procreation, for it is his magic power that allows the donkey progenitor to win Pan De. But Jalindar is the direct agent of Gopi Chand's conception—reducing his handsome disciple to ashes (not for the last time) and giving them to Manavati Mother to "lick up."

Whereas Bharthari's birth story begins with a father's curse and continues with a tale of bride-winning from a male viewpoint, Gopi Chand's has a completely maternal perspective throughout. King Bharthari's sister, Manavati (called Manavati Mother or Manavati Mata), is the central character in Gopi Chand's birth story. Like his eventual initiation as a yogi, Gopi Chand's birth as a king is engineered by Manavati. Although his birth involves a divinity's personal intervention and a yogi's loan, the story is far less fanciful to villagers than that of the talking donkey and his gold and silver palaces. Indeed, to village audiences the barren woman's desperate search for divine assistance is deeply familiar.

Manavati's tale of running from deity to deity, and of making appropriately pleasing offerings to each, resembles personal experiences I often heard narrated and several times witnessed, while I was living in Ghatiyali (Gold 1988, 149–54). Even the queen mother's temporary disgust with the fruitlessness of such activities and the subsequent revelation—inspiring redoubled faith—that there is one god who has not been tried but who just may do the trick, are patterns well known to modern villagers.

Once Manavati presents herself in the yogis' camp in the Chapala Garden, we are in more exotic territory; few if any villagers have walked among crowds of yogis. Gorakh Nath strides through Bharthari's story as a lone apparition of striking and singular power, but Jalindar Nath is always surrounded by disciples (visible and invisible). Despite the extraordinary nature of their numbers and way of life, Jalindar's cohorts are portrayed in a manner that coincides with villagers' notions about run-of-the-mill yogis. They are not a terribly attractive lot. Rather, except for Gopi Chand, the two chief disciples, Charpat and Hada, and Jalindar himself, the massed yogis are deficient characters: crippled, ugly, aged. In the opinion of many Rajasthani peasants yogis are a scruffy group among whom one in a thousand might be the real thing.

Charpat Nath's encounter with Hira Dasi is almost a replica of Gopi Chand's future confrontations with two sets of slave girls, as well as of Bharthari's with Pingala's maidservants. Yet a few noteworthy and revealing differences stand out within the stock exchanges, insults, and misunderstandings. Gopi Chand and Bharthari want bread, but Charpat wants milk. Sharing daily bread represents the intimacy and substantial identity that is the hallmark of family unity in rural India. Milk does not transfer pollution in the way bread does; rather it is food that can be given to higher castes or even to deities.

Gopi Chand and Bharthari vent their anger by striking an impudent slave girl on her back, but Charpat contents himself with a blow to a rock. The effect is the same: the slave girl stops arguing and takes a message to the queen. But Charpat dazzles, rather than beating her into doing his errand. Gopi Chand and Bharthari, despite their yogis' costumes, react personally and viscerally to jibes from their "purchased" women. Charpat's relative self-restraint reflects his genuine noninvolvement in the householder's world; he has come on a mission for the guru that means nothing to him. In short, Gopi

Chand and Bharthari in the guise of begging yogis are still connected
in several ways to palace life; Charpat Nath is not. Another salient
factor, of course, is that neither Bharthari nor Gopi Chand is enough
of a yogi to turn rocks to gold.

Text

"Gopi Chand, abide in prayer,[1] son,
Praise the true Master,[2] O Gopi Chand,
king and king's son, darling boy,[3]
Recite prayers, my dear darling boy,
and your body[4] will be immortal.
My son, be a yogi, my dear darling boy,
and your body will be immortal."

"My mother, the earth is ashamed, my birth-giver,
the sky is ashamed, Manavati Mother,
king's daughter.
My birth-giver, aren't you ashamed? Mother and birth-giver,
queen from the Color Palace.[5]
My mother, you have only one son, mother and birth-giver,
on whom you are forcing yoga.
My mother, God won't reward you, birth-giver,
Our stars favor prosperity.[6]

---

1. *samaraṇ samaraṇ bhajaṇoṅ. Samaraṇ* (H. *simran*) means constant recitation of
God's name or names; the verb *bhajaṇo* has eighteen glosses in the *RSK*, including
"to recite God's name" and "to be absorbed, to take refuge, to accept, to embrace."
Manavati Mata is giving her son practical advice.
2. *sāñchā ī nāth.* The term *nāth* as used here is a name of God but also evokes
the Nath yogis, among whom Gopi Chand is numbered, and the Nath *jāti*, of which
the singer is a member (see chapter 2).
3. *lālā;* a very affectionate word for male babies, used as a term of endearment
for any male younger than the speaker.
4. *kāyā;* although explicitly perishable, *kāyā* is more than *śarīr*, the physical body;
it is the perishable body endowed with a soul. Elsewhere (Gold 1988) I translated
kāyā, awkwardly, as "body-soul."
5. *rang mahal;* to translate this as "ladies' palace" because it describes where
the royal women dwell would take away the implications of *rang* or "color"—
implications of enticement and pleasure.
6. *ugamāī bhalā satārā.* According to Bhoju, the message here is that only poor
folk become yogis!

"My mother, who, when born a king,
turns yogi and departs?
Manavati Mother, king's daughter,
Tell me the hidden tale of such a one,
 my mother and birth-giver,
and I will do your bidding."

"My son, Rama was a yogi, son,
Lakshman was a yogi,
My darling boy, on Kailash Mountain, Bhola Nath,[7]
 my darling boy,
who created the earth.
My darling boy, I'll tell you someone closer,
 my dear darling boy,
your uncle Bharthari,
My son, in an instant he abandoned Ujjain's kingdom,
 darling boy.
He turned yogi and went."

"My mother, I have eleven hundred queens,
sixteen hundred slave girls,
My birth-giver, they will eat opium-poison and die,
 birth-giver,
Why did you get me married?"

"My son, whose are the queens? Gopi Chand,
whose are the slave girls?
My darling boy, Time will eat them,[8] my dear darling boy.
But your body will be immortal.

"My darling boy, the kingdom you rule, Gopi Chand,
will dissolve.[9]
My darling boy, become a yogi, my dear darling boy,
and your body will be immortal."

---

7. The first three examples that Manavati Mother glibly gives are not quite
to the point; Rama and Lakshman spent twelve years exiled in the forest but did
not renounce the world to become yogis. Bhola Nath is a name of the god Shiva,
who was never a worldly king; he is, however, famous for straddling ascetic and
worldly modes of being (O'Flaherty 1973).
   8. *khāl khā jāve;* Time (H. *kāl*) is death.
   9. *paralā ma jāsī.* Bhoju told me that *paralā* meant a torrential rain, but in the
RSK it is the Rajasthani for Sanskrit and Hindi *pralay*—the total cosmic dissolution
that occurs cyclically in Hindu time.

"My mother, give me another twelve years.
Let me rule,
let me ride horseback,
My birth-giver, I won't break this promise to you,
    birth-giver,
Later, I'll be a yogi."

"My son, twelve years? Gopi Chand,
Who gets them? My dear Gopi Chand,
My son, don't count on a moment, darling boy,
Time will eat you.
My son, be a yogi, my dear darling boy,
and your body will be immortal."

His mother had said all this,
now what did Gopi Chand declare?
"My birth-giver, without yogis, my mother and birth-giver,
you wouldn't have obtained a son,
My mother, yogis do *tapas* in the woods,
    my mother and birth-giver,
but you live in purdah.[10]
My mother, without yogis, my mother and birth-giver,
You wouldn't have obtained a son."

Sovereign Shiva! Indescribable! Indestructible!

(GC 1.1.s)

Gopi Chand was a king. His mother was childless. She had no son,
so this is what she did: every day she feasted one hundred *sādhus*[11]
and one hundred Brahmans. She served them feasts fit for Brahmans.
She also made gifts of one hundred cows. She did this for the sake
of merit.[12]

---

10. Purdah, literally a curtain, "covers" a whole set of practices that are sometimes described as "the seclusion of women" although this seclusion is more symbolic
than actual in rural life. A woman who "keeps purdah" would not normally leave
her husband's house.

11. *Sādhu* is a general term for any religious mendicant or monk or saint.

12. *puṇ;* Sanskrit and Hindi *puṇya*. The concept of merit for rural North Indian
Hindus is associated with intangible rewards gained through good works. *Puṇya* is
understood as a kind of karma or action with effect, however refined. The accumulation of *puṇya* may help a soul toward a better birth without granting the ultimate
aim of liberation from birth and death.

She gave one hundred cows every day. And she gave honorariums[13] of gold to the *sādhu*s and Brahmans, two golden coins to each.

After feasting them, she gave them honorariums of two golden coins.

[*Aside to Ann and Daniel:* Yes, she gave generously to them after feasting them, but you won't be able to give so generously to me, after having me sing. *There is general laughter.*]

Then she said to Gopi Chand, "Son, give up the kingdom and become a yogi. I brought you as a twelve-year loan. I brought you as a loan, after I served the guru and Lord Shankar. So be a yogi, son, and your body will be immortal."

"But Manavati Mother, I have fifty-two portals,[14] I have fifty-three doorways, I have the rule over twelve districts, and a court of justice in my house. And I'm married to eleven hundred queens. Now I am the master of the kingdom."

And after him there was no younger brother, none at all.

"And now if I become a yogi, then to whom will I entrust the care of my kingdom? If I become a yogi, Manavati Mother, I won't be at all satisfied. I've ruled for twelve years and you say, 'Be a yogi.' Give me twelve more years to rule. And allow me to ride, to ride horseback. And later I won't break my promise to you, mother. Later I will be a yogi. Let me rule for twelve more years."

"Who gets eleven or twelve years, son?" his mother said. "Who gets twelve years, son, you can't count on a moment. And then there's the promise to the Guru Sovereign — that promise must be fulfilled or Time will eat you. If Time eats you, and you're dead, then who will enjoy these queens and slave girls? But if you become a yogi, son, your body will be immortal."

Then Gopi Chand said, "But mother, you live in purdah inside the palace, and yogis live in the jungle. They do *tapas* by their campfires in the jungle. But you live in the palace. So, how did you come to know any yogis?

---

13. *dakṣiṇā;* in Sanskrit ritual, an additional gift, a final pay-off to a priest or preceptor.

14. *ḍoḍyāṅ;* f.pl. of *ḍoḍī,* an architectural feature of Indian castles described as, among other things, a little room that one passes through to enter a big house; since this is one definition of portal, I settled on portal. Elsewhere (misled by village informants unfamiliar with palaces) I translated *ḍoḍī* as balcony.

"Within your domain, mother, are goddesses and gods: Mataji, Bhairuji, Salagramji.[15] And there are a lot of ghosts and spirits, too. If you had worshiped them and taken a son, then you wouldn't be making me a yogi." That's what Gopi Chand said.

Manavati Mata said, "Look son, for twelve years I followed their rules,[16] for twelve years." What rules? The ones about how to worship deities.

"Besides that, for twelve years I performed dharma[17] and meditation, and besides that I feasted one hundred *sādhu*s and one hundred Brahmans, and besides that I gave gifts to one hundred cows, and I built a temple for Salagramji. And for Mataji and Bhairuji and all the deities I built shrine-platforms.[18] I staked flagpoles with waving banners above the temples at those deities' places,[19] and every day I supplied soaked chickpea-offerings[20] to all the deities. Whoever ate saltless bread and coconuts, to them I gave saltless bread and coconuts; whoever ate goats, to them I gave goats. If they ate buffalo, I offered up buffalo. Every day I offered up red paste[21] and I worshiped them all for twelve years. I performed dharma and meditation. But it wasn't in my fate. There was no son written for me."[22]

So twelve years went by, twelve years of dharma and meditation. And then she gave up dharma and meditation. She gave it up and

---

15. Mataji may refer to any village goddess; Bhairuji is a particularly important minor deity in this part of Rajasthan and is often associated with cures for barren women; Salagramji is a small black stone, worshiped as a form of Vishnu.

16. *niyam rākhnā;* not perfectly translated by "follow the rules," for it implies internal discipline as well as external precision in maintaining the good habits and ritual observances demanded by any given deity.

17. Moral conduct; here a coverall for appropriate religious acts.

18. She distinguishes thus between Salagramji who, as a form of Vishnu, would reside in a temple and the regional deities who are usually enshrined on roofless platforms.

19. A flagpole with a long pennant is one highly visible, moderately costly, and therefore pleasing offering often made to local gods in Rajasthan.

20. *baḷ bākaḷ; baḷ* is a sacrificial offering; *bākaḷā* is defined in the *RSK* as boiled grains offered to gods or ghosts but in Ghatiyali refers to soaked chickpeas—of which Bhairuji is especially fond.

21. *kāmī;* a paste made of red power and clarified butter that is smeared on icons to beautify and please them.

22. See Gold 1988, 149–54, for barren women's transactions with deities in Rajasthan of which this is a realistic, if somewhat exaggerated, description.

made a resolution:[23] "I won't give even a smidgeon of butter-offering[24] to any god at all." She made a resolution: "Now I won't even give the raw ingredients for one meal to any Brahman. And I won't even give a scrap of bread to any indigent person." She made a resolution against doing dharma and merit.

(GC 1.1.e)

"Now, I won't even toss a scrap to a stray mutt. And if any Brahman should come, if any *sādhu* should come, I won't even hand out a pinch of flour." Thus she swore an oath.

For three days after making this resolution she did nothing for dharma or merit. The third night came, the third night . . . and there was Lord Shankar, in the form of a boy, and he had locks like this on his head.

[*As he said*, like this, *Madhu Nath gestured to Ann, who had curly, unruly hair:* Like yours]

Like this, falling all over his head. And ashes, ashes were smeared on Baba, all over Lord Shankar.

[*Addressing Ann:* Do you know Lord Shankar?

Ann: Yes, I know Lord Shankar.]

Yes, it was Lord Shankar, Mahadev himself.

It was twelve midnight when he came, and the night watchman was making his rounds.

On his feet he was wearing wooden sandals, and in his hand he carried iron tongs. And on his shoulder he had a sack. And he cried "*Alakh!*" in the portal of the palace, at midnight, and sounded his horn.[25] Lord Shankar sounded his horn and said, "Manavati Mata, give alms, my mother. A yogi is standing in the portal. Give alms!"

Then Manavati Mata said, "Yogi, just go away the same way you came. I have given up dharma and merit. I have made a resolution. I will not even toss a scrap to a stray mutt. I won't give any alms to any *sādhu* or saint. So go away. For twelve years I gave away much

23. *samkalp;* a Sanskritic term for a vow or resolution normally made before some difficult religious undertaking such as a pilgrimage; its use here in the negative sense is clearly ironic.

24. *dhūp;* specifically clarified butter (*ghī*) poured over smouldering cow-dung cakes; it is the most essential ingredient for the worship of local deities in rural Rajasthan.

25. The description of Shiva's appearance and actions is typical of all descriptions of yogis in Madhu's tales.

wealth, and I had great faith in the deities, and I worshiped them a lot. But now I will give no burnt offerings to any deity, nor will I do anything for the sake of dharma or merit.

Then Lord Shankar said: "Hey Manavati Mata,

> Don't give up truth, O brave one,
> or you'll lose your honor too.
> Bound to truth is Mother Lakshmi,
> and she'll return to you.[26]

Without a pillar the sky is buttressed. Truthful work is the channel for merit."[27]

And she said, "Babaji, for twelve whole years, I feasted you *sādhus* but for three days I haven't given any feasts—that's why you have come to restore dharma. Isn't there a program for a feast somewhere else? It's three days since I've stopped giving daily feasts, as I did for twelve years, and you've come to restore truth. Just leave the same way you came. Yogi, I've given up truth and dharma. I worshiped the deities a lot and I also did a lot of dharma and meditation, but I met no son-giver on the face of the earth."

Then Lord Shankar spoke, "Manavati Mata, you must have worshiped pebbles and rocks—stones. If you had worshiped me, me, if you had worshiped me, then your job would have been perfectly done. What can come of worshiping rocks and pebbles?"

As soon as he said this, Manavati Mata opened the door of the palace and ran and clasped Shankar's feet. She fell at his feet saying "Hey, Grain-giver, who are you? Where have you been? I worshiped the thirty-three *karoṛ* of deities, but who are you? Tell me, where is your place?"

"Manavati Mata, in the Chapala Garden,[28] beneath a jasmine tree is an icon of Shankar. When did you ever worship that good Shankar?"

---

26. This rhymed couplet or *dohā* is a local saying.

27. The cumulative meaning of these enigmatic statements seems to be that Manavati Mata should have faith (as the sky stays up without a pillar), and if she continues her truthful work she will receive what she desires; Lakshmi, the goddess of prosperity and well-being, will not abandon her.

28. The Chapala Garden is a place that recurs throughout both tales—usually as a campsite for yogis, but it is also where Pingala's cremation and return to life took place in Bharthari 2.

"Alas, Grain-giver, I never worshiped you. I never even remembered Shankar. I was lost, circling around the other deities. And I never even remembered Mahadev, nor did I worship him."

"So if you never worshiped me, why are you faulting me? When did you ever worship me? And you are faulting me, and I never even ate your burnt offerings."

Manavati Mata took five Brahmans with her, and she took a tin of clarified butter. In with the butter she mixed saffron and musk, raisins and dates, almonds, raisins, and dates. And she took fine milk sweets. And she began to perform fire oblations over there. Where? In the Chapala Garden, Shankar's place.

And Manavati Mata stood on one foot. For three nights and three days, she remained standing, "Shiv, Shiv, Shiv, Shiv" she kept on praying all night and day. "O Shankar, O Shankar, O Shankar." And she had an altar set up by Brahmans. And they made butter oblations and milk-sweet oblations into the fire.

After only three days Lord Shankar was pleased, and as soon as he was pleased he came to Manavati Mata and said: "Ask and what you ask will be. If your kingdom is too small then I will double or quadruple it; if your riches and property are too little, then I will fill your treasury with diamonds and rubies; just ask, and whatever you ask will be."

She said, "O Baba, my kingdom is great, and I haven't the least shortage of riches or property, so give me a protector of the kingdom,[29] a boy, give a child, because I have no protector of the kingdom."

Lord Shankar said, "Manavati Mata, it's not in your fate. It's not written by Fortune. So where can I get you a son? You came from God's house a totally barren woman."[30]

She said, "Grain-giver, why not, why isn't it written for me?"

"It's not in your fate."

"So, Grain-giver, your promise is broken, your promise is broken, the one you made me, you gave me a promise. Over there, in the palace, you said that my job would be perfectly done. So, do my job perfectly, Baba, or else your promise is broken."

"Manavati Mata, I won't break my promise. There's another yogi

29. That is, an heir.
30. *banjharī;* a term used for a barren woman, often as an insult or a curse.

doing *tapas,* one Jalindar Nathji. Where? Right over there, in this garden. That yogi has fourteen hundred disciples doing *tapas* secretly, and fourteen hundred disciples doing *tapas* visibly, on the earth. Jalindar Baba. [Jalindar Nath/ Yes, the one with saffron burning[31] in his campfire. Go to him, fall at his feet, and that yogi will be pleased. Then I will have one of his disciples given to you."

Manavati Mata turned and left Mahadev and now—Jalindar Baba's feet.

/She falls at his feet./

(GC 1.2.e)

Manavati Mata went to Jalindar Baba, whose eyelids were lowered as he was repeating prayers. She prostrated herself, respectfully greeting the Guru Sovereign. But he didn't speak. He had lowered his eyelids. Who? Jalindar Baba.

Fourteen hundred disciples of his were doing *tapas* secretly, within the earth, and fourteen hundred disciples were doing *tapas* visibly. Among the visible disciples Charpat Nath[32] was the chief, and he stood by the campfire. Jalindar Baba had closed his eyelids.

Saffron was burning in his campfire, crackling, and Baba had shut his eyelids. As soon as Manavati Mata came she prostrated herself respectfully. "Hey Guru Sovereign," she implored him. She prostrated herself three or four times, and then she stood there for about an entire hour, but the Guru Sovereign didn't awaken. He didn't awaken, so Manavati Mata got mad. She said, "Well! A very surprising thing has happened! I am a queen, and I have prostrated myself in greeting to him, but he has taken no notice. Well, yogi, I am no less than you. You keep your eyelids closed for six months, but I will shut mine for twelve years."

Then Manavati Mata took the shawl with which she was wrapped and folded it up into a pillow and went to sleep beside the campfire.

Now Manavati Mata shut her eyes and did not awaken for twelve years. And rain poured down, in the rainy season, from *Śrāvan* to *Bhādvā.*[33] So Manavati Mata disintegrated. Termites ate her; scor-

---

31. Saffron is in India, as in the West, highly precious, so to burn it is a sign of profligacy in which only a very powerful yogi would indulge.

32. Charpat Nath is a figure mentioned in other Nath lore; verses attributed to him appear in collections of Rajasthani devotional literature.

33. June-July and July-August, when rainfall is heaviest in Rajasthan.

pions hatched in her mouth. And mango, lemon, and orange trees sprang up in the middle of her stomach, in her intestines.

She died, she actually died, and a termite hill of clay rose there.[34] She died. She went to sleep in that yogi's shelter,[35] and twelve years passed. Twelve years passed and a great big tree grew in her stomach.

Twelve years were over, and Jalindar Baba's eyelids opened. As soon as they were open, he said to Charpat Nath, "Oh no, Charpat my son, you've neglected sweeping around my campfire. Look, over here's a termite hill, and over there a tree has sprung up."

"Hey, Guru Sovereign, I sweep around the campfire every day, but King Taloki Chand's[36] queen, Manavati Mata, came into your shelter and went to sleep. She threw herself into your shelter, and you didn't wake up. Twelve years have gone by, father of a daughter! In twelve years she became a termite hill, right here. She died, so lemon and orange trees grew in her intestines. Now what will I do with her? If I sweep out the refuse, then where will I dump this queen?"

"Oh, so she's a queen is she?"

"Yes, she is King Taloki Chand's queen, Manavati Mata."

"OK, son, then uproot these trees and plant them in the garden and quickly search through that termite hill and take out her bones—find the ribs and wristbones of that one eaten by termites."

So he put Manavati Mata's fleshless bones back together, joint by joint, and over them he circled his tin with life-giving elixir.[37] As soon as he circled that tin, she was standing there, and she prostrated herself and then stood with her hands pressed together. "Hey Baba, Jalindar Baba, I did not awaken before you did. You woke up first. So now, Baba, twelve years have gone by. I've been doing *tapas*, and now I am standing at your service. Twelve years have gone by, and now you have opened your eyelids."

Having heard that much, Jalindar Baba said, "Manavati Mother, ask and whatever you ask will be. If you want wealth, then you will

34. The image of a person in meditation so deep that termites build hills on top is a conventional one in Rajasthani folklore.

35. To be in the shelter (*śaraṇ*) of a deity or powerful person has particular implications of surrender and asymmetrical reciprocity (Wadley 1975).

36. One of the few references in the text to Gopi Chand's father.

37. *sarajīvaṇ kūṁpo;* a *kūṁpo* (*kupī, RSK*) is a type of metal can in common use in the village. It is small and round with a long narrow spout in the center.

have no shortage; if you want a greater kingdom, then I will double or quadruple it; and if you want liberation then I will send you to the city of heaven."[38]

"I have no lack of wealth, and my kingdom is great. Just give me a protector of the kingdom, give me a boy. I need a child to rule the kingdom."

"Hey Manavati Mata, it's not written in your fate. You came from God's house a barren woman, and a son is not written for you."

"Baba, your promise is broken. I spent twelve years doing *tapas*, and Lord Shankar promised: 'Serve that yogi and he will be pleased, and you will get a son.' So, Baba, you're breaking Shankar's promise."

Then Jalindar Baba said, "Hey, Manavati Mata, it's not written for you, it's not written in the womb. But I can give you one of my disciples, who, after ruling for twelve years must be given back to be a yogi. I will give him for only twelve years. Twelve years as a little boy, a mere boy, laughing and playing, those I will not count. When he becomes the kingdom's king, master of the throne—he has another twelve years—let him rule. Then make him a yogi and his body will be immortal. If not, Time devours him. You may take him from among my disciples."

Then Manavati Mata said, "Hey Grain-giver, better than sonlessness is twelve years. If that's all, well, OK. If all you can give is twelve years, Grain-giver, then give it. It's not written for me, so give me twelve years only, right now, and at least the stigma of barrenness will be removed, and I will have some pleasure. Afterwards I will make him a yogi."

"Manavati Mata, come tomorrow. Now go back to your palace. In the morning a yogi will come, and you should have him served alms of milk. That's all, pour in alms of milk and your job will be done."

So Manavati Mother went back to the palace, and in the morning he sent a yogi, he sent a disciple.

(GC 1.3.e)

---

38. Liberation (*mokṣa*) refers to release from endless rounds of birth and death—the ultimate aim of life for Hindus. This sentence of Jalindar's shows the merging in popular understanding of "liberation" with "heaven" (see Gold 1988, 233–41).

The next day dawned, and the Guru Sovereign ordered Charpat Nath: "Son, go and get alms of milk from the palace of Manavati Mata. Bring back alms of milk."

So Charpat Nath took his sack-and-stuff, his iron tongs-and-stuff, and he put on his sandals-and-stuff. Then he took his gourd-and-stuff in his hand. A seated yogi's a stake in the ground, but a yogi once up is a fistful of wind. The Nath took the wind's own form and turned his face toward the land of Bengal.

As soon as he entered the city he went to the palace. He passed through one portal, he passed through a second portal, and in the third portal he called, "*Alakh!*" He called "*Alakh!*" and he sounded his horn instrument. Who? Charpat Nath. As soon as he called "*Alakh!*" his voice came to Manavati Mother's ears. And as soon as she heard it, she said to her slave girl, "Slave girl, today a yogi is calling "*Alakh!*" at the gate. Fill a platter with diamonds and rubies and take it to him, give him alms. Ask for a blessing, and give him fine alms."

Then the slave girl filled a golden platter with diamonds and rubies and placed it on the palm of her hand. She passed through one portal, she passed through the second portal. In the third portal was a yogi to whom she called: "Hey, yogi, from which city do you come and go, for you strike me as an established Nath.[39] Raise your eyelids, Baba Nath, I have come to take your *darśan*."

Once she had said this, Charpat Nath raised his eyelids. Then she said, "Take these alms, Baba, I have come to take your *darśan*, and I have brought a platter filled with diamonds and rubies."

"Oh slave girl, why have you brought these pebbles and rocks, why have you brought a platter filled with stones? I will take alms of milk."

Then the slave girl said, "Is this a holy man or a prankster—a yogi or what? You're not a yogi at all, you seem to me to be sick. A yogi, father of a daughter! Yesterday or day before yesterday, troubled by hunger, you were a householder's boy, dying of hunger, and that's why you became a yogi, so it seems. So now you desire a scrap of bread for your alms. You're no yogi! I brought a platter filled with diamonds and rubies. If you took them, yogi, you could bathe

---

39. *ṭhakāṇā hālo;* literally, someone from a large estate—in other words not a piece of human flotsam.

in Malva,[40] go to Gujarat, go to all Four Established Places.[41] For the rest of your lifetime, all you'd have to do would be sleep and eat, and still you wouldn't use it up—a platter of diamonds and rubies. But you have called them pebbles and stones. Yogi, if there were leaves in the middle of your destiny, then they would fly away, but it seems that a big rock is tangled there. That's why you have called diamonds and rubies 'pebbles.'"[42]

As soon as she had spoken, Charpat replied, "OK, slave girl, there's a big stone caught in my fate. Do these rocks serve the purpose of food, huh? Nowadays do we wander about for money? Do we wander about for currency notes? Are they something to eat? What use are these pebbles and stones, these diamonds and rubies? They are hardly good for eating. Slave girl, bring me some alms of milk."

"Look at the yogi! It's a platter of diamonds and rubies and he's crying for milk."

Then Charpat Nath got angry. There was a big flat stone lying there, weighing five or ten maunds,[43] and he struck it with his tongs, saying, "If you want wealth, take this from me," and he turned the entire stone to gold.

As soon as he turned it to gold, the slave girl shut her eyes. "Uh oh! This yogi is some weird miracle-worker!" And the slave girl ran away. She ran away and said to the queen, "Hey Grain-giver, honored queen, today it's your son-giver. He struck a flat rock with his tongs and turned it to gold, so go at once."

Manavati Mata rushed to the balcony to see the baba: "Hey Baba, what can I do for you?"

"Hey Manavati Mata, I have a desire for milk, bring me milk."

She said to the slave girl, "Bring our kingdom's twelve huge milk pots, and fill his gourd."

40. Malva is a region of Madhya Pradesh—idyllic pastoral country in Rajasthani lore.

41. *chār dhām;* four major pilgrimage centers (Badarinath, Puri, Rameshvaram, and Dvarka) located in each of the cardinal directions on the subcontinent; to journey to all four sites is beyond the financial means and adventurous spirit of most rural Rajasthanis.

42. This speech is almost identical with other speeches made by slave girls to Gopi Chand in parts 2 and 3. Charpat's response, however, is very different from Gopi Chand's.

43. One maund, a unit of weight that seems to have passed from India into British usage at some point, is currently considered equal to forty kilograms.

Then the slave girl emptied one milk pot into his gourd but the milk didn't even cover the bottom. She emptied the second, and the bottom was not covered. She emptied seven or eight pots. Then Queen Manavati Mata came: "Girl, let's see if there isn't a hole in this gourd."

"Manavati Mother, when this gourd overflows with milk, then your promise will be fulfilled. If not, then it won't be."

She said to the slave girl, "Pour in all the milk from our twelve milk pots, and run to the village, and demand the villagers' milk. Have it collected, for . . . 'When the king gives a summons old women come running'[44] . . . so we'll be able to fill the gourd."

"No, Manavati Mother, I won't take the milk of others."

/I will take only yours./

"That's enough, I will take only yours." So she emptied in seven pots, she emptied eight, she emptied ten, she emptied eleven. As soon as she emptied the twelfth pot the gourd overflowed.

That was enough. Baba was pleased and said, "Enough, you have filled up my gourd."

She said, "Baba, your desire is fulfilled, so now what?"

"Manavati Mata, the Guru Sovereign orders you to come in the morning to his campfire in the garden."

So Charpat Nath left, and his gourd was full. He went back to the garden and emptied his gourd into a huge cauldron, and all the yogis filled their gourds from it. He gave all the yogis milk to drink. The disciples drank alms of milk, and the Guru Sovereign drank too, and all of them were pleased. And as soon as day broke, Manavati Mata came back. She came to get a son.

(GC 1.4.e)

> Manavati Mata
> at the break of day
> went into the garden.[45]
> Mother went to the campfire,
> the guru's campfire.
> Mother went to the campfire
> and fell at the yogi's feet.

44. Here this proverb may simply imply that as queen, Manavati can commandeer the villagers' milk if she desires.

45. This is the final sung segment of GC 1.

As soon as she fell at his feet,
   what did Baba Jalindar say?
"Mother, no son is written for you, birth-giver,
   I shall give you one disciple.

"For twelve years
   have him rule the kingdom,
   Have the kingdom ruled, Mother.
Later make him a yogi, my mother and birth-giver,
   as a yogi he'll be immortal.

"If you don't bring him to yoga,
   then Time will eat him,
   Time will eat him.
But if you make him a yogi, my mother and birth-giver,
   as a yogi he'll be immortal.

"Fourteen hundred disciples of mine
   are doing *tapas* visibly,
   Mother, doing *tapas* visibly.
Go, and pick one of these fourteen hundred disciples,
      the one that pleases you,
   and that's the disciple you will receive."

Now Manavati Mata looked at
   the fourteen hundred disciples,
   their campfires were burning,
   as the yogis recited prayers.
Seated amidst them all
   was Gopi Chand.
Gopi Chand's campfire was in the center;
   there he stayed amidst the yogis.

On his foot a lotus
   sparkled,
   on his left arm a jewel
   gleamed, it gleamed
   on Gopi Chand,
And on his forehead a moon so bright, it seemed as if
      the sun were rising in the garden;
   Mother was pleased.

"Baba, a boy has pleased me today, yogi,
  now you please me.

"Baba, on his foot a lotus
  sparkles, and on his left arm
  a jewel gleams.
Baba, on his forehead a moon, yogi,
  so that's the boy for me."

When Manavati Mother had said this much,
what did Jalindar Baba say
    to Mother?
"Mother, don't tear out my liver, my mother
    and birth-giver,
  many disciples fill the garden."

"Baba, lend me that disciple,
  give that very one to me.
If not you break your promise, Baba Nath yogi,
  you break your promise to me.

"How can you break your promise, yogi,
  how can you break it?"
So Baba called to Gopi Chand,
"Come here,
  Son, go now, Gopi Chand, my darling boy,
  Now you must rule the kingdom."

Baba called Gopi Chand,
  called Gopi Chand,
  and seated him by the campfire.
The yogi took his ashes-armband,[46]
    circled it over him,
  and turned Gopi Chand to ashes.

He turned him to ashes
  and gave them to Mother.

---

46. A well-known demon in Hindu mythology possessed such an armband and
was finally tricked into destroying himself with it; usually Madhu Nath refers not
to an armband but to a "tin" that reduces to ashes, just as Jalindar's other tin
brings the dead to life.

"Mother, now eat them, my mother, then go,
and you will have a son.

"Mother, you asked for only one,
you asked for one,
but I give you two.
Mother, one is Gopi Chand, but this sister of his,
Champa De, I also give.

"For twelve years take this bliss
in your hands, take it,
and have the kingdom ruled, too.
Later, make him a yogi, my mother and birth-giver,
as a yogi he'll be immortal."

Shivji Sovereign!

(GC 1.5.s)

At daybreak Manavati Mata went to the Chapala Garden. There, fourteen hundred of Jalindar Baba's disciples were doing *tapas* secretly and fourteen hundred were doing *tapas* visibly. At once, she fell at his feet: "Hey, Guru Sovereign, for twelve years I did *tapas*." Manavati Mata fell at his feet, "Hey Baba, give me a son, Grain-giver. Now my twelve years of service are complete. So now, Baba, fulfill your promise."

"Manavati Mata, these fourteen hundred disciples are doing *tapas*. Whichever one of them pleases you, that's the boy I will give to you."

So Manavati Mata went into the garden where the fourteen hundred disciples were doing *tapas*. She went among them, but some had twisted limbs and some were bearded, and some were long-haired, and some were crooked-mouthed—such sons! Some were old and some had white hairs. But Gopi Chand was a boy like Shambhurya [Nathu Nath's nephew, a handsome well-groomed youth present at the time], and on his foot a lotus was sparkling and on his left arm a jewel was gleaming and on his forehead was a moon, as bright as if the sun were rising—just as if in the middle of the garden the sun were rising. He was in the center of everything, in the midst of the campfires, and on both sides of him the other *sādhu*s sat—but the light stayed only with him—with Gopi Chand.

Manavati Mata was pleased with him: "Oh my oh my! This is the very boy I will take for myself. What will I do with such bearded fellows? What will I do with such twisted limbs, or ones like this who don't even understand speech? [*Madhu Nath gestures toward Ann and there is general laughter.*] What will I do with them?"

Manavati Mata said, "After my twelve years of *tapas*, I will take a boy like this one." She was pleased with Gopi Chand alone, among all the fourteen hundred disciples. She went to the Guru Sovereign's campfire, and stood there: "Hey, Guru Sovereign, a disciple has pleased me, and Grain-giver, the one who pleases me, that is the very one I ought to receive."

"Yes, Manavati Mata, which disciple? Which disciple pleases you?"

"Hey, Guru Sovereign, on his foot a lotus is sparkling and on his left arm a jewel is gleaming and on his forehead is a moon giving light—that's the boy that I will take."

Jalindar Baba said, "Manavati Mata, you are sonless. I am giving you a loan, and yet you have put your hand into my liver. The light of my entire assembly—that light is his only. He is the moon,[47] Gopi Chand, and if I give him to you then I will live in darkness."

"Well Baba, then you break your promise. I did twelve years of *tapas*, I gave up my life-breath completely. Then your eyelids opened. What's your pain in the liver compared to mine? Trees grew in me, termites ate me! And now you are giving a disciple, and you say I have put my hand in your liver? If you don't give this boy then your promise is broken!"

/It's true!/

"How can you break your promise?"

"All right, Manavati Mother, go ahead and take the one who pleases you." The guru had given a promise.

"Son, Gopi Chand, come here." As soon as the guru gave the command, Gopi Chand came over there, asking, "Guru Sovereign?"

"Go, son, for twelve years rule the kingdom; marry queens and slave girls and rule the kingdom."

"Hey Guru Sovereign, why are you making me leave my devotional prayers? I won't go! What do they have over there in the

47. The second half of Gopi Chand's name, Chand, means "moon" but is also a very common Kshatriya surname. Other legendary heroes in India, such as Chandra Lekha, also have moons on their foreheads.

kingdom? In the householder life stage[48] one only falls into the noose of *māyā*'s net."[49]

"No son, go; recite your prayers and go, son. Rule the kingdom for twelve years, and enjoy yourself among the queens and slave girls. Rule, son, I am sending you."

"Guru Sovereign, I didn't expect this."

"No son, sit down." And he sat Gopi Chand down and circled his turn-to-ash tin over him, and burned him up into one pinch of sacred ash.[50] Who? Gopi Chand. Then he took the sacred ash and gave it to Manavati Mata. "Lick it up," he said, and she licked it up with her mouth.

"Go, Manavati Mata, this Gopi Chand will be yours, and he will have a sister, too, Champa De. Go, I promised you one but I have given you two, sister and brother. Champa De is yours for her entire life, but Gopi Chand is given as a loan. Have him rule the kingdom for twelve years, and then make him a yogi. If you don't make him a yogi, Time will devour him."

Now he is born. These were the circumstances of Gopi Chand's birth.

(GC 1.5.e)

48. A reference to the theory of four stages of life (*chār āśrama*) in Hindu social codes.

49. *māyā jāl; māyā* or illusion encompasses all the pleasures and concerns of a householder's existence. Its snares are a recurrent theme in the tale.

50. Although the word *bhasm* is used for ashes in the preceding phrase, those that Jalindar feeds to Manavati are called *bhabhūt*—often translated as "sacred ash"—a term applied only to ashes of burnt offerings made to deities. This sacred ash has a variety of ritual uses and curative properties; yogis smear their bodies with it.

Part 2

Gopi Chand Begs from Queen Patam De

Introduction

As part 1 closes, Manavati has completed her account to Gopi Chand of how she acquired him as a loan from Jalindar Nath. The point of this narrative is to persuade Gopi Chand of the necessity to submit to his destiny and renounce his kingdom. Part 2 opens, then, with Gopi Chand's response to his mother's advice: he pushes his guru down a well. Following his performance of the birth story, Madhu had informally previewed these events for me. From that telling I had gathered that Gopi Chand alone had conceived this bright idea of how to dispose of Jalindar. Several weeks later, when Madhu performed the episode as it appears here, he made it clear that it was "Royal Servants and relatives" who "misguided" Gopi Chand in advising this remedy for his distress.

No matter whose idea the mischief is, the opening events of part 2 hardly follow the course that Manavati had in mind. Gopi Chand marches in pomp to the guru's camp and boldly attempts to do away with him. Note that the sung portion refers in one verse only to Jalindar's captivity in the well and then takes up the consequences in greater detail. In the explanation, however, Madhu Nath elaborates considerably on the well episode, to everyone's enjoyment. This is a no-lose entertainment situation. Since nothing can really hurt or shame a powerful yogi like Jalindar Nath, to picture him buried under horse manure offers unmitigated delight.

That Jalindar, despite being buried under horse manure, is able to smoke a pipe with Gorakh Nath and—between the two of them—to free Gopi Chand from Death's Messengers is also an enjoyable representation and trumpeting of yogis' superior power. Neither Death's Messengers nor the anonymous "god" who deployed them puts up much of a fight when Gorakh Nath brandishes his tongs. Note too the unstated causal connection between Manavati's vow to Jalindar that she will spend one and one-quarter *lākh* of rupees on good works should Gopi Chand come back to life, and the yogis' prompt rescue of her son. This link sustains her role as Gopi Chand's protectress and birth-giver. Also sustained is the familiar pattern of bargaining materially with divine powers established in the birth story. When Gopi Chand regains consciousness and tells Manavati with poignant simplicity and wonder what it was like being dead, she insists that he carry out her vow and distribute the cash even before fulfilling his destiny as a yogi.

The melodrama of Gopi Chand's tale reaches one of its several peaks in his encounter with Patam De Rani and the multiple keening chorus of concubines and slave girls. The conflicted identity experienced by Gopi Chand—who despite all Jalindar's efforts to make him a firm disciple never seems fully transformed (Gold 1989)— emerges vividly as he approaches his former palaces as a begging yogi.

Spatially, this entire episode is a movement inward. Gopi Chand's emotional crises grow more intense as he travels from forest to waterside to Jewel Square to portal to the interior of the Color Palace. There—surrounded by wailing queens and slave girls, his little daughter clinging to his neck—he is completely drowned in sound and sentiment. Patam De's reproaches to Gopi Chand are different from Pingala's to Bharthari. Pingala accuses Bharthari of ruining her life by marrying her when he was born to be a yogi. She had plenty of other suitors. She could have stayed a virgin.

Patam De's reproaches have less to do with status, more with relationship, and thus are more intimate. "You like the guru better than you like me" seems to be her most acute complaint. Unlike Pingala she has a daughter, so she cannot lament her childlessness, nor does she care that Gopi Chand has left the kingdom without a male heir. Rather, for her the crux of misery is that her husband, her man, has denied their former marital bond by calling her "Mother" and spurned her charms in favor of the guru's. Everything Patam De says is reinforced by the hundreds of other wailing women; her final acceptance of Gopi Chand's new status is forced on her by her mother-in-law.

Whereas Bharthari succeeds in walking away from Pingala with alms for the guru, Gopi Chand fails. From his complete immersion in an inner abyss of emotional rhetoric and copious tears, he cannot emerge on his own. He needs help from both his motherly guru and his mother to extricate himself. Reduced to ashes for the second time, he is restored to life a third time in Manavati Mother's palace, where she is able to feed and advise him. As she hurries off to succor her son, Manavati's parting words to the queens—"You've killed my son, now take a rest!"—are biting but also true. The destructive, burning power of passionate love has taken its toll. By the grace of Jalindar's infinite patience, however, Gopi Chand escapes death once again.

It is in keeping with the maternal bias of Gopi Chand's entire tale, versus the paternal stress and scheme of Bharthari's, that Jalindar is a soft, forgiving, "motherly" guru where Gorakh Nath is hard and strict. Gorakh Nath is Bharthari's father's guru. He shocks Bharthari into enlightenment and neither coaxes nor coaches him. Jalindar is Gopi Chand's mother's teacher and benefactor. He nourishes, encourages, and supports his disciple in every way. In one of Madhu's rather rare asides during an *arthāv*, he noted and praised the special quality of Jalindar's care for Gopi Chand, contrasting it with the indifference of contemporary gurus.

Text

"Gopi Chand, abide in prayer, son,
  Praise the true Master, O Gopi Chand,
  king and king's son, darling boy.
  Recite prayers, my dear darling boy,
  and your body will be immortal.

"My son, from piling up pebbles
  the castle was built, Gopi Chand,
  the castle was built.
  But it's not our lot to live there,
    my dear, darling boy
  You must take fakirhood."

Jalindar Baba was covered up

with horse manure,[1]
completely covered up with horse manure.
Gopi Chand was sleeping in the palace, Lord,
    in the early afternoon,
when Death's Messengers[2] came.

The eleven hundred queens
were fanning him,
the sixteen hundred slave girls
were standing in the Color Palace.
When Death's Messengers came for Gopi Chand,
they grabbed him and took him.

They took Gopi Chand, and
he truly died.
Eleven hundred queens were wailing
in the Color Palace,
Sixteen hundred slave girls were wailing
in the Color Palace.
Manavati Mata came from her Color Palace:
"Why are you wailing, slave girls and queens?"
Mother came into Gopi Chand's castle
    while eleven hundred
queens and slave girls were wailing.

As soon as she came
Manavati saw;
and she placed her hand on Gopi Chand's chest,
she placed her hand, but
Gopi Chand had no heartbeat at all,
He had truly died.

What did Manavati Mata
say to Jalindar Nath?
"Baba, I shall make a resolution,[3]

---

1. Only here does the singing refer to Gopi Chand's attempt to get rid of his guru; the *arthāv* that follows will explain what happened.

2. *jam kā dūt;* these are familiar figures in Hindu mythology.

3. Manavati's resolution in part 1 was ironically conceived, but this one is sincere and reflects the usual practice of village religion where a large offering is promised if and only if a greatly desired boon is granted.

of one and one-quarter *lākh*,[4] Baba,
I shall make a resolution.
If Gopi Chand returns to life, my guru,
I will have that much distributed for dharma."

This much had happened,
when the yogis Jalindar Baba
and Gorakh Baba
were smoking hashish
in the Chapala Garden.
What did Gorakh Baba say
to Jalindar?
"My guru Jalindar,
You said you gave Gopi Chand,
But where did you give him?

"Death's Messengers
are taking Gopi Chand, look!
Death's Messengers took him."
When Gorakh Nath had said this much,
what did Jalindar Baba
say to Gorakhji?
"Gorakh Nath, I did give Gopi Chand,
I gave him to Mother.
Set Gopi Chand free, Gorakh Baba,
hurry up, set Gopi Chand free."

When Jalindar Nath had said this much,
Gorakh Baba the yogi
took the form of the wind,
took his iron tongs,
and flew up in the sky.
As soon as he got there he gave Death's Messengers
a couple of whacks with his tongs.

"Why are you taking
this disciple of ours?

---

4. One *lākh* equals 100,000; presumably Manavati means she will spend 125,000 rupees. The amount "one and one-quarter" (*savā*) is commonly used in offerings both of cash and kind at Rajasthani shrines and is often associated with the removal of inauspiciousness.

Did God give him to you?
He was given from my disciples, so
How can God ask for one of ours?"

(GC 2.1.s)

So, the first time when he went to become a yogi there were
seventy-three hundred drums, and seventy-two hundred noblemen.
They went with great drums and flags and armies, to a military
drumbeat. He was going to be a yogi, and many Royal Bards and
Genealogists were calling out respectful greetings. They were wailing,
"Hey Grain-giver, you are the Hindu Sun!" Seven hundred thousand horses were going before him and seven hundred thousand were
going behind him, and Gopi Chand was enthroned on an elephant's
back.

"Grain-giver, are you going to become a yogi?"

He said, "Brothers, my mother is forcing me."

"Burn your mother.[5] Where did your mother get this notion?"

Then they misguided him. Who? His companions. Who were
they? His relatives, and the Royal Servants: "Grain-giver, where is
your guru?"

"On the edge of the blind well in the Chapala Garden."

"You prostrate yourself to him and I'll get behind him and push
him into the well. Then, after that, who will make you a yogi?"

So they pushed him into the well from behind, brother. They
pushed him and now they came and said to Gopi Chand, "Grain-
giver, your mother keeps crying like this, but now your guru is dead.
We have pushed him in the well and put a flat rock on top of him.
So tomorrow get the dung of seven hundred and fifty horses, fill up
carts with it, and use it to fill up the well. Press it down thoroughly.
Fill up the well with horse manure. So the Guru Sovereign really
will die. Who then will make you into a yogi?"

"Yes, this is also a good idea." The next day he gave an order.
Gopi Chand commanded all the Cultivators and Gardeners[6] in his
kingdom to give free labor[7]—and fill the blind well with horse

---

5. *thāṅkī mātā bāḍī lagāvo;* a conventional curse.

6. Two populous peasant castes in the bard's village and area are *loḍā* (cultivators)
and *mālī* (gardeners).

7. *begār;* labor conscripted by the ruler from his peasants with no pay.

manure. Those Cultivators got up at the time of flour-grinding[8] and called to one another, "Brother let's go and do the king's labor." Laboring for the king, they filled carts with horse manure and pressed it all into the blind well and filled it up. They worked for four or five days. They made an entire heap. They filled it and pressed it down, so that was it: the problem of the Guru Sovereign was finished. And Gopi Chand continued to rule the kingdom.

Gopi Chand did not become a yogi although Manavati Mata had ceaselessly pleaded with him.

"I sent Gopi Chand to be a yogi. Why has he come back?"

Then some Royal Servant or other said, "Mother, he threw his guru down the well and then he covered him up with horse manure and pressed it down thoroughly. Gopi Chand won't be a yogi."

"What, Gopi Chand won't be a yogi?"

"No, he won't."

"Alas, he'll die, my son will die, now what can I do, he will die. Things have turned out strangely. O sorrow-makers, oh dear, what to do?"

She kept after him for a few days, but the last chance came and went. Whose? Gopi Chand's. Now the twelve promised years were over, and on that very day Gopi Chand was sleeping in the early afternoon. He had eaten a good meal and he lay down for a comfortable siesta. His eleven hundred queens were fanning him; his sixteen hundred slave girls were in attendance.

Then Death's Messengers arrived. As soon as they came up to Gopi Chand they touched him with their sticks.[9] They yanked out Gopi Chand's breath and took out his soul.

They threw down a palanquin and laid him on it and then four of Death's Messengers took Gopi Chand. As soon as they took him, he died. Death's Messengers took him.

Now all eleven hundred queens and sixteen hundred slave girls were crying hard, their eyes filled with Indra's misty rain; they were wailing.[10] The sixteen hundred slave girls' resonant weeping[11] filled the whole palace.

---

8. A convention of traditional time-reckoning: about 4 A.M., the hour when, before the introduction of electric flour-mills, all village women used to rise to grind grain for the day's bread.

9. *kuterā;* 3- to $3\frac{1}{2}$-foot-long sticks, such as policemen carry.

10. The first two references to the ladies' weeping are exactly the same as those

Now his mother's palace was separate. She thought to herself, Uh oh! The queens and slave girls are happy and content. So why are they wailing? With a little stick in her hand and wooden sandals on her feet[12] Manavati Mata went to Gopi Chand's palace. The eleven hundred queens and sixteen hundred slave girls were beating their chests. What had happened? Gopi Chand had died. Oh my! Manavati Mata saw that something very strange had happened. Just today he was very happy and content. He had neither pain nor flatulence.[13] So what happened to Gopi Chand?

Quickly Manavati Mata went and grabbed his hand, but she found no signs of life whatsoever, no pulse. She laid her hand on his chest, but there wasn't any heartbeat.

/He had arrived./[14]

"Oh no! He's gone, Gopi Chand. O son, Gopi Chand, for many days I've been telling you, 'Be a yogi, son, and your body will be immortal.' But you didn't accept what I said, and you had the Guru Sovereign pushed into a well and covered him up with horse manure.

"Hey Guru Sovereign, I vow to give one and one-quarter *lākh*, Grain-giver, one and one-quarter *lākh* of rupees. If my Gopi Chand comes back to life, Guru Sovereign, then I will distribute one and one-quarter *lākh* for dharma and merit, and then straightaway I myself will make him a yogi. But he must come back to life, Guru Sovereign. I was heedless for too long, but now I won't let him go with anyone else—I'll take him myself. As soon as Gopi Chand comes back to life, first I'll have one and one-quarter *lākh* distributed for dharma; then I will go with him. I'll take him to the garden and make him a yogi. But Guru Sovereign, my Gopi Chand ought to come back to life, Guru Sovereign."

Over here, then, Manavati Mata made a vow to spend one and

---

applied again and again to Gopi Chand's own crying; the third, *kurḷārī*, is by contrast never done by Gopi Chand. One of its meanings is the wailing that women do at death. More generally, it is any crying out in unison.

11. *ranohī jāgarī*. The aural image here is of a resonant echoing within buildings.

12. Why the queen mother carries a little stick is unclear; she wears wooden sandals, perhaps because of her affinity with yogis.

13. *koī khaī dukhyo na pāḍyo na;* a common expression meaning that not the least thing was wrong with him.

14. That is, he had arrived elsewhere, left this world.

one-quarter *lākh* for dharma. And over there were Jalindar Baba and
Gorakh Nathji, smoking hashish. Where? Over there in the garden.
On the edge of that blind well.

When he meets water, then he's water. Who? Jalindar Baba. And
when he meets wind, then he's wind. And when he meets flame, then
he's flame.[15] So he hardly remained buried in the well—he also
came out.[16]

So, Jalindar Baba and Gorakh Nath Sovereign were smoking
hashish, and Death's Messengers had seized and taken Gopi Chand.
Then Gorakh Nath Sovereign looked up. "Jalindar Baba, you said,
'I have given Gopi Chand.' You said, 'From my disciples I gave one
disciple to Manavati Mother.' But Death's Messengers have taken
Gopi Chand."

"What?"

"Yes, they are taking him."

"Oh, the sister-fuckers! Why are they taking my disciple, my
disciple that I myself gave. To whom? I gave him to Manavati
Mother. And that little-God-fellow,[17] why is he asking for him? He is
hardly the one who gave him."

"They've taken him, Death's Messengers have grabbed him."

"Oh, run, Gorakh Nath. Beat those sister-fuckers with your tongs
and free Gopi Chand and bring him here."

Then Gorakh Nath Sovereign took the wind's form. He took his
tongs and flew up in the sky. Meanwhile, inside the palanquin, the
four Death's Messengers had thrown Gopi Chand face down, with
his hands bound behind his back, and they carried him like a
rolled-up banner. Thus they were taking him when Gorakh Nath
Sovereign came along and gave each of them a whack with his tongs.
He struck Death's Messengers: "Oh, you sister-fuckers! Why are you
taking our disciple? Do you think God gave him? He is our disciple!
We gave this disciple, and that sister-fucker God is hardly the one
who gave him, so why has God demanded him?"[18]

As soon as he said this, and as soon as he dealt them one or two

---

15. According to Bhoju, these phrases describe a "*siddh puruṣ*" or perfected being
who may at will take on the characteristics of any medium. The meaning here is
that Jalindar Baba is not affected by being pushed down a well.

16. As we will see in part 4, he did remain buried and must be excavated.

17. *bhagvānyo;* a disrespectful diminutive of *bhagvān.*

18. Recall that Manavati Mata came from God's door a barren woman.

blows with his tongs, Death's Messengers released Gopi Chand and went far away.

As soon as they released him, he came back into the palace and returned to life at once. "Oh my! I've slept very deeply." The wailing queens saw him. "Oh my! I've slept very well." And Manavati Mother was standing near.

"O son, Gopi Chand. What came over you? For many days I've been telling you to be a yogi, and then your body would be immortal. And the Guru Sovereign's deadline arrived, and you did not become a yogi. Son, what came over you?"

"Mother, they really took me."

"Look, the queens and the slave girls are wailing. Where is your royal throne, and your horse-drawn chariot and palanquin? Did they go with you? Just now they took you and if the guru hadn't freed you, then who would have freed you?"

"Mother, there was a *sādhu* with hair this long and with tongs this big, and he came. I was bound with my hands behind my back, and they were taking me. And he gave them each one blow with his tongs. He told Death's Messengers: 'Hey, it's our disciple and hardly yours, hardly God-given—it's our disciple. And you sister-fuckers, why has God demanded him? And why are you taking him, sister-fuckers? Let go!'

"Then he let them have it with his tongs, and they released me and ran away."

"Son, they released you. Now be a yogi or else Death will eat you. And these queens and slave girls will remain right here, and your royal throne will remain right here. Nothing goes with you. I made a resolution to distribute one and one-quarter *lākh* for dharma—so you must do that."

So he distributed one and one-quarter *lākh* for dharma, in order to fulfill her resolution.

Then the son and mother went together, informing no relatives, informing no queens and slave girls, informing no one.

(GC 2.1.e)

Hurriedly, before dawn, Manavati Mata grabbed Gopi Chand by the hand: "Let's go, son, I will make you a yogi." So Manavati Mata pushed Gopi Chand in front of her, saying, "There is no meaning in these things, son, Time will eat them. The queens and slave girls will stay over here wailing. You died, but if you become a yogi your body will be immortal."

This sermon affected Gopi Chand, because he had died. From dying, he really found out[19] that we must all die. So Manavati Mother took Gopi Chand into the Chapala Garden.

They entered through the gateway. In the distance they could see Gorakh Nathji Sovereign and Jalindar Baba, over there, doing *tapas* by the campfire. Gopi Chand went before her, and Manavati said, "Go, son, sit by your guru, clasp his feet." But suddenly both gurus became nine-hand-tall lions. They became nine-hand-tall lions and came at Gopi Chand as if to kill him, in order to frighten him, brother, to scare him away. They both came at him, roaring.

Gopi Chand said, "Hey Guru Sovereign, it was my fault, Grain-giver. I pushed you down under horse manure. Forgive my error, Grain-giver."

Gopi Chand shut his eyes tight. And then he clasped the paws of those who had become lions. "If they want to eat me, let them eat me. There's nothing left for me to do but die or become a yogi. So, fine, let them eat me, and my misdeed will be removed."

As soon as he clasped their paws, then Jalindar Baba and Gorakh Nath Sovereign turned back into yogis. When they were yogis, Jalindar Baba said, "Son, Gopi Chand."

"Yes, Guru Sovereign."

"Go son, your desires are not yet satiated.[20] Go rule the kingdom for another twelve years. You've had twelve years of queens and slave girls, but your desires are not satiated. So go, son, rule for another twelve years. Go, run away."

"Guru Sovereign, now I won't go. Now, I will be a yogi. I will become your disciple, I won't go back."

"Oh go back, sister-fucker, you will ruin my karma.[21] Sister-fucker, your cravings for queens and slave girls have not yet been

---

19. *marṇāū jach gī; jachṇo* means "to examine and find out" or "to learn through experience."

20. *dhāpyo;* the common village term for having had enough, used at the end of a meal, for example.

21. The Rajasthani *karam* is sometimes equated with an uncontrollable fate or destiny (*kismat, lekh, takdīr*, etc.). But at times its meaning approaches that of Hindi and Sanskrit *karma*—in that responsibility for all individuals' destinies is attributable to their past or present actions. Here Jalindar Nath is worried that his karma will be stained by initiating someone who is unprepared for renunciation.

removed. And your desires for the throne of rule are not satiated. Go back!"

"No, Guru Sovereign, I won't go."

"You won't go?"

"I won't go."

"OK, then sit down by the campfire." He seated him in a posture of meditation. And Jalindar Nath Sovereign took out his dagger with four blades. As soon as he took out his four-bladed dagger he told Gopi Chand, "Say 'Shiv! Shiv!'"

So first Jalindar Nath Sovereign pierced Gopi Chand's left ear. As soon as he pierced the left ear, milk came out. And he drove a wooden peg into it. As soon as he had driven in the peg, he then turned to put the dagger in the second ear. But Gopi Chand thought, "Now, the game of life is spoiled. That's it. He gives one blow with the dagger and the game of life is spoiled . . . queens and slave girls . . . the whole kingdom has turned to dust."

While Gopi Chand's imagination was running on like this, the guru raised the dagger and pierced his right ear and blood came out. Blood came out, and the Guru Sovereign was incensed: "You sister-fucker! I told you that your mind wasn't satiated with queens and slave girls, your mind wasn't satiated with ruling the kingdom. I told you to go and rule for another twelve years and, sister-fucker, you didn't go. But still your spirit is led astray in the net of illusion."[22]

"Guru Sovereign, what is to happen happens."

"You have spoiled my karma. Milk used to come out of my yogis' ears. Milk came out; but now blood has begun to come out. It's a sign of things to come."[23]

He inserted a wooden peg in the ear, made from *nīm*,[24] and then he put an iron platter weighing one and one-quarter maunds[25] on

22. *māyā jāḷ ma jīv na ḍulā diyo; ḍulāṛno* is to be *caused* to be restless, demoralized, nervous, fickle, unsteady, deviated, or astray. The suggestion is that Gopi Chand is more helpless than culpable.

23. *lāg jāy āindā se;* according to Bhoju the phrase implies that from this day only blood will come out.

24. The *nīm* tree's leaves and wood have many ritual and healing uses in rural Rajasthan.

25. *suvaman;* as noted above, the sum of one and one-quarter is associated with the removal of inauspiciousness; here, the heat of the flames cooks or heals the wounds in Gopi Chand's ears and averts inauspicious influences thought to threaten the healing process.

Gopi Chand's head. On top of the platter he ignited a wood fire and the flames rose up. He put the platter on a cloth pad on Gopi Chand's head, and took him on a pilgrimage tour. The flames rose up, so that the fire at times hung down over his ears.

After the pilgrimage tour the Guru Sovereign took him to our campfire.[26] Where? In the Kajali Woods. Over there in the Kajali Woods, fourteen hundred of the Guru Sovereign's disciples were doing *tapas* invisibly. And fourteen hundred visible disciples were doing *tapas*.

As soon as they got there, the Guru Sovereign took the iron platter down from Gopi Chand's head and said, "Son, you have become a firm[27] disciple. Now you have become a yoga-holder. So take your tongs, son, and take this sack, and take this deer-horn instrument, and wear these wooden sandals on your feet.[28] Now son, this is the kind of work that needs to be done. You have become a yogi."

"Yes sir."

"Go into your castle and get alms. Say 'Mother' to your special wife, Patam De Rani, and beg for alms and bring them back. Then your yoga will be fulfilled."

"Hey Guru Sovereign, Patam De Rani is my woman. How can I call her 'Mother'? I have scattered all her leaves and smelled all her flowers.[29] She is my woman, Guru Sovereign. It would shame my saintly guru[30] and my mother's milk. How can I call her 'Mother'?"

"Yes, son, Gopi Chand. Patam De Rani was your woman, but that was in your ruling time. Now you have become a yogi, a yoga-holder, so son, now in the time of yoga she is your mother. Call her 'Mother' and bring back alms, and then your yoga will be fulfilled."

"Well, you have given the order, the Guru Sovereign's order, and if you say it, it must be done."

"Yes. So son, come on the roads and go on the roads and call all

26. Here the singer identifies himself with the legendary Nath yogis.

27. *pakko chelo;* H. *pakkā* has many meanings including ripe, cooked, unassailable, genuine, fried.

28. Thus the guru bestows the emblems of a yogi's identity on his cooked disciple.

29. *Ūnai pānā pānā baroḷī phūlā phūlā dhūmarī;* according to Bhoju, this poetic saying means that he knows each part of his wife's body as well as a gardener knows the leaves and flowers on his plants.

30. *guru-pīr;* actually a pairing of Hindu and Islamic terms for a religious teacher.

women 'Mother' and 'Sister.' And don't bring shame to your yogi's robes. Hurry and get alms from Patam De."

So let's see what happens to Gopi Chand, and what alms he will bring.

(GC 2.2.e)

So Gopi Chand put on his wooden sandals, picked up his tongs, picked up his sack, and took his deer-horn instrument. A seated yogi's a stake in the ground, but a yogi once up is a fistful of wind. The Nath took the wind's form and turned his face toward Gaur Bengal.[31]

He crossed one woods, he crossed a second woods, in the third woods Gopi Chand came to the border. As soon as he came to the border, his white, white castles came into view, and Gopi Chand remembered the things of his ruling time. As soon as he remembered, it was just like when a spark falls into one hundred maunds of gunpowder. When a wick is set to one hundred maunds of gunpowder— then flames shoot up. Just so, flames rose up violently in Gopi Chand's mind.

He thought, Oh, a very astonishing thing has taken place! There was a day that once rose for me when I would sport at hunting lions in the jungle. Seven hundred thousand horses were in my company, and I rode in a throne on the back of an elephant, whisks waving over me. Many Royal Bards were shouting my praises.

But today look at the splendor with which Gopi Chand was going into the palace. On his fair body he was wearing a loincloth, and on his fair neck spread matted locks, and his whole body was smeared with ashes. In his hand he had tongs and on his shoulders was a sack and there was no one to herald his coming.

Remembering the things of his ruling time, Gopi Chand was crying hard, his eyes filled with Indra's misty rain. Water poured from his eyes. "Hey Guru Sovereign, how has my condition changed so fast? There is no one to herald my coming. No one to say 'Victory to Shiva!'"

He was crying over there. Gopi Chand cried a lot, he cried so much. There used to be fifty-two portals and fifty-three doorways and twelve districts' rule and a home court of justice and today—nothing at all.

"Today sacred ash is smeared all over me, look, and on my

31. Madhu pronounces this location *Gor;* see chapter 2.

shoulders there's a sack and in my hand tongs. I'm wearing a loincloth, and I am all alone in the jungle, wailing. But if things hadn't turned out like this, thousands, hundreds of thousands of men were in my service."

Gopi Chand was crying hard, his eyes filled with Indra's misty rain. Water poured from his eyes. And he besought[32] his guru. "Hey Guru Sovereign, I beseech you, quickly come, Baba Nath. Your fireplace in Kajali Woods is far away, and Guru Sovereign, my castle also is far away, and Grain-giver, now in the jungle I'm wretched."

So he besought his guru with body and mind, and as soon as he besought the guru, Jalindar Baba came. As soon as he came, he rebuked Gopi Chand:

"O son, if you're already wretched here in the jungle, what will your condition be when you're near the queens and slave girls?"

Gopi Chand was crying hard, his eyes filled with Indra's misty rain. Water poured from his eyes. He said to his guru, "Hey, Guru Sovereign, you have no knowledge of these things, to cry or not to cry about them. What do you know? I have eleven hundred queens in the castles weeping, sixteen hundred slave girls weeping, and Manavati Mata, my old mother, she is crying very hard. And in my kingdom were fifty-two portals, fifty-three doorways, twelve districts' rule, and a home court of justice. But now the court is deserted and the great drum lies upside down. And Guru Sovereign, you have no knowledge of these things. You were thrown down from the sky and caught by Earth Mother,[33] and you have neither mother nor father, nor any woman, nor any nanny goats, nor any sister, nor any nieces."[34]

"Calm down, son. Go on reciting prayers and keep your attention on those prayers. Go thus to your palaces, meet your queens and slave girls, get some alms and hurry back, son."

(GC 2.3.e)

---

32. *arodhyā;* a variant of *ārādhno,* meaning to pray or praise. This term always occurs when Gopi Chand implores Jalindar Nath for help and in no other context in the two tales. To distinguish it from *samaran* or the calm recitation of prayers, I shall translate it "beseech" throughout.

33. Gopi Chand refers to Jalindar's presumably mythic birth and elaborates the argument in subsequent encounters when the guru chides him for "tangling in *māyā*'s net." See Gold 1989.

34. Note that, except for "father," everything the guru lacks is female.

A seated yogi's a stake in the ground, but a yogi once up is a fistful of wind. The Nath took the wind's own form, and turned his face toward Bengal. Gaur Bengal, that was his village, and Dhak Bengal was his sister's place, her marital home.[35] He crossed one woods, he crossed a second woods, and in the middle of the third woods he reached the waterside. As soon as he reached the waterside in Bengal, Gopi Chand set up his meditation seat and ignited his yogi's campfire. He sat in a meditation posture and began reciting prayers.

So, Gopi Chand had lowered his eyelids and was reciting prayers when the sixteen hundred slave girls came from the palace with their double water pots, to fetch water.

They emerged from the village and looked out over the waterside. There they saw a yogi doing *tapas*. Among them was Hira Dasi.[36] They were talking of other things when Hira Dasi spoke: "Hey, slave girls, burn up all other matters. Today there's a yogi doing *tapas* on the waterside. Today's our lucky day! Our king became a yogi. So we will ask this yogi about him, we will ask for news of our king—where our yogi king went and where he didn't go—whether he's well, whether he's sad or happy, we'll find out about our king."

They didn't know if he had really become a yogi, or if he had just got angry and left. The queens and slave girls knew nothing at all. So right away the sixteen hundred went and set their double water pots down on the waterside, and surrounded Gopi Chand, as I am surrounded here [Madhu refers to the audience surrounding him at the time of telling]. He had set up his campfire, and on all four sides of him were women, nothing but women, slave girls. Now what did they say to Gopi Chand? As soon as they had surrounded him, Hira Dasi spoke.

(GC 2.4.e)

"Hey, yogi, from which city do you come and go? You seem to be an established Nath. Raise your eyelids, Baba Nath, we have come to take your *darśan*."

As soon as this much was said, Gopi Chand thought, Brother, some truthful servant[37] has come to serve me. Someone has brought flour and things, things to cook with. Let me see. And he raised his

---

35. Madhu offers this clarification of geography as an aside.
36. When Dasi is part of a name I do not translate it.
37. *sevak;* derived from *sevā* or service, a term with religious implications.

eyelids and saw that his campfire was surrounded by nothing but slave girls—sixteen hundred were standing there. As soon as he saw them, Gopi Chand knew. "Brother, these are my own slave girls who have come. But if they recognize me, then look out! Illusion's net will spread here."

As soon as he raised his eyelids, Hira De Dasi spoke: "O, Guru Sovereign, O Great Soul, O noble Grain-giver, our king became a yogi, and went away. Noble Grain-giver, tell us about him. We will take you into the palace, and Guru Sovereign, we will serve you. Our king became a yogi. Is he happy or is he sad? In what country are he and his guru? Did he pierce his ears or didn't he pierce them?" These are the kinds of things she asked.

"O brother, I know nothing about your king and I know nothing about any queen. I am a wandering *sādhu* who has come, what should I know?"

There were sixteen hundred slave girls surrounding him. And they were crying hard. And as they cried they were asking him news of Gopi Chand. "Hey Guru Sovereign, our king had sixteen hundred slave girls and eleven hundred queens, and because of him all of us in the Color Palace are wearing long blouses.

"And his Manavati Mother—may she burn up!—she made her son a yogi secretly. Our king had fifty-two portals and fifty-three doorways, twelve districts' rule, and seven hundred thousand horses were raised in his company. He rode in a throne on an elephant's back, with whisks waving over him. But the kingdom has become desolate. And the great drum is lying upside down.

"Noble Grain-giver, please tell us about our king! We will take you into the palaces and serve you." The sixteen hundred slave girls were crying very hard. "Noble Grain-giver, our king resembled you. He had a face just like yours. Our king became a yogi, and we yearn for him. Where is our king?"

Gopi Chand was wretched. "Now if these sluts recognize me here then *māyā*'s net will spread." So Gopi Chand braced himself and lifted his tongs from the middle of his campfire. He brandished his tongs at the slave girls, the sluts who kept on crying. "Get out of here, I have no knowledge of your king or of any queen. Why have you come here bothering me? Get going or else I will beat each one of you with my tongs, you sister-fuckers."

After he had rebuked them, the slave girls filled their water pots.

Lifting up their pots, they returned to the palace. As soon as they entered the palace, they put down their double pots. Queen Patam De took her whip from its peg and gave Hira De a couple of whacks.

"Slave girl, you left in the morning to get water, so where have you been sitting the whole day? Wanton slut, who knows where? Maybe you went to see some show? Where were you sitting, getting water, for the whole day, all sixteen hundred of you?"

So she gave her a couple of whacks. Then, crying, Hira De said, "O Mistress, send me away if you like, or if you like take away my life, but there's a yogi doing *tapas*. Where? At the waterside. So I joined my hands in greeting to that yogi and asked him to tell me some information about our king, and I offered to serve him and to bring him into the palace. I asked, 'Is the king sad or happy? In what country is he? At whose campfire has he become a disciple? Who is his guru? Where is he? Give me information about my king.' I only asked for this kind of information, Grain-giver, and that's why I was late."

"You slut, I was burned and now you're putting salt in my wounds. You'll be the death of me, if every day you go to get water and meet some yogi and ask him for information. You're putting salt in my burns, and you'll be the death of me. My king became a yogi, and that's why you feel free to taunt me."

Such was her justice.[38]

(GC 2.5.e)

Meanwhile, Gopi Chand picked up his sack and his tongs from the waterside. He put on his sandals and . . . a seated yogi's a stake in the ground, but a yogi once up is a fistful of wind. The Nath took the wind's own form and fixed his consciousness in Gaur Bengal. He entered the city. Gopi Chand was wearing a loincloth on his fair body, and matted locks spread over his fair neck. He had tongs in his hands and a sack on his shoulder.

As Gopi Chand was going along, he remembered the times when he ruled. "Oh my! What an amazing thing has happened!"

Gopi Chand was crying hard, his eyes filled with Indra's misty rain. In the center of the city, he entered the marketplace. It used to be that people went before him crying "Grain-giver, greetings!

38. *nyāy hoyo;* an ironic comment on her treatment of the slave girls, who were only trying to help.

Grain-giver!" They would cry "Greetings, Giver of grain!" But today, no one even glanced.

"I'm still the same man I was before. But look! No one even says 'Victory to Mahadev!' [People could at least remark,] 'Brother, there's a *sādhu* going along, and for this reason we will cry victory to Mahadev!'"

Gopi Chand was crying hard, his eyes filled with Indra's misty rain. Water poured from his eyes. He entered the main market. Crying hard he went along, thinking, No one even says, "Sovereign, where do you live? Victory to Mahadev! Come and be seated please." No one even says "*Rām Rām*."[39]

Gopi Chand was crying hard, his eyes filled with Indra's misty rain. Water poured from his eyes. He went into the Jewel Square, and after passing through the gateway, he saw an elephant tied up. Where? To the fodder trough. It was Mangano Hathi, the one he used to ride.

From this side Gopi Chand was coming, crying hard, and as soon as he saw Mangano Hathi, Gopi Chand shrieked. From the other side Mangano Hathi too began to bellow. "Hey Grain-giver, O king, what have you done? You became a yogi and left and there is no one to feed me bread and no one to give me fodder and water. Grain-giver, what troubles have come into my life! I don't even get any water, there is no one to look after me at all."

"O brother Mangano, now what to do? Fortune has inscribed this destiny in my karma with thick writing: immortal fakirhood. There is no one to remove it."

"But Grain-giver, what is to become of me?"

"Son, this was written for me, in my *kismat*.[40] Yours also is written: to die of hunger. So go and die."

Gopi Chand passed through one portal and a second portal, and then he came to the third portal, where he lit his campfire. And he set up his meditation seat. Then Gopi Chand gave a rousing "*Alakh!*" He gave a rousing "*Alakh!*" and sounded his deer-horn instrument in the portal. As soon as he sounded his horn, the sound reached the

39. *Rām Rām* is the most common greeting between equals in the bard's region. Thus Gopi Chand seems to crave any human intercourse, not just the adulation he received as a king or should receive as a yogi.

40. Yet another word for fate, from the Urdu-Persian tradition, and one very common in village talk.

ears of Patam De Rani. As soon as the sound reached the ears of Patam De Rani, she spoke to Hira De Dasi.

"Slave girl!"

"Yes, Grain-giver."

"Go! Today, after many days, a yogi has come and given us a rousing '*Alakh!*' Our king became a yogi and left. Previously, many yogis used to come but this is the first yogi to come since our king left. So fill a platter with diamonds and rubies, and give very fine alms to the yogi. And ask for a fine blessing and bring it from the yogi. Go right away and do it. Go at once, because it's a yogi and he might get angry and go away, and then he will curse us."[41]

As soon as she said this, the slave girl put on a skirt with eighty pleats and wrapped herself in a flowered Gujarati sari and put on her nose ring and her toe rings and a three-ring set of hollow anklets. She put on many delicate ankle chains, and eyeliner and henna, and she threaded pearls in her hairs. She smeared on eyeshadow, and she put on necklaces—one strand, two strands, seven strands, so she became like the flame of Holi, and like lightning in a black cloud.[42]

If the wind blows this way she bends this way, and if the wind blows that way she bends that way, and if the wind should blow in all four directions then that slave girl would break into pieces.[43] And if an opium-eater like brother Hardev [a member of the audience] met her, then he would take her for a dose of opium and eat her up.

(GC 2.6.e)

The bondwoman now filled a platter with
diamonds, rubies, and pearls.[44]
Hira, my slave girl,

---

41. If a yogi goes away empty-handed, he may well curse the uncharitable house. Patan De seems to have forgotten her previous rage at the slave girls' mentioning yogis.

42. Metaphors of fire and lightning evoke danger as well as beauty and are particularly appropriate for a dangerous woman.

43. This same image of extremely delicate yet dangerous female beauty occurs in the Rajasthani Dev Narayanji epic to describe Rani Jaimti—an incarnation of the goddess whose aim is to destroy the heroes.

44. This sung portion is more than double the length of most, indicating that Madhu may have simply become carried away while singing and neglected to break at the usual place. He begins his *arthāv* at a point in the narrative that omits a portion of the sung story. I therefore translate the singing until the *arthāv* catches up with it.

passed through one portal,
the bondwoman passed the second portal,
now she came to the third portal.
When she reached the third portal, Lord,
what did she say to the yogi?

"Take these, Baba,
spread open your sack,
and hold out your cup, yogi.
I have a platter filled with diamonds and rubies, yogi,
now your poverty has fled."

When Hira had said this much,
Gopi Chand raised his eyelids
and gazed at the slave girl.
"My bondwoman, why have you brought a platter
    filled with stones and pebbles?
What will I do with these pebbles?

"Such stones and pebbles
I left behind at home,
Hira De, my slave girl.
Slave girl, bring me a stale, leftover scrap,
a feast from Patam De Rani's hands."

"O Yogi, you don't seem to be a yogi,
it seems to me you're sick,
princely yogi.
Yesterday or the day before you were
a householder's boy, dying of hunger,
and that's why you became a yogi.
Up until now your hunger hasn't left you, yogi,
and that's why you crave a scrap of bread.

"Yogi, were there leaves
in the middle of your fate
they might fly away,
but there must be a boulder in the middle of your fate, yogi,
if you're calling diamonds 'pebbles.'"

When Hira De had said this much,
what did Gopi Chand reply?

"Hira De, my bondwoman,
O bondwoman, there was once a day
that rose for me when
they would gnaw on my polluted[45] scraps,
but today, bondwoman, people speak to me any old way."

"O Yogi, you don't seem to be a yogi,
it seems to me you're sick,
princely yogi.
Yogi, quit saying 'bondwoman,' yogi,
or I'll let fly my bamboo.
Yogi, I will hang you high from the bitter *nīm* tree,
and rub your wounds with salt.

"Yogi, I am the queen,
Yogi, I am the queen.
Yogi, I alone am mistress of the fort:
You won't get away with calling me 'bondwoman'!"

"Bondwoman, your front teeth stick out
and your forehead's ugly![46]
Bondwoman, your fate is shattered.
Bondwoman, where have you come from,
claiming to be my Queen Patam De?"

"Yogi, the mistress of the kingdom
doesn't call me 'bondwoman,'
yogi, nor do the city people call me 'girl,'
princely yogi.

"You just quit this 'bondwoman' business, yogi,
or I will split your skin with my bamboo.
Yogi, I will hang you high from the bitter *nīm* tree,
and rub your wounds with salt."

(GC 2.7.s)

---

45. *uṭhyārā;* Rajasthani for *jhūṭhā,* or polluted by saliva. Presumably he refers in the third person to the slave girls, who would have eaten his leftovers.

46. *thāri bhūṇḍi cha ye lalāḍī; bhūṇḍi* can mean ugly or inauspicious or improper; *lalāḍī* is another of the many words that in rural Rajasthan refer to preordained fate. Literally, however, it means the "forehead"—where fate is written. This phrase thus carries a double meaning: your face is ugly, your fate is inauspicious.

So this is what happened with the bondwoman. She said to Gopi Chand, "Yogi you aren't really a yogi, it seems to me you're sick! I will hang you high from the bitter *nīm* and rub your wounds with salt."

But it was Gopi Chand. Gopi Chand was muttering, dizzy, all in a flurry, till he burst out in rage and fury.[47] Gopi Chand thrust his tongs into the middle of his campfire, right in the burning coals, until they got red hot. Then he struck the bondwoman in the middle of her back, and she went rolling. Her platter of diamonds and rubies scattered all over the portal, and the bondwoman went rolling and falling. He had struck her once on the back, but two streaks swelled up just as when a sick animal is branded.[48] And she was weeping loudly, she was crying very hard, her eyes filled with Indra's misty rain. Water poured from her eyes.

She returned to the Color Palace and went lamenting to Patam De Rani. Then Patam De Rani spoke:

"Slave girl, Hira De, I sent you laughing; why have you come crying? What kind of a yogi is it, a magician? a death-spell wielder? Did he feed you roasted hashish, so that you've come wailing and stoned?"

Then the slave girl said, "Mistress, you can have your job, and I will take two oxen and be a farmer. Should I eat blows from any yogi's tongs?"

Then Patam De Rani spoke, "Bondwoman, are you making useless excuses? Where did the yogi shove his dagger in you?"[49]

Hira was wrapped in that flowered Gujarati sari, but the pearls in her hair had scattered when he whacked her with the tongs. Now when Patam De said this, Hira De unwrapped her sari and balled it up and tossed it behind the queen. Then she ran and threw herself face down, and as soon as she did, Patam De Rani looked at her back.

From her neck right down to her buttocks were swollen welts like

---

47. This is a stock phrase: *Gopi Chand ka āyo sarnāṭo ar ghasgyo bharnāṭo ar ros āgyo gāḍo. Sarnāṭo* refers to the sound of a loud or rushing wind and may imply angry muttering; it is also an intoxication resulting from excitement and restlessness. *Bharnāṭo* means *chakkar* or dizziness. *Ros* translates literally as anger.

48. A tongs has two strips of iron, but Bhoju interprets the two welts from one blow to result from the blow's prodigious force. The term I translate "streaks" evokes lightning. Branding is a treatment still practiced on livestock.

49. I was convinced that by this statement Patam De suggests that the yogi might have sexually assaulted Hira De; according to Bhoju she only asks sarcastically, "Where does it hurt?"

lightning streaks. "Bondwoman, he gave you one whack but two streaks have swollen on your back. It looks just like when a sick animal is branded in the middle of the back. What kind of a pitiless yogi is this? How could he treat you this way? That yogi has no compassion inside his hollow frame,[50] if he uses his tongs like this. Suppose you die, then what?"

Hira De kept crying, "Mistress, what does that yogi understand? He understands nothing of pity, there's no pity at all in his heart. Mistress, run him out of the portal. He almost took my life away. And if he had taken my life away, then who would take care of my children?"

And she wept like a waterfall. "Mistress, that yogi almost took away my life."

Patam De got angry and said, "Girl, what use is a yogi like that who doesn't even have compassion? A yogi is supposed to have compassion inside of him. But this one is a wicked one. He's not a yogi at all, he's sick! So, slave girl, go and call the sixteen hundred slave girls. All of you beat him with bamboo sticks and make that yogi's skin fly. Chase him out of the castle."

Hira De went running at once to call the sixteen hundred slave girls. She called them and they gathered in the presence of the queen. The queen ordered Hira to give each of them one bamboo stick, but instead she gave each of them two. Oh son of a ...! She gave two bamboo sticks to each person. "Now let's go get that yogi!"

(GC 2.7.e)

As they were going, she called to them from the balcony above— who?—Patam De Rani: "Hey, girls, wait, and listen to what I say. Don't kill the yogi, just frighten him and chase him out of the palace. O sluts, if you kill a Brahman, then you meet destruction, for age upon age.[51] And if you kill a yogi, then your lineage will truly sink, sluts, he'll curse us. And our kingdom is without a son, our kingdom is without a ruler, so if the yogi gives a curse, the kingdom will be

---

50. *ghaṭ;* literally a clay jug, often a reference to the body as a container of something more important; here, however, is the opposite implication—the yogi has nothing inside.

51. *jug jug hatyā hojyā; hatyā* is literally murder or slaughter. Powerful beings must be treated with care, for to damage them is to incur great damages to oneself in the Hindu karmic economy.

lost. Don't kill the yogi but just frighten him and chase him out of the palace."[52]

They passed through one portal, they passed the second portal, and they came to the third portal and challenged the yogi.

"Yogi, now pack up your bag and baggage, your club and gourd. We will make you remember the whack you gave with your tongs. Many days have gone by, and who knows whom you have beaten with your tongs. But today, we will make you remember it. We'll hang you high from the bitter *nīm* tree and rub your wounds with salt. We'll beat you with bamboo sticks, and then you'll understand what kind of slave girls we are!"

While they were saying this, Gopi Chand raised his eyelids and gazed around the portal. In the month of *Śrāvan*, clouds of Indra the Great King mount in the sky; thus were the sixteen hundred slave girls like a red and yellow[53] cloud bank. And their bamboo sticks overshadowed him.

Gopi Chand squeezed his eyes shut. Oh my! If all these sluts hit me with their bamboo sticks then I will die.

"Look, you bondwomen, once the day rose for me when I had fifty-two portals and fifty-three doorways, twelve districts' rule and a home court of judgment. And today look at me! I have fallen into the company of poverty and you sixteen hundred slave girls—you who were brought up on my scraps—are raising bamboo sticks over me. You have become ungrateful wretches, you who are my bought goods."

"Yogi, you're no yogi at all, you're sick! We will make you remember the blow you gave with your tongs. Now you try to make yourself into our king. Now you're afraid of being beaten so you pretend to be our king. But we don't count such a king. We will make your skin fly off with our bamboo sticks and we will rub your wounds with salt."

Meanwhile, son of a ...! They had surrounded Gopi Chand, and some prodded him, and some grabbed his matted locks, and some

52. Obviously Patam De Rani is a little overexcited and confused here. Her kingdom is already in big trouble, her lineage already "sunk" with no male heir and the king a renouncer. Her statement reflects the culturally prevalent fear of angry yogis.

53. These colors are favored by Rajasthani women for outer wraps.

began to toss his club and gourd and all his bag and baggage here and there.

Gopi Chand thought, Son of a . . . ! These sluts won't accept me. Gopi Chand was crying hard, his eyes filled with Indra's misty rain. Water poured from his eyes. And he besought his guru. "O Guru Sovereign, I beseech you, come quickly Baba Nath! O Jalindar Baba, these sluts who were nourished on my scraps are going to spoil my honor."

He mediated on the guru with body and mind, and he besought the guru with body and mind. "Jalindar Baba, Guru Sovereign, come quickly." He was such a truthful manly disciple, and Jalindar was such a truth-speaking guru, that immediately upon Gopi Chand's beseeching him, he was standing there.

[As an aside, Madhu adds: The gurus of today have become such that even if their disciples cry out in agony, still they don't glance in their direction.]

The guru came at once, and as soon as he came he said, "Well, Gopi Chand?"

"Guru Sovereign, these sluts, raised on my scraps, have spoiled my honor."

"O son, Gopi Chand, they will not accept you as you are. So take a square of cloth and get it wet; in your gourd is water—wet a square of cloth with it, and remove all the offering-ash from your body. Reveal the face of your ruling times, son, and right away all of those sluts will fall at your feet."

So, Gopi Chand took water from his gourd and wet a square of cloth and began to wipe off the offering-ash with the wet cloth.

As soon as he had wiped off the offering-ash—on his foot a lotus sparkled, and on his left arm a jewel gleamed, and on his head was the moon, so that it seemed as if the sun had risen in the portal. As soon as the sun rose, as soon as they saw the face of his ruling times, all of the sluts immediately threw down their bamboo sticks and fell at his feet.

They said to Gopi Chand, "Hey, Grain-giver, King, Baba, we are your purchased goods, and we have become ungrateful wretches. We came holding bamboo sticks above you, Grain-giver, and we are sluts reared on your scraps."

All sixteen hundred slave girls went falling and rolling and weeping into the Color Palace. Then Queen Patam De spoke: "O slave girls, first I sent one and she came back weeping, and just now I sent sixteen hundred and they all have come back crying.

"O girls, O bondwomen, I sent you laughing. Why have you come weeping like this? What kind of a yogi is it, a black magician? a death-spell wielder? Did he feed you roasted hashish, that you have come stoned—all sixteen hundred slave girls crying, huh? Is it some kind of a yogi magician who fed you powdered green hashish and you have come weeping, stoned on hashish?"

(GC 2.8.e)

So Hira De Dasi said to Queen Patam De, "Mistress, you may scold me or beat me or take away my life. But your fate is shattered. Your husband has come as a yogi. Gopi Chand is standing here as a yogi. Meeting is good and parting is bad and the noose of *māyā's* net is always very bad. Mistress, it's a carnival of parting. Your husband has come to your door, and if you want to take his *darśan* then go to the balcony. If you don't, then it's a yogi's bane.[54] If he gets up and goes, you'll never even have seen his face.

"Mistress, break and scatter these pearls in your hair; break and scatter these ivory bangles, too; break and scatter the sixteen kinds of ornaments you are wearing, for now you must put on a long blouse. Gopi Chand has come as a yogi. On his foot a lotus sparkles, and on his left arm a jewel gleams, and on his forehead is the moon so bright that it's as if the sun had just risen in the midst of the portal. Go onto the balcony and take your husband's *darśan*. If you like, beat me with the whip, and then go and look with your eyes.

"If the yogi gets up and goes empty-handed, he might give a yogi's curse. If he goes empty-handed, then the desire to see his face will stay with you the rest of your days."

Patam De Rani thought, Let's see, let's see from the balcony. She put wooden sandals on her feet and took a little stick in her hand.[55] And she went onto the balcony and looked into the portal. On his foot a lotus sparkled, and on his left arm a jewel gleamed, and on his

54. *jogī kī phaṭkār;* this can mean the influence of yoga but here seems analogous to worry about any ordinary yogi, leaving empty-handed and sending back angry emanations.

55. Why does the queen wear wooden sandals and carry a little stick? Later Manavati Mother comes in this fashion, more appropriate for a female yogi than a queen. Perhaps Madhu describes Patam De as shortly he will describe Manavati.

forehead the moon was as bright as if the sun had just risen in the portal.

Oh my! She went and saw his face, Gopi Chand's face, and Patam De Rani was satisfied. Oh my, look, how beautiful! What a king he is! But he has come under the spell of yogis.[56]

"Hey, King, so I seem bitter to you. And these Color Palaces and everything seem bitter to you and you met some yogi who seemed good. So you smeared yourself with offering-ash, and put great big rings in your ears. So I seem bitter to you, but that yogi seems good."

As she was saying this, Gopi Chand was looking up at the balcony, and Gopi Chand cried "*Alakh!*" and sounded his deer-horn instrument. He sounded it, and he held out his begging bowl in his hand: "Hey Patam Mother, drop in alms, my mother. This is my guru's strict order: Give me alms."

Oh my! As soon as he had said this, Patam De Rani beat her head against the wall, and said, "My own husband has called me 'Mother.' Better to die than to live." She beat her head against the wall and jumped off the balcony, and she fell into the portal.

As soon as she fell the queen lost consciousness. Then the sixteen hundred slave girls picked her up and began to massage her. They took her into the palace and wrapped her in a bedroll and massaged her. She had fainted. The eleven hundred queens were weeping and the sixteen hundred slave girls were weeping, and the combined resonance echoed through the palaces.

Manavati Mata lived in a different palace. "Why are the queens and slave girls weeping? What has happened?" Manavati Mother put on her sandals and picked up her little stick and hurried to Patam De's palace. As soon as she came, she asked, "O girls, why oh why are you weeping today? What has happened to make all the queens and slave girls weep? Are you in some kind of pain?"

Then the slave girls spoke, "Hey Mother-in-law, our Grain-giver is in the portal. Your son has come as a yogi. It's Gopi Chand: on his foot a lotus sparkles and on his left arm a jewel gleams and on his forehead is the moon so bright it seems as if the sun had just risen in the portal. Patam De Rani went to take his *darśan* and fell from above into the portal. She fell from the balcony and we have taken her into

---

56. *jogyāṅ kī phaṭkār ma āgyo; phaṭkār* here is less yogis' evil emanation than their influence. Thus Patam De explains to herself her husband's desertion.

the palace to massage her. Grain-giver, Gopi Chand has come as
a yogi."

"Why are you stirring up mischief? Many yogis come into the
portal. What would Gopi Chand come here to take? Gopi Chand will
not come here."

"Mistress, accept it if you like, or don't accept it. Mother-in-law,
go out on the balcony and see for yourself."

(GC 2.9.e)

Manavati Mata
went onto the balcony.[57]
Mother now saw Gopi Chand in the portal,
and bowed her head to him.

She bowed her head
to Gopi Chand,
and spoke to Gopi Chand:

"My son tell me what news
is in your heart?
Son, why did the guru send you here?
Why did you come to these castles?"

"For nine months, mother,
you kept me in your womb, Manavati Mother,
daughter and sister of kings.
It shames my saintly guru that my birth-giver
bows her head to me.

"Moreover, my birth-giver,
it shames your milk
if you prostrate yourself to me."

When Gopi Chand had said that much,
now what did Mother say?
"My Gopi Chand, King,
my darling boy, I didn't bow to you, my son,
I bowed to the guru's robes.

57. This sung part is also oversize. As above, I give the singing for which there
is no *arthāv*.

"Son, it's no shame to your saintly guru,
  nor does it shame
  your mother's milk.
My son, tell me your heart's news:
Why did the guru send you?"

"My mother, the guru sent me
  for this:
'Son, go to your Queen Patam De's palace,
  and cry "*Alakh!*" in the palace.
Gopi Chand, go and call Patam De "Mother,"
Gopi Chand, bring back alms.

"'Then your yoga
  will be fulfilled.'
Thus the guru sent me.
Mother, if I get alms
  from Patam De,
Then my yoga will be fulfilled."

When Gopi Chand had said this much,
  then his mother said,
"Gopi Chand, I'll have alms given you,
  but you must brace yourself.

"Illusion's net will fiercely spread,
  so you must fiercely brace yourself.
When she gives you alms,
  my son,
  your yoga will be fulfilled."[58]

So, as soon as she had said this much, Manavati Mother went back
into the palaces. As she was going she rebuked the queens and slave
girls. "O you sluts, why are you crying for no reason? Many yogis
come this way into the portals, calling "*Alakh!*""

But the slave girls said, "Mistress, we didn't believe what we heard,
but we came and saw for ourselves."

---

58. The following paragraphs are not sung but spoken: Madhu keeps strumming
the *sārangī* as he talks and at the end resumes his singing. Because the passage
advances rather than recapitulates the tale, it is not *arthāv*. This is one of only two
occasions when Madhu Nath's performance style thus briefly shifted.

"Shut up your useless wailing, sluts!"
Then she went over to Patam De, lifted off the bedding, grabbed
her hand, and sat her up.

Manavati Mata now lifted the bedding
from Patam De Rani.
"Patam De, give alms, my son,[59]
many yogis come.

"Son, why are you choosing misery?
Patam son,
many yogis come into the portals."

"O Mother-in-law, I didn't believe
what I heard from others,
Mother-in-law, I didn't believe
what the girls said.
But Mother-in-law, I saw from the balcony today:
your son has come as a yogi.

"Mother-in-law, my husband
called me 'Mother.'
Better to die than to live."

When Patam De had said this much,
what did Mother say?
"A yogi's breathed upon him,[60]
Son, but your husband is hungry and thirsty.

"Son, your husband has come
to your house,
you must feed him a good meal.
My son, make a meal for him,
Patam son,
Then bring him into the palace."

---

59. In affectionate affection, a Rajasthani mother-in-law or mother may call
a daughter-in-law or daughter "son." Manavati Mata uses this device now when
the greatest strength is required of her daughter-in-law.

60. *jogī kī lāgarī ye ūkai ab phūk;* this phrase means that Gopi Chand is under a
guru's control, has received a mantra at initiation. Meaning 2 in the *RSK* for *phūk*
is *mantra paṛte hue muh se chhoṛī jāne vāle vāyu:* "the breath that leaves the mouth when
reciting mantras."

"Mother-in-law, I will feed him a good meal,
I will feed him a good meal.
Mother-in-law, if he doesn't speak the sound 'Mother,'
then I will feed him a good meal."

"Patam, son, a yogi's breathed
upon Gopi Chand.
Feed your husband a good meal, son,
he has come to your door in hunger and thirst.

"Or else, son, the yogi will get up
and quit the portal today.
As he came, hungry, he'll leave.
Your husband has
given you *darśan*,
now you give him a good meal!"

(GC 2.10.s)

So the eleven hundred queens and the sixteen hundred slave girls prepared a feast, and Manavati Mata took the fresh warm food, nine kinds of festive food, and placed it on a platter. She placed a golden water jug on the platter. Then she took it to the portal. The eleven hundred queens and the sixteen hundred slave girls went weeping. And there was Gopi Chand, who immediately called *"Alakh!"* and sounded his deer-horn instrument. "Patam Mother give me alms, my mother, it is the guru's strict order."

But as soon as he said "Mother," she about-faced and went back. "If he is going to call me 'Mother' then I won't give it, I won't give him alms. It would be better to die than to live. Why has my husband called me 'Mother'?"

So Gopi Chand won't take alms without saying "Mother." And Patam Mother won't give alms.

When Patam De came back, Manavati Mata said, "Son, he is under the spell of yogis. Give him alms, and then afterwards we'll bring him into the palaces. And we'll give him a bath and we'll dress him in clothes. He's become a yogi, but now we'll keep him here.[61] Son, give him alms."

"Mother-in-law, he is calling me 'Mother,' so I won't give him alms."

---

61. Clearly this speech is intended to deceive Patam De.

"He has come under the spell of yogis, son, and you must give them." Pushing her, she brought her near to Gopi Chand.

"Patam Mother give me alms, my mother. It is the guru's strict order."

The queen backed up again, but Manavati Mother grabbed her wrist and pulled her and forced her to empty the platter. As soon as she had spilled the food into his cup, he took the alms, and as soon as he had taken them, the eleven hundred queens surrounded him and the sixteen hundred slave girls surrounded him, and took him in their midst.

Patam De said, "Grain-giver, I taste bitter to you, but you think that yogi's just swell. He shoved a loincloth up your ass and put these earrings on you. He pierced your ears and put these great big earrings[62] in them, and he gave you these long, spreading, matted locks of hair. You used to wear a fine coat and shirt, but now in their place you've smeared ashes. Grain-giver, these palaces taste bitter to you because the guru made you think the jungle's swell."

They took him in their midst, and then they brought the little princess, just so big—Phulam De, Gopi Chand and Patam De Rani's daughter—and they flung her on to him. As soon as they flung her, she recognized her father, because he used to play with her, and so she clung to his neck. She clung to his neck, holding on with intertwined fingers. The girl was weeping and nearby the queens and slave girls were weeping too.

And Gopi Chand too was crying hard, his eyes filled with Indra's misty rain. Gopi Chand was miserable.

"Hey Guru Sovereign, if you want to take care of me, then do it, or else, Guru Sovereign, I will go back and take care of my kingdom. Yes, I will take care of my kingdom, because over here the net of illusion is spreading fiercely.

"And the queens and slave girls are weeping. Hey, Guru Sovereign, as I beseech you, come quickly, Baba Nath. If you want to take care of me then do it, or else I will go back to taking care of my kingdom.

---

62. *murakā;* a special term for a man's ear ornament but not one of the several special terms for yogis' earrings—defined in the *RSK* simply as a "small earring" worn by men. Patam De says "great big *murakās*" either because she disdains yogis' earrings and will not accept Gopi Chand's having them (my theory) or because she is ignorant of the correct terminology (Bhoju's opinion).

And as for these earrings-and-stuff,[63] I'll get rid of them.

"Yes, I'll take care of my kingdom. Keep taking care of me, do."[64]

So he besought his guru with body and mind. And as soon as he besought him, then the Guru Sovereign, who had gone to the Kajali Woods, picked up his turn-to-ash tin and hurried to see what was happening.

The eleven hundred queens had surrounded Gopi Chand and the sixteen hundred slave girls were there too, and little princess Phulam De was hanging on his neck. And she was weeping, and the queens and slave girls were weeping, and from their mingled cries a single resonance arose.

Manavata Mata forbade them, but they wouldn't accept it.

The Guru Sovereign saw that whirlpool[65] and said, "Uh oh! Illusion's net is spreading very fiercely around here." So the Guru Sovereign took his turn-to-ash tin and circled it over Gopi Chand and burned him into a pile of ash.

Over here he turned Gopi Chand into ashes; at the same time he pushed him over there into his mother's palace. But right in front of the queens' and slave girls' faces he turned him to a pile of ashes. Manavati Mother looked toward her palace and saw Gopi Chand ascending into it. As soon as she saw him going in,[66] she said, "Weep, sluts! You've killed my son, now take a rest. May you all burn up! How many times did I explain to you, 'Don't cry, sluts, don't cry, don't surround him!' But you've killed my son, so take a rest, sluts! Now you can rest in comfort. You grabbed him and surrounded him, weeping. Now you've really killed him, he's dead."

Gopi Chand was seated in his mother's castle. When his mother got there, she lit the stove and prepared food. She prepared food and gave Gopi Chand a good meal.

(GC 2.10.e)

What did Manavati Mother say to Gopi Chand?[67]

63. *murakyāṅ vurakāṅ;* here Gopi Chand seems to follow Patam De's lead in speaking disrespectfully of the sacred earrings.

64. The consecutive but contradictory statements are typical of Gopi Chand's perpetual uncertainty about his renunciation.

65. *chakkar;* also dizziness, circle, confusion.

66. Manavati therefore knows Gopi Chand is all right; she makes the following speech to deceive his women.

67. This is the final segment of GC 2; no *arthāv* follows.

"Feast on this meal, my darling boy,
and take the guru his special portion.
Don't go forward my son,
don't go backwards.[68]
Yes, my darling boy, don't go to the land of Bengal,
your mother forbids it.
My son, don't go to the land of Bengal,
your mother forbids it."

"Mother, I've looked ahead, my birth-giver,
and I have looked behind,
Manavati Mata, king's sister and daughter.
But I've never seen the land of Bengal.
Birth-giver, who lives over there?

"Reveal their mystery to me,
my mother,
and I will do your bidding."

"My son, on one branch
were two fruits,
King Gopi Chand,
King's son and brother.[69]
My darling boy, younger than you is your sister:
Now she will die in tears.

"My darling boy she'll eat
opium-poison and die:
'My brother has come as a yogi.'"

"My mother, eleven hundred queens,
my birth-giver, sixteen hundred slave girls
Yet, birth-giver, none of these ate poison and died.
So why will my sister die?
Reveal this mystery to me,
my mother,
and I will do your bidding."

---

68. The sense is probably something like, "Don't leave the straight and narrow path; don't vacillate."

69. Of course, Gopi Chand has no brother; the phrase "king's son and brother" is a convention.

"My darling boy, those eleven hundred queens, Gopi Chand,
those sixteen hundred slave girls
were born of others,
King Gopi Chand,
King's brother and son.
But, my darling boy, you and your sister had
    the same birth-giver,
my darling boy, she will die in tears.

"My son she will eat
opium-poison and die:
'My brother has come as a yogi.'"

"For nine months, my mother,
you kept me in your womb,
Manavati Mata,
King's sister and daughter.
Yes, my birth-giver, you slept in the wet,
and you laid me to sleep in the dry.[70]

"But mother, you didn't eat poison,
you didn't die, so
Why should my sister die?
Reveal this mystery to me,
my mother,
and I will do your bidding."

"My son for twelve years
I served the guru,
Gopi Chand King.
My darling boy, I served Shankar, Bhola Nath,
and brought you as a loan.
My son, be a yogi,
my dear,
and your body will be immortal."

"My mother, meeting is good, my birth-giver,
    parting is bad,

70. That is, she slept with him when he was a wetting infant, and when he soaked
the sheets she traded places with him.

It's a carnival of parting, my birth-giver, so I will surely
meet with my sister, Champa De."

"My son, if you go
to Bengal today
don't show them your king's face.
My darling boy, or Champa De is dead,
your sister.
Gopi Chand, don't show your face.
Son, now take a special portion
for the guru,
and go and make prostrations to him,
from me as well.
Go, son, and reach his campfire."

When Manavati had said this much,
Gopi Chand crossed one woods,
the yogi crossed a second woods,
then he came to the third woods.
In the Kajali Woods was the guru,
he bowed his head to the guru.

[*Madhu Nath's signature*][71]

The village, oh the city, is Ghatiyali,
Madhu Nath sang Gopi Chand.
Now praise Ram,
all brothers,
and recite Shankar's name.

Speak victory to Lord Shankar!
Victory to King Gopi Chand!

(GC 2.11.s)

---

71. This is the only closing where Madhu actually sang a formal *chhāp* or signature.

Part 3

Gopi Chand's Journey to Bengal

Introduction

Madhu Nath's account of Gopi Chand's journey to Bengal is twice as long as any other segment of the tale.[1] Moreover, the actual encounter with his sister, Champa De, accounts for a minute portion of this bulk. Elaborated, rather, are the several ways in which Gopi Chand is tormented by female Bengali magicians, and how his guru sends one rescue party that fails and then accompanies another that succeeds in rescuing him and subduing the rebellious women. Comedy and adventure as much as pathos set the mood here.

Initially, the contest between innocent Gopi Chand and his accomplished enemies is thoroughly one-sided. For the village audience, Gopi Chand's travails as an ox prodded in the rear end by a magician's slave girls, or as a donkey loaded with dirty skirts and mounted by a laundress, are exuberant fun. The magicians themselves are gleefully bad characters, completely duplicitous not only toward Gopi Chand but toward one another. Their magic, just like that of the yogis, is subsumed in ordinary life. Thus they use their magically acquired slave to aid in their tedious low-caste labors.

When required to explain the origins of their new work beast, Gangali Telin and Kapuri Dhobin in succession respond by fabricating stories of a newborn nephew and the return gift that a brother makes to his sister for her participation in protective rituals for his

1. The original title for this part was "Gopi Chand Goes to Dhak Bengal to Get Alms from His Sister, Champa De." It is the only one of Madhu Nath's titles that I modify.

child. In rural Rajasthan such rituals are indeed appropriate occasions to make valuable gifts to sisters. The lady magicians, wild and dangerous as they are, are not so different from ordinary women—a message that has a double edge: don't dismiss female power; or, watch out for female treachery.

The conflicts between Gopi Chand's fellow disciples and the Bengali women plus their disciples eventually escalate into a global battle of the sexes. These escalating conflicts offer a hyperbolic catastrophic vision of what would happen if a few independent women were allowed to influence the rest. When the women are finally defeated there follows an anticlimactic and unsuspenseful battle between male householders and renouncers. If the lady magicians were almost a match for Jalindar Nath and his yogis, the men of Bengal are pushovers.

Like the village audience, I too reveled in the temporary but glorious victories of the Bengali lady magicians when I first heard this part performed. The Rajasthani women I knew were high-spirited and outspoken but in my view a bit too dedicated to their household chores. After more than a year of living in their company, I was completely enchanted by the spunk and playfulness of Madhu's "Bengali women," ready to drop their babies and rolling pins and play games with yogis at a moment's notice. These were thrilling visions.

In the end, however, the women are defeated and punished. After at last transforming the Bengali women into donkeys, the guru tells his disciples, "Take your revenge," and they beat the she-asses until "marked . . . with all sorts of lines and stripes" they "dropped piles of shit all over." This scene is described with gusto, if no more than was the magicians' previous victory over the yogis. But I had filtered it out of my conscious memory, until I did the word-for-word translation. Then it made me unhappy. When I listened to the tapes and heard both Madhu and his audience chuckling happily during this moment of revenge, I was troubled.

Gopi Chand part 3 raises issues of anger, violence, and misogyny, even as the yogis raise their red-hot tongs to beat various adversaries. Beyond the collective violence against the she-asses, there are also individual blows—the first struck by Charpat Nath upon the male gardener's back, the second by the meek and mild Gopi Chand upon his sister's slave girl.

What is the point of these moments of violence? In part, I fear, they are funny. But why? Violence is a low form of action; wise yogis with restrained passions are not supposed to get mad. It is therefore comical when Jalindar rouses his disciples by declaring, "If you can't win with magic and spells, then use your tongs, give those sluts your tongs, beat them." But it is also shocking.

The lady magicians, regarding the welts on the gardener's back, sum it up: "What kind of pitiless yogi is that? . . . If they've given such a brand, these yogis don't understand pity. They don't even know the word for pity." Patam De in part 2 and Champa De later in part 3 make similar comments upon regarding the damage done by a yogi's tongs. Any involvement in the world is degrading for yogis, but violence is a particularly low form of involvement.

Just as there is a stock phrase for weeping—"Gopi Chand was crying hard, his eyes filled with Indra's misty rain. Water poured from his eyes"—so there is for anger: "X was muttering, dizzy, all in a flurry, till he [or she] burst out in rage and fury." The stylization of overwhelming emotion may be a trick to deny its disruptive, internal, individualistic dimension. Once again, the tale has it both ways. These yogis are not uncontrollably angry; they are acting a part. So the audience can laugh at a brutal yogi, feel disgusted with him, but at the same time reserve judgment.

Issues of kingship surface once more in Gopi Chand part 3. Just as in Bharthari 1, the dreaded specter of a kingdom without subjects is raised. In Bharthari the king must give up his daughter to set matters right with yogic powers. Here it requires rather more complex negotiations, and these are managed by a woman. Gopi Chand's sister, Champa De, tells her husband the king just how to abase himself sufficiently before the yogis, of whom he is frankly terrified. The result is to make the kingdom safe for begging yogis, as it surely was not while the wishes of the lady magicians held sway.

Gopi Chand's sister stands out even among the outstanding women of the epic. She demonstrates a sagacious diplomacy in instructing her husband in his dealings with Jalindar. Her intimacy with Gopi Chand is clearly unique. Not only is she the only woman who dies for him but, once revived by Jalindar's elixir, she is the only one who will eventually follow him, herself dressing as a female renouncer and wandering the forest in search of her yogi brother. She thus confirms Manavati's pronouncement that a sister, a fruit from the same branch, is the one who will display the greatest devotion. Yet even with Champa De the yogi's sustained ambivalence toward women is voiced. She is momentarily vulnerable when, in a split second of concern for her home, she lets Gopi Chand slip away. Madhu does not miss this chance to castigate her as "just like a woman"—with all the phrase's attendant implications of fickleness and material-mindedness.

Gopi Chand's emotional persona really dies when Champa De, his twin, dies in his arms. His parting from her is virtually the end of his story (Gold 1989). He will reappear, but not in a speaking role, only at the very end of part 4 where he passively partakes of the immortality that Gorakh Nath tricks Jalindar into giving him.

Text

Gopi Chand came from Manavati's palace with alms.[2] He had called Patam De Rani 'Mother' and brought alms from her hand. He had begged for the guru's special portion. Gopi Chand came to the guru, prostrated himself, and greeted him respectfully. He said, "Guru Sovereign, I have called my Queen Patam De 'Mother,' and I have brought alms from her, and I have brought alms from my mother's palace, too. I have brought you a special portion from my mother's palace. Guru Sovereign, it's enough, my aim has been fulfilled."

"Good, son. Now, Gopi Chand, praise God, son, and do *tapas* by the campfire."

"But Guru Sovereign, I still have one more desire. Grain-giver, my sister is in Dhaka, in Bengal, my sister, Champa De. My heart is set on meeting her.[3] So I will go and meet my sister, Guru Sovereign, and then come back."

Then Jalindar Baba said, "Gopi Chand, son, why are you tangling in illusion's net? You ought to praise God and recite his name. You are missing the chance to pray. Sister-fucker, why are you tangled up in illusion's net? How can you possibly wander in sorrow to your sister's place?"

2. Madhu strums the tune on his *sārangī* but talks rather than sings; note that no sung segment begins this part.
3. Literally, "the desire to meet with her is affecting my mind very powerfully." Indian psychology does not consider the "mind" (*man*) a good guide for the religiously inclined; rather it is often a willful opponent.

"No, Guru Sovereign, my consciousness[4] won't adjust to prayer until I have met with my sister."

Then the Guru Sovereign said, "Look, son, Gopi Chand, your sister, Champa De, lives in Dhaka. Over there, they won't allow you to meet your sister."

"Who won't allow me to meet her, Baba?"

"Over there is a land of magicians . . . seven lady magicians."

"Who?"

"Behri Yogin and Gangali Telin and Kapuri Dhobin, Setali Khamari and Luna Chamari and Bajori Kanjari and Chamani Kalali.[5]

/There are seven sisters./

"There are that many lady magicians, so, son, they will never allow you to meet with your sister."

Then Gopi Chand spoke, "Hey Guru Sovereign, I have in you such an all-powerful guru—so should I be afraid of magic spells?"

Then the Guru Sovereign said, "OK, Gopi Chand, so go and visit your sister. Come on the road and go on the road, and call all women 'Mother' or 'Sister.'" That was the Guru Sovereign's order. He gave it, and Gopi Chand bowed his head to the Guru Sovereign and left.

(GC 3.1.e)

Gopi Chand, abide in prayer, my son,
Praise the true Master,
Gopi Chand, king and king's son.
Yes, darling boy, from prayers and praises, my darling boy,
your body will be immortal.

Gopi Chand took his sack, his sack,
the yogi picked up his iron tongs.
Gopi Chand put on his sandals
and sounded his deer-horn instrument.

---

4. *cat* (H. *cit*); consciousness with a potential for enlightenment that mind lacks.

5. The caste names of these women translate as Yogin, Oil-presser, Washerwoman, Potteress, Leatherworker, Butcher, and Wine-seller. See Crooke 1926, 134, 437–38, for references to a "noted witch," called Lona Chamārin (the salt one), who strips naked in order to plant rice seedlings. I am indebted for this reference to David White, whose research on alchemical imagery in yogic teachings convinces him that "she is in some way a demonization of the corrosive powers of caustic substances" (personal communication 1987). *Lūṇ* is the Rajasthani word for salt.

A seated yogi's a stake in the ground,
but a yogi once up is a fistful of wind.
Yes, the Nath took the wind's own form
and turned his face toward Bengal.

Gopi Chand crossed one forest,
the yogi crossed a second forest,
now he came to the third forest.
Yes, in the third forest, Lord,
he reached the borders of Bengal.
When he reached the borders
his sister's
white, white palaces appeared.
[*Madhu mutters something and changes melodies.*]
The palaces appeared, and Gopi Chand,
the yogi, remembered things
about his ruling time.
Gopi Chand was crying hard, his eyes filled with
    Indra's misty rain.
Water poured from his eyes.

"How did such a day arise
for me, Gopi Chand,
how did it arise?
Seven hundred thousand horses
used to ride in my company,
used to ride in my company!
And I'd sit in a throne on an elephant's back,
whisks waving over me.

"There once was a day when
I'd arrive at my sister's
with such magnificence.
But with what magnificence have I come
to my sister's today?
On my fair body
a loincloth is wrapped,
on my fair neck
matted locks have spread,
now my whole body is smeared with ash, Lord,
today I come in poverty."

Gopi Chand was crying hard,
his eyes filled with Indra's misty rain.
Water poured from his eyes.
"There was a day when I had
fifty-two portals,
I had fifty-three doors,
I had twelve districts' rule, Lord,
but today I come in poverty."

Gopi Chand was crying hard,
his eyes filled with Indra's misty rain.
Water poured from his eyes,
and he meditated on the guru.
"Guru, my sister's palaces
are still distant,
my Guru Jalindar,
Guru, your campfire too,
is far away,
my Guru Jalindar.
Guru, in the jungle I feel great misery, Honored Guru,
from my beseeching please come.
Guru, as I beseech you, come, Baba Nath, sorrow-giver,
Oh please take care of me!"

(GC 3.2.s)

So Gopi Chand put on his sandals, took his tongs, took his sack,
picked up his deer-horn instrument, called *"Alakh!"* and bowed his
head to the Guru Sovereign. As soon as he had bowed his head . . . a
seated yogi's a stake in the ground, but a yogi once up is a fistful of
wind. The Nath took the wind's own form and turned his face toward
Bengal, in order to visit his sister.

He crossed one forest and a second forest, and within the third
forest he reached the borders of Bengal. As soon as he reached the
borders, his sister's white, white castles appeared. As soon as he saw
the white, white castles . . . for Gopi Chand it was as if a flaming wick
were set to one hundred maunds of gunpowder. Flames exploded,
like that.

"Oh ho, what an amazing thing has happened! There was a day
when I used to arrive at my sister's with such magnificence. There
were seven hundred thousand horses riding in my company and I sat

in a throne on an elephant's back with whisks waving over me and bards chorusing, 'Have mercy, Grain-giver, giver of grains!' And with what magnificence have I come to my sister's today!"

So Gopi Chand remembered his ruling times. Gopi Chand was crying hard, his eyes filled with Indra's misty rain. Water poured from his eyes. In the midst of the jungle he was weeping and wailing.

[Gopi Chand laments his changed condition and weeps for the guru here just as he did on approaching his wives' palaces. And, just as he did then, Jalindar comes and spurs him onward.]

(GC 3.2–3.e)

Gopi Chand continued on his way. A seated yogi's a stake in the ground, but a yogi once up is a fistful of wind. The Nath took the wind's form. He crossed one forest, he crossed the second forest, in the third forest he came to Bengal's waterside.

As soon as he reached the waterside, he set up his campfire-and-stuff, and he set up his meditation seat, and at once he began to meditate, began to turn his prayer beads, lowered his eyelids. So, Gopi Chand had come to Bengal's waterside and was meditating.

From over there all seven lady magicians were coming to get water. Lady magicians.

/All seven./

Seven, seven were coming.

/*Ann:* Of different castes?/

Of different castes. One was Behri Yogin, and Gangali Telin, and Kapuri Dhobin, Setali Khamari, Luna Chamari, Bajori Kanjari.

/*Ann:* Women?/

Yes, women: Setali Khamari and Chamani Kalali. The seven lady magicians were coming to the waterside to get water, and they were talking. In front of all the rest was Behri Yogin, for she was the guru-queen of them all. Among them was Gangali Telin, who looked onto the waterside and spotted Gopi Chand. That yogi appeared to be doing *tapas*.

Now Gangali Telin spoke: "Sisters, listen! Burn up all other matters and listen to me."

"What is it?"

"Look, over on the waterside, there's a yogi doing *tapas*. Many days have gone by since we've played a contest,[6] but today's our lucky

6. *bād rachāsyā;* literally, create a dispute.

day. So burn up all other matters and let's hurry to the waterside, for today we'll have a contest with this yogi."

As soon as she said this everyone got excited and, going to the waterside, they put down their double water pots. There was Gopi Chand, seated in meditation, his eyelids lowered, reciting prayers. So they surrounded Gopi Chand, all seven of them.

Then Behri Yogin said to Gopi Chand, "Yogi, where are you from? You look like an established Nath. Raise your eyelids, Baba Nath, I have come to take your *darśan*."

As soon as she said this, Gopi Chand thought, Brother, some devotee has come to offer service to me. He was hungry too, and thought, Someone must have brought food for me to cook, and then I will eat.

Gopi Chand raised his eyelids and looked around, and everywhere he looked he saw *women*. Silently he counted them and there were a full seven.

As soon as he had counted a full seven, Gopi Chand, who was hungry, stopped feeling hungry. Uh oh! Guru Sovereign said something about "seven lady magicians" and they seem to have come right here to the waterside. They didn't even let me into the city. They look like lady magicians and I don't even know magic, I don't even know spells. And now, who knows what they will do? Oh brother! So right away he lowered his eyelids again.

As soon as he had lowered his eyelids, Behri Yogin spoke: "Hey yogi, where are you from? Raise your eyelids, Baba Nath, I have come to take your *darśan*. Why do you shut your eyes now? Talk a little with your mouth. Who is your guru? What is your village and what is your name? Tell everything, or else we will play a contest with you."

As soon as she had said this, Gopi Chand spoke: "O sisters, I don't know contests nor do I know contesting, O Bengali women. And I am a yogi who was shaved only yesterday; I am a new-made yogi. So I know neither contests nor contesting. And I have come wandering aimlessly into Bengal."

Then Behri Yogin said, "Yogi, it seems you are a knowledge wielder, a love-spell wielder, a death-spell wielder,[7] since you have come into

---

7. *jāṅ jugāro* (someone who possesses knowledge), *kāmaṇ gāro* (often refers in the village to the magic used by Rajput women on bridegrooms), and *muṣṭgāro* (can refer to the action of injuring or killing with a particular *mudra* or hand gesture).

Bengal; otherwise you wouldn't even have glanced over here in Bengal. If you knew nothing, then how did you come into Bengal?"

"O sisters, I came to wander."

"Does this look like some public meeting place?[8] Without asking you have come to Bengal, and this is hardly a public meeting place. This is Bengal! How did you arrive if you know no magic and spells?"

"O sisters, I know nothing. I came only to wander."

"Yogi, now watch out for your magic, watch out for your spells! If you don't tell me all about yourself, then I will send you flying, I will send your campfire flying, I will turn your iron cane into a crow, I will turn your sack into a vulture, and that gourd of drinking water I will turn into a tortoise.[9] And I will send you flying in the sky. How did you come here into Bengal if you know nothing?"

Then Gopi Chand said, "Sister, I am a new-made yogi. Do as you please with me, sister. If you wish to fly me in the sky, that's fine; and if you wish to keep me on the earth, that's fine. But I have come as a new yogi, and sisters, *chhoṭ*[10] is striking my ears, so keep away from me."

Behri Yogin said, "Brother, nobody is allowed to come here."

"So is this your father's kingdom? Do you give the orders here?"

"Yes, I give the orders."

"Fine, sister, I won't come again, sister, I've come and now I'll go."

"Yogi, you seem to be a knowledge wielder, a death-spell wielder, and now watch out for your wisdom."

So right away Behri Yogin recited magic, and she recited spells, and she struck the magic blow.[11] Gopi Chand, poor thing, he knew nothing, he was a new-made yogi. And no one had taught him magic spells, and he had just come to visit his sister. Behri Yogin struck the magic blow and turned Gopi Chand into a parrot. Yes, she turned him into a parrot and put him in her sack.

---

8. The term used is *paṭelāṅ kī pol*—the entranceway to a headman or *paṭel*'s house. Inevitably involved in factional politics and settling disputes, a *paṭel* must keep open house for enemies as well as friends.

9. Behri Yogin address her threats to virtual emblems of yogic identity (Gold 1989).

10. An emanation harmful to any healing wound, one particularly associated with mentruating women.

11. *jādū kī phaṭkār;* in the *RSK phaṭkār* may be a vital blow, a shock, a curse, an angry look.

Then at the waterside all seven lady magicians filled their double water pots, put them on their heads, and returned to the city. They returned to the city, and there they went their separate ways. They each were heading home, but at just this moment, Gangali Telin spoke to her Guru Sovereign—to whom? to Behri Yogin.

(GC 3.4.e)

Gangali Telin said to Behri Yogin, "Hey, Guru Sovereign." /She was the chief disciple./

Yes, she said, "Guru Sovereign, what are you going to do with this parrot?"

"Sister, I will put him in a hanging cage in my house and give him food to peck; what else will I do? What's on your mind?"

"Guru Sovereign, give me this parrot, and I will put him in a hanging cage, and I'll have fine conversations with him."

"Look, Gangali Telin, if I give the parrot to you, then you will give the yogi sorrow."

"Grain-giver, would I give the yogi sorrow? I will give him lentils mixed with butter to peck and sweet sweet Ganges water to drink. I promise not to give this yogi any sorrow. I will love this parrot better than my own soul. Guru Sovereign, give me this parrot."

"Well, you'll really keep him with love, you'll love him better than your own soul?"

"Yes, Guru Sovereign, give me this parrot."

So Behri Yogin took him out from her sack and gave him to the Oil-presser woman. Then they split up, each going to her own house. Gangali Telin put him in her sack and went home. At her home she had three hundred fifty oil presses going. When she got there she took down her double water pots and put them in the water niche.[12] Then she put her hand in her sack and took out the parrot.

She took the parrot out of her sack, put him down, and recited magic. She recited spells and struck the magic blow and spoiled the parrot. She turned him into a young ox. She made an ox, and she pierced his nose and inserted a thick nose rope.

She had sixteen hundred slave girls. Who did? That Oil-presser woman. And she said to them, "You sluts, how can you be so slack,

---

12. Notice this homey detail, which also shows that the lady magicians, despite their dirty dealings with yogis, follow the life patterns of ordinary women.

when I am standing here with a virgin[13] ox? Take this ox and yoke him to the oil press and drive him day and night. Don't let this ox go, because he cost a lot of money. He was very expensive, and he is a virgin ox."

After she said this several of her slave girls came running and surrounded the ox. They grabbed him and bound his eyes,[14] and making soothing sounds they took him to the circular track and delicately put the yoke on him. They put on the yoke and the leather harness and struck his back with the nine-tailed whip, and as soon as they struck him, Gopi Chand leaped forward so that twenty kilos of oil seeds were pressed in just a few minutes. After all, he had been a ruler.

"Girls," said Gangali Telin, "don't set the ox free. Grind oil seeds in twenty-kilo batches, one after another. Make him go day and night, and if he goes slowly then beat him with the nine-tailed whip and poke him with the iron spike. Push him forcefully from behind. Don't let him go, this is a virgin ox."

Gopi Chand ground up one batch of seeds and a second one and a third. While he was grinding the fourth batch Gopi Chand's spirit withered.[15] Gopi Chand was crying hard, his eyes filled with Indra's misty rain. Water poured from his eyes. Plop, plop, his tears were falling, and he went slowly, and they beat him with the nine-tailed whip and shoved him from the rear with the toothed iron spike, so that the moon and the sun were printed on both his buttocks.[16] Gopi Chand was beginning to get hungry and he was tired; he had pressed four batches of seed, and the fifth was poured into the press. Now how far could he go? Gopi Chand was crying hard, and he besought his Guru Sovereign:

"Hey Guru Sovereign! Oh, father of a daughter! How nicely I have

13. *āsūdho;* can refer to a virgin, to one who has not worked for a long time, to a man who has not had sex with a woman in a long time, to a field that has lain fallow, or to one who cannot be exhausted in any way.

14. Oxen attached to oil presses are normally blindfolded—the only way, I was told, to fool them into walking in endless circles.

15. *khamalāgya;* Bhoju describes this as "to be finished like a flower after blooming."

16. Recall that in his ruling condition Gopi Chand is described as having the moon on his forehead, giving off such brightness that it is as if the sun were rising. Therefore, this branding of his rump has especial pathetic and ironic power. The conjunction of sun and moon carries sexual significance in Tantric yoga (Dasgupta 1969, 238).

visited my sister! Here I am yoked to the oil press and the sluts are poking all over my body. Wherever they please they are sliding the iron spike and striking me with the whip, and I am dying of hunger. Hey Guru Sovereign, now my life's breath will leave me. Guru Sovereign, I beseech you, come quickly, Baba Nath, for my breath is leaving me, and now I am in no condition to turn the oil press."

Gopi Chand was crying hard, his eyes filled with Indra's misty rain. Water poured from his eyes. He was turning the press very slowly. And such grace came to pass[17] that Kapuri Dhobin arrived to fetch some oil from the Oil-presser woman's house. There she saw the ox going, and a stream of his tears flowing, Gopi Chand's tears. They were beating him with the nine-tailed whip and welts were raised on his hide. And the moon and sun were printed on his buttocks by the iron spike.

"Hey you sluts, this ox is crying ceaselessly, his condition is completely spoiled. The moon and the sun are printed on his two buttocks, and his tears are falling, plop plop, and his complexion has blackened and the hairs of his body are standing on end. Now let the poor thing go."

"Mistress, how can we let him go?"

"Sluts, you will make him breathe his last. Let him go, his condition is ruined, he's crying hard."

"Mistress, Kapuri Mother, how shall we let him go, mistress? You know she ordered us to drive him night and day, and not to let him go, because he cost a lot of money. She said, 'Whip him with the nine-tailed whip, and prod him with the iron spike; drive this ox night and day!' So how can we let him go without her command?"

"Hey, let me in, who does your mistress think she is? Let me in to see that slut." So Lady Kapuri went in to see Gangali.

(GC 3.5.e)

She went up to Gangali Telin and asked her, "O Lady Gangali, Gangali lady, where did you get this ox? Yesterday I came to your house and there was none. So where did this ox come from today? This ox you have brought is a handsome one. Where did you get it?"

---

17. *asī kṛipā hoī;* a remark perhaps intentionally ironic, because the Washerwoman saves him from the oil press only to give him even more wretchedness. In the sung version Kapuri Dhobin comes to take laundry rather than to fetch oil.

Then what did Gangali say? "Kapuri Dhobin, don't keep saying 'handsome, handsome' lest the evil eye strike my ox. You said it two or three times, so now spit from your mouth, spit lest the evil eye strike my ox.[18]

"My brother went to a lot of trouble to give it to me, so that I could live off its earnings. Look, Kapuri, in my natal home my nephew was born. So I took bracelets and necklaces, and my brother gave me the ox as a return gift.[19] So, spit from your mouth, lest the evil eye strike my ox and my ox die. Spit then."

When she had said this much, Kapuri Dhobin was muttering, dizzy, all in a flurry, till she burst out in rage and fury. Thus enraged, Kapuri Dhobin began to recite magic, and having recited magic she recited spells, and having recited spells she struck the magic blow and spoiled the ox. She released it from the oil press and turned it into a donkey, and she grabbed the donkey's ears and brought it home with her. She brought it home and tied it to a stake and went running all around Bengal.

She ran around Bengal, and from some she took skirts and from some turbans; she took skirts and wraps from all the women of Bengal. She took them in order to wash them. She brought them and loaded them on top of the donkey. She piled them on the donkey, and she sat herself on top of the pile and went to the pond. She tied up the donkey and washed the clothes, and she piled the wet clothes back on him, and she, the Washerwoman, sat on top. Gopi Chand was crying hard, his eyes filled with Indra's misty rain. Water poured from his eyes.

Gopi Chand wailed, "Oh me oh my, Guru Sovereign, you must come. Your eyelids are closed over there in the Kajali Woods, but I am your disciple, and how my condition has been spoiled today! The clothes from all of Bengal, skirts and wraps, are on top of me, on top of the king. It doesn't seem possible that someone would pile up skirts and wraps on top of King Gopi Chand, but there it is, Guru

---

18. *nazar* or the "evil eye" refers to the destructive effects of looking with admiration on another's prized possession. Spitting is an antidote.

19. *ḍhūṇḍ ma;* literally, in the *ḍhūṇḍ*. That is, she brought ornaments to her brother's wife and child on the occasion of *ḍhūṇḍanā*—a ritual for the protection of a new son to which sisters must bear gifts. An ox would be an exceptionally fine but not unheard of return gift from a brother.

Sovereign.[20] And what's more, the Washerwoman has seated herself on top of me—a Washerwoman is seated on top! So Grain-giver, if this were my ruling time, and a Washerwoman sat down on top of me, then I would bury her deep and have horses trample her, or else I would make her fly from a cannon's mouth. But I am being controlled by others, and Guru Sovereign, I beseech you to hurry today, Baba Nath, O sorrow-giver, take care of me!"

Gopi Chand was crying hard, his eyes filled with Indra's misty rain. Water poured from his eyes. The Washerwoman kept on driving Gopi Chand back to her house. There she tied him to a stake and put the clothes out to dry. So he spent the night there and the next day came. On that day, who came to the house? The Washerman had drunk wine, so Chamani Kalali, the Wine-seller woman, came to ask for payment.

(GC 3.6.e)

As soon as she got there, she saw the donkey tied up. And she said to Kapuri Dhobin, "Kapuri, lady, where did you get that donkey? Yesterday you hadn't a donkey. So where did you get it? Lady, that donkey strikes me as handsome! You have brought a very fine thing."

When she had said this, Kapuri Dhobin spoke. "Look, sister, spit from your mouth, lest the evil eye strike my donkey. If my donkey dies now then what of yours will be spoiled? In my natal home my nephew was born. I brought them auspicious designs and auspicious hangings, and I also brought puffed grains.[21] I went to my nephew's protection rite and my brother gave me this donkey so I could live off its earnings. Chamani Kalali, spit from your mouth, slut, lest the evil eye strike my donkey. Spit, because my brother is a great miser, and he gave it unwillingly. Yes, and you will kill it, the evil eye will strike it."

When she had said this much, Chamani Kalali was muttering, dizzy, all in a flurry, till she burst out in rage and fury. Thus enraged,

---

20. In Rajasthan the mention of soiled skirts cannot but evoke the potential of menstrual pollution. I was told that even the skirt of a non-menstruating woman was polluting because it must have come into contact with menstrual blood.

21. Colored designs (*sāṭyā*) are made on paper and placed by the door of a new mother, usually not for *dhūṇḍanā* but on the day of the postpartum cleansing ritual and sun god worship. Wreaths (*bāndarvāl*) are hung over the doorway during celebrations of childbirth. Grains (*dhāṇī*) are usually barley or wheat.

she recited magic, Chamani recited spells, and she struck the magic blow. As soon as she struck the magic blow, she spoiled the donkey and turned him into a rooster, a cock. She made him a rooster and put him in her sack and took him to her house. And the Washerwoman just stood there staring.

She took him and began to teach the rooster. She taught him to speak—"Cockadoodle doo!"—and sat him on the rooftop.

Gopi Chand had fifty-two portals, he had fifty-three doorways, he had twelve districts' rule, and a court of judgment in his home—and he had seven hundred thousand horses. When he went out with his horse company, seven hundred thousand horses went out. And he rode on an elephant, upon a royal seat, and whisks were waved over him, and his praises were constantly shouted out by numerous bards. How did a condition like Gopi Chand's get ruined?

Chamani Kalali had made Gopi Chand into a rooster and seated him up on her rooftop and taught him to speak in a fine voice as the sun was rising.

Now Behri Yogin's husband was Asamal Yogi. So he was the Wine-seller's elder sister's husband.[22] Who?—Asamal Yogi. He lived at Asan where Ogar Nath lives.[23] Behri Yogin lived there, at Asan, and there Asamal Yogi had set up his campfire, for doing *tapas*. He kept on doing *tapas* all day. And all alone he played sixteen flutes at once.[24] Who? Asamal Yogi. And he remained absorbed in the melody. So at daybreak Behri Yogin would take her sack and go begging for flour. Begging for flour, she went to Chamani Kalali's.

(GC 3.7.e)

> Behri Behri Yogin, the slut,[25]
> took her sack, the slut
> took her tongs,
> put on her sandals and

22. *jījājī;* because of the guru-sister relationship that unites the lady magicians.

23. This is another instance of Madhu's half-joking location of his story in local scenery; Ogar Nath is a member of Madhu's family who lives as a renouncer on the grounds of a village Shiva temple called Asan—literally "Meditation Seat." See Gold 1988, 48–50.

24. *soḷā puṅgyāṅ na ekalo bajāvai;* I thought this might allude to some difficult meditation practice, but villagers understand it to mean that he actually has sixteen flutes in his mouth.

25. A few lines of singing are not covered by *arthāv*.

sounded her deer-horn instrument.[26]
Now throughout Bengal, today the lady yogi
is going to beg for flour.

Begging for flour
she arrived at
Chamani Kalali's house.
The lady yogi arrived at the house,
and called "*Alakh!*"
and sounded her deer-horn instrument.
She sounded her horn and
looked up on the roof
and saw a rooster
sitting there.
The lady yogi saw the rooster, and what did Behri Yogin say
to the Wine-seller woman?
"Wine-seller woman, where did you pick up
this extra yogi, slut?

"One slut turned him
into an ox,
and yoked him to the oil press.
One slut turned him
into a donkey
and one made him a rooster.
O slut, where did you pick up
this extra yogi, slut?"

When Behri Yogin had said this much,
Chamani came outside.
Chamani came outside, prostrated
to the lady yogi,
then stood with her palms joined.
"My guru, I have given your yogi
no trouble at all.
My guru, yesterday I went to the Washerwoman's
and she kept him as a donkey.
My guru, I turned the donkey into a rooster,

26. Note that she prepares to go begging just as a male yogi would.

I only brought him yesterday.
My guru, I have given this yogi no trouble, dear guru,
what do I want with a yogi?
My guru, take away the yogi, dear guru,
what do I want with him?"

When Chamani had said this much,
the slut Behri Yogin
began to recite magic,
the lady yogi began to recite spells.
The lady yogi struck the magic blow
and turned the rooster back into a parrot.

(GC 3.8.s)

So Behri Yogin turned him into a parrot and put him in her sack
and brought him from Chamani Kalali's place. Begging flour as she
went she continued on her way until she came to Asan. As soon as
she came to Asan, there was her husband, playing one melody on
sixteen flutes. He was filled with the flutes' melody and was sitting in
a meditation posture, like this, and the crackling fire was burning,
and the yogi was intoxicated by the melody. Just then Behri Yogin
came and said, "Hey, my husband, you are intoxicated by the
melody, but I have brought a surprise for us."

As soon as she said this, Asamal Yogi stopped the melody of all the
flutes and raised his eyelids and said to Behri Yogin, "Ho, lady yogi,
what surprise have you brought? Tell me. What have you brought?"

At once, Behri Yogin put her hand into her sack and took out the
parrot. She took out the parrot and put it at the feet of Asamal Yogi.
As soon as she put down the parrot, Asamal Yogi looked at it. He
looked at the parrot with attention, and he shook his head, like this
[*in disapproval, as Madhu demonstrates*]. "You've done something awful,
lady yogi. You've done something awful! Why have you brought it?
O, you sorrow-giving slut, what crime did it do?"

"O Grain-giver, what happened, tell the truth. Why are you
shaking your head?"

"O slut, why have you brought your death? Your death has come.
Put him back where you got him."

Behri Yogin said, "What do you mean, my death?"

"He is the king of Gaur Bengal. His name is Gopi Chand, and he
is the real brother-in-law of our own king, and he is our queen's real

brother. So when king finds out he will bury you deep and have horses trample you, or he will send you flying from a cannon's mouth. Whom? All seven of you sluts. And if it so happens that our king and queen don't find out, well he is Jalindar Nath's disciple, Jalindar Nath! In the Kajali Woods his fourteen hundred invisible disciples are gathered, doing *tapas*, and his fourteen hundred visible disciples are doing *tapas*, and his fire burns with saffron. So Jalindar Baba will come and lay waste to the whole city. And he will turn you all into donkeys and beat you with tongs until your skin flies off. Braying 'Tibhu tibhu' you will wander here and there.

"Put him back where you got him. He is your death. Take him back wherever you found him. Let him go. There's no use keeping him, so hurry up and put him back. If you are saved from the sword's blade you will be slain with the point, and if you are saved from the point, then you will be slain with the blade."[27]

After Asamal Yogi had said this much, Behri Yogin was muttering, dizzy, all in a flurry, till she burst out in rage and fury. Picking up the parrot she put him in her sack, saying, "My pockets are filled with many such as Jalindar Baba. I keep them in my pockets. But you, Baba, you are uselessly absorbed in the melody of sixteen flutes."

She put him in her sack. There was a two-story building there, in Asan, and she climbed upstairs, saying to herself, "Many like Asamal Yogi play in my pockets." But as she was running, Asamal Yogi spoke, "Ho, lady yogi, one day your pockets will split and Jalindar Baba will emerge. Your pockets will burst, and on that day I won't come to help you."

"Fine, don't come! My pockets are filled with many such as him, Babaji." And she climbed to the top floor, set out her cot, hung the parrot in a cage, and lay down to sleep.

(GC 3.8.e)

Behri Yogin tossed this way and that, but she couldn't get to sleep. A train of thought[28] filled her mind. Her thoughts ran on about what Asamal Yogi had said. Her eyes were shut, but she couldn't get to sleep. She thought, My husband Asamal Yogi said: "This is the king

---

27. That is, if you escape the king then Jalindar Baba will get you, and vice versa.
28. *veg* or *beg;* literally "speed," but used for an interior stream of thought that is uncontrollable.

of Gaur Bengal, and put him back where you got him." So let's see, is it the king of Gaur Bengal? He said it was Gopi Chand, so let's see, a king's face is hardly unrecognizable. Let's make him into a man and look at his face and see if his face is a king's beautiful one.

In the attic Behri Yogin quickly took down the cage and took the parrot out of the cage. At once she recited magic and recited spells and struck the magic blow, and she turned the parrot into a man. As soon as she made it a man, it was Gopi Chand, the king's son. On his foot a lotus sparkled and on his left arm a jewel glittered and on his forehead was the moon, so it seemed as if the sun had risen on the top floor. As soon as that sun rose, Behri Yogin turned her full gaze in his direction, Behri Yogin looked, and as soon as she looked she became dizzy, dazzled by the king's radiance, she fell face down. Behri Yogin was not able to endure the king's heat, so she fell on her face and for two hours she remained without consciousness, without knowledge.

Gopi Chand saw. "Now she's unconscious. But if I kill her, then what will happen? There are too many others—what good will it do to kill just one? Brother, if I kill this lady yogi the others are ready. Asamal Yogi is ready, and there are seven lady magicians ready, there is all of Bengal full of powerful magic-wielders. They will not let me go safely. So what's the use of killing her? Let me beseech the guru!

"By now, so many days have passed when I've been in animal bodies. Some days I was a donkey, and some days I was a parrot, and some days I was a rooster, and some days I was an ox and yoked to the oil press. But now I'm inside a human body, so with body and mind let me meditate on the guru."

So Gopi Chand besought the guru with body and mind, "Hey Guru Sovereign, from my beseeching quickly come, Baba Nath, O sorrow-giver, if you would take care of me then please do, because my soul is very confused.

"And Baba, I have endured so many troubles. Just now I am in a human body, and in my human body I am meditating on you. Guru Sovereign, remove my troubles, Guru Sovereign, then I will never come back to Bengal."

So with his body and mind Gopi Chand remembered and praised his guru, up on the top floor. As soon as he remembered him, the guru's meditation seat in the Kajali Woods began to shake. There were fourteen hundred disciples doing *tapas* invisibly and fourteen hundred doing *tapas* visibly. Among these, Charpat Nath, was the chief disciple. Charpat Nath stood at the campfire, serving the guru, and right away the Guru Sovereign's eyelids opened, and as soon as he opened his eyes, he said to Charpat Nath, "Son, Charpat?"

"Yes, Guru Sovereign?"

"Son, what king's kingdom is swaying? Son, what ascetic's asceticism has diminished, what truthful person has swayed from truth? Say, son, my meditation seat trembled and my eyelids opened— what's going on?"

Then spoke who? Charpat Nath. Palms joined together, he spoke, "Hey Guru Sovereign, hey Jalindar Baba, you made Gopi Chand, the king of Gaur Bengal, your disciple. You made him your disciple, Baba, and you put yogis' earrings in his ears and caused him to put on renouncers' clothes and caused his hair to grow and spread and smeared him with ash and sent him into Bengal to visit his sister. But he hasn't met his sister, and, Guru Sovereign, over there he met the other sisters, on the road, the other sisters, the seven lady magicians. And, Guru Sovereign, Gopi Chand's condition has been greatly spoiled. Grain-giver, take care of him at once. You made him a disciple and you sent him, and he knew nothing at all, nothing. You sent him to visit his sister and he has suffered a great deal of sorrow, a great deal. His tears are flowing. You had better take care of Gopi Chand right away."

"Good, good, son, let's do it right now."

Meanwhile, two hours passed completely, and Behri Yogin regained consciousness. As soon as she regained consciousness, "Oh me oh my, the father-eater! If he had wanted to kill me, he could have done it, he could have kicked me. It's weird that I lost consciousness."

Having regained consciousness, she recited magic and she recited spells and she struck the magic blow. As soon as she struck the magic blow, she turned Gopi Chand back into a parrot. She made him a parrot and shut him in the cage and took it to a dark pit[29] in the middle of Asan. It was a chest-deep hole, and she buried him with the cage, so deep, and pushed a flat stone on top.

"We'll see, if Jalindar Baba comes, how will he search and who will give him the address?

29. *khāī;* according to Bhoju this can refer to a ditch, moat, or trench, such as rich people have beneath their houses to hide money and valuables.

/Even the wind can't go near him./
"We'll see who will give him Gopi Chand's address."
And now let's see about Jalindar ourselves.

(GC 3.9.e)

Jalindar Nath said to Charpat Nath, "Call the fourteen hundred disciples. We will send them into Bengal to search for Gopi Chand and bring him back." So as soon as he got the Guru Sovereign's order, Charpat Nath went. And he brought the fourteen hundred disciples who were doing *tapas*, and they stood in the exalted presence of the Guru Sovereign. The Guru Sovereign said, "O sons, fourteen hundred disciples, go to Bengal now, and search for Gopi Chand and bring him back at once."

The fourteen hundred disciples said, "Guru Sovereign, we will shit right here but we won't put a foot in Bengal!" [*Laughter*]

"Why, what's the matter?"

"Grain-giver, we know nothing and—son of a . . . !—as soon as we get there, they will make us into donkeys. What can we do by going there? We won't have the tiniest effect. As soon as we get there, they'll turn us into donkeys, so we won't go to Bengal at all."

Then the fourteen hundred disciples said, "Guru Sovereign, send Charpat Nath with us to Bengal, send the chief disciple, and then we will go otherwise, as soon as we get there, my son's . . . they will make us into donkeys. So send Charpat Nath with us and then we will go."

When they had spoken the Guru Sovereign said, "OK, son, Charpat Nath?"

"Yes, Guru Sovereign?"

"You go, son, and search for Gopi Chand and take care of him and quickly bring him back."

Then Charpat Nath said, "Hey Guru Sovereign, send me too, but later take care of me quickly, so I won't end up a donkey braying in the wilderness, because of those sluts. I don't want to bray in the wilderness while you're over here with your eyelids lowered."

"That would be a big surprise. The sister-fuckers . . . go! How can those sluts make donkeys out of you?"

Then the fourteen hundred disciples took their sacks, picked up their tongs, put on their sandals and lifted their horn instruments. Then they bowed their heads to their Guru Sovereign. A seated yogi's a stake in the ground, but a yogi once up is a fistful of wind. The Naths took the wind's own form and turned their faces toward Bengal. They crossed one forest, they crossed a second forest, and in the third forest they reached the garden of Bengal. As soon as they reached the garden, there was the garden-keeper[30] standing in the entranceway, Bhairu Mali.

"Hey garden-keeper."

"Yes, Sovereign."

"OK, brother, open the gate. Here are fourteen hundred yogis, who will do *tapas* in the garden."

Then the garden-keeper said, "Loincloth-wearers, what connection does this place have with Babajis? If I let you in, you will spoil the king's garden. Scram into the jungle! Do *tapas* in the jungle. If you set up your campfires here, you will break the mango and lemon and orange trees. So go into the jungle. What business do Babajis have in the garden?"

Then Charpat Nath said, "Garden-keeper, these yogis don't do *tapas* in the jungle, they do *tapas* only in gardens. So open the gate."

"O loincloth-wearers, didn't I say you have no business in this garden? Go in the jungle to heat yourselves at fires. This is the king's garden and you will spoil it. There is no order to let you enter it."

"So, there's no order?"

"Yes."

At this point Charpat Nath was muttering, dizzy, all in a flurry, till he burst out in rage and fury. He gave the garden-keeper a blow on the back with his tongs that sent him rolling. Falling and rolling went the Gardener. He had given just one blow to the Gardener, but two welts rose up on his back, just like when sick livestock are branded.

And he went rolling and wailing, he fled into Bengal. Over there at the waterside all seven lady magicians—Gangali Telin, Kapuri Dhobin, Setali Khamari, Luna Chamari, Bajori Kanjari, and Chamani Kalali, all seven lady magicians[31] were filling their pots with water. And here came the garden-keeper, crying and crying.

---

30. *bāgavān;* I translate this term, referring to a particular post, as "garden-keeper," and for the caste name *Mālī* I use Gardener. Bhairu is the name of a member of the audience who is of the Gardener caste.

31. He has left out Behri Yogin, probably by accident.

/After having been branded./

After having been branded. [*Laughter*]

Then all seven love-spell wielders spoke. "O garden-keeper, Bhairu, Oh father of a daughter! What happened? Why are you crying? What terrible trouble has befallen you? What's the matter? Tell the truth—what are you crying about?"

"What am I crying about? I am crying to you, O sluts, to you. You did it, you must have committed some crime and what has happened? Well, you are lady magicians and you have suspended all of Bengal in midair with your magic.[32] But what's the big accomplishment of doing magic here in our own village? Fourteen hundred yogis have come into the garden. Do some magic on them, and then I'll know your magic is true. O sluts, you can frighten anyone in the village, but let's see you do some magic on these yogis who have come, fourteen hundred of them. Make them run away, and then I will know that your magic is true."

"Hey, we will go at once."

"Uh uh! Don't say you're going yet—first look at my back." Then he ran right up to them and spread himself face down before them. From the back of his neck right down to his hips, there appeared two stripes.

/He was branded./

He was branded. As soon as they saw the brands, they shut their eyes. "O garden-keeper, Bhairu, father of a daughter! What kind of pitiless yogi is this? He gave you one blow on the back, but two welts have risen, just like when sick livestock are branded. If they've given such a brand, these yogis don't understand pity. They don't even know the word for pity."

"Now don't you go, in forgetfulness and trust. Don't go. They gave me one blow, but if you go they will decorate[33] you. Don't go in forgetfulness and trust, for they'll beat you with their tongs until your skin flies off. That's the kind of yogis they are."

"They're like that?"

"Yes, like that. Don't you go."

---

32. *ākhā Bangāḷā na adhar kar melyo ho jādū kā ghālyā;* as noted previously, to be in midair, or betwixt and between, is a bad condition.

33. *manḍṇā;* to make designs of white paste such as women use to enhance the beauty and auspiciousness of their courtyard floors.

After hearing this much they decided, "Let's go back to the village and get everyone together. We'll send around invitations."

So, they returned to the village, and each of the seven lady magicians bought seven maunds of rice and stained it yellow, tossed it in the frying pan and made it yellow. Then they sent invitations, each to her own disciples.[34] Each one of them had seven hundred disciples.

(GC 3.10.e)

Well, brothers, they brought along those who weren't disciples, too, just to see the show. "Come along with us, we'll have a contest with the Babajis." So they gathered at the waterside, some wrapped in striped wraps or wraps with silver trim, some wearing flowered skirts. Dressed like that they came, in splendid multicolors, on the pretext of getting water. They gathered from the whole village, from the whole city.

In front of them all were the seven lady magicians, and in front of the seven was the guru-queen, Behri Yogin. They hurried to the garden. They went through the gate, and the fourteen hundred yogis had lowered their eyelids, and their campfires were crackling. They had put logs in their campfires and they had lowered their eyelids, and they were reciting "Shiv Shiv."

The garden filled with all the women of Bengal. Behri Yogin went up to the yogis and said, "Hey yogis, from which city do you come and go, because you seem to be established Naths. Open your eyelids, Baba Nath, for I have come to take *darśan*."

Meanwhile, Charpat Nath raised his eyelids and looked. As soon as he raised his eyelids he saw. "Oh my! Just as clouds mount in the month of *Srāvan* coming from the place of Indra, like those clouds, mounting and mounting, are these women dressed in red and yellow." The garden was filled and a procession of women spanned the village reaching all the way to the waterside. "O Lord, if they are all magicians, then there won't be enough of us to go around—how will they share us out?"

Charpat Nath closed his eyes, "Hey Lord, are there so many blasted lady magicians here? No matter, it's all to be done by the Guru Sovereign."

---

34. Even today traditional Rajasthani invitations are sent via messengers bearing grains of yellow rice.

Behri Yogin had come, and she said, "Hey yogis, where do you come from and where are you going? You seem to be established Naths. Raise your eyelids, Baba Nath, I have come to take your *darśan*. At which campfire were you initiated, who is your guru? What is your name and what is your village? How is it that you have come in such a mass? Give me this information; if not I'll play a contest with you."

"O sisters, I don't know contests and I don't know contesting, O Bengali women. Why have you come to quarrel with meditating *sādhus*? Go home. I have lost my central and priceless pearl[35] and I've come to Bengal to search for it."

"O yogis, you must be knowledge wielders, you must be love-spell wielders, you must be death-spell wielders, for you have come into Bengal, and if you weren't then you couldn't have come. What priceless pearl have you lost? You must be knowledge wielders and for this reason have come here to give us a test. Now tell everything, or else, yogi, I will play a contest with you."

"O sisters, I don't know contests and I don't know contesting."

"You don't know? Does this look like some public meeting place where you can come without asking?"

"I didn't know, lady, that your wishes were commands here, or I wouldn't have come."

"O yogi, knowledge wielder, love-spell wielder, death-spell wielder, watch out for your wisdom now. Because I am going to send you and your campfires and your gourds and your iron tongs and your sacks all flying in the sky."

"Let them fly." As he said this, Charpat was muttering, dizzy, all in a flurry, till he burst out in rage and fury. And Charpat Nath recited magic and recited spells and struck the magic blow and turned all the sluts into donkeys—every single one of them. Charpat Nath made them all into donkeys. But, my son's . . . ! Behri Yogin remained standing.

She stood there and challenged Charpat Nath: "Yogi, if you are holding back some of your wisdom, then swear on your guru a hundred thousand oaths! As much wisdom as you've got, let it come over

35. *khān;* according to Bhoju, this is a variant spelling of *kāṅn,* one of the names of Krishna, and implies that Gopi Chand is as special among Jalindar's disciples as Krishna was among the Gopis.

me. You have made all the city's women into donkeys. But now let your wisdom come on me, let it come now!"

Charpat Nath once more recited magic, recited spells, struck the magical blow. He said spells into many pebbles and threw them, but not one struck Behri Yogin. After a bit she said, "Have you finished?"

"Lakshmi,[36] my magic doesn't work on you."

"So, Charpat Nath, better be careful because my skill is coming." And Behri Yogin recited magic, she recited spells, she struck a magic blow, and as soon as she had struck a magic blow, she turned all the disciples into donkeys. After this clash, Charpat Nath alone remained standing. And on the other side, only the lady yogi. That's it, the others were made into donkeys. But sister-shamed Charpat Nath! While she alone remained standing, if only he had given her a couple of blows with his tongs, then he might have been able to stop the lady yogi. But he missed his chance. Charpat Nath again recited magic and recited spells, but nothing happened. That was it, he was defeated. "Enough, enough, now what can I send over you, Lakshmi?"

She said, "Charpat Nath, be careful, now my skill is coming." And she recited magic. After reciting magic she recited spells, and she struck the magic blow. Son of a . . . ! The lady yogi turned Charpat Nath into a camel. She made him a camel and then the lady yogi turned the women who were donkeys back into women. Who? Behri Yogin.

Yes the fourteen hundred disciples were made donkeys, and the women beat them soundly with sticks, and they threw clumps of earth at them. "Run off, let's go!" They drove them into the wilderness and left them there.

Having left them in the jungle they came back. They had won, and came singing victory songs, son of a . . . ! They were happy! And they went into the village. And the women said to those who had not gone, "My sister-in-law, if only you had come with us! Fourteen hundred yogis were made into donkeys and driven into the jungle. We played a contest today and had a lot of fun."

"O big sister-in-law, take me with you next time, take me with you. Next time, sister-in-law, don't leave me behind." So right away the others were ready. The women were talking like that, and

---

36. It is common in the village to address a woman who is giving you a hard time as the goddess of good fortune and prosperity.

the fourteen hundred disciples were braying, "Tibhu tibhu," and beseeching the Guru Sovereign. "Hey, Guru Sovereign, we beseech you, come quickly, Baba Nath."

(GC 3.11.e)

So, the fourteen hundred disciples had eaten up all the grass. And now what was left to eat in the wilderness? Charpat disciple, who was turned into a camel, had stripped off and eaten the leaves of all the *nīm* and *khejaṛā* trees. And he besought the Guru Sovereign. He was crying hard, his eyes filled with Indra's misty rain. Water poured from his eyes. He besought the guru, "Hey Guru Sovereign, come here quickly, Baba Nath, O sorrow-giver, now take care of us. Those lady magician sluts have turned our fourteen hundred disciples into donkeys and driven them into the jungle."

The fourteen hundred disciples were crying hard, their eyes filled with Indra's misty rain. Water poured from their eyes. Whose eyes? The donkeys'. They had turned the fourteen hundred into donkeys, and the chief disciple, Charpat Nath, they turned into a camel. The camel in the jungle was crying and beseeching the guru with body and mind, and the fourteen hundred disciples were beseeching the Guru Sovereign: "Baba, we pray, come here quickly, Baba Nath, we are turned into donkeys and Grain-giver, you have your eyelids lowered over there, but the seven lady magicians of Bengal turned us into donkeys and drove us into the jungle."

As soon as they besought the guru with body and mind, the Guru Sovereign's eyelids rose in the Kajali forest. There were fourteen hundred disciples doing *tapas* invisibly, among whom the chief disciple was Hada, the king of Bundi's prince. He was a Hada Rajput.[37] He was Guru Jalindar Baba's disciple. [Hada has an exchange with Jalindar identical to Charpat Nath's previous conversation. Jalindar, as before, commands his fourteen hundred disciples to go and rescue Gopi Chand, and when they protest he orders Hada to go with them. When Hada expresses his own reluctance to deal with the lady magicians, Jalindar is annoyed.]

(GC 3.12.e)

---

37. Bundi was a small princely state not far from Ajmer district. The name of Bundi's ruling clan was Hada.

"Sister-fucker! Are there thousands and millions of lady magician sluts in Bengal that you can't win? Well, sister-fuckers, if you can't win with magic and spells, then use your tongs, give those sluts your tongs, beat them. Fourteen hundred and fourteen hundred is twenty-eight hundred.[38] So lift up my meditation seat, I will go with you."

Wonderful! The Guru Sovereign's coming too.

At once they picked up the Guru Sovereign's meditation seat, and they took their sacks, they took their tongs, they put on their sandals . . . a seated yogi's a stake in the ground, but a yogi once up is a fistful of wind. The Naths took the wind's own form and turned their faces toward Bengal. They crossed one forest, they crossed another forest, in the third forest they came to the Bengal garden.

As soon as they entered the Bengal garden and passed through its gates, they came to where the fourteen hundred yogis had been doing *tapas*. Then they saw that the campfires were burning like this [Madhu and his listeners are seated around a fire] — the campfires of the first ones who were made into donkeys. Fourteen hundred campfires were just as they had left them, with the wood burning, but not a single disciple.

Jalindar Baba looked and laughed. He said, "O Hada disciple."

"Yes, Guru Sovereign?"

"Fourteen hundred campfires are burning but there's not one disciple! The sluts have eaten all of them, they have eaten up all fourteen hundred disciples, those lady magicians, my daughters!"

"Oh, who knows what happened, Baba."

"Well, sons, sit at these fourteen hundred campfires, they are burning. Set up your meditation seats, and Hada disciple, let's see, let's lower our eyelids and take care of our disciples."

Saffron is burning in the Guru Jalindar Baba's campfire. He fixed up his meditation seat and burned saffron in his campfire. And all the other disciples sat at the burning campfires and Hada disciple set up his meditation seat and lowered his eyelids and began to take care. He set his mind to take care of the fourteen hundred disciples who were turned into donkeys in the jungle. They were braying in the wilderness, here and there. And Charpat Nath, who himself was a

38. That is, we must outnumber them.

camel, was stripping and eating the bark from the *nīm* and *khejarā* trees.

As soon as he raised his eyelids, Hada disciple said, "Hey Guru Sovereign, your fourteen hundred disciples are turned into donkeys and Charpat Nath has become a camel and is stripping the *nīm* and *khejarā* trees and eating them."

Fine! Now let's see the orders given to Bhairu and Hanuman.[39] Guru Sovereign!

(GC 3.13.e)

He gave an order to Bhairu and Hanuman. "Sons, go and bring the fourteen hundred disciples." Bhairu and Hanuman went at once, and they gathered the fourteen hundred disciples together and brought them into the garden. As soon as they entered, then Hada disciple began to recite magic, he began to recite spells, he struck the magic blow, and as soon as he struck the magic blow he turned the donkeys back into disciples. And Charpat Nath who was a camel, he made him back into Charpat Nath, and as soon as he was himself again Charpat Nath prostrated to the guru. "O Guru Sovereign, even though I have an all-powerful guru such as you, still those sluts were able to do magic on me. They made me into a camel, Grain-giver. And they made all the other disciples into donkeys."

Then the Guru Sovereign said, "Sons."

"Yes?"

"Each of you set up a separate campfire and cut wet green wood from the garden trees, mango, lemon, orange, and all. Cut it and put it on the campfires. And all together call "*Alakh!*" and all together sound your horn instruments. Now day will become night in Bengal. And the whole of Bengal will shiver, shake, and tremble. And right away, without our calling them, the seven lady magician sluts will come here."

So they each lit separate campfires and cut the green, wet wood of mango, lemon, and orange trees and piled it on their campfires, and

---

39. Bhairu is an agent of Shiva; Hanuman's mythological persona is—like Bhairu's—an active errand-doer, but he is associated with Rama. To my inquiry on their pairing, Madhu Nath said, "These two always stay together." Philip Lutgendorf has clarified this association: "Though a Vaishnava figure, the celibate, physically immortal Hanuman is considered to be a Mahayogi and full of shakti. Hence he has great appeal to Shaivas" (personal communication 1990).

smoke rose up from within the Chapala Garden.[40] Billows of smoke rose up and went into Bengal; Bengal became filled with smoke, and day became night in Bengal. As soon as day became night in Bengal, they all called "*Alakh!*" and they all sounded their horn instruments so the whole of Bengal trembled and shook and swayed.

Then the seven lady magicians thought, A powerful yogi seems to have come. Like Ladu Nath.[41] Right now a powerful yogi has come, day has turned to night in Bengal, and the whole of Bengal trembles and shakes. Right now a yogi who is very powerful seems to have come.

And they thought, This time we must take all our disciples with us. So at once they purchased seven maunds of rice and made invitations, they made yellow rice and sent around invitations.

Behri Yogin had seven hundred disciples and Kapuri Dhobin had seven hundred and that Oil-presser woman, Gangali Telin, had seven hundred, and Setali Khamari had seven hundred and Luna Chamari had seven hundred and Bajori Kanjari and Setali Khamari and Phula Malin[42]—each one of them had seven hundred disciples. And they sent yellow rice to all of them: "Let's go at once. Come quickly onto the waterside. Many yogis have come, more than before."

"Hey, big brother's wife, last time you didn't take me with you. The first time fourteen hundred yogis were turned into donkeys, and this time I want to go too." So at once, without delay, in order to see the fun and play the contest, for the thrill of it, all of them took their double pots and they gathered at the waterside.

They were dying from anticipation. If one slut was grinding flour, she left the flour in the mill; and if one was rolling bread, she left the flour in the dough dish, she left the dough: "Later I will roll it." And if one was nursing a boy or girl, she tied him in the cradle: "We will be late for the show and miss the fun, so let's go now and nurse later." The sluts, all the women of the city, acted this way. The women gathered at the waterside. Now let's see them go into the garden.

(GC 3.14.e)

40. Either Madhu misnames the "garden of Bengal" here, or any garden full of yogis becomes a "Chapala Garden."

41. Madhu jokes with his relative Ladu Nath.

42. This is the first we hear of a Gardener magician; she would be the eighth.

[The encounter between Behri Yogin with her cohorts and Jalindar and Hada Nath with theirs proceeds in an identical fashion to the earlier encounter between the lady magicians and Charpat. Hada, not Jalindar, acts as yogi spokesperson, until Behri announces:]

"I will send all of you twenty-eight hundred yogis flying and spinning in the sky."

As soon as she said this, Hada disciple thought, Oh, son of a . . . ! She will send us flying in the sky! [*Much laughter*] That's pretty amazing!

Then the Guru Sovereign said, "All right, I will tell. Shall I tell you all about myself?"

"Yes, tell about yourself."

"But, brother, if I tell you everything about myself, then you won't send me flying in the sky?"

"I won't send you flying if you tell everything."

"Sister, on Kailash Mountain, Lord Shankar's campfire burns nine *jojan*s tall.[43] That is my guru's place! And Lord Shankar, the king of Kailash, is my guru. And every day we are gathered . . . so where do we come from? From over there, on Kailash Mountain, where there is a masterworker who fashions human forms[44] out of rocks. As he fashions them, he places them on the road to Bengal. So they come into Bengal. You imagine that you will wipe out yogis so not a seed remains—that you will finish off yogis. But we yogis are taking birth from rocks. The masterworker keeps fashioning us out of rocks, and we set out immediately on the road to Bengal. So you might think that you will finish off yogis, but let me tell you that when the stones of the earth are finished, that's when we yogis will be finished. So now I have told you all about my campfire; and Bhola Nath of Kailash Mountain is my guru!"[45]

"O yogi, knowledge wielder, love-spell wielder, death-spell wielder, then we will have a contest with you."

"I told you all about myself and you still want to have a contest?"

---

43. Kailash is the traditional dwelling place of Shiva; one *jojan* equals 12 *koś* or 24 miles.

44. The term used here is *mūrtī*, but it refers less to an icon than to a stone figure.

45. Innocent or Simple Nath, one of Shiva's most common epithets. Although by familiar tradition Shiva is Jalindar's guru, I found no other references to yogis being made of stone; I interpret this speech as an imaginative expression of Jalindar's bravado in the face of the threatening Bengali magicians.

"Yes, brother, we will have one."

Then Jalindar Nath said to Hada disciple, "OK, Hada disciple, play a contest with them, but be careful!" Then Hada disciple recited magic, and after reciting magic he began to recite spells and he struck the magic blow. As soon as he recited spells, he turned every single one of those Bengali sluts, all the women, into donkeys. But during this clash, Behri Yogin was not affected. My daughter! She alone remained standing.

"Yes, yogi, swear a hundred thousand oaths on your guru, and then let as much knowledge as you have come over me."

At this, Charpath Nath said, "Hada Grandpa, those other sluts don't mean anything—I made them into donkeys myself! But, son of a...! This Behri Yogin is a bag of hot chilis! Hada Grandpa, she turned me into a camel! This one's a magician, and my magic didn't work on her."

Meanwhile, Hada disciple once more recited magic, and having recited magic he began to recite spells, and he struck the magic blow and turned Behri Yogin into a she-camel.

Then the Guru Sovereign said to all the disciples, "There are burning coals in your campfires, so make your tongs red hot. Then, sons, close the gates for a little while, and take your revenge." So they closed the gates and—all the sluts were turned into donkeys—and they began to beat them with iron canes, red hot ones, until they marked them with all sorts of lines and stripes [*Told with great zest and laughter*].

They looked like they were wrapped in decorative blankets. Braying and braying, "Tibhu tibhu," they ran around the garden, and they dropped piles of shit all over.

Afterwards the Guru Sovereign said, "Now, sons, open the gates and drive them into the wilderness where you were grazing and leave them." Then they rounded them up and drove them into the jungle, where the disciples had already eaten up all the green grass fodder. And now the sluts licked the dust and wandered in the jungle, braying "Tibhu tibhu."

All the women of the city were turned into donkeys! You couldn't have the vision of a Bengali woman anywhere. In the villages there was nothing you could even call a woman. The Guru Sovereign drove them into the jungle and left them there. Not a woman remained to be seen in the city, so that you could say, 'Brother, at so-and-so's house a woman remains." Now they were not women, they were donkeys.

Now only men were left; they were searching among themselves, and the boys and girls in the cradles were crying. And Hardev [a member of the audience] said, "Oh no, my son Nathu's wife hasn't come. I myself will go and search for her."

Some said, "My sons' and daughters' mother hasn't come back." And some said, "Oh no! Mine left the dough in the kneading bowl." Others said, "O dear, at my house the bread is burning on the griddle." But others shouted: "Let the bread burn, but my boys and girls are crying in the cradle and whose breast will suckle them, where has she gone?"

Talking in this way all the men of Bengal gathered at the council place.[46] When they had gathered there, that gardener who was still burning like red peppers—the one who was beaten with the tongs yesterday—joined the assembly. Then the gardener said, "Your women are in the jungle."

"What do you mean, 'in the jungle'?"

"Many yogis came into the garden, and the women went to play a contest with them. The first time your women made all the yogis into donkeys and drove them out. But this time a big guru came and they gathered again. They went to play another contest, and the yogis made your women into donkeys, and they are braying in the berry wilderness.[47] If you don't believe me, then look at my back."

Who said this? The gardener. "Look at my back, it has welts like streaks of lightning, and the same kind of stripes are on your sluts. Those who were the lady magicians' disciples went and those who weren't came along to see the show."

So now, what to do? Ladu Nath said, "Let's all take ear-high sticks. And let's all go, all the men of the city, and aim our sticks at the yogis. We will show them our magic spells! We men may not have any magic spells, but we have plain stick magic, and from one blow with a stick five loincloth-wearers will fall." [*Much audience response and hearty laughter*].

(GC 3.15.e)

46. *hatāi;* usually refers to a designated neighborhood or caste meeting spot.
47. *bor kā mangarā;* another example of local setting that refers to an area just outside Ghatiyali where berries used to be plentiful.

And they all took sticks as tall as their ears, and said, "We don't know magic spells, but let's all go search for every single one of our women, my son's Babaji![48] They have plucked all our women."

So grouped together, all the men of the whole city went to the garden. They took ear-high sticks and went through the gateway, and then the leader of the whole village and city spoke: "Hey yogis, how is it that so many of you have come and gathered here? And tell me where our women are."

Then the Guru Sovereign Jalindar Baba said, "O brothers, what do I want with your women? It was because of women trouble that I first became a yogi. I became a yogi to get away from women. What need have I of women? There aren't any women around here, and we don't even know your women. And what would women have come to get from *sādhus* like us?"

"O yogis, we don't know magic and we don't know spells but we have plain stick magic. So tell us nicely about our women or else, with one stick, right now, five loincloth-wearers will fall. Tell us nicely about our women; you may have magic spells, but we have clubs!"

As soon as he had said this, Jalindar Baba said to Hada disciple, "Oh son, Hada."

"Yes Guru Sovereign."

"Son, they don't know spells. They are bumpkins like Hardev. They beat with sticks as soon as they come. As soon as they raise their sticks, they apply them, and afterwards, son, we won't remember any magic spells, after sticks have fallen. So will you speak spells or eat sticks? You won't remember magic spells, son, so take care in advance: the sticks are about to start flying."

Hada disciple recited magic, and he recited spells, and he struck the magic blow. As soon as he struck the magic blow, all the men of Bengal were turned into donkeys. Then Charpat Nath said to the fourteen hundred disciples: "Now let them take care of their women, sons. Round them up and take them into the wilderness, so that the he-asses shall be with the she-asses." They began braying, "Tibhu, tibhu," and went running and running throughout the whole wasteland.

Enough, the jungle of Bengal was now populated, but over there in the city just a couple of old folks were left. All of Bengal was deserted. Then the old folks talked among themselves, "The children

48. This is an insult to the yogis.

are howling and dying of hunger." The old folks gathered together, "Brother, now what to do? Where did the men go? The men don't come and the women don't come, and something strange has happened."

Later they got the news: many yogis came to the garden and they're the ones who caused the whole city to become deserted. And they made the women and the men into she-asses and he-asses. And they drove them into the wilderness and left them.

Then the old folks gathered and went to the king, to Gopi Chand's sister's husband, to his elder sister's husband. He was on his way to meet with his sister. Gopi Chand's elder sister's husband was the king, and the old folks went to him to lodge a complaint.

"We have a complaint, Grain-giver."

"Old folks, who has committed a crime against you?"

"Grain-giver, out of the whole population of the city, only us, a couple of old folks are left. All that there are, have come."

"So where are all the men and women of the village?"

"Even if you search, you won't find them anywhere."

"Why, where have they gone, old folks?"

"Grain-giver, fourteen hundred and another fourteen hundred yogis came to the garden. And they made all the women into she-asses. And afterwards the men went to search for them, and they made all the men into he-asses and drove them into the jungle and left them. Your jungle has become populated, but your whole city is deserted. Grain-giver, only us, a few old folks remain—and you remain, so do as you will."

"Why, old folks, now what do you want?"

"Grain-giver, we will go and you come along with us, and together we'll get the city repopulated: we'll fall at the yogis' feet."

The king said, "Old folks, why, I'm the only man left and it seems as if you want me to be made into a donkey, too. I'm the only man left in Bengal and you're thinking, 'Brother, let's make the king into a donkey, too.' This seems to be your desire."

"No, Grain-giver, but you are the king, and if you join your hands to them then they will repopulate the city."

"Old folks, I will shit right here but I won't put my foot there. They will make me a donkey. And my queen will be left here in the palace. And I'll wander braying in the jungle over there. We can settle another city. Let them burn up."

But Lady Champa De spoke. Who? Gopi Chand's sister. Gopi

Chand's sister spoke to the king. "Hey King, on account of our subjects, we are called kings. Over what will we rule when Bengal has become deserted? This is what you must do. Your rule is luckless. It's all because there were lady magicians in the city, and they played a contest with the yogis. That's why they made the whole of Bengal deserted. In my natal home, yogis came every day, calling '*Alakh!*' in the portals. And alms were set out for them. But I have been given in marriage into a luckless kingdom, a luckless land. And I haven't had the vision of a single yogi. Yogis never call '*Alakh!*' at my door. In my natal home, every day, every other day, a yogi came, calling '*Alakh!*' I always set out alms for them, and my brother was given as a loan. Ours was the *māyā* of yogis.[49] But over here in your kingdom, what is going on?

"King, this is what you must do: take these old folks with you, tie your hands behind your back with raw thread, and go over there bare-headed and bare-footed, and fall at the yogis' feet."

(GC 3.16.e)

The queen explained it all to him: "Go, he will never ever make you a donkey. It's becaue of the lady magicians never letting yogis into the city—that's why he made your city deserted by turning everyone into donkeys.

"Tie your hands behind your back with raw thread, O King, and take a couple of old ladies with you and go bare-headed and bare-footed and fall at the yogis' feet.

> Humility is great, so in the world bow low,
> as the green grasses bend in the river's flow.
> Why does the *erand* climb so high with its haughty power,
> Why does the mango bend so low, with its humble power?[50]

---

49. *mākai to jogyā kī hī māyā;* this lovely phrase seems ambiguous. It could mean "we got our prosperity from yogis" or "we lived our illusory lives by the good grace of yogis."

50.
> *nūvan barī hai sansār ma ra na nūbai jyo nīch,*
> *phānī melo gundalo nūbai nandī ka bīc;*
> *erand to kyo charhai hai ūchau ka ūnī kararāyī ka pān,*
> *ar ām nīcho kyo lulai ūkī naramāi ka pān*

The message of these couplets is that one must be humble in order to survive, like grasses or mango trees. A mango bends low and people can reach its fruit without harming the tree, but people cut down the *erand* (whose seeds are used for machine oil) because otherwise,they cannot reach its fruit.

"Even if the yogi looks darkly at you, say 'Grain-giver' and fall at his feet. Prostrate yourself to him and admit your mistake. And he will repopulate your city. Whatever he says, agree with him."

On hearing this the king began to hope, but he said, "Look here, Queen, he will turn me into a donkey, and then I will wander hungry in the jungle and you will remain in the palace."

"He won't turn you into anything. Humility is great. Fall at the yogi's feet."

So, at once the king had his hands tied behind his back with raw thread, and he went bare-headed and barefoot, taking a few old ladies with him. With his hands tied behind his back, the king went to the garden. As he was about to enter, from the gateway, he saw the yogi doing *tapas*, but to the king it looked like a nine-hand-tall lion seated there, and he began to tremble. He stood trembling in the gateway and did not go inside. The king had no strength to speak. "Now if I speak, he'll make me a donkey, then what?"

So Jalindar Baba raised his eyelids and there was the king, it was King Bhoj.[51] Jalindar Baba noticed that he was trembling, so Jalindar Baba said, "Hey, King, why are you trembling here? What do you want?"

"Grain-giver, later I'll tell you many things, but first, don't make me into a donkey. I agree to everything else, but don't make me a donkey, Grain-giver."

"Good, I won't make you one. What do you want?"

"Grain-giver, whatever you say, that I'll do, and I will serve you. But, Grain-giver, repopulate my city."

"King, anything else, whatever strikes you as fine. But if you speak of repopulating the city, then I'll make you a donkey."

So the king began to tremble, "Hey Grain-giver, don't make me a donkey. If you prefer it that way, don't repopulate the city."

"Sister-fucker! Your rule is such a blind one! You're the king but your rule is such a blind one. In your village you have such trouble-making sluts—Behri Yogin, Gangali Telin, Kapuri Dhobin, and all the rest of those lady magicians. When our yoga-born come, they don't let them beg and eat. They make some into roosters, and they make some into parrots, and they make some into oxen and yoke

51. According to Bhoju, King Bhoj was a king of Ujjain; Madhu just used the first king's name that came into his head.

them to the oil press. Those trouble-making sluts made my disciple into a rooster, yoked him to the oil press, made him into a parrot, and buried him in a hole. Your rule is such a blind one."

"O Great King, I will have an edict engraved: 'No sluts will play any games with any robe-wearers.' The punishment is burial and to be trampled by horses. The edict will require them to vow, Hindus on cows and Muslims on pigs,[52] not to play any contests with any yogis at all. In this way, Grain-giver, I will serve you. So please repopulate the whole city."

Then Jalindar Baba spoke, "Fine, King, have an edict engraved."

"Yes, I will erect a stone edict."

"Yes, so go, order an edict to be engraved and have it erected."

So he called the workmen from several villages, and had an edict engraved. Hindus had to swear on cows and Muslims on pigs: "If any yogi comes, no slut will play a contest with him." Anyone who did would be buried deep and horses set to trample her from above. And each one had to swear a hundred thousand oaths on her own guru: "If any robe-wearer comes, I won't play a contest." Thus an edict was engraved and erected in the ground.

Now the Guru Sovereign gave an order to Bhairu and Hanuman. "Sons, go get the he-asses and she-asses and bring them back."

(GC 3.17.e)

Here's what Bhairu and Hanuman did: they produced bees, and they sent them. The bees went to where the he-asses and she-asses were grazing and braying. The bees attacked them and brought them. Then the garden was filled with he-asses and she-asses.

As soon as the garden was filled, the Guru Sovereign said: "Hada disciple, turn the men back into men and the women back into women." But Charpat Nath spoke: "Wait, Guru Sovereign, you're going to repopulate the city? But you still haven't taken care of Gopi Chand, and the whole affair was on account of Gopi Chand. You have begun to repopulate the city but no—Gopi Chand ought to come first."

Then the Guru Sovereign said, "Right, son. OK, Hada, call Gopi Chand." Hada disciple began to meditate, he began to recite and

---

52. That is, should they break the vow, Hindus must eat cow and Muslims must eat pig flesh—equally abhorrent although for different reasons.

pray. There was a dark pit, with a slab of stone pushed over its top, and he made that slab fly off. Inside the chest-deep dark pit, inside a cage, made into a parrot, Gopi Chand was buried. By the power of magic, he took the cage out from inside the dark pit and made it fly. Gopi Chand was shut up in that cage, and Hada disciple made it fly into the garden.

"Look," said the Guru Sovereign, "Look, King, at what those sluts did. This is a king. This is Gopi Chand, the son of King Taloki Chand."

At once he recited magic and he recited spells and he struck the magic blow and turned the parrot into Gopi Chand. As soon as he made him into Gopi Chand, on his foot a lotus sparkled, and on his left arm a jewel gleamed, and on his forehead was the moon. It was just as if the sun had risen in the garden. Gopi Chand was crying hard, his eyes filled with Indra's misty rain. Water poured from his eyes. He fell at the Guru Sovereign's feet: "Hey Guru Sovereign, it took you so many days to take care of me. But I have died. Some days I was yoked to the oil press, and some days I was turned into a donkey, and some days I was turned into a cock. And this Behri Yogin is a real slut—she shut me in a cage, and Guru Sovereign, she put me in a deep pit."

Then the Guru Sovereign said, "Son, you are just one single soul but, Gopi Chand, just look at your revenge: the garden is completely filled with he-asses and she-asses. I have made the whole city desolate, and these he-asses and she-asses are standing right before you. I made the whole city desolate for your soul's revenge. And now an edict has been engraved and erected so these lady magician sluts will never play with anyone again, now no one need fear."

Then the Guru Sovereign gave the order to Hada disciple and Hada disciple recited magic, he recited spells, and he struck the magic blow—turning the he-asses into men and the she-asses into women. "Sisters, take care of your boys and girls, and roll out bread and eat." And, to the men, "Take care of your women."

And he separated the seven lady magicians. He separated them and Charpat Nath began to beat the sluts with his tongs. Now with grass blades in their mouths and their hands before their faces,[53]

---

53. *ghās kā thūṇakalyā levai ra hāth khāvai;* according to Bhoju these are abject gestures. The women are pleading for mercy.

they fell at his feet. "Grain-giver, we won't play any more contests. No more contests. Grain-giver, we are your cows, but give us the gift of life. Now even if a yogi or a *sādhu* comes and gives us five shoe-beatings—even then we will not play contests with them. Grain-giver, the edict is erected. And we each swear a hundred thousand oaths on our gurus to play no contests with any robe-wearers."

And they made vows as required by the edict.

"Then go back and repopulate the city!" Everyone went to their own villages and houses, and they took care of the boys and girls.

Now, the Guru Sovereign said to Gopi Chand, "Good, son Gopi Chand, now these fourteen hundred yogis can go, and, son, now you go and visit your sister. Now visit your sister."

"Guru Sovereign, I tried to visit her before, and the mark is still lying here on my rump—the moon and the sun are printed—and so I've had enough of a visit with her!"

"No, son, you've come this far, so brother, meet with your sister."

Jalindar Baba's assembly went back to the Kajali Woods. The city was repopulated. And now Gopi Chand is going to his sister's.

(GC 3.18.e)

[Gopi Chand for a second time experiences sorrow at his changed condition while approaching his sister's domain. However, this time when he reaches the portals of her palace and calls *"Alakh!"* Champa De sends her slave girl Moti De with jewels for the yogi. Gopi Chand's encounter with Moti De, the girl's return to her mistress, the subsequent attack of all Champa De's eleven hundred slave girls on the yogi, and his revelation—after Jalindar tells him what to do—of his true identity all follow exactly the same pattern as the encounter with Patam De's slave girls in GC 2. I return to the text with the final sung segment of GC 3, at the moment when the slave girls, aware of who has come, go wailing to the queen.]

The eleven hundred slave girls
went wailing,
they went stumbling and falling.[54]

All eleven hundred bondwomen, the sluts,
went wailing into the palace.

---

54. This is the final sung portion of GC 3.

"O girls, I sent you off laughing, bondwomen,
why do you now come crying?
What kind of yogi is this,
a magician?
What kind of yogi is this,
a death-spell wielder?
O bondwomen, did he feed you roasted hashish,
that you have come stoned and wailing?"

When the queen had said this much
what did Moti De Dasi, the bondwoman,
say to her mistress?
"No, Mistress, the yogi is no
magic-worker, Mistress,
the yogi is no
death-spell wielder.
No, Mistress, he didn't feed us roasted hashish.
Mistress, your brother has come as a yogi.
Mistress Champa De, your fortune has burst, your brother
Gopi Chand stands as a yogi."

When Moti De had said this much,
Lady Champa De took down
a whip from its peg.
The lady struck Moti De twice:
"Slut, you're making my brother a yogi!
Slut, I'll use my bamboo to make your skin fly off!
How can you make my brother a yogi!"

When the queen had said this much:
"Mistress, beat me if you wish,
drive me away if you wish,
take away my life, Mistress,
take away my life.
Meeting is good,
parting is bad,
Mistress, it's a carnival of parting, oh Lord!
Mistress, you won't meet your brother again.

"On your brother's foot
a lotus is sparkling,

on his left arm
a jewel is gleaming.
On his forehead is the moon, Lord,
Now go, sister, and meet with your brother!"

When Moti De had said this much,
Lady Champa De went to the portal,
she went to the portal
and saw Gopi Chand's countenance.
On her brother's left arm
a jewel was gleaming,
and on his forehead the moon.
Gopi Chand stood shining,
and this sister, Champa De, ran and
wrapped herself around Gopi Chand's shoulders.

"Brother, you had eleven hundred queens
and sixteen hundred slave girls,
when did you leave them?
And our old mother,
when did you leave her and come?
O my brother, to whom did you entrust the kingdom?"
And she gave her brother a hug.

Both sister and brother
are crying hard.
Champa De hung on his shoulders,
dying of anguish,
Champa De stopped breathing.
Champa De, his sister, died,
but remained stuck to his shoulders.
Gopi Chand is crying hard in the portal,
"Now what has happened to me?"

(GC 3.23.s)

The slave girls went falling and stumbling and wailing into the Color Palace. When they got there, Queen Champa De said, "O girls, I sent you laughing so why have you come crying? What kind of a yogi is he, a magician? a death-spell wielder? Did he feed you roasted hashish that you have come stoned and wailing, all you eleven hundred slave girls?"

They were crying hard, all eleven hundred slave girls, their eyes filled with Indra's misty rain. They kept wailing, and then one said to the queen, "Mistress, that yogi is no magician, no death-spell wielder and he did not feed us roasted hashish. O Mistress, your fortune has burst, your brother Gopi Chand has come as a yogi."

As soon as she said this, Champa De took the whip down from the peg and gave a couple of blows . . . to whom? . . . to that Moti De who had already been beaten before with the tongs. She was the chief slave girl. "Why, slut, are you making my brother a yogi? I have only one brother, you wicked slut!"

"Mistress, beat me if you wish, or even take away my life. But meeting is good and parting is bad and the noose of *māyā*'s net is always very bad. It's a carnival of parting. Gopi Chand has become a yogi and come into the portal; if you like, take away my life . . . but it's a carnival of parting from your brother—go and meet him. On his foot a lotus is sparkling and on his left arm a jewel is gleaming and on his forehead is the moon, as if the sun had risen in the portal. And meeting is good but parting is bad. Meet with your brother, go and meet him, or else if he picks up his campfire and leaves, then afterwards you will never meet again."

While she was saying this, sister Champa De got up. She got up and went to the portal and there—on his foot a lotus was sparkling and on his left arm a jewel was gleaming and on his forehead was the moon. As soon as she saw Gopi Chand's countenance, she wept and weeping she went and at once threw her arms around Gopi Chand.

"O my brother, you had eleven hundred queens and sixteen hundred slave girls, fifty-two portals, fifty-three doorways, twelve districts' rule, and our old mother—when did you leave them and come? And how did you come to take on yoga, and what caused you to put yogis' earrings[55] in your ears? What is this you have done?"

Saying these things, she threw her arms around him and embraced him, and she began to wail. Then she really breathed her last. Really, clinging to his shoulders, Champa De died.

Gopi Chand was crying hard, his eyes filled with Indra's misty rain. Water poured from his eyes. He was wailing in the portal, "Hey Guru Sovereign, hey Grain-giver, I came to visit my sister and my

55. *mandarā;* note that unlike Patam De, Champa De uses one of the correct terms.

sister has died but remains stuck to my shoulders. Something very inauspicious has happened to me. My sister has died. And now what will the world[56] say? They'll say, 'Her brother became a yogi and came, and then Queen Champa De died. A crime has occurred.'"

Then with his body and mind he besought the Guru Sovereign. Who did? Gopi Chand. "Hey Guru Sovereign, I am beseeching you so come quickly, Baba Nath, Grain-giver, why have you afflicted me with this lifelong blemish?" He besought the Guru Sovereign with his body and mind and while he was beseeching him, the Guru Sovereign came. "Son?"

"What's happened, Grain-giver? See me before you. You sent me to visit, but did you send me to kill my sister? Moreover, as I was on the way to meet her I had a lot of trouble. And Grain-giver, now what sorrow have you given to my spirit? My sister, Champa De, really died and remains stuck to my shoulders, and the world will call it evil: 'Who knows what Babaji came and really killed her?' Why have you afflicted me with this lifelong blemish, the stain of a virgin?"[57]

At once, the Guru Sovereign took his tin with the elixir of life. He sprinkled the *chameli* tree and took out Gopi Chand's sister's soul.[58] He grabbed it and put it back inside her and sprinkled her with the elixir of life.

As soon as he sprinkled her, he made Lady Champa De stand right up again. And she brought her brother into the palace and they had a good time, laughing and chatting, both sister and brother for a few days. She kept him very comfortably inside the palace, and thus sister and brother remained. But she would not let Gopi Chand go. If he went, then she would go with him. "Take me with you, and I will be a yogini, too."

Gopi Chand was standing in the portal, ready to go, but she wouldn't let him go. "I'll go with you, brother. I will be a yogini, and go."

56. *samsār;* even as a yogi, Gopi Chand seems worried about what people will think, about his reputation. Bhoju modifies my judgment: he's worried about *yogis'* reputations.

57. That is, a sin resulting from killing a chaste woman.

58. Apparently Champa De's soul had entered this tree (a fact not previously mentioned); *chameli* is a type of jasmine, and *champa* is also a sweet-smelling flower.

Now how could Gopi Chand take his sister with him?
/He can't take her./

In the portal he said, "Lady, look out, your palace is on fire. Fire struck, your palace is burning!" So she looked back to see if it were true ... just like a woman.[59]

She looked back. "Is it really on fire? He said fire had struck, so let's see if our palace has burnt." In that much time Gopi Chand disappeared. He turned into wind. Becoming wind, that's all, he left.

Later she became a lady yogi. She put on ochre clothing and for six months she searched, wandering in the jungle. But she didn't find Gopi Chand. For six months she wandered, searching in the jungle as a lady yogi, but she didn't find Gopi Chand.

[*Madhu to Ann:* Now go to sleep, it's over.]

(GC 3.23.e)

---

59. *tariyā kī jāt hai;* literally, "That's the species of women."

Part 4

Instruction from Gorakh Nath

Introduction

A persistent legend in India tells of a land to the east that is "ruled by women." For Rajasthanis this is imagined to be in Bengal; for Bengalis it is in Assam; for Assamese, it is probably Burma. The story of how the Nath yogi Gorakh Nath goes to rescue his guru, Machhindar, from entanglement or enslavement in such a kingdom is one of the most popular pieces of Nath folklore. I have even seen it enacted in the Hindi film *Maya Macchendra*. In Madhu Nath's version, as elsewhere in Nath literature, the episode is initiated by mutual taunting between Gorakh Nath and Jalindar's disciple Kanni Pavji—who makes his first appearance here—concerning their respective gurus' current conditions. "Your guru is in Bengal ruling a kingdom and enjoying women," one of Kanni Pav's disciples taunts Gorakh Nath with ill-advised rancor. "Your guru is smothering under horse manure," returns Gorakh Nath. This horse manure provides the direct link between the main action of Gopi Chand 4 and the preceding three parts of the tale. Gopi Chand is, after all, responsible for Jalindar Nath's being at the bottom of a well covered with horse manure in the first place.

Other than the manure, the backstage role of Manavati as patron of yogis, and the reappearance of Gopi Chand at the end when it comes time for him to be made immortal, several evident thematic patterns link this final segment of the Gopi Chand epic to the preceding three. Most obviously, the motif of royal renunciation is replayed yet again in the wrenching of Machhindar Nath away from his Bengal. Here, however, rather than a born king who must be persuaded to turn yogi we have a born yogi who has turned king and must be lured back to the ascetic fold. Like Gopi Chand, Machhindar is reluctant to leave the pleasures of royal life. And, even after quitting throne and wives under Gorakh Nath's persuasive entreaty, he clings first to his sons and, after they are lost, even more absurdly and tenaciously to his four gold bricks.

Echoes of Gopi Chand's adventures in part 3 are certainly evident in Machhindar's captivity by female magicians in a place called Bengal, and Gorakh Nath's rescue mission. Whereas the low-caste lady magicians' sexual use of captive Gopi Chand was only implied by their prodding, riding, and "teaching him to sing," Machhindar's queens explicitly "keep him a parrot by day but make him a man at night" until he settles into domestic life so nicely that they feel it safe to stop enchanting him. They have not, however, reckoned on the determination of Gorakh Nath and are quite readily disposed of by that master. This outcome contrasts strongly with the preceding two parts of Gopi Chand's tale where the aspiring yogi grapples endlessly with females and the victory is often less stunning than the fray. Gorakh has a much more difficult time, however, detaching Machhindar from his two sons.

The violence of Gorakh Nath toward Machhindar's sons may be more disturbing than the iron tong whacks delivered by various yogis in part 3. Rather than the result of explosive and stylized anger, it is premeditated, calculated, and truly devoid of human feeling on Gorakh Nath's part. Madhu employs a fair amount of realism in describing Nim Nath's and Paras Nath's sufferings ("drops of blood sprinkled and splattered.... The boys... were calling in a terrible way"). The non-Indian reader may well be able to understand how much little boys are loved in the village and appreciate this fearsome example of a truly detached yogi's indifference to human feelings. Perhaps less accessible to the foreigner is the shock that will tangibly ripple through an Indian audience when Gorakh Nath—who needs a dead animal as a prop for his plot to pollute his guru's sons—walks up to a "Cow Mother" and tells her politely to die. (He does, of course, conscientiously restore her life after her carcass has served his purposes.)

Most of Gopi Chand part 4 concerns rivalries among males, beginning with Gorakh Nath's conflict with Kanni Pavji's party, continuing through his extermination of Machhindar's sons, and finally coming back to the internecine quarrels of the yogi gurus. This brings the gender stresses in the epic cycle full circle. Bharthari began with male rivalries but concluded with the machinations of women. Gopi Chand begins with women's affairs and female characters are its motivating force until the very end when it returns to a male world.

Gopi Chand 4 is, among other things, about the caste identity of its performer. It contains a number of origin stories for objects and groups important to Naths. These include the crystal used to fashion yogis' earrings; the locusts over which the Naths' power was once a major source of their livelihood; the Jain yogi sect founded by Nim Nath and Paras Nath; and the nomadic Snake Charmers (*kālbeliyā*) led by Jalindar's disciple Kanni Pavji.[1]

Out of the blind well where Jalindar Nath was buried come two rather different products: seven species of locusts and the fruit of immortality. These could be thought of as representing the Nath caste's occupational identity and the Nath sect's claims to religious achievements. The Nath caste's control over locusts provided their traditional claim to worth and salary in rural Rajasthan (see chapter 2). Here Gorakh instructs the locusts to "maintain the honor" of yogis' robes and "keep their stomachs full of bread." The fruit of immortality transforms Gopi Chand and Bharthari into eternal immortals. Full stomachs and immortality are coexistent goals, it would seem, in these popular yogis' stories. Just as the contrapuntal values of love and detachment have been interwoven and interplayed throughout the two tales, so the renouncer's triumph over bodily limits and the householder's need to satisfy bodily hunger both have a place in the finale.

Text

"Gopi Chand, abide in prayer, son,
  Recite prayers with devotion, son,
  Praise the true Master, King Gopi Chand.
  O my son, recite prayers, my dear darling boy,
  and your body will be immortal."

"My mother, the earth is ashamed, my birth-giver,

---

1. *Kālbeliyā* is a caste in modern Rajasthan. Many of its members still live nomadic lives and perform as musicians and snake charmers. Kanni Pavji is known as this caste's guru.

the sky is ashamed, Manavati Mother,
O King's Queen.
My birth-giver, I will stake my word:
Later I'll be a yogi!

"Mother, give me twelve years more,
and let me rule the kingdom.
Let me ride horseback,
Manavati Mother,
king's daughter and sister.
My birth-giver, I won't break this promise I'm making,
Birth-giver, later I'll be a yogi."

"My son, twelve years? Gopi Chand,
who gets them, King Gopi Chand,
king's brother and darling boy?
My son, death is buzzing[2] around you
and it won't leave you.

"My son, the guru's promise,
Gopi Chand, will be fulfilled,
Gopi Chand King,
and king's darling boy.
O my son, recite prayers, my dear darling boy,
and your body will be immortal."

Now Gorakh, Gorakh Baba
in Gaur Bengal
was doing *tapas* at a Potter's house.[3]
Gorakh Baba was doing *tapas*.
Kanni Pavji, Jalindar Baba's disciple,
Jalindar Baba's disciple,
Kanni Pavji, came with his assembly
into the Chapala Garden.

The fourteen hundred disciples
ignited their campfires,

---

2. *bhunvai;* Gopi Chand is like a flower, and death is a bee buzzing around him.
3. Potters are frequently portrayed as devotees, Bhoju says, because of their traditional role as water-givers. To supply water to thirsty people is highly meritorious.

added more wood,
and praised God.

He sent one disciple to the palace,
he sent him to Manavati Mata.

"Mother, an assembly has come
of fourteen hundred yogis
in the Chapala Garden.
Mother, send them a feast, my mother and birth-giver,
and send wood for their campfires too."

When the disciple had said this much,
she summoned the people
to give free labor.
Mother had them hitch up their carts,
she had them hitch up their carts.
"Fourteen hundred yogis are doing *tapas* in the garden,
so fill up these carts with their feast."

She had the carts filled
with five festive treats,[4]
laddūs and *jalebīs*[5]
she sent to the garden,
Mother sent to the garden.
Now Gorakh came
from the Potter's door.
He had set up his campfire,
and was doing *tapas*
by the road.
Baba was doing *tapas*
when a cart came along, loaded with goods.
What did Gorakh Baba say?
"O Cart-man, what load do you carry, brother?
Reveal to me what you've brought."

---

4. *pāñch pakvān;* in the village this is the most elaborate feast given, consisting of
fried wheat bread, three fried sweets, and one crisp spicy treat.

5. *Laddūs* are round balls of sugary, deep-fried chickpea flour. *Jalebīs* are often
described as "sweet pretzels" because of their shape. They are made of deep-fried
dough that is soaked in sugar syrup.

"Baba, many yogis have come
to the Chapala Garden.
From the palace the queen sends them blessed food:[6]
We're loaded with *laḍḍūs* and *jalebīs*."

When the cart-man had said this much,
now what did Gorakh Baba
say to the cart-man?
What did he say to the driver?
"O son, I too am a yogi, so you should give me
just as much stuff.
Now you'd better fill my cup, because all the yogis
will feast in the garden."

When Gorakh had said this much,
what did Hardev Patel[7] say?
"Babaji, if you want to feast then
let's go to the garden, yogi.
Here it would all get polluted.
We're serving food at the campfires, yogi,
that's where we're serving it!
If I give you blessed food in the middle, yogi,
the blessed food will all get polluted."[8]

(GC 4.1.s)

So Jalindar Nath's disciple . . . Who? Kanni Pavji—the guru of the
Snake Charmers—Kanni Pavji was Jalindar Nath's disciple, and a
great miracle-worker. He had fourteen hundred disciples. Now Gopi
Chand was a loan from Jalindar Baba—so now she always serves
yogis. Who? Manavati Mata. No matter how many yogis come into
the garden, she gives them all tea and water and feasts them. As many
yogis as come, that's how many she feasts, Manavati Mata, Gopi
Chand's mother. She sends the food into the Chapala Garden.

So there were fourteen hundred disciples. Whose? Kanni Pavji's.
His assembly came. And Kanni Pavji too came. They entered the

6. *prasād;* the treats are so called because they are offered to god-like yogis and,
according to Bhoju, because they are not a whole meal.

7. Once again, an audience member's name is incorporated into the story.

8. Here is another reference to "the middle" as a bad place. A plate of food once
eaten from is polluted. But if Gorakh were to eat from his own cup, that should not
by ordinary definitions pollute the rest of the cart load.

Chapala Garden and they lit their campfires. They were eating and sounding their conch shells a lot and reciting God's names.

Kanni Pavji sent a disciple into Gopi Chand's palace. "Go to Manavati Mother and tell her 'Fourteen hundred yogis are doing *tapas* here, in your garden, so please send them blessed food. And send them wood for their fires, and send things for tea and water.'"

One yogi went into Manavati Mother's palace and he called "*Alakh!* Manavati Mother, fourteen hundred yogis, Kanni Pav's assembly, have come. Fourteen hundred yogis are doing *tapas* in the garden, so send them treats and tea and water, and send them equipment for preparing hashish and *bhāng.*"[9]

"Fine, brother, I'll send it all." Then she summoned the Cultivators and the Gardeners[10] to give free labor. She told them to bring their carts. And she had them fill these with *laḍḍūs* and *jalebīs* and sent them to the garden.

But on the way they met Gorakh Nath Sovereign. He was staying with a Potter, doing *tapas* at his house. In that very city. Gorakh Nathji learned that that sister-fucker Kanni Pavji's assembly had come, and all these things were being sent for them. So he said to the Potter, "Prajapat?"

"Yes, Guru Sovereign?"

"Your donkeys are tied up and hungry. Untie them, and I will take them to graze."

"What, Guru Sovereign, you will graze the donkeys?"

"Oh untie them, they're hungry."

So the Potter untied the donkeys. He untied them and Gorakh Nath took five or so and he came to a road. Near the road was some shade, where he set up his campfire. Then he sent a stream from his penis, and he made green grass spring up right there, so the donkeys could graze on it. He let the donkeys graze, right there, on that green grass.

Now the carts came along. What was in them? They were filled with *laḍḍūs, jalebīs, sātalyā, purīs, peṭha-veṭhā.*[11] Now as soon as the

---

9. *Bhāng* is a drink made with marijuana. Shaivite ascetics often partake of these intoxicating substances, as the deity Shiva is thought to do.

10. As in GC 1, labor is conscripted from *lodās* and *mālīs*.

11. Here Madhu elaborates on the delicious tempting treats, adding three more. *Sātalyā* is a deep-fried and crunchy sweet made of white wheat flour; *purīs* are fried wheat breads; *peṭha* is a milk sweet, and the echo-word implies still other delicacies.

first cart came along, Gorakh Nathji Sovereign said to the driver,
"Hey, what have you got in there?"

Then Hardev brother spoke, "I'm loaded up with *laḍḍū*s and
*jalebī*s."

"Where are you taking them?"

"To the Chapala Garden. Fourteen hundred yogis are doing *tapas*
there, and so blessed food is going there. Sovereign, you should
go too."

"Oh but I'm grazing donkeys, and if these donkeys get loose, then
there will be a lot of trouble. I will eat as much stuff as you put in
my cup. You're taking blessed food there for the sake of yogis. I too
am a yogi, and I will eat as much stuff as you can fit in my cup."

Then the cart-man spoke—who? Him, Hardev Patel. "Babaji, if
you want to feast, then let's go over there. If I give it to you here,
then you will pollute the blessed food. Over there are yogis and we're
serving this feast at their campfires. I'm not going to make it polluted
in the middle of the road. I won't put any in your cup now. Let's go
to the garden where the yogis are; you're a yogi too, so feast!"

"But brother, my donkey will get lost."

"Where will he get lost? Now, brother, feast or graze your donkey.
You can't do both. Let's go over there, Sovereign, and feast."

He didn't give Gorakh Nathji Sovereign any.

Later along came another cart-man with tired oxen, lagging
behind.

(GC 4.1.e)

"O brother, What is your cart filled up with?"

"Sovereign, I've got *laḍḍū*s, *jalebī*s, *sātalyā*, *purī*s, and all kinds of
vegetables too."

"O child, I too am a yogi. What yogis are you taking these
things for?"

"Yes, Sovereign, you're a yogi. Fourteen hundred yogis are doing
tapas over there. So I am going for those yogis."

"Oh, but I too am a yogi, sister-fucker! I too will eat. Give me
as much stuff as my cup will hold."

"Go over there, Sovereign."

"But I am grazing this donkey and it might go astray. Sister-
fucker, I'm only one human body. So fill my cup one time."

He was compassionate. "Sovereign, over there yogis are eating—

but if you won't come, well, you too are a yogi, so I will fill your cup."

So he took the cup and filled it, Gorakh Nathji Sovereign's. As soon as he filled it, Gorakh Nathji Sovereign said, "Hey *laṇḍī!*" and clapped his hands.[12] "Let all the prosperity[13] come into this cart and let the one ahead be filled with pebbles and stones, the sister-fucker!"

Baba said, "Let all the good things from the first cart come into this one." But in the first cart where once there were *laḍḍūs* and *jalebīs* and *sātalyā* and *purīs* and such things, nothing remained of them: they had turned into speckled stones, rocks, and white pebbles.

Now the fourteen hundred yogi disciples were doing *tapas*, and Ladu Nath, too, was there with them. So as soon as the first cart came, he was hungry, and he went over to the cart. Ladu Nath picked up his tongs and asked, "What all have you brought?"

"Sovereign, I have brought what will satisfy you: *laḍḍūs*, *jalebīs*, *sātalyā*, *purīs*, all these things."

But he lifted the cover and looked to see what was in it. "It is rocks, only rocks—that's what you have loaded and brought."

"Sovereign, I brought *laḍḍūs*, *jalebīs*, *sātalyā*, and *purīs*. They must not be in your fate. What shall I do about it? On the road they turned into rocks. What can I do?"

The driver had uncovered his cart, and piled up there were speckled rocks, pebbles, and stones. The whole assembly of yogis got up. "O you sister-fucker, what have you brought?"

"Great kings, I brought *sātalyā*, *purīs*, *laḍḍūs*, *jalebīs*, all seven kinds of festive food. If they're not written in your fate, what can I do about it?"

"Oh that sister-fucker Manavati Mata sent rocks for us, now did she?"

"Manavati Mother sent feast-food. But on the road this happened ... what can we do about it?"

"Oh my, a weird thing has happened."

In the meantime the driver with tired oxen, the last one, was coming from behind. All the yogis were feeling very regretful: "Sister-

12. As in Bharthari 2, Gorakh Nath summons the female spirits or *śakti*s who serve him.

13. *riddhi;* a term used for Lakshmi.

fucker, how did we end up with rocks? You are saying that you brought *laddūs* and *jalebīs*."

Then the last driver, the one with the tired oxen, arrived.

(GC 4.2.e)

In the first cart there were pebbles and stones. When the rear cart came, they looked inside it—they were hungry, those *sādhus*, so they thought, Let's look in the last cart and see if it too has nothing but pebbles and stones.

/They were feeling a great craving./

So they uncovered the cart, and it was filled up with *laddūs* and *jalebīs* and *sātalyā* and *purīs*—all nine kinds of festive food, all five fried treats. It was filled to the brim!

"The other one came first, but only you have delivered the goods."

"Yes Sovereign, but both were filled with the same stuff."

"But this sister-fucker brought rocks, he brought pebbles and stones, the sister-fucker. Where did he drop the goods, and pick up these pebbles and stones?"

"Sir, I have no idea. I was going very slowly with my oxen, so I have come from behind."

"Oh, and who did you meet? Did you meet anyone on the way? Did you meet any *sādhu* or saint?"

"Yes, Sovereign, there was one over there on the road doing *tapas*, one *sādhu*."

"So did you give him some?"

"Yes, he said, 'O brother you have *laddūs* and *jalebīs* in your cart, and I'm a *sādhu* too, I'm a yogi too. You're bringing this for yogis, so fill my vessel, or else my donkey will go astray.' So I filled it, Sovereign."

"Good." Then Kanni Pavji asked the first driver, "Did he beg from you too?"

"Yes, he begged from me, but I forbade it. I said, 'Let's go over there and feast. If I serve it here, it will get polluted; we are serving the feast at the campfires."

"Then . . . my son! he turned them into rocks. But for the one who gave him alms, he kept the *laddūs* and *jalebīs*."

Then Kanni Pavji said to his disciples, "Ask the cart-men if there were people with him."

"No, he was a solitary human form."

"Good, then you seven hundred disciples go and grab Gorakh Nath[14] and bring him here." Kanni Pavji ordered seven hundred disciples.

Then the seven hundred disciples picked up their sacks and took their iron tongs and put on their sandals. A seated yogi's a stake in the ground, but a yogi once up is a fistful of wind. The Naths took the wind's own form. They were going to where Gorakh Nathji was doing *tapas*.

As they approached him, Gorakh Nathji Sovereign saw that seven hundred were coming, so Gorakh Nathji made fourteen hundred disciples stand up. He lifted his tongs, like Ladu Nath, like this. [*Madhu gestures as if brandishing tongs.*] Gorakh Nathji thought, Let the sister-fuckers come, and we'll see how they are going to grab me!

Then the seven hundred disciples approached, but from a distance they saw fourteen hundred and thought: Our beans won't cook[15]— let's go back. Because we are seven hundred and they are fourteen hundred—they will beat us up. Let's go back. So they went back and said to Kanni Pavji, "Grain-giver, you sent us, Guru Sovereign, but we are just seven hundred and over there near Gorakh Nathji fourteen hundred disciples are standing."

"What, fourteen hundred? But the cart-men said that he was alone. Then he was alone, ask the cart-men, he was alone. He must have created them—that sister-fucking Gorakh Nath—so all fourteen hundred of you go."

"Sovereign, if we go as fourteen hundred then he will make twenty-eight hundred. He is Gorakh Nath. We won't be able to do this."

"OK, so you can't do it?"

"Nope."

"OK, then I will go alone, and speaking with sweet tones I will bring him. Yes, I will go alone, for we won't get him to come by fighting."

(GC 4.3.e)

---

14. They realize immediately that it must have been the rival guru, Gorakh Nath, who has played such a trick on them.

15. *na galai ápaṇī dāl;* literally, "our *dāl* won't soften"—a phrase meaning, "we won't succeed."

Kanni Pavji took his sack and picked up his tongs and put on his sandals. A seated yogi's a stake in the ground, but a yogi once up is a fistful of wind. The Nath became the wind's own form. Gorakh Nathji had set up his campfire by the road, by the wayside. He was chanting, "*āmaṅ sāṅmā rāmā sāmaṅ.*"

Kanni Pavji greeted him respectfully. "Guru Brother, blessed food has come from Mother in the castle. And my assembly is in the garden. Let's go, Guru Brother, and let's eat blessed food over there. Let's feast on blessed food and let's smoke hashish and drink *bhāng*—we'll smoke a hash pipe together. We'll prepare *bhāng* and almond milk.[16] Let's go, Guru Brother."

"O, brother, Kanni Pav... if we go over there, what about your disciples, what will they say? I won't be able to stand it."

"No, Guru Sovereign, let's go, Guru Brother, you've got to come, surely you'll come."

"OK, brother, let's go."

So Gorakh Nathji Sovereign too took his sack and his tongs and...a seated yogi's a stake in the ground, but a yogi once up is a fistful of wind. The Naths took the wind's own form. And Kanni Pavji and Gorakh Nathji Sovereign went to the Chapala Garden.

"Indescribable, indestructible, take some, Baba, Lord Shankar.[17] Gorakh Nathji Sovereign, you have some too."

So Kanni Pavji used sweet talk and soothed Gorakh Nathji and he began to prepare hashish and *bhāng*. The two guru brothers fixed up their meditation seats at the campfire and sat down. They were preparing a hashish pipe, and Kanni Pavji said, "Fix some *bhāng* and almond milk, too, because I have brought Gorakh Nathji Sovereign as our guest."

So the two guru brothers, Gorakh Nathji Sovereign and Kanni Pavji, were smoking dope together. But there was a bastard[18] among Kanni Pavji's fourteen hundred disciples who said, "This is a bad thing. Look at this Gorakh Nath. He turned our blessed food into

---

16. *ṭhaṇḍāī;* milk-based drinks rich with ground almonds and sweet spices. These are either mixed with *bhāng* or used as "chasers" to counteract its heating effect (Roxanne Gupta, personal communication 1991).

17. *Alakh alakh abhinyāsī bābā leṇā Shankar Bhagvān;* a prayer or dedication spoken while smoking.

18. *dogalo;* not an insult that I often heard. According to the *RSK* it can refer to a person whose parents are of different castes or to one fathered by the mother's lover.

rocks. Manavati Mother sent us blessed food from her castle—*laḍḍūs,*
jalebīs, sātalyā, and *purīs*—and he turned it into speckled stones,
pebbles, and white rocks. And he doesn't even know about his guru.
Machhindar Nathji, Gorakh Nathji's guru, is over there in the land
of Bengal enjoying himself with sluts—and he has had two sons! But
look, Gorakh Nath's not even ashamed, and he spoiled our blessed
food."

Gorakh Nathji Sovereign is over here smoking dope, but his ears
are listening over there: "Let's see what kind of gossip they're telling
about me."

They were connected like brothers, but still there was enmity between them.[19] Kanni Pavji's disciples were whispering, but Gorakh
Nathji Sovereign heard, and so he asked, "Hey brother, my guru
is in the land of Bengal, enjoying sluts, and he has two sons?"

"Yes sir, he has."

"He has had two sons, and he's enjoying sluts over there?
Machhindar Nathji? Well, Ladu Nath, maybe my guru is enjoying
sluts, but your guru is smothered under horse manure. Jalindar
Nathji is smothering under horse manure. He is smothered under
Gopi Chand's seven hundred and fifty horses' shit. He is smothered,
sister-fucker, and he hasn't come out. My guru's alive and enjoying
sluts and ruling the kingdom. And your guru is smothering under
horse manure, buried in the blind well. The sister-fucker, he hasn't
come out from there."

As he was saying this, they thought, Let's get our guru out now!
We'll get him out of the blind well filled with horse manure, right
now.

"And I'll bring back my guru, too. I'm hardly any worse off than
you are. So get your guru out of the horse manure in the blind well,
and I'll bring my guru right now."

Then the fourteen hundred disciples took up their pickaxes and
their shovels, and Kanni Pavji told them to take baskets and begin.
"Let's dig him out right now, today!"

(GC 4.4.e)

Gorakh Nathji Sovereign was smoking dope, and meanwhile the
fourteen hundred disciples started in. My witch! They took shovels
and pickaxes and baskets and started in. So they emptied half the

19. In families brothers are similarly rivals, so this is not really a contradiction.

well. It was filled with horse manure and Jalindar Baba was inside, smothered underneath. Beneath the horse manure he was reciting God's names.

Kanni Pavji's fourteen hundred disciples started right in, using their shovels to fill up basket after basket with horse manure and then dumping it. It took quite a while for the well was filled to the top. They would throw down fourteen hundred baskets all together.

Gorakh Nathji Sovereign was smoking dope. He got up and put on his sandals and took his tongs and took his sack and stood and looked at the well. By the time he came, stoned, half the well was emptied. And Gorakh Nathji Sovereign thought, My son! They've already half emptied it by now. And I haven't even left this place. I must go to get my own guru. And it is fifteen hundred miles away from here. My Guru Sovereign is in Bengal, fifteen hundred miles away. I will go to Bengal, and who knows what will happen over there—will the guru come or won't he come? Who knows what kind of mess he's snared in? My son! They'll empty it in just one day, but my guru ought to come before theirs does.

So Gorakh Nathji Sovereign took off his sandal: "*Laṇḍī*, double in the day and quadruple in the night!" He struck his sandal three times: "Double in the day and quadruple in the night until I come back, sister-fucker! I shall come, even if it takes six months. Whatever they dig out from there, it will refill; in the day it will double, and in the night it will quadruple."

And . . . a seated yogi's a stake in the ground, but a yogi once up is a fistful of wind. The Nath took the wind's own form and turned his face toward Bengal. He crossed one forest; he crossed a second forest; in the third forest Gorakh Nathji Sovereign came to the borders of Bengal. He reached Machhindar Nathji Sovereign's borders.

Machhindar Nathji Sovereign had gone to Bengal to wander. But Rajput lady magicians,[20] Rajput women, took him into their power. They made Machhindar Nath into a parrot. They made him into a parrot and hung him up. For a few days they kept him as a parrot only. Later, in the night they made him a man, and in the day they made him a parrot. They kept on doing this until Machhindar

20. They are thus clearly distinguished from the other Bengali lady magicians who are low-caste.

Nath's enchantment held firm. After that they didn't make him into any parrot, and they fell in love with him. The Rajput ladies made him their king. They made Machhindar Nathji their king and he fathered two sons, Nim Nath and Paras Nath—boys of five and seven years of age. Now Machhindar Nathji Sovereign had become a king.

He thought, If that sister-fucker Gorakh Nath comes, then he will take me away; he will make me leave my kingdom; he will make me leave these queens. If Gorakh Nath comes, he will take me. So I'll place watchmen on our borders. And if any Babaji comes, anyone with even a scrap of ochre cloth,[21] he can't enter. So that's why he placed watchmen everywhere a road crossed his boundaries.

"Brother, no yogis can come into Bengal. Fine, let others come and go, but no yogi, no one wearing matted locks, no one carrying tongs and a sack, no one in ochre cloth, no yogi ought to be able to come."

"Good, sir, we won't let them come."

Now Gorakh Nathji Sovereign came along and he went up to the border, walking along heedlessly. The watchman was sitting there.

"Ho Sovereign!"

"Brother?"

"Where are you going?"

"Brother, I am going into the land of Bengal."

"By the king's order, you may not go."

"Who may not?"

"You."

"Why?"

"No one in ochre can come over here, it is the king's order."

"Oh, I'm just going to wander."

"Sovereign, there are many countries around here, and you should wander in them. Wander in other countries, but I won't let you come into this one."

"So, you won't let me come?"

"Yes, I won't let you come. I can't let ochre-cloth wearers come.

21. *bhagavān thekalī; bhagavān* is the red-orange color of cloth that distinguishes renouncers' robes and that the Nath caste wears only as turbans. The implication here is that no one with even a patch of ochre-colored cloth upon his person will be allowed into Machhindar's kingdom.

This is the king's will, and I get my salary for enforcing it. Please go somewhere else to wander, not here. There are many other countries around."

Gorakh Nathji saw the situation: Son of a...! Now what will I do?

"You won't let me in, brother?"

"Sovereign, please go back."

"OK, brother, I'll go back, brother... Now they won't let me in, now what?"

Gorakh Nathji Sovereign very regretfully turned back. "Sister-fucker! My son! I wandered all this way and now they won't let me in! It's turned out strangely. And they've probably emptied the well—they will take out Jalindar Nathji."

Thinking in this way, he went back about two miles. Who? Gorakh Nathji Sovereign.

Some performers were on their way, five or ten of them, theater people. They had loaded up some oxen, they had a couple of pack oxen. The performers were going along.

"O brothers, who are you?"

"Sovereign, we are performers."

"What will you do, and into what land will you go?"

"Sovereign, we are performers and we put on plays. We are going into Bengal."

"Good, you are going into Bengal?"

"Yes, we are going to Bengal, Sovereign."

"O brothers, do what I say."

"Yes, say it, Sovereign."

"Take me with you. I will watch over your camp, and I will bring fodder for your oxen."

"What pay will you take?"

"Oh, nothing at all, what do I need with a salary? I will watch over your camp and I will graze your oxen. I will take no salary."

Then the players said, "Oh a man without a salary is fine with us. You can be the camp watchman. When we put on our plays then you keep watch over the camp and graze our oxen."

"Yes, I will graze the oxen."

He bundled up his ochre robes and everything else in a white cloth—and he didn't keep his long locks. He bundled up his stuff and put it on an ox. Now who could tell he was a yogi?

/He changed his costume./[22]

He changed his costume and went with the players. They came to where the watchman was sitting: "O brothers, who are you?"

"We are all players."

"Is there any yogi among you, any person with ochre cloth, any yogi at all? Because if there were a yogi, there is an order against him."

"No, we have seen no yogi at all. We are theater people."

"OK, then go."

They went, sir. When they came to the first village on this side, they put on their play. They put on the play and he grazed the oxen. In the day he went and sent a stream from his penis. Then right there grass spread. Grass spread and the oxen were satiated. And then he gathered and tied up bundles of fodder and loaded them on the oxen and brought them back. And in the night he watched over the camp.

The players saw. "My witch! This man without a salary is good, our oxen are completely satisfied. He brings dark green grasses even in the hot season. This man is good for us; he applies his hand even without a salary."

(GC 4.5.e)

So they went on their way, putting on plays in Bengal. Machhindar Nath was ruling the kingdom, in the capital city. When the performers reached that city and went into the bazaar, everyone came running: "The performers have come, today the performers have come! They're about to put on a play."

/They decided to hold it at Four-Arms./[23]

They chose Four-Arms Temple as the site for the play. They called to one and all, throughout the village: "Brothers, today the performers will put on a play!" All the women and men gathered.

---

22. *bhes badalgyā;* a nice play on the double meaning of *bhes* as disguise and yogis' robes.

23. A member of the audience suggests the most appropriate location in our village for such a production—before the temple of Four-Armed Vishnu. In the part of Rajasthan where Madhu comes from almost every village, including his own, has a centrally located Temple of Four-Armed Vishnu where public performances, most often on religious subjects, occur.

Gorakh Nathji Sovereign spoke to the players: "O brothers, today I too will join the show."

"Sovereign, what will you do?"

"Whatever you say, I will do."

"But tell us what kind of things you do?"

"Well, if you say so, then I will play the drum. I know how to play the drum, or I will play the *tablā*. If you say so, I will play the *sārangī*. If you say so, I will play hand cymbals. I can play everything. If you say 'Sing,' then I will sing too."

"OK brother, let's go."

Gorakh Nath Sovereign went along with the performers, and the play began. As soon as the play began, Gorakh Nathji Sovereign played the drum. He played the drum, and its beat went far. With one drumbeat the Word[24] resounded in the netherworld, and one drumbeat resounded in the sky, and the third drumbeat resounded in the play. Those who were watching the play watched, but they became absorbed in the drumming. Who? The entire village was entranced by that drum's attractions, spreading around.

Whoever heard that drumbeat became entranced: "Oh my, such a player has never come to us before."

They made five hundred rupees in the city. The players knew that it was all because of that man, our Gorakh Nathji. "Our fortune is made! Today he came and today we earned five hundred rupees." They were totally satisfied and they thought that their days of hunger were past.

Everyone in the village was very pleased. The Royal Servants, their brothers, and sons had come to see the play, and the next day they went into the fort.

"Oh, Grain-giver," they said to the king, Machhindar Nath. "Grain-giver, excellent performers have come."

"Uh huh?"

"They put on a play in the bazaar, and it made everyone blissful. The drummer gave a great deal of pleasure. One of his drumbeats made the Word resound in the netherworld, and one of his drumbeats resounded in the sky, and one resounded in the play. Our stomachs ache from laughing so much, and from the effects of the drumbeat. It was really a great play!"

---

24. *sabad;* can and here certainly does refer to divine sound.

Then Machhindar Nathji spoke. "Today let them perform their play in my own Jewel Square."

"Whatever the Grain-giver orders should be."

"Then go right away and say to the performers, 'Brothers, today your company will perform in the fort.' If they like, then I will serve them food and supply their water."

So now let's see how the players perform in the fort...

(GC 4.6.e)

The players went to prepare for the show, and Gorakh Nathji Sovereign went too. As they were going, people said, "O brother, today they'll put on the play in the fort!" They were dying of excitement. "Last night he played the drum in three different ways, so today let's go to the fort!" Dying of excitement, the whole village crowded into the fort, and the performance began, and the drummer gave the beat.

Gorakh Nathji Sovereign played his drum so that one drumbeat resounded in the netherworld, and one resounded in the sky, and one resounded in the play. The play had started, and as the play was starting, everyone who was near him became very affected. Gorakh Nathji Sovereign took everyone into his power.[25]

Now half the play was over, and Machhindar Nathji was sitting on a chair, and his Nim Nath and Paras Nath were seated on his knees. Then when half the play was over, Gorakh Nathji Sovereign changed the drumbeat.

He changed the first drumbeat, and he changed the second drumbeat, and that drumbeat of its own accord began to play:

> Wake Machhindar, Gorakh has come!
> Wake Machhindar, Gorakh has come!
> From East and West I've called to you,
> Why sleep such sleep, O great guru?
> I'm a disciple but you're the guru true.[26]

Now the drumbeat was talking like that, and everyone was

---

25. *baśikaraṇ;* this same expression was used to describe the lady magicians' conquest of Machhindar Nath. Gorakh Nath is their match.

26.   *jāg Machindar Gorakh āyā.*
        ar agam pachham diyā helā jī.
        asoṛī nīnd kaī sūtā parem guru
        āp satguru ma celā hū.

laughing, "Oh this drum, what has it started saying?"

> Wake Machhindar, Gorakh has come!
> Wake Machhindar, Gorakh has come!
> From East and West I've called to you,
> Why sleep such sleep, O great guru?
> I'm a disciple but you're the guru true.

Now the drum began to talk like this, and Machhindar Nathji paid attention: "That sister-fucker Gorakh Nath has come. Brother, no one but Gorakh Nath could do this mischief. That sister-fucker Gorakh Nath must be among the players."

And the drumbeat was saying:

> Wake Machhindar, Gorakh has come!
> Wake Machhindar, Gorakh has come!
> From East and West I've called to you,
> Why sleep such sleep, O great guru?
> I'm a disciple but you're the guru true.

Machhindar Nathji thought, O, sister-fucker Gorakh Nath has come. Nobody else could play such a drumbeat except for that sister-fucker.

Meanwhile, Gorakh Nath got up, and he prostrated himself and respectfully greeted the Guru Sovereign. As Gorakh Nath was doing this, Machhindar took Nim Nath and Paras Nath, who had been sitting in his lap, and put them aside. He set them on a table. "Sit over here." And he seated Gorakh Nathji on his knees, because he was his first disciple.

He seated him, and said to the players, "Brothers, keep playing. Later on we can talk together. But you players, don't ruin the play, don't wreck it, keep the play going."

So they went on watching the play. Nim Nath and Paras Nath, the boys five or seven years of age, were sitting there. And Gorakh Nathji saw them—Nim Nath and Paras Nath—watching the play. So a little while later, Gorakh Nathji contrived to make them need to piss and shit. Who? Those two boys.

The play was going on and they said to Machhindar Nathji, to the ruler, "Father..." And one said, "I want to shit," and one said, "I want to pee."

"Oh, right now watch the play."

"Uh uh, Father, I have to poop." And the other said, "I have to pee."

Then Machhindar Nathji Sovereign said, "O, Gorakh Nath."

"Yes, Guru Sovereign."

"Take them to shit and pee."

"Sure," so he grabbed them by the wrists: "Let's go, I will take you to shit and I will take you to pee." He took them out, and he sat them down, both boys. He took his dagger out of his sack, and he said: "Just shit or just pee or else I will stab you with this dagger, sister-fuckers. Do one work, don't do two, either shit only or pee only. If you do both, then I will stab you with the dagger."

Now, son of a . . . ! Shit comes, and then pee also comes, doesn't it? /It comes./

[*There is a great deal of laughter and many audience comments here.*]

Now the boys were frightened. They thought, If we shit, then pee will come and then he will stab us with his dagger. So they didn't shit or pee, they were dying of fright.

"Let's go back, that's enough, did you shit?"

"Yes I shit."

"You didn't pee?"

"Uh uh, I didn't pee."

But neither one of them had shit or peed. They were dying of fear. So he brought them back and seated them. And they began to watch the play. They began to watch the play, but a little while later, he made them want to shit and pee even worse. Who did? Gorakh Nathji.

As soon as they felt it one said to Machhindar Nathji, "Father, I have to poop." And the other one said, "I have to pee."

"But Gorakh Nath just took you to shit and pee."

"Yes, but we have to go again."

Gorakh Nathji afflicted them very very strongly with the need to shit. "Oh no, we have to go we have to go." One said, "I have to shit," and the other said, "I have to pee." So they were very miserable, while they were watching the play.

Then Machhindar Nathji said, "Gorakh Nath."

"Yes, Guru Sovereign."

"Take those sister-fuckers to shit. Take them nicely and help them shit."[27]

---

27. *yannai jhāṛ pachhāṭ hangār lyā bhenchod na. jhāṛ pachhāṭ ra juvā ra lyā ka yannai hangālyā ka.*

"Yes, Guru Sovereign, I'll go."

(GC 4.7.e)

"Make sure they shit nicely."[28]

Now the Guru Sovereign's words[29] came to Gorakh Nath. So should it be done or not done?

/It must be done./

"Gorakh Nath, go and make sure they shit nicely."

Gorakh Nathji Sovereign got up and grabbed both boys by the wrists and took them to a platform outside the fort. It was made of stone, and he took them onto it and began to smash both boys. And he took off their skins and piled up their bones and flesh, stripping off the skins.

He took off the skins and hung them on the back of the Guru Sovereign's chair. And then he began to watch the play. Machhindar Nathji saw that Gorakh Nathji had come; why hadn't he brought Nim Nath and Paras Nath?

"O Gorakh Nath."

"Yes, Guru Sovereign."

"Where are Nim Nath and Paras Nath?"

"They are watching the play, Guru Sovereign."

Then he looked here and there. That's the way mothers and fathers worry. He didn't see the children. So how could he enjoy the play?[30] Then he said, "Gorakh Nath, where are Nim Nath and Paras Nath? You took them to shit and piss, so where are they? They're not here at the play."

"Guru Sovereign, they are watching the play."

"Where?"

"They are hanging on the chair. Their skins are drying, I hung up their hides over there."

"Gorakh Nath, you sister-fucker, you just got here and you've killed my Nim Nath and Paras Nath. You sister-fucker, what crime have you committed, you so-and-so!"

"Guru Sovereign, remember your words! What did you say? You said, 'Gorakh Nath, go and smash them thoroughly!'[31] I acted upon

---

28. *yānnai jhār pachhāṅṭ ra juvālyā*
29. *vachan;* can be more powerful: vow, promise.
30. Note the un-yogi-like mentality depicted here.
31. *jā kha ka yānnai Gorakh Nāth jhār pachhāṅṭ ra juvā ra lyā;* a play on words is

the words you said. If you tell me to smash them thoroughly, then I smash them. Your words are powerful, words said by the Guru Sovereign, right out of your mouth. So I acted upon them."

"Oh, sister-fucker, I was talking about having them shit and piss,[32] but you really smashed them thoroughly, you didn't spare a bone, and you brought back nothing but skins."

"Guru Sovereign, I only did what you said to do."

"Yes, sister-fucker, you've sure done a lot for me! Burn up, you sister-fucker! I didn't allow any renouncers to cross my boundaries but you joined the performers and came in. And now, you just got here, and you killed my Nim Nath and Paras Nath, you killed them, sister-fucker, you caused me a lot of trouble and you interrupted the play too."

"Guru Sovereign, are you angry?"

"Yes, and if you didn't want me to be angry then you shouldn't have killed the children."

"Guru Sovereign, don't be angry." Then he took the skins and filled them back up with the bones and things he had piled up, and then he circled his tin with the elixir of life over them. No sooner had he done this than the boys came to life, just as they had been before.

"Guru Sovereign, don't be angry."

The Guru Sovereign was happy. There were his boys, just as before: Nim Nath and Paras Nath.

The play was over, it was light.[33] Gorakh Nath bade farewell to the performers. "Go, brothers, that's enough, this is where I wanted to be."

"But Guru Sovereign, all our play's profits are due to you. It's been just incredible!"

"But I just wanted to come to this village."

"It would have been better for us if we had taken you somewhere else."

---

involved here. The dictionary meaning of *jhāṛno* is "to strike a blow; to beat; to erase; to destroy." *Pachaṭno* is "to beat as when slapping clothes on a rock to get the dirt out of them." Thus the destructive instructions are easy to read. It is more difficult to find "Make sure they shit nicely," in the words *jhāṛ pachhāṅṭ ra juvālyā*. This is local language and I have to accept Bhoju's interpretation on faith. However, in Ghatiyali *jhāṛai* refers to a runny bowel movement and the *RSK* gives "to send" for *pachaṭhno*.

32. *mūṅ to jhāṛai juvābā vāstai mūtbā vāstai khiyo.*

33. As is often true in India, this was an all-night performance.

"Enough, brothers, all I wanted was to come here."

So the performers left. Gorakh Nathji stayed a few days with his Guru Sovereign and began to tell tales to him. "Guru Sovereign, you have to go. Over there, I had a bad quarrel with Kanni Pavji's assembly. I said, 'Brother your guru is smothering under horse manure,' and they said, 'Your guru is in Bengal ruling a kingdom and enjoying women.' So Grain-giver, we had some harsh words among us, and I said, 'Now I'll bring my guru,' and they said, 'Now we'll get out our guru.' That's the quarrel that we had, so Guru Sovereign, we really must go. Later if you want to come back, that's fine."

"O Gorakh Nath, these lady magician sluts won't let us go."

"The lady magician sluts won't let you go?"

"They will do magic. They will transform us magically. They will make us into roosters, they will make us into donkeys, these lady magicians. They'll do magic on me, and if you try to take me and they find out, the sluts will kill you."

"O Guru Sovereign, I'm just telling you to go. You shouldn't even think about those sluts. You come with me because I have a quarrel to settle over there, with Kanni Pavji's assembly. So it is necessary for you, the Guru Sovereign, to go."

So he persuaded him. But then he said, "O brother, I want to take Nim Nath and Paras Nath. I will leave my kingdom and my queens, but I will take both my boys, my Nim Nath and Paras Nath."

"Yes Guru Sovereign, take them. Let Nim Nath and Paras Nath live here or take them, as you like—it's up to you. But over there the yogis have gathered together."

"OK, Gorakh Nath, let's go. We'll leave in the middle of the night. At midnight. Then the sluts will be sleeping. And I'll send Nim Nath and Paras Nath ahead. At midnight no one will see, no dogs will bark. Let's go."

"OK."

"But, Gorakh Nath, if the sluts catch us before we get to the boundaries, then they will kill us."

"You go in front, Guru Sovereign, and don't give any thought to those sluts."

(GC 4.8.e)

They left at midnight. Machhindar Nath Sovereign filled his bag with four golden bricks. "Brother, there's an assembly of *sādhu*s and saints over there, and I'll give them a feast of blessed food. I'll pay for one day's feast." He put four golden bricks in his bag, and took his sack, took his tongs, put on his sandals, and sounded his deer-horn instrument. He sent Paras Nath and Nim Nath ahead.

A seated yogi's a stake in the ground, but a yogi once up is a fistful of wind. The Naths took the wind's own form. And now they left Bengal. They crossed one forest, they crossed a second forest, and in the third forest, they came to the border.

Now Machhindar Nath's queens were four lady magicians. And one of them realized that Gorakh Nath had taken them.

"Why are you sleeping, sluts, he took him! And he took the princes Nim Nath and Paras Nath, too. He took them and he has reached the border."

"Yes he took them!" Throughout the whole palace there was a great commotion.

"O sluts, what are you doing sleeping? He took them, the father and the princes, too! He took Machhindar Nathji, Gorakh Nath took them!"

"Oh, he took them and now they've reached the border."

Son of a . . . ! One queen became a she-ass and one became a big vulture, the kind with a red neck,[34] and one became a white vulture.[35] And they came flying, whizzing after them, when they had reached the border.

As soon as they came flying after them, Machhindar Nath spoke: "Gorakh Nath, they have come. The sluts will kill us right now."

"I understand that they have come. Guru Sovereign, don't look back, don't give it a thought."

So they kept coming and one had became a she-ass and was braying as she came, and he struck her with his tongs. She was a she-ass so he gave her to the Potters: "Load her heavily and feed her little."[36]

And one had become a white vulture, and he struck her with his

---

34. *khanchar banyo ū rātyā galtā ko kāṅvalo; khanchar* is not in the *RSK*, but *kāṅvalo* is identified as a kite, a white vulture, or a large crow. I am not certain of the zoology in *khanchar*'s case, but it is an unpleasant bird of prey.

35. Note that only three transformations have been identified here, although there are four queens. Madhu forgot to mention the queen who became the smallpox goddess, Sitala Mother, as we will learn shortly.

36. An accurate description of a donkey's existence.

tongs and even today she still flies in the sky. The one who became Sitala, Gorakh Baba installed her outside the village.[37] That was Nim Nath and Paras Nath's mother. She is worshiped over here.

Then the fourth came, the one who had become a big vulture with a long neck—the kind that eats the bones of dead animals, that one with a red neck. He made her stay a vulture and said, "Slut, you keep flying in the sky." So she keeps flying in the sky.

So Gorakh Nathji Sovereign finished off all four lady magicians just like that and came along with Nim Nath and Paras Nath and Machhindar Nath.

So they went along, and when they came to a city or a village they would set up their campfires at dusk. Then Gorakh Nathji Sovereign would go into the settlement to beg and bring back cold stale scraps—for the guru and to feed Nim Nath and Paras Nath.

One day they came to a certain city and were going to spend the night there. Now Gorakh Nathji Sovereign said to Machhindar Nath, "Guru Sovereign."

"Yes son?"

"Grain-giver, should I go alone into the settlement? We are four persons, and what use is it if I go alone into the settlement? We ought to teach these boys, Nim Nath and Paras Nath, to beg. It is our yogis' work so we ought to teach them, and take them around the settlement."

"But they are king's sons! [*Spoken with a perfect sense of delicate outrage*] What do they know of begging, Gorakh Nath you sister-fucker?"

"Guru Sovereign, it is necessary to teach them."

"Yes, we'll have to teach them, but they'll learn little by little."

"Come Guru Sovereign, I'll take them into this neighborhood. Let them fill their own bellies, guru. I'll take the disciples and let them get as much flour as they need to live."

But Gorakh Nathji was *thinking*, I'll destroy them on the way, so those sons of penis-eaters[38] over there don't see them and say, "Look, your guru enjoyed sluts and had sons." Yes, I'll get rid of them so no one can say that.

---

37. Sitala Mother is the goddess of smallpox; her shrine is outside the village.

38. *phoḍākhāṇī;* this harsh insult refers to Kanni Pavji's group of yogis who taunted Gorakh with his guru's laxity. As an insult to the mother, it implies not sexual perversity but excessive desire.

But to Machhindar Nathji Sovereign he said, "Grain-giver sir, we should put wooden sandals on them and give them tongs to carry and sacks and smear them with ashes. And let them go into the settlement to beg and I'll go a different way. Let our disciples bring enough to fill their stomachs."

"All right, son, go. Nim Nath, Paras Nath you go too."

"But Guru Sovereign, we have never begged, '*Alakh! Alakh!*'"

"Yogis' begging is easy, isn't it, sister-fuckers? If people are true they'll come forward and give to you, and those without truth won't give."

[*spoken with* sārangī *background music*] Gorakh Nath Sovereign took them forward—whom? Nim Nath and Paras Nath. There was a Merchant's funeral feast[39] going on over there in that city, and the place was filling up with Merchants and Brahmans.

(GC 4.9.e)

Gorakh Nath took Nim Nath and Paras Nath into the city. "You go into that neighborhood, and I'll go into this neighborhood. Afterwards, you come back to the campfire, and I'll come back there too. That's the order."

"*Alakh alakh alakh alakh!*" they went calling.

Gorakh Nathji Sovereign called "*Alakh!*" as he went into the bazaar that was filled with many Merchants and Brahmans. "O it looks like a feast!"

"Yes it's a Merchant's feast, sir."

"So which house is the feast-giver's?"

"It's this one, sir."

A cow was standing over here, near Ratan Well.[40]

"Cow Mother, what are you doing over here? Go to the feast-giver's gateway and die in the gateway." So Cow Mother did this, she went to the gate, right near the threshold, and sat down and died.[41]

And Gorakh Nathji Sovereign went on to the next street.

---

39. Funeral feasts are of great importance in village social life; they often involve feeding hundreds or even thousands of guests. Madhu uses two words that I translate "Merchant": *Mājanā* and *Bānyā;* in Ghatiyali both refer to members of a relatively wealthy caste who act as shopkeepers and are all Jains.

40. This is a named well in Ghatiyali, near the Brahman neighborhood.

41. Gorakh Nath's ruthlessness toward the cow foreshadows his ruthlessness toward the boys.

Now, where the food lines were set up,[42] the Merchants' and Brahmans' feasting shut down.

"O, *Rām Rām Rām* a cow died! Where can we eat if a cow died?[43] And there's no one to take it away. How can the platter-bearers serve the feast? A cow died, and you've got to remove it first, brother. Then we'll feast."

Now who is going to remove a cow all of a sudden?

So this strange thing had happened, and in the midst of the confusion, Nim Nath and Paras Nath came calling "*Alakh! Alakh!* Hey brother, Merchant Father, you're doing some big cooking today! Feast us and give us a special portion for our Guru Sovereign."

Those boys were making a racket. "O brother Merchant Father, feast us, and give us a special portion for our Guru Sovereign."

There was one bastard of a Merchant there, and he said, "Hey boys, don't make such a hullabaloo."

"O Merchant Father, then feast us. And give us a special portion for our Guru Sovereign."

He said, "This cow died, and, sure, we'll feast you and we'll give you a special portion for your Guru Sovereign. But first one of you grab the horn and one of you grab the tail and push the cow over by Ratan Well, by the wall. Then we'll start feasting again, and we'll feast you too and we'll fill your cups for the Guru Sovereign. This cow died over here by the gate, and so the feasting has stopped. If you want to eat then you must pull."

One of them, Nim Nath, said, "If Gorakh Nathji sees us then he'll beat us."

But Paras Nath said, "Oh, who knows what alley Gorakh Nath has gone into. You grab the horn and I'll grab the tail and then they'll feast us and they'll fill our cups too. Otherwise, these are Merchants and my son! they'll never feast us!"[44]

So one brother grabbed the horn and one brother grabbed the tail. And they pulled that cow over by the wall of Ratan Well and put it down there. As soon as they had pulled it, the Merchants set

42. At village feasts, guests are seated before leaf plates in lines that may be in the courtyard but usually extend outside into the street.

43. A dead animal is polluting and food must not be eaten in its vicinity. The very essence of low-caste service in the village is the removal of dead animals.

44. Merchants are notoriously stingy and almost always badly portrayed in folklore.

up their eating lines again. "Brother, now the cow is removed, brother, now be seated."

They sat down in the eating lines, and they made the boys sit down too. "Here, boys, you feast too." So they feasted them.

"Give us a special portion for our Guru Sovereign."

"Brothers, take this special portion." And so they filled their cups. As soon as they had their cups filled, and they had eaten their fill, they went back to the Guru Sovereign's campfire.

They got there and said to the Guru Sovereign, "Guru Sovereign, look, take this. Gorakh Nathji brings stale cold scraps and today we have brought five fried treats. Today we went for the first time and we brought five fried treats!"

When they told this to the Guru Sovereign, he was very happy. "Yes, my sons, today you have brought some excellent goods, but that sister-fucker Gorakh Nath brings stale cold scraps that I can't even chew."

Meanwhile, Gorakh Nathji Sovereign had been making his rounds, and then he came back to the Merchant's gate. The dead cow was lying there, and Gorakh Nathji Sovereign sprinkled it with the elixir of life and said, "Cow Mother there's no grazing over here, what are you doing?" She came back to life and Cow Mother went on her way.[45]

No one had feasted Gorakh Nathji. He had stale cold scraps in his bag when he went back to the campfire. At the campfire he said, "Take some, Guru Sovereign, eat."

"Yeah, sister-fucking Gorakh Nath, you bring sister-fucking cold stale scraps that an old man like me can't eat. But today my Nim Nath and Paras Nath went, and they brought five fried treats."

"Guru Sovereign, these cold stale scraps are Truth's. And these five fried treats are Untruth's."

"Sure sister-fucker, my Nim Nath and Paras Nath brought them and that's why they've become Untruth's, but your scraps are Truth's."

"Yes Guru Sovereign, those are Sin's and these are Dharma's."

"Sister-fucker, how are these Sin's?"

"Guru Sovereign, cover them up. And cover up these scraps too."

So he covered them up with a sheet. He covered the boys' cups

45. Gorakh Nath thus repairs his sin of cow-killing, however anticlimactically.

and he covered the scraps too. As soon as he covered them, sister-fucker! Prosperity entered the scraps, but the boys' turned into pus and blood. So their cup had pus and blood, but Gorakh Nath's scraps turned into five treats.

"All right, Gorakh Nath, what's the meaning of this?"

"Guru Sovereign, they brought this for pulling a cow. They brought it for pulling a dead cow, so that's why it has pus and maggots. Now these two can't be our disciples any longer. They're dead, the sister-fuckers. They have turned into Leatherworkers.[46] They are low cow-pullers.[47] They have no more meaning for us. They have become Leatherworkers."[48]

"Well, sister-fuckers, you removed a cow?"

"Yes, Grain-giver sir. There was a Merchant, and he wouldn't feast us, and there was a dead cow lying there, outside his house, and we grabbed its horns and tail and dragged it aside. We just gave it a little push."

"Well, sister-fuckers, you're spoiled. You have become low cow-pullers."

Gorakh Nath said, "Guru Sovereign, they're spoiled, and they're no use to us anymore, so now what will we do with them? What will we do with the sister-fuckers? What do we need them for? They have become cow-pullers and they can't live with us. They can't smoke or share tobacco with us."

"So those Merchants, those cunts—why did they spoil our disciples?"

"Let's take them there."

So Machhindar Nath grabbed one of their wrists and Gorakh Nath grabbed the other one's wrist. And they went to the Merchant's gate. There was a big flat rock lying there and they began striking them on it. They grabbed their feet and threw them against it, and drops of blood sprinkled and splattered.

The Merchant and his wife fell at their feet and joined their hands and begged forgiveness. "Oh, Grain-givers, don't kill them."

---

46. *regar;* one of the two leatherworking castes in Ghatiyali.

47. *ḍheḍ;* the *RSK* gives the caste name *chamār* for this, but according to Bhoju it is less a caste name than an insulting designation specific to the work of pulling dead animals.

48. *chamār;* the other local leatherworking group.

"O you sister-fuckers, you didn't feast them. Why did you ruin our disciples, why did you have them pull a cow from your place? O sister-fuckers why did you turn them into Leatherworkers? O cowards,[49] you didn't feast them, you sister-fuckers. Why did you have our disciples pull a cow? What good are they to us now? They're no good at all. So we are going to kill them at your gateway. Why did you make them into Leatherworkers? Why did you have them pull a cow?"

"O Guru Sovereign, who told you this story? I didn't even talk to them at my party."

"O yes, you sister-fucker, you turned them into Leatherworkers. We are yogis and what good are they to us now? We will kill them at your gateway, sister-fucker."

"Hey Grain-giver, don't kill them."

"So what should I do then?"

"Grain-giver, leave them with us, and we will feed them plenty of bread in a nice way and take good care of them."

"Sure, sister-fucker, you did this to our disciples and you'll give bread! I'll kill them right here at your gateway, sister-fucker."

So he struck them and struck them. He grabbed their feet and smashed them, again and again, the way we smash a blanket.[50] Blood spattered, and the boys Nim Nath and Paras Nath were calling in a terrible way. The Merchant and his wife begged forgiveness and fell at his feet, "Oh Grain-giver don't kill them."

"So if I don't kill them what will I do with them?"

"Hey Grain-giver, don't kill them and we will make them our deities, we will call them Thakurji."[51]

"So, you will make them Thakurjis?"

"Yes sir, we will make them Thakurjis, and we will worship them with rice. That's what we'll do from one generation to another."

"Good, show me the temple."

So right away he took them to the temple. There was a temple

---

49. *leḍyāvo;* an insult meaning "coward" that is particularly appropriate for Merchants, according to Bhoju, because Merchants are notoriously unwilling to fight.

50. That is, slap it down again and again, as clothes are washed in rural India.

51. A title used for deities in many local temples of Rajasthan, its primary meaning is a local landlord or ruler.

with no icons, in which they put both brothers standing side by side. Gorakh Nathji Sovereign turned them to stone.

Then he said to the Merchants and Brahmans, "Offer up water on these and drink the nectar from their dicks[52] or else you'll be destroyed. Worship them with rice and serve them well, or else you'll be destroyed."

So the Merchants and Brahmans offered water and accepted it from their penises,[53] saying, "Grain-giver, Thakurji Sovereign, Grain-giver."

So that's how the Merchants' sect came to be, and Nim Nath and Paras Nath became Thakurjis.[54] And Gorakh Nathji Sovereign's sorrow was erased. "Now nobody can say, 'Look, brother, your guru enjoyed sluts and had sons.'"

Now they left that place where they had made Nim Nath and Paras Nath into Thakurjis.

(GC 4.10.e)

The guru and disciple were going along together. As they went down the road, Gorakh Nathji said, "Guru Sovereign, you're walking like a cripple with that sack, you're going as slowly as an old man. Give that sack to me. It must have something heavy in it, so let me carry it."

But the Guru Sovereign wasn't about to give up his gold bricks. Brother, that Gorakh Nath, who knows where he'll throw them down, my son!

/And who knows how he'll trick me!/

Yes, he'll play a trick with my gold bricks. He's not likely to give them to Gorakh Nath!

He said, "No, no, Gorakh Nath."

"Come, Guru Sovereign, it looks like there's a weight in there, give me your sack."

"No."

So the Guru Sovereign went slowly along. And on the road they came to a banyan tree and a step-well.[55]

52. Because the icons in Jain temples are naked, water poured on their heads is likely to run over their penises. The word for male organ here is not *lingam* but *indarī*, which Bhoju tells me villagers use for little boys' penises.

53. *langī;* another term probably related to *lingam*.

54. According to Bhoju, Nim Nath and Paras Nath are included among the twenty-four Jain *tīrthankars*.

55. *baṛ bāvaṛī;* in Rajasthani folklore travelers often come upon these two paired comforts of shade and water.

Machhindar Nath said, "Gorakh Nath let's take a little rest here. Let's have a smoke and let's take an afternoon rest and wash our hands and faces."[56]

"Yes, Guru Sovereign, let's wash our hands and faces."

"They sat down in the shade of the banyan tree over there by the step-well. And they smoked the hashish pipe, and Machhindar said, "Gorakh Nath, I shall go wash my hands and face."

"Yes, Guru Sovereign, go wash."

"Brother Gorakh Nath, this is the thing."

"Yes, Grain-giver, tell me."

"You beat time. [*Madhu claps to demonstrate.*] And while you're clapping I'll wash my hands and face and come back."

Now whatever the guru says must be done. Mustn't it be done? /It must be done./

The Guru Sovereign thought, To protect my sack I will start him clapping first, and then go. Otherwise he'll throw the bricks that I've loaded in it into the step-well, and then what will I do?

So he started him clapping. [*Madhu continues to demonstrate and laughs.*] "As soon as he's keeping time I'll go over there." The Guru Sovereign said to him, "Yes, son, you beat time and I'll go into the jungle."

"Yes, go Guru Sovereign." Gorakh Nathji began to keep time.

"You keep on counting and we'll see if I come back in the beat."

"Yes, Guru Sovereign, I am counting." The Guru Sovereign went and after a while he squatted on the other side of the thorn bush. As soon as he squatted, Gorakh Nath Sovereign kept beating time. [*Madhu claps.*] But he began to beat his thigh. And with one hand only he checked out the sack. And he didn't skip a beat.

"Let's see what weight the Guru Sovereign has crammed into his sack that makes him walk so slowly. Let's search it."

So he searched the sack and found inside it so much golden money! Four bricks were lying there. Oh the Guru Sovereign has filled his sack with stones. So then how can he walk—the son of a penis-eater? He has loaded this burden of rocks in his sack. The Guru Sovereign has put them there improperly, sinfully. Why has he filled his sack with these stones? [*Madhu is laughing, enjoying this story a lot.*]

That cunt—with one hand he kept time and didn't skip a beat and with one hand only he took them and Splash! Splash! Splash!

---

56. *hāth mūṇḍā dholyāṅ;* a standard euphemism in the village for defecation.

Splash!—with four separate splashes he threw them in the well.

As soon as he heard the four separate splashes outside the beat, the Guru Sovereign didn't care if he had shit or not shit, he washed his ass and got up. He got up so fast he didn't even tie up his loincloth, like Ladu Nath, he didn't knot his loincloth.

And the Guru Sovereign rushed back to check on his sack. As soon as he checked it out, he found out it was empty. "Sister-fucker, Gorakh Nath, you threw my four gold bricks into the well, you sister-fucker!"

"What, Guru Sovereign? What did I throw where?"

He said, "Where did you throw them? There were four splashes just now. You threw all four bricks; they broke the rhythm."

"Oh my, Guru Sovereign, why did you fill your sack with this senseless burden of rocks? Guru Sovereign, you were walking like a cripple and that's how I knew, brother. 'Why did he bring these rocks?' Guru Sovereign, I threw them away."

"Sister-fucker Gorakh Nath, I won't go with you. Sister-fucker, you made me leave my kingdom and my queens, too. You made some into donkeys and some into vultures and you spoiled my kingdom and my court. And Nim Nath and Paras Nath were my princes, whom you caused to be killed, sister-fucker, and had made into Merchant deities. And the little bit that I brought for my expenses you threw in the well. Yes, sister-fucker, you suppose that I'll go with you?"

He had made the Guru Sovereign angry.

Now Gorakh Nathji Sovereign thought, My witch! Look, the old man is angry, brother, now what am I going to do? He prostrated himself and blocked his path. He blocked the Guru Sovereign's path and joined his hands. But he turned his back on him and passed him.

"No, Gorakh Nath, don't block my path, I won't go with you. You are a knave, sister-fucker!"

And now Gorakh Nathji Sovereign said, "Guru Sovereign, you've become angry?"

"Yes, sister-fucker, you've ruined my house, sister-fucker. And now you even took my gold that I brought for expenses."

/Yes he made him leave his place and ruined everything!/

"You ruined everything, and you had my princes killed, and you made me leave my kingdom, and you made me leave my queens, and you had my princes killed. And, sister-fucker, I brought four golden bricks for my expenses, that I was going to use to feast the *sādhu*s and saints, and even those you threw in the well, sister-fucker! You have left me empty-handed, resourceless."[57]

Then Gorakh Nathji Sovereign got angry and said, "Guru Sovereign, you're really distraught?"

"Yes, sister-fucker, I'm distraught."

Just then Gorakh Nathji Sovereign threw down his tongs on the hill of Jaypalji.[58] And as soon as he threw down his tongs, the whole hill began sparkle-sparkle-sparkling: it had turned to gold!

"Guru Sovereign, take as much as you can pack. Pick up the whole hill and take it. You were going away mad, believing in four golden brick-pebbles. Now pick up this whole hill and take all this gold, nothing but gold."

Oh my! The Guru Sovereign was happy. "Hey, Gorakh Nath."

"Yes, Guru Sovereign?"

"Son, it has become permanent."[59]

"It was the grace of the Guru Sovereign that made it that way. So pick it up. Pick up the hill."

"Hey sister-fucker, you think I can carry this hill?"

"OK, Guru Sovereign, just pick up as much as four bricks' worth. Pick up four rocks and put them in your sack. And then let's go, take them and go. Guru Sovereign, are you happy now?"

"Yes, son, I'm happy."

"Good, so take them and let's go."

They began to go and then they looked back. Machhindar Nathji looked back and saw the form of riches[60]—the golden hill was sparkling.

"Oh, Gorakh Nath."

"Yes, Guru Sovereign."

"Son, spoil this golden hill again."

"Why, Guru Sovereign?"

57. *abhyāgat* can be a renouncer, as well as just a poor person. Both meanings could merge here, as Gorakh Nath takes away Machhindar's resources to make him, once again, a renouncer.

58. *Jaypāljī* is a shrine tended by the Nath caste located on a hill so named behind the Nath neighborhood.

59. *pakkā;* cooked, firm, used to distinguish houses and roads made of concrete or brick or stone from those made of mud and dirt.

60. *māyā rūpī;* could also be rendered "form of illusion."

"O sister-fucker, the king of over here will say, 'It's within my borders' and the king of over there will say, 'It's within my borders,' and then, sister-fucker, many armies will cut one another, and, sister-fucker, the sin will be ours. The slaughter will be our fault, sister-fucker—thousands of men cutting one another, sister-fucker. So spoil it again."[61]

So Gorakh Nath Sovereign hawked and spit on it—on that hill. As soon as he had spit, it turned into Kashmiri stones—from which these marble icons come.[62] And these *darśaṇī* that we wear in our ears. Our yogis' *darśaṇī* that we wear in our ears are made from that hill, from that Kashmiri stone. Like the *darśaṇī* I wear in my ears, like that.

So he spoiled it, and they went on their way: "Let's go."

The Guru Sovereign was happy. So now Gorakh Nathji and Machhindar Nathji Sovereign are going along.

(GC 4.11.e)

A seated yogi's a stake in the ground, but a yogi once up is a fistful of wind. The Naths took the wind's own form and fixed their consciousness on Gaur Bengal. They crossed one woods, they crossed a second woods, and in the third woods they came to the garden of Gaur Bengal, the Chapala Garden.

When they reached the Chapala Garden, they saw Kanni Pavji's disciples looking down-at-the-mouth. They had filled their shovels again and again, but it doubled in the day and quadrupled in the night so they were miserable, and six months had gone by since that day. The well wasn't empty—it doubled in the day and quadrupled in the night.

So Gorakh Nathji Sovereign said, "O sister-fuckers, I have brought my guru fourteen hundred miles, and, sister-fuckers, you haven't taken out your guru. It's been six months and you still haven't got your guru out."

"Father of a daughter! Gorakh Nath! You've beaten us. It doubles in the day and in the night it quadruples. Son of a penis-eater. We do the same kind of work every day, but it is never finished."

---

61. This is the only moment when Machhindar seems wiser than Gorakh; he understands the ways of kings.

62. According to Bhoju the Kashmiri stone is the same as Hindi *billauri*, a kind of quartz or crystal. Madhu is confused here; the crystal for earrings and marble for icons are two different kinds of stone.

"Yes, sister-fuckers, you'll never finish it. Quit trying. This is what you should do. Call all the gurus' disciples. Jalindar Baba has fourteen hundred disciples doing *tapas* underground. Call them. And call too his fourteen hundred disciples who do *tapas* visibly. Fourteen times two is twenty-eight. Twenty-eight hundred disciples of Jalindar Baba. And fourteen hundred disciples of Gorakh Nathji Sovereign and fourteen hundred disciples of Machhindar Nath, and fourteen hundred of Kanni Pavji."

The garden filled up completely.

Now this is what Gorakh Nathji Sovereign did. He struck seven times with his sandal. And he took out seven groups of locusts from that horse manure in the blind well.

He took out one green group, he took out one white group, he took out one black group, he took out one red group, and one dappled group. He took out one oil-colored group. And so he took out seven kinds of locusts. He took those separate groups from inside there.

He took out the groups of locusts and made them swear an oath: "Brothers, when yogis tell you go, then go. And maintain the honor of robe-wearers. Help them to earn their livings. Keep wandering around in the world, and when yogis and yoginis come, accept their magic circles[63] and maintain the honor of their robes. And keep their stomachs full of bread."

He took the locusts out of the horse manure. So we speak spells like "Om guru in the western land is the deep well where the locusts were born."[64]

The locusts were born in the blind well. In Gopi Chand's horses' dung.

And now the groups of locusts were emptied out, and the well was completely emptied. Inside it was the big flat stone upon which he had set up his meditation seat. Who? Jalindar Baba. And he was reciting God's names.

"Now take out your Guru Sovereign," he said to them.

"How shall we take out the Guru Sovereign? He won't come out."

63. *kār dhār;* a circle inscribed on the ground and empowered by spells that can keep locusts inside or outside its line.

64. *Aum gurujī paccham deś majj kā go jyāṅ ṭiḍī kā jalam hoyā;* this is a fragment of an actual spell used to remove locusts. There is no harm in revealing the spells because their potency derives as much from the sayer's accumulated meditative prowess as from the words themselves.

"All right brother." So they called Gopi Chand and Bharthari. And Gorakh Nathji Sovereign asked for *ḍāb* grass. He asked for *ḍāb* and he used it to make dolls of both of them,[65] of Gopi Chand and of Bharthari. Then he set down a big drum. Where? He set down a big drum on the edge of the blind well, and Gopi Chand and Bharthari began to play it. And now they will become immortal, right here, Gopi Chand and Bharthari.

(GC 4.12.e)

He made these dolls,
and set down the drum on the edge.[66]
He set down the drum on the edge,
and Gopi Chand and Bharthari
began to play the drum.
They began to play,
they played "*dam dam*" on the drum
and the sound went into the blind well.

From the blind well
Jalindar Baba spoke:
"Who is going '*dam dam*'?"
Gorakh Baba said,
"Baba, Gopi Chand and Bharthari,
Baba, Gopi Chand and Bharthari."
A voice emerged from Baba's mouth: "Ashes!
Gopi Chand and Bharthari are ashes."

As the speech "Ashes" emerged
the dolls burned up.
The dolls burned up, and then
a second time
he made dolls
and gave them their names,
and they began playing.
Baba yelled, "Wasn't my speech accepted?
Now who's going '*dam dam*'?"

65. *Ḍāb* is a special green grass used in Sanskritic rituals; in other versions of Gopi Chand's story these dolls are made of seven metals, or of three metals, hinting at associations with an alchemical pursuit of immortality.

66. This is the final sung segment of GC 4.

"My guru, it's Gopi Chand and Bharthari, Baba,
Gopi Chand and Bharthari."
The guru's voice came out of the well, "Ashes!
Let Gopi Chand and Bharthari be ashes!"

Outside the dolls
burned up, outside
they burned up.
For the third and last time
the yogi made dolls,
he made dolls.
Then Gopi Chand and Bharthari
played the drum,
he had them play the drum.
Now the sound *"dam dam"* went into the well
and Jalindar Baba demanded:

"Who's going '*dam dam*' today?
Who is doing it,
who is doing it?"
"My guru, Gopi Chand and Bharthari are doing it, Guruji,
It's Gopi Chand and Bharthari."

After this had happened,
the guru's promise emerged:
"As long as earth shall be
live Gopi Chand and
Bharthari! O sons,
Bharthari will live."[67]
The guru's speech "Immortal" emerged,
and Gopi Chand became immortal.

(GC 4.13.s)

So the blind well was emptied of the locusts, and Jalindar Baba
was in there doing *tapas,* reciting God's names.[68] Now to get the Guru
Sovereign out...

"Do this: call Gopi Chand and Bharthari. Gopi Chand and
Bharthari are in this company, among Jalindar Baba's disciples."

---

67. An echo of the proverb, *jab tak akās dhartarī tab tak Gopī Chand Bhartharī.*
68. This begins the final spoken segment of Madhu Nath's Gopi Chand epic.

Then Gorakh Nath made dolls out of *ḍāb* grass. He made two grass dolls: one was Gopi Chand and the other was Bharthari. He named them separately. And he had Gopi Chand and Bharthari start to beat the drum. "*Dam dam dam dam*," they beat the drum. And the sound of the drum playing "*dam dam*" went into the blind well, and Jalindar Baba's eyelids opened. From inside came a voice. "Hey, sister-fucker, who is going '*dam dam*' over here?"

Then Gorakh Nathji Sovereign said, "Sovereign, it is Gopi Chand and Bharthari."

"Sister-fuckers—ashes!"

As soon as the speech "Ashes" emerged then, crackle crackle those dolls burned up. The dolls Gorakh Nath had made . . . because Jalindar said, "Let Gopi Chand and Bharthari burn to ashes!" but Gorakh Nathji had given their names to the dolls.

So as soon as the dolls burned up, then he made a second set of dolls. So we'll try, and third time proves all.[69] Yes, let's see, if they will become immortal with three chances.

The first set of dolls turned to ash, and then he made more dolls of *ḍāb* grass. "That one's Gopi Chand and that one's Bharthari," and he had them begin to play the drum.

"*Dam dam dam*" it went, and as soon as it went "*dam dam dam*" then the Guru Sovereign said, "Hey sister-fuckers, who is there? What sister-fucker is making this '*dam dam dam*' racket?"

Gorakh Nathji Sovereign said, "Sovereign, Guru Sovereign, it's Gopi Chand and Bharthari."

"Those sister-fuckers—ashes!"

Then the dolls burned up right there. And as soon as the dolls burned up, then Gorakh Nath made more dolls. "Let's see! Now comes the third, and the third time proves all. If the speech 'Immortality' emerges, then they'll be immortal. But if the speech 'Ashes' emerges, then they're dead."

So he made the dolls for the third and last chance. "Brother, that one's Gopi Chand and that one's Bharthari."

And he had Gopi Chand and Bharthari begin to play the drum.

---

69. *lok patijāṅ;* according to Bhoju this expression occurs in contests where the "best of three" is the winner. I cannot explain the literal meaning, which may concern the three "worlds" (*lok*) in cosmology. I translate as "third time proves all" rather than "best of three" because in two out of three times Jalindar gave the curse of "ashes."

And it went *"dam dam dam"* and as soon as it did, then Jalindar Baba yelled, "Hey sister-fucker, who is going *'dam dam dam'* and isn't accepting what I say?"

"Guru Sovereign it's Gopi Chand and Bharthari."

"Yes, you sister-fuckers, as long as the earth remains, so will Gopi Chand and Bharthari."

That word[70] emerged from the Guru Sovereign. That did it. The speech "Immortality" emerged and they became immortal. Then Gorakh Nath stretched out his arm. "Come out, Guru Sovereign."

"Why?"

"Why? Because the whole assembly is watching and calling you. So come out."

Then Gorakh Nath stretched out his arm and grabbed the guru's hands with his and brought out Jalindar Baba.

He had been doing *tapas* for years in the blind well, he had been doing *tapas* for so long that from his truth's complete success a fruit of immortality had been produced there.[71]

He brought that fruit of immortality in his sack, and as soon as he came out, he took it out and with his own hand he gave the immortal fruit to Gopi Chand and Bharthari. He fed half to Gopi Chand and he fed half to Bharthari, so they became immortal, brother.[72]

So they took out Jalindar Baba. As soon as they took him out, he set up his campfire, and fixed up his meditation seat . . . he had saffron burning in his campfire. Everyone was saying, "The Guru Sovereign has come, the Guru Sovereign has emerged!"

So then they said, "The whole assembly is here, Guru Sovereign. We ought to have a big feast, of all the gurus."

Jalindar Baba was the senior guru,[73] and so he had to provide the first feast. It was a wish-feast.[74] "Eat a lot, a lot of *laddūs* and *jalebīs*."

---

70. *śabad*.

71. *jīkā satt kā parmāṇ se amar phal paidā hogyo uthai;* this could also be construed as "from the evidence of his truth." It is the only mention in either of Madhu's epics of an *amar phal*—around which certain versions of Bharthari's story revolve (see chapter 3).

72. The events that follow were not included in the singing, but Madhu's narrative flowed into them without pause.

73. Machhindar Nath is usually identified as the first of the Nath yogi gurus, but Madhu Nath says Jalindar is the eldest.

74. Here the expression "wish-feast" (*manasā bhojan*) involves a nice assortment of desirable sweets; see below for Gorakh Nath's magical wish-feast.

So all the assemblies of yogis had a feast at the guru's expense. They cooked masses of food and all the yogis feasted well.

/They had a wonderful time!/

Now the next day—whose turn was it? Machhindar Nath Sovereign's. Machhindar Nath was junior to Jalindar Nath. So Machhindar Nath took his four bricks, his gold bricks. He gave them and said, "Brothers, take these four gold bricks and bring all the stuff and then eat plenty of *laḍḍūs* and *jalebīs*." That was it: the stuff came and then Machhindar Nath Baba's feast took place, in a very fine way . . . his cooking . . . his party.

So now? Now it was Kanni Pavji's turn. And Kanni Pavji also gave a great party for everybody.

But now his number[75] comes up. Now Gorakh Nathji is left.

Gorakh Nathji's number came up. And he thought, Brother, I haven't any feast stuff, nothing at all. I haven't any cash, and I haven't any firewood, and I haven't any beans, and I haven't any stuff at all . . . I'm a yogi, I am. Let the sister-fuckers drink offering-ash tomorrow!

When evening came, Gorakh Nathji Sovereign called, "O assemblies, listen, all you assemblies. Tomorrow Gorakh Nathji Sovereign invites you at twelve o'clock for a feast, for a wish-feast. The invitation is for whatever you desire.

"Everyone bring his own cup right side up, covered with a cloth. Whatever you desire to eat, then put your hand on your cup and ask for it. That very food will come."

So he gave that invitation, and then Gorakh Nathji Sovereign went to sleep.

Now day dawned. And as soon as day dawned, and they had washed their hands and faces, the yogis turned their prayer beads. At eleven o'clock they went to Gorakh Nathji Sovereign and said, "The time has come. Get up, you don't have any stuff yet, nothing at all! Where are you going to get stores of grain, cooking pots, flour, all the things? You promised twelve o'clock. O brother, where are the goods going to come from?"

"You just take your baths, brothers, and wash your hands and faces."

---

75. This is one of the few moments when Madhu Nath uses an English word; "number" commonly means "turn" in rural Rajasthan.

"Well, we already bathed and washed and we're hungry. Yesterday you said there would be a feast at twelve o'clock. So it's twelve o'clock and Sovereign, we're dying of hunger!"

"Good, brothers, you're hungry?"

"Everyone is hungry."

"Good, then sit down. Sit down in eating lines. Let each guru's own disciples sit in separate eating lines."

So they sat down in separate lines. In one line were Jalindar Baba's disciples. In one line were Machhindar Nath's disciples. In one line were Gorakh Nath's. In one line were Kanni Pavji's.

"Now, brothers, this is what you should do. There are leaf plates set out. Everyone hold his own cup right side up and sit down. Take your cup and sit down, everyone."

Now Kanni Pavji's disciples were feeling enmity. Why? Because he had turned their food into rocks previously. Gorakh Nathji had turned that cartload of cooked food that was coming into rocks. They were feeling enmity.

Gorakh Nathji Sovereign said, "OK, brothers, set down your cups, with their mouths up, and cover them, cover them with a cloth." They covered them with a cloth.

This was his wish-feast, Gorakh Nathji's cooking.

"Everyone put your hand on your cup and ask for your desire, whatever you want to eat. And that very thing will come."

Now one of Kanni Pavji's disciples said, "That cunt—let's ask for improper things. He spoiled our feast-food. He turned it into rocks. So let us spoil his cooking. How? Some of you ask for snakes in your cup, and some of you ask for scorpions, and some of you ask for goats' heads, and some of you ask for buffalo, buffalo heads. Some of you ask for big snakes and some for jackals, foxes, lizards, fat lizards . . . we'll ask for all these different things and see where Gorakh Nath will grab them."

"Yeah, then it will be spoiled, where will he get living animals and bring them? He said we'd have a feast in our cups. But where will Gorakh Nath get scorpions, poisonous lizards, snakes, or water snakes?"

So they covered them up, and my son! They were dying of enmity. And some asked for snakes, and some asked for lizards, and some asked for goats' heads and some buffalo heads, and some asked for jackals and foxes and fat lizards. They asked for them in their cups.

Gorakh Nathji Sovereign said, "Yes, brothers, everyone is invited to my wish-feast. Put your hands on your cups, which are curtained, and ask for any kind of food. Ask!"

Well, Machhindar Nath's and Gorakh Nath's and Jalindar Nath's disciples asked for *sātalyā* and *purīs*, and *laḍḍūs* and *jalebīs*, and delicate breads and lentils. They asked for what they wanted. And they asked only for things to eat.

But Kanni Pavji's disciples . . . some asked for jackals and some for foxes and scorpions, poisonous animals, lizards and poisonous lizards and goats' heads and big snakes. They asked for black snakes and things like that, brother!

And it all came into their cups. Gorakh Nathji Sovereign made everything come, because he had invited them to a wish-feast.

Now which gurus were senior to Gorakh Nathji Sovereign? The one whom he took out from the blind well, Jalindar Baba. And Machhindar Nathji—and he went to their campfires.

He said, "Guru Sovereigns?"

"Yes, brother Gorakh Nath?"

"Well, Guru Sovereigns, I made a promise in the night. I gave invitations to a wish-feast of mine. So, Guru Sovereigns, whatever they desire they ask for it, and it comes into their cup."

"So they eat what they ask for."

"And suppose they ask for something improper, then, Guru Sovereigns, what should they do?"

"Let the sister-fuckers eat it, or beat them with tongs! It was an invitation to a wish-feast so why should they ask for improper things? And if they ask for improper things, the sister-fuckers have to eat them!"

Then Gorakh Nathji Sovereign said, "Yes, brothers, everyone uncover his own cup and feast."

So everyone took off the piece of cloth. And Machhindar Nathji's and Gorakh Nathji's and Jalindar Baba's disciples began to feast. They had asked for good feasts. Some had *laḍḍūs* and *sātalyā* and *purīs*, things to eat. And if they asked for vegetables, then they got vegetables. And if they asked for vegetables with *purīs*—whatever they asked for, all five festive foods, they got.

But those who asked for other things had piles of lizards and scorpions. Some had fat snakes and some had goats' heads and some had buffalo heads and they looked . . .

"Eat Eat!" [*Laughter*]

Now how would they eat?

Gorakh Nathji Sovereign said, "Jalindar Baba..."

"Yes, brother Gorakh Nath."

"Why aren't these disciples of Kanni Pavji eating?"

"Hey, you should eat!"

"Yes, Guru Sovereign." [*Spoken in a nasal whine*]

"Stand up, all you Guru Sovereigns, stand up... Machhindar Nathji, Jalindar Baba, look! What things have they got to eat? Improper, improper things to eat are lying there in their cups."

So they looked in them.

"O sister-fuckers, what have you done? So feast on it!"

"Grain-givers, how can we feast on this? Snakes and lizards, look! Goats' heads and buffalo heads."

"O sister-fuckers," the Guru Sovereigns said. "Did it come without asking or did you ask for it?"

"Guru Sovereigns, we asked!" [*Spoken like terrified children confessing to a prank*]

"How would it come without asking? Gorakh Nathji made a promise: 'Ask for whatever you wish, ask and eat.' So you asked and now the things have come. There are snakes and lizards and buffalo heads, goats' heads, sister-fuckers, foxes and jackals. Fat lizards and poisonous lizards... sister-fuckers! That's what you'll eat! You asked for them to eat."

"Guru Sovereigns, we asked out of enmity."

"What kind of enmity?"

"From before, when he turned our feast into rocks."

"If you had asked for rocks, maybe we could have helped you. But you asked for jackals and foxes. Eat them, sister-fuckers."

"Grain-giver, how can we eat them?"

"Now I'll make my tongs fly, sister-fuckers, why did you ask? Were you trying to destroy Gorakh Nath's wisdom? Where will he get scorpions, where will he get fat lizards, where will he grab jackals, where will he get snakes, where will he cut off animals' heads?' Well, sister-fuckers, he put them in your cups, you have really spoiled his honor! Eat them, sister-fuckers!"[76]

So he beat them with his tongs and fed them, the Snake Charmers.

---

76. Jalindar seems to be the speaker and actor here, but the text is ambiguous.

He fed them and gave them a fraction of knowledge, but to us he gave a full measure.[77]

"Go, sister-fuckers, and don't settle in any village. You have to live in the jungle and play the flute.[78] And catch snakes, sister-fuckers, and make them dance. Eat snakes, search for lizards, kill jackals and foxes and eat them. Sister-fuckers, live in the jungle only."

That's it, this will be their destiny. When any Snake Charmer comes, we keep him outside. He gave them a fraction of knowledge, and to us he gave a full measure of knowledge.

And our sect settled many retreats and could make lions and cows live together. In many places we turned the hills to gold, and sometimes five hundred *bīghās*[79] of land were assigned for our retreats, for the service of Mahadev. We could keep a cow with a lion, that's the kind of wisdom we had! When armies die, then we make the king a disciple and bring his army back to life. We bring it back to life and make the king a disciple.

That's it. Now Gopi Chand has become immortal, and that's it, Gopi Chand is complete.

(GC. 4.13.e)

77. Literally he gave the Snake Charmers "one and one-quarter of one-quarter of a *ser*" and gave the rest "one and one-quarter of a whole *ser*." A *ser* is a little over two pounds.

78. *pūṅgī;* an instrument associated with tribal groups.

79. One *bīghā* equals five-eighths of an acre.

Afterword:
Politics, Love, Death, and Destiny

Stories have a remarkable capacity to travel, soaring like yogis as a "fistful of wind" across all manner of linguistic, cultural, and political boundaries. Ethnography generally involves more sluggish and encumbered crosscultural treks. That may be why so many of us who seek to interpret other cultures hitch rides on stories.[1] Many interpretive flights would be possible on the wings of Madhu Nath's tales. The zigzagging course I shall take in the following pages was charted by my response to the persuasive power of Madhu's voice and reflects preexisting intellectual and personal interests. One fine hope I have for this book is that readers who bring other predispositions to it will be moved to explore its richness in ways that never occurred to me. Yet I do feel convinced that the tentative and oscillating nature of my interpretation is at least partially intrinsic to the narrative structure and performative life of these stories of yogis told by and for householders. No tidy resolutions are offered. Few if any who hear these stories decide to renounce the world, and neither tale as I recorded it ends on a note of divine detachment. The one

---

1. The English word "narrative" is etymologically connected with "knowledge," deriving from the Sanskrit root *gna* meaning "know" (White 1981, 1). Thus *gyān*— the very knowledge of which the bard Madhu Nath claims a full measure in the closing passage of his epic performance—has an ancient and crosscultural association with stories. See Narayan 1989 for many insights into the use of narratives as religious teaching.

311

thing we are sure of is that Gopi Chand and Bharthari live ever after; whether happily or not is hard to say.

Recall the last lines Madhu sings of Bharthari. The king addresses guru Gorakh Nath with these words: "Baba, now feast on your food, from the queen today, from my Queen Pingala." Thus he reaffirms possession even as he fulfills his yogic severance. And at the close of Gopi Chand, Madhu does not stop with Gopi Chand's receiving the fruit of immortality but goes on to describe the quarrel between Kanni Pavji's disciples and Gorakh Nath that results in the degradation of the former. Here Madhu claims that his own group received a full measure of "knowledge" (*gyān*) and the degraded group a fractional measure. His own group received land grants for many pleasant retreats, but the degraded group had to live in the jungle and eat snakes.

At first I was unhappy about this ending; I was tempted to excise it; it struck me as off-key—an almost melancholy reincorporation of hierarchy and worldly concerns into the renouncers' world, after they had flushed out love. Here was a sorry commentary on what religion had to offer. That reaction, I fear, displayed a genuine deafness to the texts' original voice, and a refusal to grant the teller his interpretive rights (Tedlock 1983). Madhu trumpets this ending and enjoys in it a strong reaffirmation of his identity with powerful yogis, and a claim for his own worth as part of that group—even if the part to which he belongs had slipped into marriage and owning property.

If the ending of each tale dangles, each dangles differently. Indeed, two very different characters appear when we place Gopi Chand and Bharthari side by side. The recurrent refrain, the theme song, of Gopi Chand's tale is his mother's advice:

> My son, be a yogi, my dear darling boy,
> and your body will be immortal.

Gopi Chand's mother, to save her son's life, commits him to yoga. His response is repeated emotional revolt, followed by an eventual resigned submission to his fate.

The recurrent refrain in Bharthari is Pingala's lament.

> You must realize, Bharthari Panvar of Dhara Nagar,
> You're the master of my union but
> you've gone and left me destitute.

Bharthari's wife, Queen Pingala, wants to prevent Bharthari from becoming a yogi, for it destroys her well-being as an auspiciously married woman. Bharthari's response to Pingala is to tell her to "quit being stubborn," because his yogic destiny is preordained, thickly writtern.

Thus although both epics are about kings who leave the world, each creates a different atmosphere with different stresses as it describes the process. Gopi Chand's is about persuasion toward yoga, which eventually works. Bharthari's is about persuasion against it, which eventually fails. I first became interested in Gopi Chand because he was so sentimental and wishy-washy, and because he had deep empathy for females (Gold 1989). On the basis of Gopi Chand's tale alone, I hypothesized that the householder status of the performer's caste, and the high valuation of women in rural Rajasthan's folklore community, allowed a sympathy for love in the world to overwhelm the yogic detachment valued in the original tradition (Gold 1991).

Bharthari, however—that donkey's progeny—is a stubborn boor, making up his mind and sticking with it no matter how much it hurts other beings—usually female ones. Even his crazed grief over Pingala's death is selfish and harmful to others. No one weeps with him, as people do with Gopi Chand. Madhu Nath makes high comedy of Bharthari's mourning scene.

Despite the uncle's and nephew's shared immortal destiny each reaches it by a different path. Nonetheless, it must be possible to find commonalities of meaning in the two tales. They are joined not only in Madhu Nath's limited repertoire but throughout various performed and literary genres, from secular Hindi theater to Nath sect hagiography. I went back to India explicitly to record Bharthari in order to balance my interpretation of Gopi Chand. In this closing chapter I deliberately seek the deep meanings that rise from both tales.

I shall highlight three recurring concerns and one overarching non-concern that I find evident in both texts. Both tales are about kings, and also about kingdoms—populated political entities located in space, subject to disruption and reconstitution, and dependent on good relations with yogis. Both tales have much to do with the intimate ties of kinship, and how these are bound and unbound. Both tales are about final partings, ambiguously construed, sometimes in terms of yogic detachment and immortality, sometimes merging with human mortality. Finally, both tales frequently evoke as ultimate authority the causal black hole of predestination. Yet, I shall suggest, they are not sucked in by its explanatory power.

In exploring the ways that such configurations of story and meaning form and interpenetrate in Madhu Nath's tales I have taken these "crazy stories" (so my mother calls them) to be deep (*gehrā*) and serious (*gambhīr*). But as any reader who has come this far knows, pervading all of Madhu Nath's performance, like a fifth dimension, is a comic flair. Yogis warn us not to take politics, love, death, or destiny too seriously—still less the conclusions of our errant and ego-ridden minds.

Demographic Surges through Landscapes of Meaning

As I translated these tales I was struck by a recurrent motif best described as the motion or flux of populations. Twice in Bharthari's tale and once in Gopi Chand's entire populaces are temporarily displaced. Bharthari's tale also narrates the permanent settlement of a new kingdom. In each case these events were obviously connected with demonstrations of how a king is not only responsible for, but dependent on, his subjects. And, not surprisingly, each of these movements of peoples is directly or indirectly related to the active power of yogis.

Because my interest in the tales initially focused on what I felt to be their extraordinary concern with and insight into the psychological turmoil of separate persons, I found the narratives' apparent fascination with demographic surges puzzling and (I confess) not so gripping. What, after all, could these episodes have to do with either the teachings of yogis or the emotions of householders? Yet the tale-teller lavishes considerable attention on these scenes.

Consider the episode in Bharthari 1 when Pachyo Potter decides to quit his city because his donkey Khukanyo, a disciple of Gorakh Nath, is embarrassing him and endangering his life by loudly demanding to marry a princess. The potter's move precipitates that of the rest of the populace. Royal servants inform the king of the trouble brewing:

"Grain-giver, over whom are you ruling here? Only owls are left here in the village, only owls hooting. The whole city is empty. Not even a child remains."

"Why?"

"Who knows why they left. But, I'm telling you, sir, there are no human beings left here."

"So they left. Well what was troubling them?"

"Who knows? They told of no trouble. They left and went to the border."

In Gopi Chand 3, all of Bengal is depopulated because of the contest between lady magicians and yogis. After the yogis have turned not only the tricky ill-doing women but their innocent husbands into braying donkeys who must forage in the wilderness, a very similar moment arises. Only a few old folks remain and they go to the king.

"Grain-giver, out of the whole population of the city, only us, a couple of old folks, are left. All that there are, have come."

"So where are all the men and women of the village?"

"Even if you search, you won't find them anywhere."

"Why, where have they gone, old folks?"

"Grain-giver, fourteen hundred . . . yogis came to the garden. . . . Your jungle has become populated, but your whole city is deserted. Grain-giver, only us, a few old folks remain—and you remain, so do as you will."

In both cases matters are set right when the king personally negotiates with powerful beings or their agents—the donkey in the first case, the yogi-guru Jalindar Nath himself in the second. But a simple subordination of kings to yogis is not all that is happening.

None of these episodes is intelligible without some grasp of spatial concepts in the world of the tales. This is a world where spaces are politicized, gendered, and bounded. But the boundaries are made for passage, not containment. The center, innermost realm—the Color Palace—belongs to queens. As implied by its name, the Color Palace (*rang mahal*) is a place of passion and strongly associated with the intimate relationships to which yoga puts an end. Outside the Color Palace we find the Jewel Square or bazaar, where the commerce of ordinary city life goes on. Beyond lie two important locales for both stories: the garden and the waterside. These are places on the edge, between city and country, meeting grounds. In Bharthari, the garden is where Pingala burns and Gorakh Nath instructs the raving king; in Gopi Chand a garden is the site of the contest between women magicians and yogis.

All the places I have named thus far are part of the greater city. Beyond them lie the jungle, the wastelands, the woods, the uninhabited countryside—and there is a plethora of subtly distinct Rajasthani and Hindi words for these areas. Somewhere in this no-man's-land lies the Kajali Woods where yogis camp. Intercourse between castle and city, and the surrounding jungle or forest is critical to the action of both tales. Recall the hilarious scene in Bharthari's birth story when the king promises the demanding donkey his daughter as a bride if the donkey is able to surround his city overnight with double walls of copper and brass. Not trusting a king's word of honor, the donkey makes his walls (by stamping his hoof and calling on guru Gorakh Nath) without gates.

The population wakes up to this dreadful situation, just as the donkey had predicted:

> "When someone has to go to the latrine they will beat their head on the wall. As for the livestock, how will they take them to graze? Where will the people go to shit? When it's dark they can squat near the wall, but where will they go once it's light?"

The king has no choice but to go through with the shameful marriage. Like his subjects, a king too must have an ongoing physical connection with the land beyond the city walls. Part 2 of Bharthari's story opens with Pingala taunting Bharthari by saying that his kingship is "worthless" because he never rides hunting in the woods.[2]

What have yogis to do with these configurations? Associated with the jungle, they are dependent for alms on the city. And just as much as the people who live inside need a way out, yogis who live outside need to be sure that their way in is not barred. When they wish, yogis are capable of great disruptive acts. Their *līlā* or divine play may well cause havoc to healthy social relationships—whether they drive people out of the city or trap them in it. But this *līlā* is allowed to go only so far.

The stories clearly sustain a commitment to maintaining social order, once the imperative demands of yogis are met. For ultimately yogis require a smoothly functioning kingdom for their own subsistence. In Bharthari's tale, when Bharthari is mourning Pingala in the garden—a liminal space—all the people of his kingdom assemble there and then cannot return home and cook while their king's

2. For an interesting discussion of the connections of kings to the jungle in a South Indian epic tradition see Beck 1982; see also Heesterman 1985, 118.

madness and death pollution continue. This constitutes a situation so unseemly as to shake the kingdom of heaven. Gorakh Nath is sent by God not to convert King Bharthari to a yogic perspective (although such is the result), but to bring Bharthari to his senses so that the people can "light the cooking fires" and get on with ordinary life.

Thus, although the tales show yogis aloof from ordinary people and capable of controlling them, they also demonstrate the desirability for yogis of a well-ordered society, appropriately arranged in space. Gopi Chand and Bharthari finally follow their yogi teachers to the remote wilderness, but mass departures are emphatically not recommended.

Yogis have a peculiarly ambiguous relation to the inner female space strongly associated in these tales with love, sorrow, and food. Even though Manavati has won the boon of a son twice over through ascetic prowess, she is not "given" Gopi Chand until a begging yogi receives alms of milk in her inner portal. Similarly, even though Gopi Chand and Bharthari have been initiated and tempered by fire and pilgrimage, neither will be "completed" yogis until they return from jungle to palace and claim a share of food.

Shared bread is a substantial image of family unity pervasive in Indian culture. The cold stale scrap of bread that both kings demand when they reach the domain of women immediately evokes a continuing membership in their abandoned families. But when their wives hand them the food as alms to a yogi beggar, it becomes a token of release and severance. They must bear it from the inner rooms to the guru's camp in the desolate jungle. Like so many images in the stories, the bread in its passage from royal palace to ascetic campfire is moving in more ways than one.

Unmaking Love

Margaret Trawick in her remarkable book *Notes on Love in a Tamil Family* says, "for them love was by nature and by right hidden" (1990, 91). She observes that in Tamil Nad there is a public ethos of denial, and this is just as true in Rajasthan: a mother must not gaze at her child nor a wife speak her husband's name. Yet beneath the facade of denial are tangled webs of intimate relations that Trawick's study of a family reveals in exquisite complexity and subtlety.

Folk epics are not generally known for their psychological complexity and subtlety. Yet what the tales of Gopi Chand and Bharthari have to say about the ties that bind—an English phrase that is remarkably apt in Hindu settings (Peterson 1988)—is far from simple and blunt. Nowhere in Madhu Nath's tales do the several Hindi and Rajasthani words for love (*prem, sneha, pyār,* and others) appear. Yet submerged, hidden, and indirect though its manifestations may be, the power of love infiltrates and often motivates the plots. One code for love is the guru's phrase "illusion's net" (*māyā jāl*) or the "noose of illusion's net."[3]

Manavati Mother warns Gopi Chand when he comes back to his palace as a yogi, before he meets Patam De and the other queens:

> Illusion's net will fiercely spread,
> so you must fiercely brace yourself.

When first Jalindar set Gopi Chand the task of calling his wife "Mother," the disciple protested: "But she is my wife. I have scattered all her leaves and smelled all her flowers"—a poetic depiction of conjugal intimacy, based, I was told, on a gardener's relation with his plants. The guru responds carefully: "Patam De Rani was your woman, but that was in your ruling time. Now you have become a yogi." At this precarious moment in his disciple's career he stresses not the perishability of all mortal relationships but the king's removal from them after initiation. In yogis' lore, to call one's former wife "Mother" and take alms from her hands is a well-known trial for the new initiate, but it appears to contain a built-in contradiction. If all persons are truly the same to a yogi, who has died to his past, why should it take an encounter with his wife to fulfill his yoga?

The answer, I think—at least for these Nath tales of parting—is that, unspoken though it may be, the power of love is given its due. It is given its due in two ways: as a moral imperative and as a mortal impediment. That is, in the householders' world so recently abandoned and not yet forgotten by the new initiate, marital love is worth

---

3. In everyday Nepali *māyā* means "love," and *māyā jāl* is used to refer to the "snares of love." Alan Roland in his culturally sensitive psychological exploration of Indian selves writes that "*māyā* can be viewed... not simply as illusion... but rather as the strong emotional attachments of the familial self that profoundly distract the person from his or her real nature, or the spiritual self.... What is termed detachment can be viewed psychologically as increasing involvement in the spiritual self and a loosening of the powerful emotional bonds in familial-social relationships" (1988, 307).

something. Women lay claims on men, and the validity of their claims is dodged with difficulty; that is why successful denial represents such a crowning achievement for the new yogi. That is also why these tales need, as relief, low-born and lusty bad women upon whom new yogis may practice the arts of disdain and rebuffal.

And yet, at least in that treacherous land of Bengal, the entire category "woman" easily merges with that of "lady magicians." The magicians are straightforwardly the "gurus" of all Bengali women. Several times in the course of Gopi Chand 3, the rebellious women of Bengal emerge from their domestic confines to challenge yogis in the garden. After their defeat by the great guru Jalindar Nath's power, they are transformed into braying she-asses and driven into the jungle. The men of Bengal, missing their dinners and beset by crying babies, then collectively confront the "loincloth-wearers" and demand their women back. Jalindar answers them:

O brothers, what do I want with your women? It was because of women trouble that I first became a yogi. I became a yogi to get away from women. What need have I of women? There aren't any women around here, and we don't even know your women. And what would women have come to get from *sādhus* like us?

Jalindar, of course, protests too much. His disclaimer, the audience knows, is an outright lie; the yogis are indeed responsible for the Bengali women's disappearance. But, he is also speaking the official truth: yogis, and Jalindar as a leader of yogis, have nothing to do with women. Jalindar's ingenuous double-talk opens a window on the subtle ambiguities and shifting evaluations that characterize attitudes toward the female species in Madhu Nath's tales.

If it is taken for granted that the world of yogis is a world beyond women, the existence of that world is in many ways defined in reference to women. Much more than divinity, women often seem to be the center about which these tales revolve. The nature of divinity is taken for granted; it is stable, it is available for whoever has the capacity for concentration, and it has the certainty of truth. But the nature of women is elusive, unstable, and always open to doubt. Although some women are sources of strength, food, and comfort, others are menacing enemies. But for an aspiring yogi, the passionate love of a good woman is far more dangerous than the bamboo sticks or magic spells of female adversaries.

Women are to be abandoned or, as Jalindar's tone and words imply and much of the action portrays, escaped. When Bharthari realizes his kingdom is dust and decides to seek his guru, he says to himself: "I shall go behind the queen's back. Otherwise, if I try to leave in front of the queen and all the others, there isn't a chance that they'll let me go." When face to face with the wives they must leave, neither Gopi Chand nor Bharthari refers to a quest for spiritual perfection; both evade personal responsibility by referring instead to conveniently ineluctable fate or to the guru's powerful command.

Elsewhere I have discussed gender in the Gopi Chand tale alone, highlighting the associations of females with powers at once creative and beguiling. I have explored the king's relationships with his wives, sisters, and female enemies (Gold 1991). Here I shall focus on the husband-wife bond—a bond epitomized in Bharthari's story by the central act of *satī*.

To understand the place of *satī* in Madhu Nath's tales, we have to appreciate the premises prevailing in the performance context: a Rajasthan village where the decision to be *satī* transforms a woman into a deity. This is popularly perceived as an awesome and extremely rare manifestation of female power. A Rajasthani proverb, which occurs several times in the Bharthari epic, comments: "She deliberately kills her husband to become *satī*" (*maṇas mārar satī honā*). The implication is clearly that a ruthless power-hungry woman might seek out *satī*. Whatever the social realities, most of Madhu Nath's audience views *satī*, then, as access to power for a determined woman, not as oppression of a helpless one.[4]

What is interesting about the portrayals of *satī* in Bharthari's tale is that, while the story accepts the extraordinary power of the act itself, the tale could well be taken as anti-*satī* propaganda, although it was composed by yogis, not feminists. The ideal of *satī* is founded in the wife's existing only as her husband's half-body and her acceptance of her husband as a god. Yet the husbands here are evidently not worth dying for. In all three *satīs*, as portrayed by Madhu Nath, the males have acted as selfish sinners and the females know it. This has something to do with yogis' devaluation of the marriage bond as one big strand of illusion's net.

4. See Harlan 1992 for insights into *satī* in Rajasthan. For other illuminating discussions that highlight the complexity of *satī* and raise important historical questions that I have ignored here see Courtright in press; Mani 1989; Nandy 1980, 1–31; 1988.

The first of three *satī*s that take place in Bharthari 2 is that of the does, whose mate King Bharthari shoots, ironically enough, because he had taken a vow never to harm females. Moreover, the stag, who is himself a disciple of Gorakh Nath, refuses to run away from death. The does voice righteous anger with their spouse for ignoring their pleas that he flee and thus save them the terrible fate of widowhood. They address him with insults even as they prepare to become *satī* upon his horns: "While he was dying, those does said, 'O Husband-god, father of a daughter! Turn your neck up and keep it that way! We told you to run away, but you refused to run.'"

The second *satī*, the huntress, is scornful when she realizes that her husband, who has had an excessively successful hunt, is dead. She makes a karmic connection between his killing and being killed. "Oh, you killed these deer, sinner, you killed all these deer and rabbits, and you haven't even eaten them. You died and now ants are going in and out."

As he has previously watched the does in disbelief, Bharthari gawks as the low-caste huntress becomes a goddess before his eyes. His boorishness on this occasion knows no bounds. The king observes the huntress dismember herself slowly and painfully, and he makes occasional exclamations and comments. He then decides to take advantage of the presence of divinity and crassly asks for "predictions for the coming year"—a divination typically available during goddess possession and directed toward crop success and grain prices. Her answer to him is, "King Bharthari, the coming year will pass in great bliss, a very fine year lies ahead." From one viewpoint, the falsehood of this prediction drips with sarcasm: Bharthari will leave his home, become a beggar, and suffer greatly. But from a yogic perspective, this statement confirms the *satī*'s divine omniscience. What could bring more bliss than renunciation?

Thus the huntress's speech, as frequently happens in these tales, offers both sides of the coin at once: on the worldly level an appropriately nasty retort to Bharthari's callous opportunism; on the transcendent level a vision of yogic truth. The encounter concludes with her masterful put-down:

"Say, King Bharthari, do you think I'm giving a show?"

"Yes I am sitting here, so I am seeing this show."

"O King Bharthari, you may be watching this show, but your Queen Pingala burned up over there in the Chapala Garden. She has become a pinch of ash. And...all the people including women and young men are

filling the Chapala Garden. Your Queen Pingala burned up, and the world
is watching, and sister-fucker you are watching my show!"

If we look, as directed by the transfigured huntress, at Pingala's
satī, we find that rather than "truth" (from which *satī* is of course
derived) it has at its base a series of lies and improprieties. Bharthari
tests Pingala by sending a blood-soaked handkerchief with a false
message. The Royal Servant who knowingly brings evil tidings chal-
lenges the queen: "You said, 'I won't eat bread without you, without seeing your face,' but you told lies. You women are a heartless
race. If you're a *satī,* then burn, burn, because King Bharthari died."

Well aware, by virtue of a magic plant, that her husband "hasn't
even a splinter," Pingala is piqued by Bharthari's test. "Oh my, it's
strange, he is testing my *satī*-power." Yet Pingala's reaction is not to
call the king's bluff but to pray to Shiva to make her *satī.* Shiva knows
her husband is alive, but grants her request nevertheless. God is later
angry with all of them (Bharthari, Pingala, Shiva) for their irre-
sponsible behavior. The yogi Gorakh Nath rebukes Bharthari, who
has needlessly caused Pingala's death, in strong and scornful language: "King Bharthari, you sister-fucker, you killed her with your
own hands."

It is no accident that a yogis' tale thus construes *satī* so ambiguously.
The ideology of *satī* implies that the connection between united
couples extends beyond embodiment. But Nath yogis teach in many
ways that death is the end of all connections (Gold 1988, 99–123).
Thus the institution of *satī*—an important part of Rajasthan's ruling
warrior caste's identity—is appropriately mocked in Bharthari's story.
But it is mocked by stressing not the misperception of women who
take marriage seriously but the unworthiness of the males for whom
they die.

From the renouncer's perspective, no relationship is worth living,
or dying, for. But that is not the only viewpoint in these tales. Ordinary
women's motivations are strongly rooted in a familial morality, of
which *satī* is only the extreme gesture. Males may slip in and out of
this world according to the influence of yogis. Moti Stag fails his mates
because he accepts his death as the guru's will. Bharthari's despicable
actions are judged thus: "You killed her with your own hands." His
yogi's destiny is based on a different moral economy—one where he
is not blamed for his several cruelties to females. Both perspectives
are clearly voiced.

When Gopi Chand's wife, Patam De, finds that the yogi at her gates is truly her husband, her response is "Better to die than to live," and she goes into a dead faint and falls from her balcony—a *satī*-like act. Later Patam De's mother-in-law attempts to console her by saying that Gopi Chand is "under the spell of yogis" (*jogyāṅ kī phaṭkār ma āgyo*). To the high-minded yogi, women's love itself is a deceptive spell or illusion's net, but to women in the world yogis cast spells of deception. This is a telling juxtaposition, especially given the exegesis I received from my research assistant on the phrase "under the spell of yogis."

Yogis are in fact suspect characters in the village. They are thought to use spells to enchant children and lead them away.[5] Gopi Chand's mother believes in yoga as her son's only hope. But here she attempts to soothe his wife's misery by implying that Gopi Chand would stay, were he not robbed of his volition by yogis' enchantments. Many of the situations in these tales are open to such multiple interpretations.

Women loom large in Madhu Nath's stories as embodiments of illusion, or love, or intimacy, or bondage. But if women are in certain ways paradigmatic embodiments of illusion's net, they do not have exclusive dominion over attachment. In the final segment of Gopi Chand, Madhu Nath explores the father-son bond with equally fine-tuned ambivalence. This episode is part of the saga of Gorakh Nath's rescue of his guru, Machhindar, from the magician queens of Bengal. The queens present no real difficulties—perhaps because the bard has spent himself on the subject of women in telling Gopi Chand's story. The problem here is sons.

The production of sons is for Hindu householders a chief religious good. But for yogis it is problematic—a source of persistent temptation at least as powerful as sex. The guru-disciple relationship is often conceptualized as a father-son relationship, perhaps in part to promote detachment from the desire for physical progeny. Yet this substitution or displacement can play out in all kinds of surprising ways.[6]

As Madhu Nath describes Gorakh's encounter with his guru-turned-husband-and-father, it is characterized from the beginning

---

5. See Henry 1988, 186, on the reputation of *jogīs* as kidnappers in Bhojpuri-speaking North India.

6. These include disciples adopted as legally inheriting sons and sons initiated as spiritual disciples. See Gold 1983, 1987 for an illuminating discussion of the succession disputes surrounding the eighteenth-century Sant poet Charandas.

by subterfuge, rivalry, and displacement. Gorakh Nath is unable to enter Machhindar's kingdom because Machhindar anticipates just such an event; he does not want to be rescued and has made a law that no yogis shall cross his boundaries. Gorakh must remove all signs of yogic identity and join a company of dramatic performers in order to approach his guru. When the troupe is invited to perform at Machhindar's palace, Machhindar as king sits down to watch the play with his two boys on his lap.

Gorakh soon makes his presence known with his magic talking drumbeat. When, shortly thereafter, he prostrates himself before his guru, Machhindar very deliberately removes his two sons, setting them on a nearby table, and then seats Gorakh Nath on his knees, "because he was his first disciple."

The guru recognizes who truly belongs in the paternal lap. Here is an immediate sign of Gorakh Nath's impending victory and an almost touching portrayal of guru-disciple kinship. But nothing is settled yet, and Gorakh Nath's behavior soon departs from the humanly admirable. Gorakh Nath would like to smash the kids and have done with it, but he is constrained because Machhindar, to whom Gorakh owes all deference as spiritual father, is also a natural father and is unashamed of his fatherly feelings. Just as with *satī*, it seems that yogic detachment and familial loyalty are almost simultaneously valorized. Here the simultaneity is effectively established by a pun—a play on words that is also a play on two realities: that of the householder who patiently and lovingly attends to his children's lowest needs and that of the yogi who slashes through affection.

Thus Gorakh misinterprets Machhindar's order "Make sure they shit nicely" as "Smash them thoroughly." And so he does, hanging the boys' empty skins on the back of a chair. Madhu describes Machhindar's anxiety over his sons, pointedly elaborating on the way his emotional response is akin to ordinary familial sensibilities not at all proper to a high guru. "Then he looked here and there. That's the way mothers and fathers worry. He didn't see the children. So how could he enjoy the play?"

Of course Gorakh Nath has the elixir of life handy and is able to restore the children as good as new. This first gambit has got him very little. He soon persuades Machhindar Nath to run away from the queens, but the guru insists on bringing his sons along. On the road, Gorakh devises a new and highly devious scheme to rid himself of these living reminders of his guru's fall. He offers to teach the boys to beg, referring to them as "our disciples," as if he had accepted them by transforming them into spiritual successors. Driven by his desperate desire to free his guru from the snares of *māyā*, Gorakh Nath has moved from puns to pure hypocrisy, and the bard spells out his duplicity.

"Come Guru Sovereign, I'll take them into this neighborhood. Let them fill their own bellies, guru. I'll take the disciples and let them get as much flour as they need to live."

But Gorakh Nathji was *thinking*, I'll destroy them on the way, so those sons of penis-eaters over there don't see them and say, "Look, your guru enjoyed sluts and had sons." Yes, I'll get rid of them so no one can say that.

But to Machhindar Nathji Sovereign he said, "Grain-giver sir, we should put wooden sandals on them and give them tongs to carry and sacks and smear them with ashes. And let them go into the settlement to beg. . . ."

Gorakh Nath proceeds to engineer the remarkable scenario that will eventually succeed in ridding him of the boys. The first move of the plot is to "ruin" them—degrade them to untouchable, leather-worker status—by fabricating a situation where they naively agree to carry a cow's carcass in order to get choice food for their father. The proud little boys bear festive treats back to the guru's campfire, while Gorakh has brought stale scraps. Machhindar praises his sons:

"Yeah, sister-fucking Gorakh Nath, you bring sister-fucking cold stale scraps that an old man like me can't eat. But today my Nim Nath and Paras Nath went, and they brought five fried treats."

"Guru Sovereign, these cold stale scraps are Truth's. And these five fried treats are Untruth's."

You could hardly have a stronger statement of the difference between family connections and guru-disciple ones. After Machhindar agrees that his boys are "ruined," Gorakh drags them back to the home of the merchants who engaged them to do the dirty work and begins once again to smash them to death, brutally. But they are rescued by the pleas of the merchant and his wife who negotiate on their behalf with Gorakh Nath and ultimately agree to install them as icons in a handily empty nearby temple.

Gorakh Nath instructs the merchants to offer them water and

"drink the nectar from their dicks or else you'll be destroyed." The bard concludes:

And Gorakh Nathji Sovereign's sorrow was erased. "Now nobody can say, 'Look, brother, your guru enjoyed sluts and had sons.'"

That the destiny of the boys is to be merchants' icons from whose penises nectar will be drunk is in part of course just a jibe at the merchant caste, rarely favored in folklore. Merchants are Jain in this part of Rajasthan, and Jain icons are naked. Like Hindu temples, Jain temples distribute to worshipers as "nectar" the water used to bathe the icons—water that is poured over their heads and runs down their bodies to be collected from their feet. Villagers thus may joke that merchants drink nectar from penises, because this water has flowed over the naked statues. The first word Gorakh Nath uses for penis is not *lingam*—the common term for Lord Shiva's worshipable phallus—but *indarī*, a term often employed in the village for the small wetting organs of little boys. Hence this image provides what could be a slightly disgusting association with the procreative continuities valued by householders—perhaps making them take a second look at those cherished values.

Yet familial bonds are given their due in this episode by the very complexity and roundabout nature of the process whereby they may be removed or displaced or safely relocated. That even Gorakh Nath cannot simply kill the children but must go to so much trouble to deify them suggests a preciousness that no yogic hatred can deny. Moreover, little boys' penises are perceived as precious, and treated lovingly in the village.

Mortality

Death is the premise of ordinary human existence, to which yoga is opposed again and again. "Be a yogi or else Death will eat you," says Manavati Mother to Gopi Chand. Death is also the primary blind spot of those who live tangled up in *māyā*'s net. Gopi Chand initially refuses the guru's teachings, desiring to continue to rule his kingdom and enjoy his wives and slave girls. He is literally snatched from his bed among the women and rushed off by Death's Messengers. His guru rescues him, but it is the physical experience of dying, not his mother's promptings or any instruction from the wise yogi, that now convinces Gopi Chand to renounce. As Madhu succinctly puts it: "From dying he really found out."

Bharthari has a similar insight after Gorakh Nath gives him back Pingala:

> King Bharthari couldn't sleep. "O, this is all a bundle of sin! And sister-fuck! What to do inside of it? Look, take Gorakh Nathji, he is wise, and he lives as a yogi, so why should I live as a king?... When my own Queen Pingala burned up, she was really a pinch of ash, and he scattered it, but fifteen days later he made seven hundred and fifty Pingalas stand up! Oh my, this yoga is great. To hold on to yoga is great, but to live as a king is nothing at all. It is just a fall to hell."

Elsewhere I have written at length on Rajasthanis' ideas about mortality and afterdeath existence (Gold 1988). Except for those promoted by the Nath sect's performances, such ideas are largely about maintaining controlled relationships with the spirits of the dead. Nath epics tell us two things at once about death. First, death is absolute and humans must sustain no hope of connections enduring beyond the pyre. Second, death isn't absolute at all, not for yogis. Gorakh and Jalindar each have two little tins: one contains ash-making drops and the other an elixir of life. Thus they can turn a live person to ash or bring a pile of shattered bones to life with a few sprinkles. The implication is that death itself is meaningless, one of a kind with all the other mistaken perceptions to which humans are subject in the world of flux.

Just as a yogi's capacity to turn a hill to gold dramatizes the worthlessness of wealth, bringing the dead to life negates the fatality of death. But ironically and inevitably the person who cares for wealth or for other people will never have such powers. Only the perfectly detached yogi overcomes death. Unmaking love is the prerequisite to immortality, but immortality itself is a mystery that the tales do not attempt to penetrate. That it should be gained in the end by trickery—its sound emerging from Jalindar's angry mouth more like another curse than a blessing—suggests that immortality remains an uncertain good. To those strong enough to realize the utter perishability of love, yoga offers an immortal existence, but in Madhu Nath's tales that existence is veiled, remote, and slightly suspect.[7]

---

7. A popular hymn about the inevitable partings of death concludes: "Gopi Chand and Bharthari spoke: Don't anyone become immortal: We became immortal and suffered sorrow and just keep wandering in circles" (Gold 1988, 109).

Oral Performance and the Thick Writing of Fate

There are moments in both epic tales when, in identical formulaic speeches, both Bharthari and Gopi Chand evoke the all-powerful causality of fate: "Fortune has inscribed this destiny in my karma with the thickest writing: immortal fakirhood. There is no one to remove it." Indeed, it would be easy to summarize the tales of Gopi Chand and Bharthari as two stories about kings whose karma forced them to become yogis. But if you have traveled this far with Madhu Nath and me, you will appreciate how little such a reduction tells us.

In a recent provocative essay entitled "Scapegoats of the Gods: The Ideology of the Indian Epics," John D. Smith argues, and seeks to demonstrate with examples from Rajasthani folk epics among others, that such tales present a worldview where "fate is used by the gods to enslave men, and to subject them to various evils" (1989, 177).[8] However, it seems to me that in Madhu Nath's tales—and I believe this could well be extended to other folk traditions in and beyond Rajasthan—fate provides a facile and fascinating causal backdrop but remains without motivating meaning as a force in characters' lives. Rather than engineered by deities to restrict or repress human ingenuity, fate is a stage for mortal and divine affairs, as big as the sky and just as disengaged. Smith speaks of a hero's "brilliant improvisation" (1989, 193) in the grip of fate—but he speaks of it as the thrashing of the doomed. Thus we might consider Gopi Chand's tears or Pingala's lament as manifestations of hopelessness, but I think it would be wrong. The question hinges on where the stress lies—in the results or in the process. Is it the concept of immutable destiny or is it the play of human feelings that enlivens Madhu Nath's oral performance with charm and meaning for his listeners?[9]

Subordination is not resignation, as so much recent work in anthropology, history, and women's studies has shown. Just as politically or economically disempowered persons may contrive subtle subversions, practice delicate modes of resistance, and in doing so undermine the exercise and very concept of dominance, might not the "improvisa-

---

8. See also Smith 1980.

9. Many others than Smith and I have pondered the Hindu concept of destiny. See Keyes and Daniel eds. 1983 for a number of interesting perspectives. Beck's article in that volume treats the complexity of fate in a South Indian epic.

tions" of the cosmically disempowered undermine the concept of their helplessness? It is probably no accident that fate is metonymized as writing in Indian civilization where literate elite minorities hold the keys to ritual and political power over a nonliterate majority. But it is worth paying attention not only to how that thick writing is acknowledged but also to how it is revised.

In South Asian folk traditions, rather than imposing destinies on mortals while remaining immune themselves, deities are often subject to fate just as human beings are. After Madhu Nath finished singing Bharthari in 1987 I expressed some disappointment that the end had come so soon. He offered then to perform the third major piece of his narrative repertoire: "The Wedding Song of Lord Shiva" (*Śivjī kā byāvalā*). I have not translated this, but I did read through it hastily with Bhoju's help in the winter of 1989. At the time I sensed that it provided missing links in my understandings of Bharthari and Gopi Chand. Yet I tucked it back in its file folder—understandably loath to get involved with another big text. Now that we are safely nearing the end, I shall take the risk of tapping into, if not unleashing, this additional source of perplexities and pleasures.

Anyone familiar with Hindu mythology knows that storytellers have delighted for centuries in spinning yarns about the impoverished, dope-smoking ascetic Shiva's wedding celebration: paradox piles upon paradox.[10] Madhu Nath's version of Shiva's marriage begins in an ascetic camp on Kailash Mountain where Shiva and his bull companion Nandiya live in comfortable masculine companionship, consuming quantities of narcotic and hallucinogenic substances and not much wholesome food. But Nandiya gets tired of doing all the chores and suggests that Shiva use his power to create a *chelā* (male disciple) to help with the work. Shiva follows all the appropriate, time-honored steps for creating such a being, but something goes wrong. He gets a *chelī* (a female disciple). "We've no use for girls around here," Nandiya cries in alarm, and Shiva burns her to ashes. He tries again with the same dismaying results.

Nandiya scolds him: "Baba, in this degenerate era you have started to lust after women. Don't create girl disciples, Yogi. I said you should

10. See O'Flaherty's classic compendium of Shaivite mythology for many versions from the Sanskrit (1973); see Sax 1991 for one lovely folk tradition sung by women in Garhwal.

make a boy disciple, but you are making girl disciples. When she gets to be twelve years old she will ask for a husband and where will you get him from, in the jungle? Who will get married at Kailash Mountain? Don't make a girl disciple." Compliantly, wishing only to please his friend, Shiva burns her up again.

Then Nandiya who is a holy character decides he can't live with a murderer and stalks off into the jungle. Shiva attempts to placate him: "I'll bring her back to life and then I won't be marked by the sin of murder any more." So he does, and this is his undoing. For the *chelī* he has created achieves great power through her *tapas* and after threatening Shiva with the direst curses wins a boon—she will be born again as Parvati and get him for a husband. The remainder of Madhu's tale is concerned with the humorous courtship of Shiva by an utterly determined and self-possessed Parvati and ends with a great party and a lot of good food.

The wedding song of Shivji is about how an ascetic deity gets married against his will. Bharthari and Gopi Chand are about how married humans rather haplessly become ascetics—in the case of Gopi Chand, at least, against his will. Just as the humans Bharthari and Gopi Chand are fated to renounce their thrones and wives, there is nothing the omnipotent divine Shiva with his absolute power over life and death can do to avoid marrying Parvati. Yet Shiva (and the woman-hating Nandiya) both try as hard as they can to get rid of the girl, to scare away and subsequently discomfit the barber who brings the marriage offer, and so forth. Moreover, their struggle to subvert the wedding plans is just what pleases Madhu Nath's audience, all of whom are familiar with the nice way that marriage negotiations ought to be conducted. Is the message that not even the all-powerful Shiva can resist the disasters imposed by fate? Why does his struggle make such a good yarn? We could ask the same question about Gopi Chand's incessant weeping and complaining, or even about the old and not so wily guru Machhindar's attempt to stash his four gold bricks.

I do not believe that the point of these tales is to demonstrate the iron grip of destiny. On the contrary, to confront fate and not to surrender to it is a human, and divine, prerogative. Bhoju, who grew up in the village and got involved with foreigners in his early twenties, was influenced in various complex ways by Western cynicism. Once he said to me, although it wasn't exactly true, "I don't believe in the gods anymore, but I still believe in *kismat;* fate is everything." By this he was asserting a reformulated intellectual freedom, not passive fatalism.

Even if the lady magicians lose in the end, their triumph is prolonged and delightful; even if Gopi Chand renounces in the end, he has gone protesting, declaring and demonstrating his reluctance, and this is worth something. Stuck in a donkey's body, Prince Gandaraph Syan accomplishes much. At times in these stories mortals can and do exert power over destiny: Manavati Mata gets a son though none is written in her fate. Willingly and pragmatically, she accepts the terms of the bargain:

> ... better than sonlessness is twelve years.... If all you can give is twelve years, Grain-giver, then give it. It's not written for me, so give me twelve years only, right now, and at least the stigma of barrenness will be removed, and I will have some pleasure.

Oral performances, according to numerous scholars who have worked in many cultural contexts, may open up spaces for creative resistance (Abu-Lughod 1990; Limon 1981; Vatuk 1969) and emergent cultural meanings (Basso 1985; Bauman 1977, 1986). One source of oral traditions' subversive potential is the improvisational nature of the art involved in their execution. Much has been written about the formulaic and conservative qualities of oral genres, but it is equally evident that verbal art is free to play upon and interact with immediate social contexts and to insinuate subtle subversions of preexisting power structures.[11] In the case of Indian oral epic performances, it is evident that verbal artistry can illuminate the thick letters of fate with many kinds of embellishments. I suggest that the deeper meanings lie in the embellishments rather than in that which they embellish.

Let me return to Madhu Nath's telling of Gopi Chand. Consider this speech that recurs several times in the mouths of several characters: "Meeting is good and parting is bad and the noose of *māyā*'s net is

---

11. For some recent approaches to oral versus written modes of expression see Goody 1987; Ong 1982. O'Flaherty 1988, 56–73, uses Indian examples to challenge some of the accepted distinctions in Western thought between oral and written.

always very bad. It's a carnival of parting."[12] These lines are replete
with the ambiguities and sustained ambivalence that pervade the
emotional tenor of the two renouncer-kings' tales. As a comment on
the human condition, I suggest that despite insisting on an awareness
of death, these words are neither despairing nor fatalistic.

The "Meeting is good . . . " speech is evoked when a woman learns
that the yogi at her door is her loved one, but she doesn't want to
look at him and acknowledge his imminent departure. Addressed by
slave girl to queen, this constitutes advice to take one last look at a
beloved while there's still a chance. Thus the words seem to indicate
that one must accept the conditions of the noose of *māyā*'s net and act
from love anyway.

Gopi Chand himself speaks these lines to his guru, after the guru
has reproached him for his emotional weakness. For him, they are a
kind of defiant self-defense. Here, as is often the case, Gopi Chand
allies himself with women against the teachings of yoga—a characteristic that sets him apart from King Bharthari. He is trying to tell his
guru something about his own dividedness as he cries in the liminal
area between the guru's campfire and the women's palaces.

Taking each statement contained in these lines sequentially, and
allowing each its own contextually determined validity, I may, in a
concluding flourish, connect them with the thematic areas highlighted
here as common to the epics of Bharthari and Gopi Chand.

Both tales accept and value a society where king and kingdom are
in mutual harmony and support begging yogis. From the perspective
of participants in that society—a collective entity not subject to the
ravages of time—meeting, transactions, coming, and going are all
good. Meeting is also good for couples, for brothers and sisters, for
parents and children, but that goodness is continually undermined
by the doom of inevitable parting, a condition of mortal existence.
By portraying *satī*—a deed based on the highest evaluation of human
coupling but one that takes place at the funeral pyre—as an animal,
low-caste, and ultimately truthless act, the text brilliantly devalues
pairs. The debasement of beloved sons to leatherworkers and then to
naked stone icons worshiped by a disdained caste group has a similar

---

12. *malbā bhalā hai ar bachaṭbā barā hai ar māyā jāḷ kā phandā to hargaj bot barā hai.
bachaṭatā kā meḷā hai.*

effect. Parting may be bad, but wisdom lies in realizing its necessity; to cling to what is already lost is folly.

The noose of *māyā*'s net is always very bad, because it is woven of everything that keeps mortals from achieving freedom from their otherwise eternal subjection to death's dominion. But the image of human life as a carnival of parting evokes not just sorrow and the karmically determined necessity to renounce but all the colors and pleasures, the vital engagement and funny vicissitudes of the house-holders' world that is shared by Madhu Nath and his audience.

The Language of the Bard

David Magier

The bard who performed the tales translated in this book, Madhu
Natisar Nath, is from the village of Ghatiyali, in the Ajmer district of
Rajasthan. Rajasthan is a large state at the western edge of North
India, on the border with Pakistan. With an area of 135,000 square
miles and a population of more than thirty million, it encompasses a
wide range of physical, agricultural, historical, and linguistic subregions. In reading these translations we naturally ask, Which language
were these tales translated from? For reasons that will soon be made
clear, answering this question with some particular language name
would be essentially inadequate, even if it were possible. In this
appendix I extrapolate from the text of the bard's rendition of Gopi
Chand's birth story (the *janmpatrī*), and using that as a representative
sample of his dialect, I describe some of its salient features and
explore its linguistic relation to other languages and dialects of the
region.

Before launching into the actual description, I must make several
methodological points. First there is the question of the language
sample. Any linguistic description based on tapes and written texts
(rather than interactive elicitation sessions with native speakers)
must be taken as incomplete and tentative. Linguistic descriptions
are, after all, a set of hypotheses about how the language works. These
remain hypotheses until their validity can be verified by testing
alternative forms with native speakers.

Second, there is the form and context of the collected sample.
Ideally, a description of a particular language or speech variety

should be based on the casual conversations of native speakers in regular face-to-face contexts. Our sample of Madhu Nath's speech, however, is a performance which is a restricted and highly specialized context. In other words, we may well assume that the kind of language the bard uses in reciting his tales before an audience differs dramatically from the variety of speech he would use, for example, at home in casual conversation with his family. (Formal versus casual contexts seem to produce distinct speech varieties, which linguists call "registers," in all languages, but languages may differ in the degree to which these registers are distinct from one another.) Traditional performance genres like this, while certainly containing many improvisational elements, frequently stay within fairly narrow ranges of style and register, which are themselves part of the definition of the genre.

The problem is further complicated by the fact that Madhu's audience includes the researcher (who is also the primary patron for these performances). Ann Grodzins Gold is a foreigner, a person of high status, and someone who speaks Madhu's language imperfectly. Madhu also knows that she speaks Hindi (though he does not). In this context, we cannot rule out the possibility that Madhu's speech style (including perhaps pronunciation, choice of words, and even sentence structure) is influenced to some degree by Gold's presence. And, indeed, I do find certain passages in the *arthāv* (the prose sections in which he explains the plot of the story), where the performer seems to be speaking directly to the researcher, and where certain elements of his speech become "Hindified." We can begin to envision how Gold's presence might affect the performance if we imagine a traditional context such as Thanksgiving dinner, and then picture an exotic, non-English-speaking foreigner with a tape recorder sitting down at the table. The conversation around the table would undoubtedly change in subtle and nonsubtle ways and would, in any case, differ considerably from the true casual native speech of the conversants.

I have based this analysis only on the prose *arthāv* parts of the text. This makes sense because the metrical and musical parts of the performance are likely to be more strictly structured by the genre, while the *arthāv* is closer to a regular face-to-face conversation (though it too is part of the performance). Several scholars have noted that folk performances in Rajasthan (particularly folk songs) show a far greater uniformity of language than the actual spoken dialects of the performers themselves. It has even been suggested (Komal Kothari, personal communication 1982) that there is some sort of standard folk song dialect that varies very little across most of Rajasthan. If that is the case, we would expect the musical parts of Madhu's performance to conform to that dialect and his prose explanations (characterized as more spontaneous, less formulaic, less constrained by structural considerations, and involving frequent direct address to audience members, as well as participatory inputs from them) to be close to his own dialect. Also, to minimize the effect of having Gold in the audience, I have eliminated from the analysis all parts of the text where Madhu directly addresses her, as well as obvious shifts of register (as, for example, when Madhu gives an explanation in his own dialect and then repeats it in a Hindi-like sentence to make sure she has fully understood it). In these cases, the code-switching represents a kind of linguistic accommodation to the hearer.

Finally, we must make note of a fundamental methodological problem for all dialect studies. Put simply, linguists have not arrived at any logically consistent way to distinguish between a language and a dialect. The fact is, no two people speak the same way. And even a single individual, in the course of his or her life, uses a multitude of different linguistic varieties (for example, the contextually determined registers mentioned above). How different must two such varieties be before we agree to call them two dialects (rather than just two styles of the same dialect)? How different must two dialects be before we call them two different languages? Terms like language and dialect have many meanings in popular usage (the most common being that a dialect is a disvalued speech variety, as in the sentence, often heard in India, "Why study Rajasthani? It's only a dialect!"), and they rarely have anything to do with actual linguistic differences.

Even if we ignore the question of language versus dialect, there is still the problem of naming a particular speech variety. Aside from the names of their own villages (and, of course, their caste names), the labels by which the people of Rajasthan identify themselves are often those of particular subregions, with names and borders roughly corresponding to those of the former princely states and small kingdoms. Primary historical units of what is today called Rajasthan (a name coined by Colonel James Tod [see Tod 1829] for what was previously called Rajputana, after the powerful Rajput ruling caste that controlled twenty-two separate princely states there as late as

1947) include Marwar, Mewar, Shekhawati, and Harauti subregions. Such regional names also provided the popular nomenclature for the spoken languages: Marwari, Mewari, Shekhawati, Harauti, and so forth. However, there is notoriously poor agreement, on the local level, regarding Rajasthani dialect names, since the major regions of Rajasthan have been divided into smaller princely states at one time or another, and a speaker may elect to identify his speech with a name referring to one of these smaller units. Also, some dialect names are based on the family or caste names of significant rulers in the history of a region, and these may be avoided by current speakers who do not belong to that particular caste, even if their languages are identical. In short, the popular system of identifying languages is very complex and depends on all sorts of nonlinguistic factors that constitute the general system of group identity such as caste, religion, tribe, region, subregion, and educational level. This is why language information in the Indian census reports is so difficult to interpret (Khubchandani 1983; Pandit 1977).

Leaving aside for the moment the interesting question of folk taxonomy of language in Rajasthan, we find that the actual linguistic realities in the region are very hard to pin down. Since the monumental (but now somewhat outdated) survey work conducted by Grierson 1908–22 (see vol. 9, part 2 on Rajasthan), there has been nothing in the way of careful dialect geography of Rajasthan. India as a whole has always been preoccupied with its literature and its classical and prestigious tongues, almost to the exclusion of any in-depth investigation into the rich diversity of current vernaculars. Even if such surveys were attempted, many difficult problems would remain. In the traditional society of Rajasthan, as in much of India, diversity in linguistic repertoire is a regular fact of life.

Although geography plays an undeniable role in the set of languages (or dialects) an individual knows or uses, contexts of interaction requiring different social identities play an even greater part, and the range of varieties used by individuals is quite startling to anyone from a more homogeneous linguistic environment. Everyone in Rajasthan is highly multilingual and multidialectal; each of the numerous codes a person controls will be appropriate to a different set of contexts that arise routinely in daily life (see Gumperz 1961; Shapiro and Schiffman 1981).

In a nutshell, spoken language is subject to at least three distinct types of variation: geographic (i.e., people from different places speak differently), social (i.e., people from different soical groups [e.g., castes] speak differently, even in the same place), and contextual (i.e., the very same person will speak differently at different times, depending upon social context, giving rise to distinct contextual styles and registers).

Abrupt language borders probably do not exist in Rajasthan; the situation noted elsewhere in India, with a gradual continuum of slight changes from one village to the next, forming unbroken chains across tremendous tracts of land, undoubtedly holds here too. Hence the popular Marwari maxim: *bārāṁ kosāṁ bhāsā badle, tīsāṁ kosāṁ mausim* "Language changes every twelve *kos*, weather every thirty" (one *kos* equals approximately two miles).

With all this explanation as a sort of disclaimer, we now go on to a brief characterization of Rajasthani, and to an outline of certain core speech areas that have been identified (though their boundaries are very hazy). Finally, we explore how our sample of Madhu Nath's language fits in with this overall picture.

So, what is Rajasthani? Grierson (1908) divided the spoken tongues of Rajasthan into two main groups: Eastern Rajasthani and Western Rajasthani, separated by the Aravalli Hills (where Bhil tribesmen speak a language he identified as Bhili). Marwari is the largest and most important of the western dialects, and since it claims the only extensive early literature in the state, it has had relatively high prestige. The eastern dialects include those called Dhundhari (Jaipuri), Harauti, Mewati, Ahirwati, Malvi, and Nimari.

Grierson further subdivided the Western Rajasthani group into Standard Marwari (the language of the old kingdom of Marwar itself), and other Marwari dialects, including Eastern Marwari (Marwari-Dhundhari, Mewari), Southern Marwari (Godwari, Sirohi, Marwari-Gujarati), Western Marwari (Thali, Dhatki, Marwari-Sindhi), and Northern Marwari (Bikaneri, Shekhawati, Bagri) (see figure 9). Breaking with earlier scholars (e.g., Kellogg 1875), who had classed all of the "dialects of Rajputana" as varieties of Western Hindi, Grierson (1908, 15) coined the term Rajasthani (including all the eastern and western dialects mentioned above), and gave it the status of a language in its own right. The Rajasthani dialects taken as a whole seem to bear a somewhat closer resemblance to Gujarati than to Hindi.

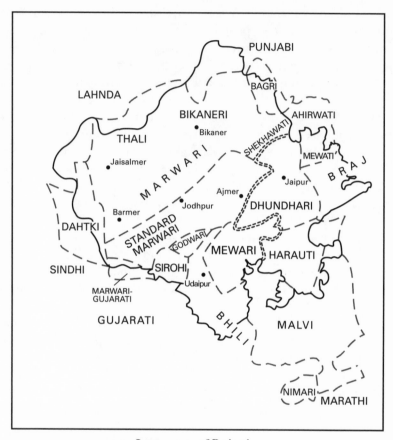

9. Languages of Rajasthan.

So where did these Rajasthani dialects come from? The Indo-Aryan languages are understood to represent one branch (the Indic branch) of Indo-Iranian, the language brought there by the Aryans migrating from the unknown original Indo-European homeland (the origin of the Germanic, Romance, Slavic, and other European language subfamilies). After the Indic branch of the Aryan tribes arrived in northern India (some time before 1200 B.C.), they codified their ancient religious hymns and preserved them in the form of the Vedas (which were not actually set down in written form till hundreds of years later). This Vedic language is the oldest attested form of Indo-Aryan. In the centuries following, there was simultaneous and separate development of the spoken Indo-Aryan vernaculars and the conservative, often artificially archaic literary languages that have been attested from different periods and genres. Various explanations of the relationships between Rajasthani, Gujarati, and Hindi have been proposed, and their divergences result from the lack of solid information about the evolution of these spoken dialects during the period between Old Indo-Aryan and the first appearance (starting around the fourteenth century) of literature in the New Indo-Aryan tongues. Given that Hindi and Gujarati are clearly distinct, and descend from different spoken Middle Indo-Aryan sources, the logical possibilities for Rajasthani are the following:

(a) Rajasthani is an offshoot from the branch that gave rise to Hindi (essentially the approach of Beames 1872–79 and Kellogg 1875, with which Grierson strongly disagreed).

(b) Rajasthani is a separate entity (Grierson's 1908 approach).

(c) Rajasthani and Gujarati are descended from a common Middle Indo-Aryan ancestor, separate from that of Hindi.

(d) Rajasthani is an amalgam of two stocks, one (Western Rajasthani) a sister to Gujarati, the other affiliated with Western Hindi (the approach taken by Tessitori 1914–16).

The problem with (c) is that it fails to notice the close affinities of Eastern Rajasthani dialects with the neighboring languages of Western Hindi. In all accounts of the similarities of Rajasthani to Gujarati, it is always Western Rajasthani (particularly Marwari) that is taken as the prime example. Since the current spoken language seems to form a continuum, it may be better to envision Rajasthani as standing between the two core areas of Hindi and Gujarati, representing elements genetically affiliated with both. This is the essence of the approach in (d).

Tessitori (1914–16), upon close analysis of some writings of the fourteenth and fifteenth centuries, came to the conclusion that "at least until the 15th century there was practically only one form of language prevailing over the whole area now covered by Modern Gujarati and a great part, or possibly most of the area of Modern Marwari." He calls this language Old Western Rajasthani and takes it to be the medieval ancestor of Gujarati and Marwari.

The scenario, as Tessitori envisions it, involved a migration between A.D. 400–600 of the Gujars (a group of Aryans) from their Himalayan homeland down into northeastern Rajasthan and then, continuing southwest, into western Rajasthan and finally Gujarat. This explains the fact that Marwari and Gujarati have certain strong similarities with Nepali. From about the thirteenth century until the end of the sixteenth (Smith 1975, 434), we see a gradual process that has been repeated many times in South Asian linguistic history. The Old Western Rajasthani (Smith calls it Old Gujarati) began to take on prestige as a literary language and spread as a verse and prose medium throughout Rajasthan. In eastern Rajasthan, where the spoken language was actually more closely related to Braj and Western Hindi, the influence of this prestigious western literary language began to be felt, and the locus of identity apparently shifted away from the Hindi midland and out to Gujarat and especially Marwar.

As Old Western Rajasthani was gaining in influence as a literary language from the thirteenth through the fifteenth centuries, it became somewhat solidified in form and hence began, again, to be somewhat archaic relative to the still-developing spoken vernaculars, where many changes were taking place. Marwari (in an early form) began to be distinct from Gujarati, and by the mid-fifteenth century, a newer literary language, more closely akin to the then current vernacular of Marwar, began to be used in certain metrical works. Within this poetic movement there developed two distinct local literary languages in western Rajasthan, both gradually replacing Old Western Rajasthani in verse writings. One is identified by Smith (1975, 434) simply as Old Rajasthani; the other is known as Diṅgal.

By the end of the sixteenth century, the now highly archaic Old Western Rajasthani began to be replaced in learned prose writing as well. The language that supplanted it in this realm, which Smith calls Middle Marwari, gained influence until it became the primary vehicle for all prose writing throughout Rajasthan. This language continued in general use throughout the region for all letters, historical tales, folk stories, learned prose, and all vernacular prose chronicles for about two hundred fifty years, "until, in modern times, the combined pressures of Urdu, Standard Hindi and English led to its ultimate abandonment in the latter half of the ninteenth century" (Smith 1975, 435). During all this period, however, the local spoken vernacular tongues of the vast majority of people of Rajasthan continued to evolve, as spoken language universally tends to do, unabated and relatively unaffected by the cyclic standardizing and archaizing developments in the literary languages.

We now come to the language of the bard himself. Madhu Nath is from a village in Ajmer district, which falls geographically on the western side of the major divide between Eastern Rajasthani and Western Rajasthani, as proposed by Grierson (see map). According to Grierson's 1908 survey, Madhu's village should fall within the dialect area designated as Standard Marwari. In fact we find that Madhu's speech is fundamentally similar to Marwari but also contains elements (especially grammatical) that differ significantly from Marwari, and that show affiliation to other Rajasthani dialects, such as Dhundhari, situated just to the east, and Mewari (to the southeast). (Comparisons with Marwari here will be based on information on that language presented in Magier 1983a, 1983b, 1985, 1987, and 1990.)

First, we note that Madhu's nouns have a system of case endings that mirrors that of Marwari (and that differs only little from most Rajasthani dialects). Masculine singular nouns have either no ending (*ṭābar* "child") or the ending *-o* (*chū̃tro* "shrine"). In the plural, masculine nouns have, again, either no ending (*mandar* "temples") or the ending *-ā* (*darvājā* "doorways"). Feminine nouns in the singular have either no ending (*rāt* "night") or the ending *-ī* (*ḍoḍī* "portal"). In the plural, all feminine nouns have the ending *-ā̃* (*rāṇiyā̃* "queens"). This dialect, like most North Indian languages, employs postpositions (words that come after the noun) where a language like English employs prepositions. Thus, where in English we say "in the room" (with the preposition "in"), in these languages one says, in effect, "room in." A particular feature of Rajasthani (as well as Hindi and most of the Indo-Aryan languages) is that nouns take special case endings whenever they are followed by a postposition (c.f., English "I" versus "me"). We call this the oblique case. In Madhu's dialect singular masculine nouns that normally end in *-o* change that ending to *-ā* (*bacchā ne* "to the boy") in the oblique case. Masculine nouns that normally have no ending, still have no ending in the singular oblique (*ṭābar ne* "to the child"). All singular feminine nouns also take no oblique ending (*banjhārī ne* "to the barren woman"). However, all nouns (regardless of gender or type of normal ending) take a special ending in the oblique plural: *-ā̃* (*bacchā̃ ne, ṭābarā̃ ne, rāṇiyā̃ ne*, etc.).

These case endings are summarized in the following chart.

	singular		plural	
	regular	oblique	regular	oblique
masc. (-*o* type)	-o	-ā	-ā	-āṅ
masc. (unmarked type)	—	—	—	-āṅ
fem. (-*ī* type)	-ī	-ī	-āṅ	-āṅ
fem. (unmarked type)	—	—	-āṅ	-āṅ

This pattern exactly parallels that of Standard Marwari. The only difference I noted was an occasional tendency to use the -ā ending for masculine singular (non-oblique) nouns; it often occurred in Madhu's speech in places that showed other evidence of an unconscious attempt to "Hindify" his speech. This divergence makes sense because the Hindi pattern differs from the one above in that it has -ā for masculine singulars. Hindi also differs in having a more complex paradigm for feminine nouns. Those that normally end in -ī take one direct plural ending (-āṅ), whereas those that do not, take another (-eṅ). Further, in Hindi, the universal oblique plural ending is -oṅ. Thus, to contrast the two feminine paradigms:

Madhu	Hindi	
rānī	rānī	"queen"
rānī ne	rānī ko	"to the queen"
rāṇiyāṅ	rāniyāṅ	"queens"
rāṇiyāṅ ne	rāniyoṅ ne	"to the queens"
bāt	bāt	"matter/word"
bāt meṅ	bāt meṅ	"in the matter/word"
bātāṅ	bāteṅ	"matters/words"
bātāṅ meṅ	bātoṅ meṅ	"in the matters/words"

These differences are relatively slight and could easily be called "dialectal" if one were inclined to classify Madhu's speech as some sort of dialect of Hindi. However, as we show below, there are other more fundamental differences.

The pronouns I found in the sample of Madhu's speech are as follows:

1st pers. sing.	mhūṅ	"I"
1st pers. plur.	mhe	"we"
2d pers. sing.	thūṅ	"you"
2d pers. plur/(honorific)	theṅ	"you"
3d pers. sing. (far) masc.	vo	"he, it, that"
fem.	vā	"she, it, that"

3d pers. sing. (near) masc.	yo	"he, it, this"
fem.	yā	"she, it, this"
3d pers. plur. (far)	ve	"they, those"
3d pers. plur. (near)	ye	"they, these"

The first thing to note, in comparing this dialect, say, with Hindi, is that the dialect makes a gender distinction among 3d person singular pronouns. Gender is totally absent from the Hindi pronoun system. Note also that Hindi has a three-tiered system of 2d person pronouns (*tū*, *tum*, and *āp*), distinguished as singular (*tū*) and plural (*tum* and *āp*), and further distinguished by levels of deference or honorific meanings (see Magier 1982). I found evidence of only two levels (singular and plural) in Madhu's dialect, but, if it is parallel to Marwari, it may have a third highly deferential pronoun (*āp*) that is used very rarely and did not occur in this corpus.

The pronouns listed above have special oblique forms for use with different postpositions. In particular, Madhu's dialect has special forms in the dative case (i.e., with the postposition *ne* "to") and in the genitive case (i.e., with the postposition *ro* "of").

	dative		*genitive*	
1st pers. sing.	mha-ne	"to me"	mhā-ro	"my"
1st pers. plur.	mhāṅ-ne	"to us"	mhāṅ-ro	"our"
2d pers. sing.	thāṅ-ne	"to you"	thāṅ-ro	"your"
2d pers. plur./(honorific)	thāṅ-ne	"to you"	thāṅ-ro	"your"
3d pers. sing. (far)	ū-ne	"to him"	ū-ro	"his"
3d pers. sing. (near)	vhā-ne	"to him"	vhā-ro	"his"
3d pers. plur./(honorific) (far)	ūṅ-ne	"to them"	ūṅ-ro	"their"
3d pers. plur./(honorific) (near)	vhāṅ-ne	"to them"	vhāṅ-ro	"their"

These forms bear little resemblance to their Hindi counterparts. The postpositions themselves are completely different (e.g., for dative Hindi has *ko* while Madhu [and Marwari] has *ne*, and for genitive Hindi has *kā* while Madhu [and Marwari] has *ro*). But comparison with Marwari yields interesting results. Most of Madhu's forms are identical to their Marwari counterparts, except for the 3d person oblique forms. The Marwari 3d person forms are:

	dative		*genitive*	
3d pers. sing. (far)	uṇ-ne	"to him"	uṇ-ro	"his"
3d pers. sing. (near)	iṇ-ne	"to him"	iṇ-ro	"his"
3d pers. plur./(honorific) (far)	vhāṅ-ne	"to them"	vhāṅ-ro	"their"
3d pers. plur./(honorific) (near)	āṅ-ne	"to them"	āṅ-ro	"their"

Also, in the non-oblique 3d person pronouns, where Madhu has *yo*, *yā*, and *ye*, Marwari has simply *o*, *ā*, and *e* (Madhu's 3d person non-oblique pronouns are, in fact, closer to those found in Mewari). One more notable difference is in the 1st person (non-oblique) pronouns. Marwari has *mheṅ* for the 1st person singular (as do most of the western dialects I observed) and *mhe* for the 1st person plural. (A special separate pronoun for 1st person plural includes the hearer, i.e., "we" meaning "you and I." This form is *āpāṅ*, and it probably exists in Madhu's dialect, though I found no instances of its use. It does not occur in Hindi.) But Madhu's pronouns, *mhūṅ* and *mhe* are, in fact, more characteristic of Mewari and some southeastern dialects of Western Rajasthani. On the whole, however, these are relatively superficial differences, and I would still be inclined to characterize this pronominal system as essentially a variant of Marwari. (But I would also want to explore the system more fully, through elicitation sessions with Madhu, before drawing any firm conclusions. See all the disclaimers above.)

The system of postpositions I found in Madhu's dialect is also essentially similar to that of Standard Marwari. The one area where I found significant variation was in the genitive postposition. Marwari uses *ro* (inflected for gender and number as *ro*, *rā*, *rī* and for oblique case as *re*) both with pronouns and with regular nouns (e.g., *chorā rī māṅ* "the boy's mother," *mhā-rī māṅ* "my mother"). What I found in Madhu's speech was the use of *ko* (likewise inflected as *ko*, *kā*, *kī* and for oblique case as *ke*), except when it occurred with the pronouns, where it tended to show up as *-ro* (etc.). In other words, his dialect seems to distinguish between a free-standing genitive postposition used with common nouns (*ko*, etc.) and a bound form of the genitive used with pronouns (*-ro*, etc.). I have not observed this distinction in any other Rajasthani dialect. It is interesting to note that the free-standing form with initial *k-* is reminiscent of Hindi, where the genitive is *kā* (inflected for gender and number as *kā*, *ke*, *kī* and for oblique case as *ke*).

The overall verbal system of Madhu's dialect is too complex for adequate description here, and in any case a limited corpus does not provide examples of all the tense and aspect forms available in the language. But I found the verbal system to be virtually identical to Marwari in nearly every detail. The only significant differences I found were as follows:

(a) Marwari uses a single verb form (i.e., without an auxiliary verb) for the simple present tense. Thus, for example, in Marwari one says *vā kaive* "she says." But in Madhu's dialect I found instances of present tense sentences using the auxiliary verb (*vā khaive he* "she says"). This pattern is found in Mewari (and is also more similar to standard Hindi than Marwari is).

(b) Madhu's language has a future tense with verb endings in *-gā* (apparently inflected for gender and number). This future is very similar to the Hindi future tense (with inflected *-gā*, *ge*, and *gī*) but differs widely from the Marwari future, which has an uninflected *-lā* ending. (Marwari also has a distinctive "inferred future" tense [Magier 1983a] that did not occur in the recorded corpus of Madhu's speech but may nonetheless exist in his dialect.)

There may be other significant differences between Madhu's dialect and Marwari that simply did not appear in our data. However, I was able to confirm that Madhu's dialect does follow the "exotic" agreement patterns found in Marwari. These are the patterns that determine the endings of the verbs, controlled by the gender, number, or person of the subject and object nouns. The system is too complex for a full description here. But it is important to note how this system differs from the one found in Hindi. Basically, the most significant differences occur in the past tense. In a past tense transitive sentence (i.e., one with a direct object), Hindi has a special case ending for the subject. It is called the "ergative" case and in Hindi is the postposition *-ne*. Also, in the case of such ergative sentences, the verb will agree in number and gender with the object rather than with the subject. Thus, to contrast Hindi present tense and past tense sentences:

maiṅ roṭī khātā hūṅ	maiṅ-ne roṭī khāī
I eat (masc.)	I-(erg.) ate (fem.)
"I eat roti"	"I ate roti"

In Marwari (and in Madhu's dialect), there is no special ergative case marker on the subject of past tense transitive sentences. But, as in Hindi, the verb does agree with the object. Thus:

mhūṅ roṭī jīmūṅ hūṅ	mhūṅ roṭī jīmī
I eat	I ate (fem.)
"I eat roti"	"I ate roti"

Interestingly, Hindi blocks the verb from agreeing with the object if the object noun (or pronoun) happens to be marked with the dative/accusative postposition. In that case, Hindi has a system for "zero-agreement." That is, the verb agrees with neither subject nor object but goes instead into a neutral form. Thus, in Hindi:

laṛkī sītā-ko	dekhtī hai	laṛkī-ne	sītā-ko	dekhā
girl Sita-(accus.)	sees (fem.)	girl-(erg.)	Sita-(accus.)	saw (neutral)
"The girl sees Sita"		"The girl saw Sita"		

Similar patterns of zero-agreement are found in Eastern Rajasthani, and even in some eastern dialects of Western Rajasthani (e.g., in Mewari). But in Madhu's dialect (as in Standard Marwari), zero-agreement patterns do not exist. Past tense transitive verbs always agree with the object, even if the object is marked by the dative case. Thus, from the text of the birth story:

mhūṅ	taitīs	karoṛ	dev-devtāṅ ne	pūj liyā
I	33	crore	deities-(accus.)	worshiped (plur.)
"I worshiped 33 crores of deities"				

One final component of the verbal agreement pattern, in which Madhu's dialect accords nicely with Marwari but differs radically from Hindi, is the pattern of personal agreement endings (which occur, for example, in the present tense forms of verbs). Hindi has separate verb endings, distinguished by nasalization of the vowel, to indicate plural agreement. Also, the simple present tense in Hindi includes a present tense participle that marks gender and number on the main verb, and person on the auxiliary verb. But Madhu's dialect (as well as Marwari and other Western Rajasthani dialects, such as Mewari) has only the personal agreement endings on the verb. This same ending appears both on the main verb and on the auxiliary (when present) and follows this agreement pattern:

	singular	*plural*
1st pers.	-ūṅ	-āṅ
2d pers.	-e	-o
3d pers.	-e	-e

Note that in this system, the verbs make no gender distinctions and in the 3d person have no distinction between singular and plural.

To summarize, we have briefly sampled a small selection of features of Madhu's dialect and compared them superficially to Hindi on the one hand, and to Marwari (and Mewari) on the other. In its gross outlines, Madhu's dialect is clearly a western dialect of Rajasthani, conforming fairly closely with Standard Marwari in most of its grammatical features. (Its phonological system, not treated here, appears to be identical to Marwari.) It shows fundamental differences from Hindi in (at least) the following areas:

(a) It has only one class of feminine nouns (all taking the ending -*āṅ* for the plural), rather than the two distinct classes found in Hindi (those pluralizing in -*āṅ* and those in -*eṅ*).

(b) It marks gender distinctions in the 3d person singular pronouns (totally absent in Hindi).

(c) It has a simpler present tense verb paradigm, which does not distinguish gender in the verb endings and does not distinguish number in the 3d person (both of which are essential parts of the Hindi verbal structure).

(d) It has no ergative case marker for past tense transitive sentences (which is usually taken as a fundamental characteristic of Hindi but is totally absent in Madhu's Rajasthani).

(e) It has no zero-agreement pattern in ergative sentences. Past tense transitive verbs always agree with direct objects, regardless of the case-marking of the latter (whereas Hindi specifically blocks verbal agreement with any case-marked noun).

(f) The parallel to the Hindi honorific 2d person pronoun (*āp*) does not seem to occur in Madhu's dialect, whereas it is quite common in Hindi.

If Madhu's dialect is like Marwari (and I believe it is), the honorific system in the pronouns is essentially two-tiered (compared to the three-tiered system of Hindi), while the verbal system allows for a much wider range of honorific distinctions than is available in Hindi. It is fascinating to note the actual usage of these pronouns. For example Gopi Chand and his mother, Manavati Mata, address each other as *thūṅ* (the expected norm in most of India, reflecting the intimacy and lack of formality between mother and child). She also addresses Lord Shankar as *thūṅ*. It is very interesting to observe that while Manavati Mata uses the first person singular (*mhūṅ*) to refer to herself, Lord Shankar uses what is apparently the "royal" we (i.e., the plural) when referring to himself, as in this exchange:

MANAVATI MATA: mha-ne putar debā-hālo na maḷyo
                "There was no one to give a child to me [sing.]
SHANKAR: mhāṅ-ne pūjtī to thāro kāraj saddh hoto
                "If you had worshiped to me [plur.] then your job would have
                been perfectly done"

Such usage patterns are determined by complex bundles of contextual and sociolinguistic factors and so cannot be adequately determined by examining a single performance text. Much more investigation (particularly of face-to-face communication) needs to be conducted in this area.

We also found a few differences with Marwari that are worth noting:

(a) Madhu's dialect has a future tense verb ending that apparently inflects for gender and number (while Marwari's future ending does not).

(b) It does not seem to have the inferred future tense that Marwari exhibits (though this difference may simply result from a gap in the data).

(c) It has a 1st person pronoun, as well as a set of 3d person pronouns that resemble those of Mewari more closely than Marwari.

(d) It seems to have distinct forms of the genitive postposition for use with pronouns. Interestingly, only the form that attaches to pronouns (*ro*) is the same as the Marwari form. Madhu's genitive postposition, which occurs with regular nouns (*ko, kā, kī*), bears a resemblance to the Hindi genitive.

The weight of the available evidence suggests that Madhu Nath's dialect is not particularly mixed or idiosyncratic. Nor is it some form of elliptical or broken Hindi. I hope I have presented enough of an analysis to suggest that it is a complete grammatical system in its own right. It has features that allow us tentatively to classify it as a dialect in the Western Rajasthani group, with close affiliations to Marwari but containing elements in common with more southeasterly dialects like Mewari. Although Ajmer district sits right near Grierson's border between Eastern and Western Rajasthani, Madhu's dialect does not display any particular features of these eastern dialects, though some elements seem to reflect an influence from Hindi.

Proper Nouns Transliterated

Individuals from Epic and History

Asamāl Jogī
Baharī Jogaṇ
Bajorī Kānjarī
Bharat Nāth
Bhartharī Paṅvār
Bhartṛihari
Chamanī Kalālī
Champā De Rānī
Charpaṭ Nāth
Gandaraph Syāṇ
Gāṅgalī Telaṇ
Gopī Chand
Gorakh Nāth
Guru Gūgā
Hāḍā Nāth
Hīrā
Jalīndar Nāth
Kannī Pāvjī
Kapūrī Dhobaṇ
Khūkanyo
Lūṇā Chamārī
Machhindar Nāth
Mān Singh
Maṇāvatī
Motījī
Nāradjī

Nīm Nāth
Pachūjī
Pān De
Pāras Nath
Pāṭam De
Phūlam De
Pīngaḷā
Prajāpat
Rājā Pīpā
Raṇjīt
Rūpsī
Setalī Khamārī
Talokī Chand
Vikramādīt (Madhu says Bakaramādīt)

Sites from Epic and History

Badarī Nārāyaṇ
Chapalā
Ḍhāṅk Bangāḷā
Dhārā Naṅgarī
Dīp Naṅgarī
Gaṅgā
Goṛ Bangāḷā
Kailāś
Kajalī Van
Mālva
Vaikunṭh Purī

Individuals from Ghatiyali and Environs

Bhojū Rām Gūjar
Gokul Nāth
Hardev Paṭel
Lāḍū Nāth
Mādhū Nāṭīsar Nāth
Nāthū
Ogaṛ Nāth
Rām Chandra
Śambhūṛyā
Śivjī Nāth

Sukhā Nāth
Ugamā Nāthjī

Sites from Ghatiyali and Environs

Āsaṇ
Būndī
Ghaṭiyālī
Jaypāljī
Khejaṛī
Moṛī
Nāpā Kheṛa
Puṣkar
Ratan Kuā
Sadārā
Sāwar

Deities

Bhairūṅjī
Bholā Nāth
Dev Nārāyaṇ
Hanumān
Hīng Lāj Māṅ
Lakṣmī
Mahādev
Pābūjī
Rāma
Śankar
Sītalā
Śiva
Ṭhākurjī

References

Abu-Lughod, Lila. 1990. "The Romance of Resistance: Tracing Transformations of Power Through Bedouin Women." *American Ethnologist* 17(2): 41–55.

Barthwal, P. D. 1978. *Traditions of Indian Mysticism*. New Delhi: Heritage Publishers.

Barz, Richard. 1976. *The Bhakti Sect of Vallabhācārya*. Faridabad, Haryanna: Thomson Press.

Bascom, William R. 1977. *Frontiers of Folklore*. Boulder, Colo.: Westview Press.

Basso, Ellen B. 1985. *A Musical View of the Universe*. Philadelphia: University of Pennsylvania Press.

Bauman, Richard. 1977. *Verbal Art as Performance*. Prospect Heights, Ill.: Waveland Press.

———. 1986. *Story, Performance, and Event*. Cambridge: Cambridge University Press.

Bayly, C. A. 1983. *Rulers, Townsmen and Bazaars: North Indian Society in the Age of British Expansion, 1770–1870*. Cambridge: Cambridge University Press.

Beames, John. 1872–79. *Comparative Grammar of the Modern Indo-Aryan Languages of India*. Reprinted 1966. New Delhi: Munshiram Manoharlal.

Beck, Brenda E. F. 1982. *The Three Twins*. Bloomington: Indiana University Press.

———. 1989. "Core Triangles in the Folk Epics of India." In *Oral Epics in India*, edited by Stuart H. Blackburn, Peter J. Claus, Joyce B. Flueckiger, and Susan S. Wadley, 155–75. Berkeley: University of California Press.

Benjamin, Walter. 1969. *Illuminations*. New York: Schocken Books.

Bertrand, Gabrielle. 1958. *Secret Lands Where Women Reign*. London: Robert Hale.

Bhanavat, Mahendra. 1968. *Kālā Gorā ro Bhārat*. Udaipur: Bharatiya Lok-Kala Mandal.

Bhattacharyya, N. N. 1982. *History of the Tantric Religion*. New Delhi: Manohar.

Bhoothalingam, Nathuram. 1982. *Stories of Vikramaditya*. New Delhi: Publications Division, Ministry of Information and Broadcasting, Government of India.

Blackburn, Stuart H. 1988. *Singing of Birth and Death*. Philadelphia: University of Pennsylvania Press.

———. 1989. "Patterns of Development for Indian Oral Epics." In *Oral Epics in India*, edited by Stuart H. Blackburn, Peter J. Claus, Joyce B. Flueckiger, and Susan S. Wadley, 15–32. Berkeley: University of California Press.

Blackburn, Stuart H., and Joyce B. Flueckiger. 1989. Introduction to *Oral Epics in India*, edited by Stuart H. Blackburn, Peter J. Claus, Joyce B. Flueckiger, and Susan S. Wadley, 1–11. Berkeley: University of California Press.

Blackburn, Stuart H., Peter J. Claus, Joyce B. Flueckiger, and Susan S. Wadley, eds. 1989. *Oral Epics in India*. Berkeley: University of California Press.

Bloomfield, Maurice. 1924. "On False Ascetics and Nuns in Hindu Fiction." *Journal of the American Oriental Society* 44: 202–42.

Bouillier, Véronique. 1979. *Naître renonçant: une caste de sannyāsi villageois au Népal central*. Nanterre: Laboratoire d'Ethnologie.

Bradford, N. J. 1985. "The Indian Renouncer: Structure and Transformation in the Lingayat Community." In *Indian Religion*, edited by Richard Burghart and Audrey Cantlie, 79–104. London: Curzon Press.

Briggs, George Weston. 1973. *Gorakhnāth and the Kānphaṭa Yogīs*. Delhi: Motilal Banarsidass.

Burghart, Richard. 1983a. "Renunciation in the Religious Traditions of South Asia." *Man* (N.S.) 18: 635–53.

———. 1983b. "Wandering Ascetics of the Rāmānandī Sect." *History of Religions* 22(4): 361–80.

Cardona, G. 1974. "The Indo-Aryan Languages." *Encyclopaedia Brittanica*. Vol. 9 (15th ed.): 439–50.

Census of India. 1921. "*Rajputana and Ajmer-Merwara*." Vol. 24, part 1. Calcutta: Superintendent of Government Printing.

Champion, Catherine. 1989. "'A contre-courant' (*ultā sādhanā*). Tradition orale du nord-est de l'Inde: l'exemple des récits chantés bhojpuri." In *Living Texts from India*, edited by Richard K. Barz and Monika Thiel-Horstmann, 63–86. Wiesbaden: Otto Harrassowitz.

Chatterjee, Suniti Kumar. 1926. *The Origin and Development of the Bengali Language*. Calcutta: University of Calcutta Press.

————. 1942. *Indo-Aryan and Hindi*. Ahmedabad: Gujarat Vernacular Society.

Chowdhury, Abdul Momin. 1967. *Dynastic History of Bengal*. Dacca: The Asiatic Society of Pakistan.

Courtright, Paul B. In press. *The Goddess and the Dreadful Practice*. New York: Oxford University Press.

Coward, Harold G. 1976. *Bhartṛhari*. Boston: Twayne Publishers.

Crooke, William. 1926. *Religion and Folklore of Northern India*. London: Oxford University Press.

Das, Veena. 1977. *Structure and Cognition*. Delhi: Oxford University Press.

Dasgupta, Shashibhusan. 1969. *Obscure Religious Cults*. Calcutta: Firma K. L. Mukhopadhyay.

Dasgupta, Surendranath. 1924. *Yoga as Philosophy and Religion*. London: Kegan Paul, Trench, Trubner and Company.

————. 1974. *Yoga Philosophy in Relation to Other Systems of Indian Thought*. Delhi: Motilal Banarsidass.

Das Gupta, Tamonash Chandra. 1935. *Aspects of Bengali Society from Old Bengali Literature*. Calcutta: University of Calcutta.

Dehlavi, Nyadar Singh. n.d. *Bharthari Pingalā*. Delhi: Agarwal Book Depot.

Dikshit, Rajesh. n.d. *Navanāth Charitra Sāgar*. Delhi: Hind Pustak Bhandar.

Duggal, K. S. 1979. *Folk Romances of Punjab*. New Delhi: Marwah Publications.

Dumont, Louis. 1970. *Religion, Politics and History in India*. Paris: Mouton.

Dvivedi, Hajariprasad. 1981. *Nāth Sampradāy*. Allahabad: Lokabharati Prakashan.

————. n.d. *Nāth Siddhoṅ kī Bāniyāṅ*. Banaras: Nagaripracarini Sabha.

Edgerton, Franklin. 1926. *Vikrama's Adventures or the Thirty-two Tales of the Throne*. Harvard Oriental Series. Cambridge, Mass.: Harvard University Press.

Eliade, Mircea. 1973. *Yoga: Immortality and Freedom*. Princeton: Princeton University Press.

Feld, Steven. 1982. *Sound and Sentiment*. Philadelphia: University of Pennsylvania Press.

Fine, Elizabeth C. 1984. *The Folklore Text from Performance to Print*. Bloomington: Indiana University Press.

Flueckiger, Joyce B. 1989. "Caste and Regional Variants in an Oral Epic Tradition." In *Oral Epics in India*, edited by Stuart H. Blackburn, Peter J. Claus, Joyce B. Flueckiger, and Susan S. Wadley, 33–54. Berkeley: University of California Press.

Ganguli, Jatindra. 1967. *Three Women Had Made Him a Saint*. Calcutta: East and West Publishers.

Gautam, Chamanlal. 1974. *Gorakṣa Samhitā*. Bareli: Sanskriti Sansthan.

————. 1986. *Śrī Gorakhnāth Charitra*. Bareli: Sanskriti Sansthan.

Ghosh, Rai Sahib Jamini Mohan. 1930. *Sannyasi and Fakir Raiders in Bengal.* Calcutta: Bengal Secretariat Book Depot.

Ghurye, G. S. 1964. *Indian Sadhus.* Bombay: Popular Prakashan.

Gill, Harjeet Singh. 1986. "The Human Condition in Puran Bhagat: An Essay in Existential Anthropology of a Punjabi Legend." In *The Word and the World,* edited by Veena Das, 133–52. New Delhi: Sage Publications.

Gokhale-Turner, Jayashree B. 1981. "Bhakti or Vidroha: Continuity and Change in Dalit Sahitya." In *Tradition and Modernity in Bhakti Movements,* edited by Jayant Lele, 29–42. Leiden: E. J. Brill.

Gold, Ann Grodzins. 1984. "Life Aims and Fruitful Journeys: The Ways of Rajasthani Pilgrims." Ph.D. dissertation, Department of Anthropology, University of Chicago.

———. 1988. *Fruitful Journeys: The Ways of Rajasthani Pilgrims.* Berkeley: University of California Press.

———. 1989. "The Once and Future Yogi: Sentiments and Signs in the Tale of a Renouncer-King." *Journal of Asian Studies* 48(4): 770–86.

———. 1991. "Gender and Illusion in a Rajasthani Yogic Tradition." In *Gender, Genre, and Power in South Asian Expressive Traditions,* edited by Arjun Appadurai, Frank Korom, and Margaret Mills, 102–35. Philadelphia: University of Pennsylvania Press.

Gold, Daniel. 1983. "Sound and Seed in Sant Succession: Crises and Transformations." Paper presented at the annual meeting of the American Academy of Religion, Dallas, Texas.

———. 1987. *The Lord as Guru: Hindi Sants in North Indian Tradition.* New York: Oxford University Press.

———. 1992. "The Rise and Fall of Yogis' Power: Jodhpur 1803–1842." *Estudios de Asia y Africa* January (in Spanish).

Gold, Daniel, and Ann Grodzins Gold. 1984. "The Fate of the Householder Nath." *History of Religions* 24(2): 113–32.

Goldstein, Kenneth S. 1967. "The Induced Natural Context: An Ethnographic Folklore Field Technique." In *Essays on the Verbal and Visual Arts,* edited by June Helm, 1–6. Seattle: University of Washington Press.

Goody, Jack. 1987. *The Interface Between the Written and the Oral.* Cambridge: Cambridge University Press.

Gray, Louis H. 1904. "The Bhartrharinirveda of Harihara, now first translated from the Sanskrit and Prākrit." *Journal of the American Oriental Society* 25: 197–230.

Grierson, G. A. 1878. "The Song of Manik Chandra." *Journal of the Asiatic Society of Bengal* 47(3): 135–238.

———. 1885. "Two Versions of the Song of Gopi Chand." *Journal of the Asiatic Society of Bengal* 54(1): 35–55.

———. 1908. *Linguistic Survey of India.* Vol. 9, part 2: "Indo-Aryan Family,

Central Group (Specimens of Rajasthani and Gujarati)." Reprinted 1968. Delhi: Motilal Banarsidass.

Gumperz, John J. 1961. "Speech Variation and the Study of Indian Civilization." *American Anthropologist* 63(5): 976–88.

Harlan, Lindsey. 1992. *Religion and Rajput Women: The Ethic of Protection in Contemporary Narratives*. Berkeley: University of California Press.

Hawley, Jack. 1987. "Morality Beyond Morality in the Lives of Three Hindu Saints." In *Saints and Virtues*, edited by Jack Hawley, 52–72. Berkeley: University of California Press.

Heesterman, J. C. 1985. *The Inner Conflict of Tradition*. Chicago: University of Chicago Press.

Henry, Edward O. 1988. *Chant the Names of God*. San Diego: San Diego State University Press.

Hess, Linda, and Shukdev Singh. 1983. *The Bījak of Kabir*. San Francisco: North Point Press.

Iyer, K. A. Subramania. 1969. *Bhartṛhari: A Study of the Vākapadīya in the Light of the Ancient Commentaries*. Poona: Deccan College.

Jackson, A. V. W. 1902. "Notes from India." *Journal of the American Oriental Society* 23: 307–17.

Johnson, Barbara. 1985. "Taking Fidelity Philosophically." In *Difference in Translation*, edited by Joseph F. Graham, 142–48. Ithaca: Cornell University Press.

Kale, M. R. 1971. *The Nīti and Vairāgya Śatakas*. Delhi: Motilal Banarsidass.

Kellogg, S. H. 1875. *A Grammar of the Hindi Language*. 3d edition. Reprinted 1965. London: Routledge and Kegan Paul.

Kelly, Louis. 1979. *The True Interpreter*. New York: St. Martin's Press.

Keyes, Charles F., and E. Valentine Daniel, eds. 1983. *Karma: An Anthropological Inquiry*. Berkeley: University of California Press.

Khubchandani, L. M. 1983. *Plural Languages, Plural Cultures: Communication, Identity, and Sociopolitical Change in Contemporary India*. East-West Center. Manoa: University of Hawaii Press.

Kolff, Dirk H. A. 1990. *Naukar, Rajput and Sepoy: The Ethnohistory of the Military Labour Market in Hindustan, 1450–1850*. Cambridge: Cambridge University Press.

Kothari, Komal. 1989. "Performers, Gods, and Heroes in the Oral Epics of Rajasthan." In *Oral Epics in India*, edited by Stuart H. Blackburn, Peter J. Claus, Joyce B. Flueckiger, and Susan S. Wadley, 102–17. Berkeley: University of California Press.

Lalas, Sitaram. 1962–78. *Rājasthānī Sabad Kos*. Jodhpur: Rajasthani Shodh Sansthan.

Lapoint, Elwyn C. 1978. "The Epic of Guga: A North Indian Oral Tradition." In *American Studies in the Anthropology of India*, edited by Sylvia Vatuk, 281–308. New Delhi: Manohar.

Leslie, Julia. 1988. *The Perfect Wife*. London: Oxford University Press.

Limon, Jose E. 1981. "The Folk Performance of 'Chicano' and the Cultural Limits of Political Ideology." In *"And Other Neighborly Names": Social Process and Cultural Image in Texas Folklore*, edited by Richard Bauman and Roger D. Abrahams, 197–225. Austin: University of Texas Press.

Lynch, Owen M. 1990. "The Mastrām: Emotion and Person Among Mathura's Chaubes." In *Divine Passions: The Social Construction of Emotion in India*, edited by Owen M. Lynch, 91–115. Berkeley: University of California Press.

McGregor, Ronald Stuart. 1984. *Hindi Literature from Its Beginnings to the Nineteenth Century*. Vol. 8, no. 6 of *A History of Indian Literature*, edited by Jan Gonda. Wiesbaden: Otto Harrassowitz.

McLeod, W. H. 1968. *Guru Nanak and the Sikh Religion*. Delhi: Oxford University Press.

Madan, T. N. 1987. *Non-Renunciation: Themes and Interpretations of Hindu Culture*. Delhi: Oxford University Press.

———, ed. 1981. *Way of Life: King, Householder, Renouncer*. New Delhi: Vikas Publishing House.

Magier, David. 1982. "Marwari Honorifics." In *Studies in South Asian Languages and Linguistics*, edited by P. J. Mistry (July 1982). Special issue of *South Asian Review* 6(3): 160–73. South Asian Literary Association (MLA).

———. 1983a. "Topics in the Grammar of Marwari." Ph.D. dissertation, Department of Linguistics, University of California, Berkeley.

———. 1983b. "Components of Ergativity in Marwari." In *Papers from the Nineteenth Regional Meeting of the Chicago Linguistic Society*.

———. 1985. "Case and Transitivity in Marwari." In *The Semantics of Participant Roles: South Asia and Adjacent Areas*, edited by Arlene Zide, David Magier, and Eric Schiller (Proceedings of the ancillary meeting held in conjunction with the twentieth Annual Meeting of the Chicago Linguistic Society). Bloomington: Indiana University Linguistics Club.

———. 1987. "The Transitivity Prototype: Evidence from Hindi." *Word* 38(3): 187–99.

———. 1990. "Dative/accusative Subjects in Marwari." In *Experiencer Subjects in South Asian Languages: Proceedings of the Madison Conference on South Asian Languages*, edited by Manindra Verma. Stanford: Center for the Study of Language and Information.

Mahapatra, Piyushkanti. 1972. *The Folk Cults of Bengal*. Calcutta: Indian Publications.

Maheshwari, Hiralal. 1980. *History of Rājasthānī Literature*. New Delhi: Sahitya Akademi.

Majumdar, Ramesh Chandra. 1940. "Lama Taranatha's Account of Bengal." *Indian Historical Quarterly* 16(2): 219–38.

Malamoud, Charles. 1989. *Cuire le monde: rite et pensée dans l'Inde ancienne.* Paris: Editions La Découverte.

Mani, Lata. 1989. "Contentious Traditions: The Debate on Sati in Colonial India." In *Recasting Women: Essays in Colonial History,* edited by Kumkum Sangari and Sudesh Vaid, 88–126. New Delhi: Kali for Women.

Markandaya, Kamala. 1960. *A Silence of Desire.* New York: John Day.

———. 1963. *Possession.* New York: John Day Company.

Mārwāṛ Census. n.d. "Jogī." 235–54. Jodhpur. Files of the author.

Meissner, Konrad. 1985. *Mālushāhī and Rājulā: A Ballad from Kumāūn (India).* Wiesbaden: Otto Harrassowitz.

Miller, Barbara S. 1967. Introduction to *Bhartrihari: Poems,* edited by Barbara S. Miller, xv–xxviv. New York: Columbia University Press.

Misra, B. G. 1967. "Historical Phonology of Modern Standard Hindi: Proto-Indo-European to the Present." Ph.D. dissertation, Department of Modern Languages and Linguistics, Cornell University, Ithaca.

Nandy, Ashis. 1980. *At the Edge of Psychology: Essays in Politics and Culture.* Delhi: Oxford University Press.

———. 1988. "The Human Factor." *Illustrated Weekly of India* (January 17): 20–23.

Narayan, Kirin. 1989. *Storytellers, Saints, and Scoundrels: Folk Narrative in Hindu Religious Teaching.* Philadelphia: University of Pennsylvania Press.

Narayan, R. K. 1980. *The Guide.* New York: Penguin Books.

O'Flaherty, Wendy Doniger. 1973. *Asceticism and Eroticism in the Mythology of Śiva.* London: Oxford University Press.

———. 1984. *Dreams, Illusion, and Other Realities.* Chicago: University of Chicago Press.

———. 1988. *Other People's Myths.* New York: Macmillan.

Oman, John Campbell. 1905. *The Mystics, Ascetics, and Saints of India.* London: T. Fisher Unwin.

Ong, Walter J. 1982. *Orality and Literacy.* London: Methuen.

Pande, Trilochan. 1963. "The Concept of Folklore in India and Pakistan." *Schweizerisches Archiv für Volkskunde* 59: 25–30.

Pandey, Divakar. 1980. *Gorakhnāth evam unkī paramparā kā sāhitya.* Gorakhpur: Gorakhnath Mandir Shodh Sansthan.

Pandit, P. B. 1977. *Language in a Plural Society: The Case of India.* New Delhi: Dev Raj Chanana Memorial Committee.

Peterson, Indira V. 1988. "The Tie That Binds: Brothers and Sisters in North and South India." *South Asian Social Scientist* 4(1): 25–51.

Platts, John T. 1974. *A Dictionary of Urdū, Classical Hindī, and English.* London: Oxford University Press.

Pritchett, Frances W. 1985. *Marvelous Encounters: Folk Romance in Urdu and Hindi.* New Delhi: Manohar.

Pujari, Thakur Prasad. 1926. "The Fruit of Immortality." *The Indian Antiquary* 55: 213.

Raheja, Gloria Goodwin, and Ann Grodzins Gold. Forthcoming. *Songs, Stories, Lives: Listening to Women in North India.* Berkeley: University of California Press.

Raju, P. T. 1985. *Structural Depths of Indian Thought.* Albany: State University of New York Press.

Ramanujan, A. K. 1973. *Speaking of Śiva.* Baltimore: Penguin Books.

Risley, H. H. 1891. *The Tribes and Castes of Bengal.* Calcutta: Bengal Secretariat Press.

Roland, Alan. 1988. *In Search of Self in India and Japan.* Princeton: Princeton University Press.

Rose, H. A. 1914. *A Glossary of the Tribes and Castes of the Punjab and North-West Frontier Province.* Reprinted 1970. Punjab: Languages Department.

Rowlands, J. Helen. 1930. *La Femme bengalie dans la littérature du moyen-âge.* Paris: Librairie d'Amérique et d'Orient.

Sarkar, Sir Jadu-Nath. 1948. *The History of Bengal.* Dacca: University of Dacca.

———. n.d. *A History of Dasnami Naga Sanyasis.* Allahabad: Sri Panchayati Akhara Mahanirvani.

Sax, William. 1991. *Mountain Goddess: Gender and Politics in a Himalayan Pilgrimage.* New York: Oxford University Press.

Schimmel, Annemarie. 1975. *Mystical Dimensions of Islam.* Chapel Hill: University of North Carolina Press.

Schomer, Karine. 1987. "The Dohā as a Vehicle of Sant Teachings." In *The Sants: Studies in a Devotional Tradition of India,* edited by Karine Schomer and W. H. McLeod, 61–90. Religious Studies Series. Berkeley: Graduate Theological Union.

Seeger, Anthony. 1987. *Why Suya Sing.* Cambridge: Cambridge University Press.

Seitel, Peter. 1980. *See So That We May See: Performances and Interpretations of Traditional Tales from Tanzania.* Bloomington: Indiana University Press.

Sen, Dinesh Chandra. 1954. *History of Bengali Language and Literature.* Calcutta: University of Calcutta.

Sen, Kshitimohan. 1974. *Medieval Mysticism of India.* New Delhi: Munshiram Manoharlal.

Sen, Sukumar. 1960. *History of Bengali Literature.* New Delhi: Sahitya Akademi.

Shah, Waris. 1976. *Hir Ranjha,* translated by Charles Frederick Usborne. New Delhi: Orient Paperbacks.

Shapiro, M. C., and H. F. Schiffman. 1981. *Language and Society in South Asia.* Delhi: Motilal Banarsidass.

Sharma, Kailashchandra. 1983. *Bhaktamālā aur hindī kāvya meṅ uskī paramparā.* Rohtak, Hariyana: Manthan Publications.

Sharma, Padmaja. 1972. *Maharaja Mansingh of Jodhpur and His Times*. Agra: Shiva Lal Agarwala and Company.

Siegel, Lee. 1987. *Laughing Matters: Comic Tradition in India*. Chicago: University of Chicago Press.

Singh, Mohan. 1937. *Gorakhnath and Medieval Hindu Mysticism*. Lahore: Oriental College.

Singh, Zabar. 1973. *The East India Company and Marwar*. Jaipur: Panchsheel Prakashan.

Sinh, Pancham. 1975. *The Hatha Yoga Pradipika*. New Delhi: Munshiram Manoharlal.

Sinha, Surajit, and Baidyanath Saraswati. 1978. *Ascetics of Kashi*. Varanasi: N. K. Bose Memorial Foundation.

Sircar, D. C. 1969. *Ancient Malwa and the Vikramāditya Tradition*. New Delhi: Munshiram Manoharlal.

Sircar, Kanika, trans. n.d. "Gopicander Pancali." Files of the author.

Smith, John D. 1975. "An introduction to the language of the historical documents from Rajasthan." *Modern Asian Studies* 9(4): 433–64.

———. 1980. "Old Indian: The Two Sanskrit Epics." In *Traditions of Heroic and Epic Poetry*, edited by A. T. Hatto, 48–78. London: Modern Humanities Research Association.

———. 1986. "Where the Plot Thickens: 'Epic Moments' in Pabuji." *South Asian Studies* 2: 53–64.

———. 1989. "Scapegoats of the Gods: The Ideology of the Indian Epics." In *Oral Epics in India*, edited by Stuart H. Blackburn, Peter J. Claus, Joyce B. Flueckiger, and Susan S. Wadley, 176–94. Berkeley: University of California Press.

———. 1991. *The Epic of Pābūjī: A Study, Transcription and Translation*. Cambridge: Cambridge University Press.

Sundardas, Shyam. 1965. *Hindī Śabdsāgar*. Varanasi: Nagari Pracharini Sabha.

Swynnerton, Charles. 1903. *Romantic Tales from the Panjāb*. Westminster: Archibald Constable and Company.

Tedlock, Dennis. 1983. *The Spoken Word and the Work of Interpretation*. Philadelphia: University of Pennsylvania Press.

Temple, Sir Richard. 1884. *The Legends of the Punjab*. Vols. 1–3. Reprinted 1962. Patiala: Department of Languages, Punjab.

Tessitori, L. P. 1914–16. "Notes on the grammar of the Old Western Rajasthani, with special reference to Apabhramça and to Gujarati and Marwari." *The Indian Antiquary* 43–45.

Tiwari, Bhan Pratap. 1892. "The Common Legend of Bhartri Nath." *North Indian Notes and Queries* 2(8): 129.

Tod, James. 1829. *Annals and Antiquities of Rajasthan or the Central and Western Rajpoot States of India*. London: Smith, Elder and Company.

Trawick, Margaret. 1990. *Notes on Love in a Tamil Family.* Berkeley: University of California Press.

Tripathi, B. D. 1978. *Sadhus of India.* Bombay: Popular Prakashan.

Upadhyay, Nagendranath. 1976. *Gorakṣanāth.* Varanasi: Nagari Pracharini Sabha.

Vaidya, Babu Haridas. 1984. *Vairāgya-Shatak.* Mathura: Haridas and Company.

van Buitenen, J. A. B. 1959. "The Indian Hero as a *Vidyādhara.*" In *Traditional India: Structure and Change,* edited by Milton Singer, 99–105. Philadelphia: American Folklore Society.

van der Veer, Peter. 1988. *Gods on Earth: The Management of Religious Experience and Identity in a North Indian Pilgrimage Centre.* London: Athlone Press.

Varenne, Jean. 1976. *Yoga and the Hindu Tradition.* Chicago: University of Chicago Press.

Vatuk, Ved Prakash. 1969. *Thieves in My House: Four Studies in Indian Folklore of Protest and Change.* Varanasi: Vishwavidyalaya Prakashan.

Vaudeville, Charlotte. 1962. *Les Duhā de Dhola-Mārū.* Pondichery: Institut français d'Indologie.

——. 1974. *Kabīr.* London: Oxford University Press.

——. 1986. *Bārahmāsā in Indian Literatures.* Delhi: Motilal Banarsidass.

Wadley, Susan S. 1978. "Texts in Contexts: Oral Traditions and the Study of Religion in Karimpur." In *American Studies in the Anthropology of India,* edited by Sylvia Vatuk, 309–41. Delhi: Manohar.

——. 1983. "The Rains of Estrangement: Understanding the Hindu Yearly Cycle." *Contributions to Indian Sociology* (N.S.) 17(1): 51–86.

——. 1989. "Choosing a Path: Performance Strategies in a North Indian Epic." In *Oral Epics in India,* edited by Stuart H. Blackburn, Peter J. Claus, Joyce B. Flueckiger, and Susan S. Wadley, 75–101. Berkeley: University of California Press.

——. 1991. "Beyond Texts: Tunes and Contexts in Indian Folk Music." In *Texts, Tunes and Tones,* edited by Bonnie Wade. Delhi: Oxford University Press.

Watson, Major John W. 1873. "Story of Rānī Pinglā." *The Indian Antiquary* August: 215–16.

White, Hayden. 1981. "The Value of Narrativity in the Representation of Reality." In *On Narrative,* edited by W. J. T. Mitchell, 1–23. Chicago: University of Chicago Press.

Woods, James Haughton. 1972. *The Yoga-System of Patanjali.* Harvard Oriental Series. Delhi: Motilal Banarsidass.

Wortham, Reverend B. Hale. 1886. *Śatakas of Bhartrihari.* London: Trubner and Company.

Yogishvar, Balakram. n.d. *Bhakt Gopīchand Bhartharī*. Delhi: Agarwal Book Depot.

Zbavitel, Dusan. 1976. *Bengali Literature*. Vol. 9, no. 3 of *A History of Indian Literature*, edited by Jan Gonda. Wiesbaden: Otto Harrassowitz.

Zelliot, Eleanor. 1981. "Chokhamela and Eknath: Two Bhakti Modes of Legitimacy for Modern Change." In *Tradition and Modernity in Bhakti Movements*, edited by Jayant Lele, 136–56. Leiden: E. J. Brill.

Zvelebil, Kamil V. 1987. *Two Tamil Folktales*. Delhi: Motilal Banarsidass.

Index

Note: The translated texts have not been indexed.

Compositor: Thomson Press (India) Limited
Text: 11/13 Baskerville
Display: Baskerville
Printer: Thomson-Shore, Inc.
Binder: Thomson-Shore, Inc.